FATAL FAULTLINES

Irfan Husain was born in Amritsar, India, in 1944 and migrated with his family to the newly created state of Pakistan three years later. Educated in Karachi, Paris and Ankara, he joined the civil service in 1967 after obtaining a Master's degree in economics. He has pursued a parallel and covert career as a freelance journalist for most of his working life, writing under a succession of pseudonyms. As Mazdak, he became a popular columnist on the Internet edition of *Dawn*, a newspaper he has been writing for over the last two decades. Since 2002, he divides his time between the UK, Pakistan and Sri Lanka.

FATAL FAULTLINES

PAKISTAN, ISLAM AND THE WEST

IRFAN HUSAIN

HarperCollins *Publishers* India

First published in India in by
HarperCollins *Publishers* in 2012

Building 10, Tower A, 4th Floor, DLF Cyber City, Phase II,
Gurugram Haryana – 122002, India
www.harpercollins.co.in

under special arrangement with Arc Manor Publishers, Rockville, MD, USA.

4 6 8 10 9 7 5 3

ISBN: 978-93-5029-230-3

Typeset in SabonMT 11/14
InoSoft Systems Noida

Printed and bound at
MicroPrints India, New Delhi

For my parents, Hameeda and Akhter Husain Raipuri,
with deep gratitude for their gift of tolerance; and
for my grandsons, Danyaal and Sulaiman:
may they grow up in a more peaceful world.

Contents

Foreword

Stephen P. Cohen

The notion of a free or vibrant Pakistani press—let alone a competent one—would have seemed absurd to a visitor to Pakistan during the dark days of the Zia years. Then, it was hardly worth picking up the government-sponsored newspaper, or watching the officially controlled television stations, or even looking at the ostensibly independent Pakistani papers, such as *The Muslim*. I remember reading it, and other newspapers, in the same way that Sovietologists scanned *Pravda* or the Sinologists tried to decipher the *People's Daily* looking for crumbs of truth.

So, predictions about the press would have been pessimistic when Zia died and a febrile democracy was established in Pakistan, with Benazir Bhutto as Prime Minister. However, it is a measure of the resilience of the people of Pakistan and its long-suppressed elite that these predictions turned out to be false. If anything, the Pakistani press and the electronic media are too free, but that is the small price to be paid for the process of professionalization still underway twenty years after Benazir lifted press censorship and other leaders and government agencies tried to impose it.

Irfan Husain has been on both sides of the line. He has worked for the government of Pakistan, but this book represents his unofficial side—as a long-standing contributor to Pakistan's leading newspapers and magazines, notably *Dawn*, and as an acute but acerbic critic of the follies of several governments and other key players in the Pakistani drama. You can agree or disagree, but he has always been worth reading, for he represents the positive and creative side of Pakistan. The publication of this book is especially timely because it not only gathers many of his columns, but it makes a coherent case for a liberal, 'normal' state, at peace with its neighbors and itself.

As such it is an important contribution to the wide-ranging debate in Pakistan and abroad about that country's future, and should be read by Pakistanis and non-Pakistanis alike. It is a valuable contribution to our understanding of the role of the parties, of the military, and of ideology, in a state that was created on the basis of an ideology but which struggles to adapt itself to the modern world and to Pakistan's identity as a South Asian state. Finally, it shows that beside a new crop of professional journalists, many of whom have suffered grievously for their efforts to practice their profession, Pakistan has a deep pool of former officials, such as Irfan, who can reflect wisely on both the promise and the follies of their country.

Ummah:

An Arabic word meaning 'community.' In Islamic terms, the concept of a commonwealth of believers thus, the whole Muslim world without regard for national borders, race or ethnicity.

1

Why Us?

'The Americans are arming the Taliban,' Younus declared in response to an idle question about the source of the insurgents' arms.

It was the summer of 2010, and we were in Karachi, Pakistan's biggest city. Younus was driving me home, and I was making small talk in heavy rush-hour traffic. I had asked him what he thought about a particularly bloody battle in Afghanistan's Helmand province that had resulted in heavy casualties among NATO troops. Younus worked for my old friend Zohra Yusuf—a senior advertising executive, a liberal journalist, and Chairperson of Pakistan's Human Rights Commission—so I knew his views could not have come from her. I asked him why he thought the Americans would arm the Taliban to kill their own troops.

He shrugged. 'I don't know. I read it in a newspaper.'

Ironically, Younus was not even a Muslim. He was from Pakistan's Christian community and—like other non-Muslims in the country—often faced open hostility and discrimination. He could just as easily have picked up the bizarre notion of Americans arming the Taliban from one of Pakistan's dozens of private news channels that frequently broadcast a medley of ignorant views and reactionary notions, often seeming to serve as a propaganda arm for extremist groups. One of the odd twists resulting from the liberalization of Pakistan's airwaves was that many TV chat shows revel in blatantly anti-American discussions in which participants compete to express the most outlandish idea. Any attempt to introduce a note of reality into these programmes is dismissed as 'American propaganda.' Indeed, across much of the Muslim world, the easiest way to win an argument is to accuse the interlocutor of being a CIA agent.

Over the years, I have lost count of the number of times I have been labeled a CIA agent (or a Mossad/RAW agent—the Israeli and Indian spy agencies, respectively). These charges have popped up with monotonous regularity in my inbox in response to some article or other that I have written debunking a conspiracy theory or arguing for our need to put emotion and ideology aside and join the rest of the world in the twenty-first century. This attitude of sceptical self-interest does not go down well with many of my readers. Ever since my weekly column began appearing on the Internet some fifteen years ago, I have been regularly bombarded with hate mail accusing me of attempting to appease the United States and of not being a good Muslim. Not only are these emails abusive, but many are threatening. Luckily, I also get a lot of fan mail, urging me to stick to my guns in denouncing extremism.

This compendium of opposing views reflects the ambivalence toward the United States that prevails in the Muslim world. Survey after survey shows the deep animosity and downright hatred that millions of Muslims harbour for the United States. It is fair to say that many of these negative sentiments can also be found in non-Muslim states. However, non-Muslims have not declared jihad against America and are not targeting American interests around the world.

So pervasive is this anti-Americanism that, even when Washington has gone out of its way to reach out to Muslims, these gestures have been viewed as suspect or air-brushed out of the narrative. In this charged atmosphere, I have had to remind readers that it was American intervention that prevented the complete Serbian genocide of Bosnian and Kosovar Muslims. When a massive earthquake devastated large areas in Pakistani Kashmir and its adjoining region, killing more than 60,000 people, the

United States led a major international rescue and rehabilitation effort. When more than a million people fled Pakistan's lovely Swat Valley after the local Taliban captured it in 2008, Americans were the biggest international donors to help house and feed the refugees. The Americans were also the biggest donors helping the millions of flood victims in 2010, when thousands of Pakistani villages were swamped in the wake of a huge natural calamity.

Unfortunately, these generous gestures are seldom remembered very long—or even acknowledged with gratitude at the time. The lingering suspicion remains that such efforts were always motivated by some hidden American agenda.

Yet, despite this virulent anti-American poison that has spread across the Muslim world, the outward symbols of American-led globalization are everywhere. McDonald's Golden Arches are as pervasive a logo as the Islamic crescent against a green background. Video games, the latest Hollywood blockbuster, and Microsoft are as evident in Muslim countries as they are anywhere else. Such dichotomy between the widespread hatred of American policies and the voracious appetite for the products of American creativity provides a fascinating and confusing contrast.

Immediately following the events of 9/11, I was flooded with emails from Americans who had suddenly begun exploring media websites in the Muslim world to try to understand where these suicide bombers had come from. A common subtext underscored their emails to me: 'Why us?'

In addition to visiting the United States from time to time, I spent a short stint in Washington as a diplomat. Based on my (admittedly brief) experience of America and Americans, I can see the reason why they were so shocked at being attacked. During my interactions with Americans, I have found them to be open and generous. Never once did I encounter any hostility or rudeness. Granted, these observations are based on fairly limited exposure. Nevertheless, I have nothing but pleasant memories of my time there. However, it is also true that I encountered significant ignorance about the rest of the world. My impression is that for most Americans—especially those in Middle America—their huge country is world enough. They get their news from local newspapers, radio stations, and TV channels that largely ignore international events unless they have a domestic angle. National media organizations, including CNN, also focus predominantly on national and local issues. This results in a parochial worldview that blocks out any deep understanding or empathy with how people might think and react to American policies abroad.

The other reason for this blind spot is that Americans are fortunate enough to live in a nation with a genuinely effective grassroots democracy that empowers and engages its citizens in a way that few other countries experience. Most Americans are more deeply engrossed in local issues than people living elsewhere. Broadly speaking, the system works. In addition, the last sixty years have witnessed a steady improvement in American living standards. For example, the present generation has been spared the rigours of being inducted into the armed forces, and the resulting all-volunteer army has allowed the vast majority of Americans to avoid fighting in distant wars. By insulating American society from directly experiencing the impact of its foreign policy, the United States has made war relatively pain-free for most of its citizens.

All these factors make Americans largely indifferent to what happens in the rest of the world. During my discussions with Americans about international affairs, I could almost see their eyes glazing over. Of course, there are many exceptions, but by and large, even my American friends readily admit that most of their fellow citizens are woefully ignorant about geography as well as events abroad.

Above all, most Americans see themselves as the good guys. Their interventions in foreign lands are perceived as acts of self-sacrifice for the greater good of mankind. Since most of them perceive their own government as functioning under a system of constitutional checks and balances as well as constant media scrutiny, they cannot grasp the idea that much of the world often sees America in a very different light. For example, since World

War II, America has been involved in literally dozens of armed conflicts around the world. Many of these have been relatively minor affairs, yet they have all served to build up the image of America as the bully on the block. Although they might have been packaged as police actions thrust upon the United States, the fact is that they have not won the United States many friends abroad. Thus, when foreigners condemn American highhandedness, there is a certain context. Indeed, for Muslims, the last twenty years have seen two wars against Iraq, the ongoing conflict in Afghanistan, and the US-led NATO operation against Libya. Not surprisingly, Muslims do not perceive Americans as the good guys. However, most Americans think their government is a force for good abroad and that some of their taxes are used to provide foreign aid. They genuinely cannot see why so many foreigners are ungrateful to the point of burning the Stars and Stripes at the slightest pretext.

Against this background of ignorance and indifference, I could sympathize with my new American readers who were desperately trying to figure out why nineteen Muslims had flown four airliners into the Twin Towers and the Pentagon (and the failed attempt on the Capitol) on 9/11. As I sat at my computer in Karachi, trying to explain these complex issues to people who had never before considered that their country was hated abroad, I was forced to confront the prejudices and atavistic desire for vengeance that millions of Muslims harbour.

When I mentioned the idea of this book to my Pakistani friends, several of them laughed and said it was a no-brainer: They thought it wouldn't take more than a couple of pages to list the reasons for Muslims to hate America. However, to me, this glib oversimplification overlooks the many factors that feed into this animosity. Others have also opposed American policies abroad. In London, I marched with more than a million people in Hyde Park as we protested the coming war against Iraq in 2003. Over the years, the United States' actions have attracted opposition and criticism across the world, but nowhere have they provoked the kind of visceral hatred as in the Muslim world. Clearly, something else is at work here that goes deeper than political differences. Later in this book, I will explore the historical and religious factors that separate the Muslim world from the West—especially from America.

One response to the question 'Why us?' was provided by Faisal Shahzad, the Pakistani-American terrorist who attempted to detonate a crude homemade bomb in the middle of Times Square in May 2010. When the judge at his trial in New York asked him if he had looked around at the ordinary people—especially the children—before he had tried to set off his bomb, Shahzad replied: 'Well, the people select the government. We consider them all the same. The drones, when they hit, they don't see anybody. They kill everybody. It's a war, and in war, they kill people. They're killing all Muslims…I am part of the answer to the US terrorizing the Muslim nations and the Muslim people. And, on behalf of that, I'm avenging the attack. Living in the United States, Americans only care about their own people, but they don't care about the people elsewhere in the world when they die.'

The idea that the United States is targeting Muslims around the world resonates deeply, even among highly educated people in the Islamic world. However, they are in denial about the fact that far more Muslims have been killed in recent times by other Muslims than by anybody else. The Iraq-Iran war of the 1980s alone accounted for approximately one million deaths. The Taliban in Afghanistan have slaughtered many more of their fellow countrymen than Western forces have. Similarly, drone attacks in Pakistan have accounted for a tiny fraction of the casualties inflicted by various extremist factions through suicide attacks that occur with such sickening regularity.

Shocking though it might seem to Americans, many Muslims celebrated when news about the attacks on the Twin Towers and the Pentagon reached them. Although conspiracy theorists went into overdrive when the implications of this stunning act of terrorism sank in, the initial reaction was largely one of jubilation. 'Serves the Americans right!' about sums up the feelings shared by many Muslims around the world. Of course, today millions of Muslims are in denial about who was responsible for the attacks, despite the fact that Osama bin Laden repeatedly claimed them to be Al Qaeda's handiwork. A Google search for conspiracy theories about 9/11 results in literally millions of hits and—although many non-Muslims also share these bizarre theories that somehow the Americans and/or the Israelis were behind the suicide attacks—many Muslims insist that there were mysterious agents in the United States who caused the planes to fly into their targets. One highly educated and well-travelled Sri Lankan Muslim I know seriously asserted that he thought the Japanese were behind the 9/11 attacks—'to avenge the American atom bombing of Nagasaki and Hiroshima during World War II,' he assured me solemnly.

A few days after 9/11, I was invited to speak to the students of Karachi's Institute of Business Administration (IBA), Pakistan's oldest business school that was established with American technical and financial assistance in the early 1960s. The curriculum is modelled on top American universities, and its graduates have gone on to run the country's most successful business corporations. Given the virtually guaranteed jobs its degrees confer, IBA attracts very bright young men and women who undergo stringent testing before being admitted. Speaking to such an audience, I was sure I would find strong condemnation of the 9/11 attacks. However, I was disappointed. When I pointed out that—in addition to the innocent Americans who had been killed in the Twin Towers attacks—the attacks were a disaster for the wider Muslim world, I was immediately reminded of the many crimes Americans were supposed to have committed against Muslims. In the discussion that ensued, the students seemed to justify the attacks and even praise those who had carried them out. This event took place before the American-led occupation of Afghanistan and the invasion of Iraq, so clearly such anti-Americanism has been building up for a long time among Muslims. Sadly, the ideas I encountered a decade ago among the students of IBA are now widespread among a large majority of my countrymen.

In this charged atmosphere of denial and paranoia, it is hard to engage most people in the Muslim world in a rational, meaningful discussion on relations between the United States and the Islamic world. Of course, attitudes vary from one country to another. Many Americans are prone to lump the entire arc from Indonesia to Morocco, encompassing well over a billion Muslims, into a single monolithic civilization. Nothing could be further from the truth. Each Muslim country has its own history, culture, and—very often—language. Just as attitudes toward the West vary from country to country, they also differ from one section of the population of one nation to another. Thus, to assume that all Muslims have the same opinion about any subject is to make a similarly erroneous generalization about the 2.1 billion Christians scattered around the globe.

Nevertheless, the notion of the *ummah,* or a wider Muslim nation that transcends political boundaries, is unique to Islam. Indeed, many Muslims deny the legitimacy of manmade barriers that seek to divide the brotherhood of the faithful. In this worldview, any attack on one part of the *ummah* is an attack on the entire body of Islam and thus must be resisted. This concept of a borderless pan-Islamic world clashes with the post-colonial patchwork of independent Muslim nation-states that emerged after World War II. In most of these countries, Westernized elites have assumed control after the departure of their colonial overlords, with Islamists having little say or power in this largely secular dispensation.

Gradually, as these incompetent and corrupt governments lost credibility and support, they came to be challenged by Islamic groups that were often inspired by the writings of Sayyid Qutb, probably the most influential Islamist thinker of the last century. Providing political support and inspiration to religious groups that opposed the status quo was the Muslim Brotherhood. This loosely connected network of Islamic opponents faced brutal crackdowns from unelected despots, generals and kings fearing for their grip on power. Such brutal methods included torture and arbitrary executions. Furthermore, all too often, the United States propped up these unpopular regimes, resulting in the broad belief of the country siding with the oppressors.

American foreign policy is shaped primarily by geopolitics and economics, as is the foreign policy of any power with global interests. Thus, during the Cold War, the United States supported allies and friends who signed up to prevent left-wing, pro-Soviet groups from seizing power. However, all too often, American arms, money, and training were used to crush Islamist opposition. Indeed, Egypt's President Hosni Mubarak used such American support for years until he was finally toppled in 2011. For the poor, the Muslim Brotherhood and its various franchises have a simple but stark message: You are being exploited and oppressed by our corrupt leaders because they have turned away from Islam and are being kept in power by the United States. This is a message that resonates deeply among millions of Muslims.

Side by side with this narrative runs the Muslim perception of events in Israel and Palestine. Although Israel and its many supporters in the West view the UN resolution that resulted in the creation of Israel as sufficient justification for its existence, this perception is not shared by most Muslims, who view the creation of an Israeli state in the midst of an Arab—predominantly Muslim—neighbourhood as an act of sheer injustice and highhandedness that has resulted in the displacement of hundreds of thousands of Palestinians. They see the United Nations as a body controlled by Western powers and one in which they have little or no say. Ultimately, then, they view the creation of Israel as a dagger thrust into the heart of the Middle East. Given this rejection of Israel's legal basis, widespread unanimity exists among Muslims in condemning the continuing occupation of the West Bank. Every violent Israeli act in the occupied territories is flashed across the Muslim world and feeds into the anti-American mindset. True, the harshness of the Israeli occupation now causes revulsion in many non-Muslim countries as well, but it is among Muslims that it provokes the greatest fury. The fact that the United States is Israel's biggest patron and strongest ally results in much of this anger being directed toward Washington.

Above all, Muslims cannot understand that America—for all its talk about democracy, justice and international law—does not seem to want to apply these values to Palestinians. For Muslims, only one narrative exists here, and they accuse Israelis of seeking to avenge the Holocaust on the Palestinians. Apart from the notions of right and wrong, Israel's occupation of the West Bank also serves to remind the Muslim *ummah* of how impotent they have become: A small country with a population of only 7.5 million can humiliate a combination of Arab states time after time. Given that it is easier to hold a superpower responsible for Israel's ascendancy than to accept that it is their own weakness that has contributed to this state of affairs, most Muslims naturally end up blaming America.

Meanwhile, for Americans, it is difficult to gauge the depth of feeling that this conflict arouses above all others. In addition to political and historical issues, religious beliefs are invoked as Jerusalem is the third holiest city for Muslims (after Mecca and Medina). Clerics in mosques across the world remind believers during their weekly sermons following Friday prayers that it is their duty to liberate Jerusalem.

Faith is probably the most important element in a Muslim's identity—an idea quite alien to most Westerners, who usually define themselves in terms other than purely religious ideas. If asked who they are, most Muslim believers would reply 'Muslim' before naming their nationality or ethnic group. This deep adherence to religious belief, combined with the concept of the *ummah*, makes most Muslims react to the plight of their fellow believers with a sense of outrage and urgency not found among followers of other religions. These concepts and emotions are not easy for outsiders to grasp. Thus, when a bunch of young Somali-Americans set off for Somalia—a country they have never seen before—on a quixotic quest to usher in an Islamic state, many Americans are understandably puzzled.

So the answer to 'Why us?' is complex and multi-layered. Often, a local dispute in which the United States is seen to have sided with the opposing side is the reason for anti-Americanism. In other areas, left-wing Muslims might oppose America on anti-imperial grounds. Regardless of the local differences or global ambitions, several strands are woven into this narrative.

I was invited to speak at the Centre for Regional Studies at Pakistan's Islamabad University in early 2010, where I was struck by the vehemence with which the young men and women—all post-grads—in the audience opposed the American policy of using remotely piloted drones to attack terrorist groups in the country's lawless tribal areas. Although this issue will be discussed more fully later in the book, let me mention in passing that it continues to outrage millions of Pakistanis who argue that it infringes upon their country's sovereignty. I asked the students at Islamabad University to imagine that they were American policy-makers in Washington and then tell me how they would have responded to the situation: American troops in Afghanistan were being attacked and killed by militants who then found sanctuary in Pakistan's remote tribal belt, where they could regroup and rest before crossing the border back into Afghanistan to launch fresh attacks. American troops were forbidden to follow them to their bases in Pakistan. Given these circumstances, how should the Americans react? There was no coherent or logical reply to the question, other than 'The Americans should not have come to Afghanistan in the first place.'

There are two ironies that are of particular interest here. First, the Pakistani government handed over a secret base in the province of Balochistan to the Americans, from where many of these drones operate. Second—and more crucially—the further people are from the tribal areas in which the drones operate, the greater the outrage they provoke. Those living in the tribal areas of North and South Waziristan, where drones have caused the most casualties, welcome these attacks. According to them, this is the most effective means of ridding them of the unwelcome presence of the Taliban and other militant groups. These locals go on to say that, when the Pakistani forces launch their artillery and aerial assaults on these terrorists, they are nowhere as accurate as the precision strikes carried out by the drones. Whatever the reality, the fact is that these attacks are angering and alienating millions of Pakistanis, ultimately making them more anti-American than ever.

A majority of Muslims—even the humblest—feel connected to a greater whole and consider themselves heirs to a great Islamic civilization. To a great extent, they think their present lowly status is due to dark Western forces that have brought the powerful Caliphate down, together with the mighty Muslim empires that stretched across much of the known world. As the United States presently leads the Judeo-Christian coalition, they consider it to be the chief crusading power in the millennium-long struggle. Being on the losing side of this conflict, they see the *ummah* engaged in a zero-sum game in which every American gain is a Muslim loss and vice versa. According to this worldview, the jihad is the only approach currently available to Muslims to defend their honour.

Of course, not every Muslim picks up a Kalashnikov assault rifle and heads for the hills to join Al Qaeda, yet this generally supportive attitude enables extremists to flourish. In many Muslim countries, rich businessmen donate generously to charities that fund *madressas*, where young students are indoctrinated. Some of this money finds its way to extremist groups. Although few graduates actually sign up for the jihad, the proliferation of these seminaries further helps create and sustain an environment of intolerance, xenophobia, and militancy. Most of these institutions in Pakistan are unregulated and incapable of teaching anything but the rote learning of the Qur'an and other religious texts. Graduates are ill-equipped to find jobs other than as imams leading the prayers in mosques. Even if they learn nothing else, students at *madressas* pick up a deep-seated hostility toward the West, especially the United States. All Western culture is denounced as decadent and Western values as corrupt. Over the last three decades or so, these sentiments have seeped throughout Muslim society to such an extent that they are now part of the landscape; indeed, they now shape the zeitgeist in many Muslim countries—even those that are outwardly secular.

So is this indeed 'a war without end,' in which Muslims will confront the West for the foreseeable future? Judging by the unemployment, illiteracy and poverty rates in much of the Muslim world and the incompetence of most governments in the region, it would seem that this conflict will continue for a long time. However, if we step outside the current framework and take a materialist view of history, the perspective looks very different. In this model, religious extremism becomes a reaction to the forces of globalization that have transformed the world in recent years. As primitive tribes lose power to the modernizing elements in this rapidly changing world, they lash out in rage and impotence; however, they are inherently too weak to block change. The reason they seek recourse in violence is that, ultimately, terrorism is the weapon of the weak. In this landscape, where events are shaped by economic forces, these backward groups will lose despite their use of modern communication tools like Twitter and Facebook. Their demise will come about because they have little to offer recruits beyond death and destruction. Although their nihilism will attract some disturbed individuals, they can never command a broad enough support base to seriously threaten world order.

However, this relatively benign scenario presupposes steady economic growth that spreads fairly evenly. The past five decades have witnessed unprecedented progress, with hundreds of millions being lifted out of abject poverty. As aspirations rise, young people turn their backs on traditional values and roles and join the rat race. This is not to suggest that educated, middle-class men are unlikely to join the anti-American jihad. In fact, most of the 9/11 bombers were intelligent, highly qualified young men. So was Major Nidal Hasan, the US Army psychiatrist who gunned down thirteen in the Fort Hood massacre. Fasial Shahzad received an MBA from an American college and was a professional financial analyst. Yet a handful of indoctrinated fanatics do not an army make. Thus, while jihadis will be a nuisance to American interests, they are unlikely to ever repeat their 9/11 success. Indeed, the past decade has seen a steady erosion of Al Qaeda's capabilities, and the upcoming decade will probably witness its demise, especially following Osama bin Laden's death in an American SEAL raid on May 2, 2011, in the Pakistani garrison town of Abbottabad.

As jihadi groups with global ambitions are likely to become defunct over time, Islamic groups and political parties with local and national agendas will probably replace many secular governments in the Muslim world or enter into power-sharing arrangements. This should not, in itself, be a cause for concern. Islamists are already jockeying for position in the increasing ferment gripping the Middle East and North Africa. It is entirely likely that the Muslim Brotherhood and its offshoots will find a major political role, whether alone or in coalition with secular parties. After all, the rest of the world has coped perfectly well with the successive Saudi monarchs who have run their country in accordance with the tenets of the harsh, literal Wahabi vision of Islam.

We live in an edgy, tense era in which power is shifting from the nation-state to multinational corporations. In this world, the financiers and technocrats increasingly call the shots, with ideology becoming increasingly irrelevant. Understandably, ideologues on both the left and right are feeling marginalized; some of them do more than rail against the forces of change. Armed with the certainty provided by the word of God, Islamic extremists want to drag the world back to a period in which they counted for something. In their struggle for the restoration of the Caliphate and the mythical glory of Islam it represented, they are determined to usher in a world in which they can rule supreme. As such, ultimately, this is not a struggle over belief, but for political power. The jihadis may use Islamic texts and ideology to further their ends, but they are fighting for nothing less than the control of the Muslim world, and they recognize that the United States leads the resistance to their power grab.

In his remarkably prescient book *Jihad vs. McWorld*, published in 1995, Benjamin R. Barber discusses the clash between the forces of globalization represented by McWorld and those of tribal identity and reaction, which he calls Jihad. In their contempt for borders and democratic institutions, the author sees a clear parallel between the two tendencies. Fifteen years after the publication of his book, we find ourselves in the midst of this epic struggle. History moves in uneven steps, often lurching from one point to another, but the trajectory of mankind's progress has remained remarkably steady, despite many stumbles along the way. Thus, we have reason to expect the ongoing clash between thesis and antithesis to result in a stable synthesis.

Although there are no accurate figures for the number of Muslims in the United States, some estimates place them at around 4 million. Whatever the true number, it is a tiny fraction of the total population, so to think of them as any kind of genuine threat would be to enter the realm of paranoia. There will always be a handful of disaffected youths who plot to fulfil their grandiose fantasies. Other quixotic types will wish to seek adventure by joining some extremist groups in Somalia or Afghanistan. Still others will talk tough in the local mosque, attracting the attention of the FBI. Yet by and large, Muslims—like everybody else—are too busy making a living, looking after their families, and generally getting on with life to enter into anti-American conspiracies.

As we look for the answer to the question 'Why us?', we find that it is not the no-brainer some of my friends think it to be. Rather, we discover many forces and ideas at work. Ultimately, Muslims are not a monolithic group that can be easily lumped into a single category, despite the concept of the *ummah*. This book is an attempt to examine what separates them from the West and what lies at the root of their alienation and resentment.

At the close of this introduction, I need to make it clear that I lay no claim to being an Islamic scholar or an academic. My book is an attempt to explain the causes of the resentment and anger that millions of Muslims harbour toward America and the West based on my reading, travels, conversations and email exchanges with readers. Thus, this is a largely personal exploration of ideas that I hope is readily accessible to readers interested in sharing my views on the long interaction between Islam and Christendom. Although I have attempted to substantiate most of the points I have made with references from more learned writers than me, the opinions I have formed and the conclusions I have drawn are entirely my own.

Finally, although a select bibliography appears at the end of the book, some of the ideas I have expressed might reflect those I came across in books or articles I read long ago and have not cited herein. This should not be construed as an attempt on my part to appropriate credit for the works for others; rather, it should be put down to a failing memory.

2

9/11's Long Shadow

Soon after the invasion of Afghanistan in the wake of 9/11, an apocryphal story hinting at the nightmare to come did the rounds. At a mosque in the badlands under Taliban control, a cleric declared in his sermon following the Friday prayers: 'See how mighty is Allah! Earlier, the Americans were too far away for us to kill. But now, by the grace of Allah, they have landed on our doorstep!' Such a declaration sounded somewhat funny at the time as the quick victory of the allied forces seemed to signal the end of the Taliban. His words do not sound so funny today.

We woke up on 12 September 2001, in a world that had been changed forever by the events of the preceding day. Suddenly, faith defined most Muslims in a way with which many of them were unfamiliar. Americans, shaken and shocked by the attacks, struggled to comprehend the magnitude of the terrorist atrocity and its implications.

The initial reaction among many Muslims was one of spontaneous joy. Although at first the jury was out on who was behind the attacks, the destruction caused by the three hijacked airliners showed that the mighty United States was not invulnerable. In Pakistan, the press carried accounts of sweets being distributed in the streets, which is a celebratory gesture in most of the Islamic world. In the occupied West Bank, upon receiving this gift, one man said, 'This sweet comes from bin Laden.'

An organization calling itself The Free Egyptians (not to be confused with the Free Egyptian Party that was recently formed) conducted a poll, with its volunteers posing as journalists. It issued its findings in a press release dated March 9, 2004[1]. Information gleaned from the Internet is not always easy to cross-check, so I am presenting the results of the survey with some reservations as I have no idea about the methodology used in the survey or the size of the sample. This introduction to the press release gives rise to further questions, but I reproduce it here—mistakes and all:

> By the time 9/11 terror attacks took place around 80 per cent of all Muslims were hateful, resentful and envious of America simply because they became adherents of Neoislam. To measure the reaction of the educated Egyptian-Muslim middle-class to 9/11, the Free Egyptians conducted opinion polls on a sample thereof on 9/11 and the ensuing days when an atmosphere of euphoria and rejoicing took control of and overwhelmed the Muslim street. Release of results at an earlier date was not possible for security reasons...

The organization's website could not be accessed, and an email to Mahmoud Salem—the contact name given at the end of the survey—elicited no reply. Yet it remains clear that The Free Egyptians are a virulently dissident, anti-Mubarak group. After all these disclaimers and caveats, here are the results of the opinion poll:

> Of those interviewed,
> *91 per cent said they supported and rejoiced [sic] the attacks of 9/11;
> *89 per cent said America deserved to be attacked because it is an infidel country that supports the Jews;
> *83 per cent said 9/11 inspired so much zeal in them that they themselves were willing to volunteer as suicide bombers to carry out attacks against targets in America or Israel;
> *94 per cent said that 9/11 attackers died as *shaheed* (martyrs);
> *87 per cent said that 9/11 marked the beginning of the end for America; and
> *88 per cent said they supported more attacks on America.

---

1 http://www.free-press-release.com/news/200403/1078863738.html

Although these figures—questionable as they may be—surprised me, they did not come as a shock. I was in Pakistan on 9/11 and was taken aback by the quiet satisfaction and *schadenfreude* the attacks caused. Apart from the jubilation on the streets, even the secular, educated, and generally Westernized elites were full of praise for the attackers, although their identity continued to be hotly debated. To this day, many Pakistanis are convinced that a bunch of Arabs were simply incapable of carrying out such a complex operation. This view is certainly not very flattering, yet it does carry an echo of an earlier put-down by a Pakistani prime minister. When asked why he did not side with the Arabs following the Israeli, French, and British attack on Egypt during the brief Suez conflict in 1956, the prime minister, Shaheed Hoseyn Suharwardy, said acidly of Arabs: 'Zero plus zero equals zero.' Understandably, this comment did not go down well in the Middle East and soured Pakistani relations with Arab states for some time.

Although many in the Muslim streets rejoiced after 9/11, official condemnation of the attack poured into Washington from virtually every capital in the Islamic world. Joining politicians and government spokesmen were mainstream religious leaders. These public figures immediately understood that this was no time for sitting on the fence. When George W. Bush proclaimed to the world 'Either you are with us, or you are against us,' governments took him at his word. However, this sober assessment did not resonate among most Muslims. One prominent Pakistani journalist corrected me when I used the word 'Pentagon' in the context of 9/11, stating, 'It's now Penta-gone, not Pentagon.' When I told him I didn't think he was being very funny, he launched into a long diatribe about why America had the attack coming. This was not the only time I was forced to listen to such justification of the 9/11 attacks.

The following quote shows the reaction of Yemeni journalist Rahma Hugira, who was interviewed on CBS shortly after 9/11:

> I didn't used to think that I could support violence. When I saw the World Trade Centre and the Pentagon burn, I cried, I fainted with joy. And I prayed that God would help al-Qaida ...if I have nothing else to offer, my last resort is to raise two or three children to become Sheikh Osama bin Laden's. What we all see in Osama bin Laden is the man who was able to take our revenge, to wipe the tears that have been falling for a long time for our brethren in Palestine and Iraq. Through him divine justice was achieved when America was shaken on 11 September.[2]

Once the magnitude of the attacks and their far-reaching implications began to sink in, denial took hold among many Muslims. The most common conspiracy theory that did the rounds in drawing rooms and on the Internet—and one that persists to this day—was that the US government was responsible for the suicide bombing of the Twin Towers and the Pentagon. Why would any government slaughter thousands of its own citizens in the middle of its largest city? 'Ah,' reply these conspiracy theorists, as if speaking to a dimwit, 'obviously to create a justification to attack Iraq and grab its oil.' Another variation to this conspiracy is that Mossad, the Israeli secret service, was behind the attacks. The evidence cited for this theory is that on 9/11, none of the Jews employed in the Twin Towers turned up for work. This amazing story hummed along the Internet the day after the attacks, and many believe it still. I pointed out in one column that, given that employment data in the United States does not record a person's religion, it is impossible to determine whether any Jews were among the victims or not—especially a day or two after the carnage, when bodies were still being lifted out of the rubble. Needless to say, I was roundly abused in angry emails from readers who accused me of being a CIA and/or a Mossad agent.

---

[2] Atwan, Abdel Bari, *The Secret History of al-Qa'ida,* London: Saqi, 2006, p. 86

The depth of anti-American sentiment in the Muslim world is best captured by Dr Steven Kull in this testimony he gave before the Foreign Affairs subcommittee of the House Committee on International Organizations, Human Rights and Oversight on 17 May 2007. Dr Kull is director of the Program on International Policy Attitudes (PIPA) at the University of Maryland. He is quoted here at some length due to the extensive research he has conducted as well as the clarity of the insights he has developed:

> As I discussed the last time I testified to this subcommittee, in the world as a whole negative views of the United States have increased sharply in recent years. A key factor contributing to these feelings is that the United States is perceived as unconstrained in its use of armed force by the system of international rules and institutions that the US itself took the lead in establishing in the post war period.
>
> Today I will focus on attitudes in the Muslim world. Clearly the Muslim world is of particular interest as it is a major source of violence against the US. As you have already heard, it is also an area of the world with particularly negative feelings towards the United States....
>
> Not surprisingly we did indeed find [through surveys in the Muslim world as well as in-depth studies and focus groups conducted in Egypt, Morocco, Pakistan and Indonesia] negative views towards the US even though the governments of the countries surveyed, by and large, have a positive relationship with the US government. Most negative were the Egyptians—93 per cent expressed an unfavorable view, with 86 per cent very unfavorable. In Morocco, 76 per cent had an unfavorable view, with 49 per cent very unfavorable. In Pakistan, 67 per cent had an unfavorable view, with 49 per cent very unfavorable. The most moderate responses were in Indonesia, where 66 per cent did have an unfavorable view but a more modest 16 per cent had a very unfavorable view.
>
> However these numbers do not capture what I think is the most important dynamic in the Muslim world today.
>
> For decades, polls in the Muslim world and the statements of Muslim leaders have shown a variety of resentments about US policies. Muslims share the worldwide view that the US does not

live up to its own ideals of international law and democracy. There have also been specific complaints that the US favors Israel over the Palestinians and the Arab world as a whole, that the US exploits the Middle East for its oil and that it hypocritically supports non-democratic governments that accommodate its interests. These attitudes persist.

But now there is also a new feeling about the US that has emerged in the wake of 9-11. This is not so much an intensification of negative feelings toward the US as much as a new perception of American interests. There seems to be a perception that the US has entered into a war with Islam itself.

I think perhaps the most significant finding of our study is that across the four countries, eight in ten believe that the US seeks to 'weaken and divide the Islamic world.'

We do not have the trend-line data to demonstrate that this is something new. But in the focus groups this was described as something that has arisen recently from American anger about 9-11. America is perceived as believing that it was attacked by Islam itself and as having declared war on Islam. People repeatedly brought up President Bush's use of the term 'crusade' and cited this as evidence of these underlying intentions.

In this context it is not surprising that three out of four respondents favor the goal of getting the US to withdraw its military troops from all Islamic countries.

Most disturbing there is widespread support for attacks on US troops. Overall about half of all the Muslims polled approve of attacks on US troops in Iraq, Afghanistan and the Persian Gulf. Support reached as high as nine in ten in Egypt. It appears that American troops stationed throughout the region are widely perceived as occupiers.

In focus groups, some respondents said that this sense Islam being under siege has enhanced people's identification with Islam. Polling done by the Anwar Sadat Chair at the University of Maryland in Arab countries over the last few years has found a dramatic increase in the number citing their Muslim identity as primary. In our poll seven in ten approved of the goal of requiring 'a strict application of sharia law in every Islamic country.'

So does this mean that all these negative feelings toward America have driven Muslims into the arms of al Qaeda? It does appear that Muslims are embracing the type of religiously based interpretation of the conflict with the US that is consonant with views that al Qaeda has also long promoted.

But in fact al Qaeda is not popular. Across the four countries only about three in ten express positive feelings towards Osama bin Laden and only one in seven say they both share al Qaeda's views of the US and approve of its methods.

Perhaps most significant, very large majorities reject attacks on civilians. Overwhelming majorities in all countries also specifically reject attacks on US civilians in the United States and US civilians working in Islamic countries. Most agree that such attacks are contrary to Islam.

So does that mean then that the Muslim public is basically with America against al Qaeda? The answer is no. While al Qaeda may not be popular, large majorities said they perceive al Qaeda as seeking to 'stand up to America and affirm the dignity of the Islamic people' and equally large majorities agree with this goal.

Though al Qaeda and America are both seen as largely illegitimate, America is seen as the greater threat. It is as if Muslims are living in a neighborhood where there are two warlords operating. They do not like either one, but one is much more powerful. As long as the weaker one is standing up to the stronger one, it makes sense that they are inclined to play down their dislike for the weaker one.

And in the focus groups people clearly resisted criticizing al Qaeda. Having rejected attacks on civilians as wrong they became uncomfortable and somewhat defensive when asked about 9-11. They strongly insisted that there was no proof that al Qaeda was behind the 9-11 attacks.

This pattern was present in the survey as well. When we asked the respondents who they thought was behind the 9-11, in no country did more than one in three identify al Qaeda as the culprit and in Pakistan the number was a mere 2 per cent. Some respondents blamed the US itself, some blamed Israel, and many refused to even make a guess.

> In the focus groups when I brought up the fact that there were videos in which al Qaeda leaders brag about the 9-11 attacks, a common answer was: 'Hollywood can create anything.'
>
> ...Enemies of one's enemies are not necessarily one's friends. But it is pretty normal to not spend a lot of time scrutinizing their faults.
>
> This brings us back to the question we started with: What are the consequences of anti-American feelings in the Muslim world?
>
> Our study has found that anti-American feeling is by itself not enough to lead one to actively support al Qaeda. To approve of attacks on civilians one must have views that—I am happy to report—are quite unusual in the Muslim world.
>
> However, anti-American feeling can lead Muslims to suppress their moral doubts about al Qaeda. This makes it politically more difficult for governments to take strong action against al Qaeda, it makes general publics more likely to passively accept al Qaeda and it creates an environment where it is more likely that individuals will cross the threshold into actively supporting al Qaeda. In other words it gives al Qaeda more room to maneuver.[3]

Dr Kull's findings confirm the attitudes I have encountered time and again. As a Pakistani, I find it extremely depressing that so many of my countrymen are so deep in denial. Ultimately, these findings underscore the deep chasm that has opened up between the Islamic world and the United States. This fault line also makes it much harder to fight Islamic terrorism—a virus that threatens Muslim countries more than it does the West. Given the widespread ambivalence about this threat among Muslims, it is difficult to convince them that the jihadis fighting under the Al Qaeda banner are a greater existential threat to them than to Western interests and lives.

Yet if 9/11 has pushed many Muslims into denial and delusion, it has also forced them to close ranks against the Islamophobia they

---

[3] House Foreign Affairs Transcript as quoted on www.worldpublicopinion.org

increasingly perceive among Americans. Today, a greater sense of 'us versus them' exists than ever before. Although to their credit, most Americans have not allowed 9/11 to stampede them into a campaign against Islam, but opinion polls do suggest a growing suspicion of the Muslims living in their midst. Perhaps more importantly, the Islamic world appears to have replaced the Soviet threat as the principal danger America faces today. All the security checks put in place in the wake of 9/11, combined with the draconian Homeland Security legislation that the Bush administration enacted, reinforce the feelings that many Americans share about being in constant danger of terrorist attacks. These fears become living nightmares when somebody like Major Nidal Hasan guns down a dozen soldiers at Fort Hood, and Faisal Shahzad attempts to set off a car bomb in the middle of Times Square.

Shahzad is a particularly alarming case as he represents everything any young immigrant aspires to achieve: a good education, a good job, a pretty wife and two charming children—the very embodiment of the American Dream. Yet, for no apparent reason, he filled his car with explosive substances and tried to cause mayhem among a crowd of innocent people in Times Square. In a video made before his failed attack and aired by Dubai's Al-Arabiya TV a couple of months later, Shahzad says chillingly, 'All the Muslim Arabs that have been martyred—I will take revenge on their behalf. I really wish the hearts of the Muslims will be pleased with this attack, God willing.' Calling jihad a pillar of Islam he goes on to say that 'Islam will spread on [sic] the whole world and democracy will be defeated...eight years have passed by Afghanistan, and you will see that the Muslim war has just started.'

Returning to the figures for Egyptian attitudes toward the United States issued by The Free Egyptians as well as PIPA, it is not easy to reconcile apparent Egyptian hatred of the United States with the $60 billion or so their country has received over the years from America as military and economic assistance. Indeed, before President Hosni Mubarak was toppled the country was widely viewed in the Arab world as America's poodle, meekly following Washington's policies in the region. Here lies the reason for America's unpopularity among such an alarming number of Egyptians. Among other causes, complicity in Israel's siege of Gaza did not sit well with the general Egyptian populace. In any case, most of the billions that have flowed from America following the Camp David accords of 1979 have gone into weapons for the army, thereby strengthening Mubarak's three-decade-old dictatorship. His regime cracked down ruthlessly on all signs of dissent and maintained a fig leaf of democracy through fraudulent elections that no foreign observers were allowed to independently verify. Over the last twenty years, Amnesty International has regularly documented numerous cases of torture and illegal detention. Thousands of political opponents languished in jail under Mubarak. In 2008, Amnesty International estimated that at least twenty people had died under torture, with the relatives of the victims being threatened with imprisonment if they complained.

Given this track record, it is small wonder that the Bush administration rendered several terrorist suspects to Egypt to undergo severe physical and mental torture. It should also not surprise us that so many Egyptians opposed a country that was widely viewed as supporting an oppressive dictator and forcing Egypt to adopt positions in the region that were hugely unpopular. Ordinary people struggling to make a living see no evidence of the billions of dollars their government has received as aid; thus, they have no reason to be grateful to America. However, Mubarak's removal after weeks of peaceful protests holds out the strong possibility that much of this damage will be repaired. The fact that the protestors did not resort to traditional anti-American slogans bodes well for future ties.

This pattern is repeated in other Muslim countries: Unpopular despots, kings and generals use American financial, military and political support to repress their people and perpetuate their hated regimes. Meanwhile, American politicians and diplomats never cease to preach democracy and freedom from tyranny. This disconnect between word and deed further discredits the United

States in the eyes of millions of Muslims. Jordan, Egypt, and Saudi Arabia have traditionally been America's closest allies in the Middle East; their rulers have also run some of the region's most brutally repressive regimes. Thus, when Bush and his neocon cabal spoke about using the invasion of Iraq as a springboard to spread democracy among its neighbours, few Muslims held their breath.

In the immediate aftermath of 9/11, when an enraged United States placed the Taliban government of Afghanistan in the crosshairs, few questioned its right to avenge the victims of the terrorist attacks on the Twin Towers and the Pentagon. The medieval forces of Mullah Omar had not endeared themselves to the rest of the Islamic world with their barbarous and benighted rule. The wanton destruction of the giant statues of the Buddha in Bamiyan in 2000 had especially outraged international public opinion. As such, the Taliban had few defenders anywhere when the US Navy took position off the Pakistani coast. By refusing to hand over bin Laden and his Al Qaeda fighters, as the American government had demanded, the Taliban sealed the fate of their oppressive regime.

Few tears were shed in the Muslim world or anywhere else when Mullah Omar and his government were sent packing. To this point, America had been seen as the victim and was deemed to have the moral authority to act. A United Nations Security Council resolution cemented its legal position, and a large number of countries responded to its call. Turkey sent troops; Pakistan allowed American planes to fly over its territory and provided other logistical support, including the use of several military bases. Whatever reservations some Muslims might have had toward this enterprise, few were openly critical. However, in private, many demanded to see the proof of Al Qaeda's involvement in 9/11, ignoring the fact that bin Laden had himself gone public and gloated over the attacks. As a result, although the conspiracy theorists still beat the CIA/Mossad drum, most Muslims were not unduly disturbed by the prospect of the Taliban getting kicked out of Kabul. The truth is that even conservative Muslims found the excessive zeal of the Taliban embarrassing, believing that their bizarre antics and brutal acts carried out in the name of Islam were a blot on their faith and lowered its standing in the world.

When the widely anticipated attack on Afghanistan took place in November 2001 and Mullah Omar famously escaped the rapidly advancing Northern Alliance forces on a motorbike, few in the Muslim world or elsewhere thought he would make a comeback. All eyes were on Tora Bora, where bin Laden was cornered; nobody gave bin Laden much of a chance to survive the massive bombing the Americans subjected him to. Widely written off, his escape from his mountain redoubt stirred a wave of admiration for him across Pakistan and in many other Muslim countries. Support for the underdog grew as he continued to elude his hunters, despite the $25 million bounty on his head. Osama T-shirts became popular in Peshawar, and hundreds of Muslim parents named newborn sons after him.

However, when he was finally tracked down and killed by US SEAL commandos in Abbottabad a decade later, he had become a largely forgotten figure. Few Muslims mourned his passing. In Pakistan, the raid provoked anger for America for having breached the country's sovereignty and outrage against the Pakistani defense establishment for not preventing the raid. However, there was little sympathy in evidence for bin Laden himself.

Given the ease with which the Taliban were routed and the forces arrayed against them, a number of Western pundits can be excused for declaring that the myth of Afghan resistance to foreign occupation had been exploded. Thousands of miles away, Americans glued to their TV sets watched images of their Special Forces units riding on horseback with their Afghan allies as they swept into Kabul a few days after the start of the offensive. Many Pakistani volunteers who had fought with the Taliban were captured, others escaped, and scores more were killed by the Northern Alliance.

As Muslims around the world reconciled themselves to the occupation of Afghanistan and the installation of a pro-West puppet government, an odd thing happened in Washington: Bush declared war on Iraq. The principal reason given by the US government was that Saddam Hussein was still engaged in a programme to produce weapons of mass destruction (WMDs). Thrown in for good measure was the charge that the Iraqis were collaborating with Al Qaeda. Anyone familiar with the realities of the region was aware that for a militantly secular leader like Hussein, a religious movement like Al Qaeda was clearly anathema. During his long and odious rule, the Iraqi dictator imprisoned, tortured and killed thousands of political opponents, including a large number of Islamists. He hounded Islamic militants and kept their leaders on a very short leash. During Hussein's rule, Al Qaeda could not gain a toehold in Iraq; indeed, the group was able to establish its presence there only after Saddam Hussein was obligingly deposed by the Americans.

As to WMDs, it is still a mystery how and why the American Congress, people, and media were so easily duped by Bush and company. Without any recourse to intelligence sources, I was among those who had written at the time why no such weapons or weapons programmes could have existed in Iraq. I also argued with my Western friends along these lines when they cited Tony Blair and George Bush, as well as the mainstream media, to defend the decision to attack Iraq. Basically, we pointed out the obvious: After the first Gulf War, all the vastly expensive infrastructure for a weapons programme was destroyed; to rebuild it, Hussein would have needed a lot of cash as nobody would give him credit in his straitened circumstances. Subjected to sanctions, he was not allowed to sell the country's oil in the open market, severely restricting his ability to pay for anything. Furthermore, prior to the Gulf War, major Western corporations had helped Hussein in his efforts to acquire chemical and biological weapons during his war with Iran. (These companies had been listed by the Iraqi government in a detailed report on its WMD programme prepared in compliance with a UN resolution, but their names were blacked out of the 10,000-page document by the American government as soon as it was handed over in New York.) No such technical assistance had been available since the first Gulf War. In any case, Hussein wanted these weapons in his war with Iran in the 1980s as well as to project Iraqi power in the region. After his crushing defeat in the first Gulf War, there was no chance that he would be allowed to throw his weight around ever again. Following that disaster, Hussein needed to use force to keep his own people under his heel, and conventional weapons were quite sufficient for this purpose. Finally, for a decade, American and British military aircraft had flown constant reconnaissance missions over much of Iraq, in addition to the satellites that photographed everything in the country. To imagine that Iraq could mount a costly, secret WMD programme in these circumstances is to greatly overstate Iraqi ingenuity and resources.

Given my take on the impending war, I was quite happy to join a million others in marching against it in London with my wife and stepdaughters. A wide cross-section of the British population took part in that peaceful demonstration against the war, ranging from Muslim militants to young students to left-wing activists. Mothers pushed babies in carriages, while buses arrived from across the country bringing people from distant towns to join the protest. A sea of humanity converged on Hyde Park, where a few well-known speakers harangued the good-natured crowd.

Despite this huge demonstration in London as well as in other cities, Bush and Blair had already decided to go to war and were in too much of a hurry to wait for the UN inspectors to finish their task or to get a clear-cut UN resolution. To many experts on international law, the war was illegally launched—not that this little technicality caused its authors to lose any sleep.

In the Muslim world, this war raised profound questions and concerns. Above all, nobody could understand the link between 9/11 and Iraq. Muslims everywhere felt the Iraqi people had suffered enough in the first Gulf War and the decade of sanctions that had followed. In particular, children had died by the tens of thousands due to the restrictions placed on the import of medicines. The infant mortality rate had more than tripled, growing from thirty per thousand in 1984–89 to 101 in 1999. Over the years, sympathy for the Iraqi people had mounted in the Muslim world, and they were increasingly seen as the victims of American hypocrisy and vindictiveness.

It is important to understand that, although Hussein was clearly the aggressor when he attacked and occupied neighbouring Kuwait in 1990, he was not really seen as the bad guy in most of the Islamic world. To this day, millions of Muslims assert that the United States had egged him on to attack Kuwait. In particular, they cite a statement from US ambassador April Glaspie on the eve of the Iraqi invasion of its neighbour, in which she appears to have said that the move was of no concern to the United States. The Iraqi record of her meeting with Hussein on 25 July 1990 (reproduced by the *New York Times*), the eve of the Kuwait invasion, quotes her less-than-forthright position: 'But we have no opinion on the Arab-Arab conflicts, like your border disagreement with Kuwait... All that we hope for is that these issues are solved quickly.'

For many Muslims (as well as some American observers), this feeble statement served as a wink and a nod to the Iraqi dictator, giving him the clear impression that there would be no tough response from the United States if he attacked his small, oil-rich neighbour. To many Muslims, the Americans had set a trap, and Hussein had walked into it. The supposed objective of this exercise was to give the United States the excuse to attack and weaken Iraq—the one Arab country that was seen as standing up to the West and supporting the Palestinian cause.

Given the widespread perception that Hussein was not the villain of the piece, seeing his country being subjected to a decade of sanctions that blocked the export of oil and the import of many life-saving medicines further enraged many Muslims. As the West cited UN resolutions to justify Iraqi suffering, respect for this international body plunged in the Muslim world. The general view among Muslims was—and still is—that the United Nations was an organization used by America for its own purposes. As an example, Muslims cite UN Security Council resolution 242, which calls on Israel to vacate Palestinian territory captured in 1967 and occupied since then by force. They point out that no step has been taken to implement this Security Council resolution in the last four decades, yet the full force of an international coalition was brought to bear on Iraq. The perception of double standards constantly being applied has tarnished the image of both the United States and the United Nations—and not only in the Muslim world. This view of Muslims being subjected to injustice feeds into the collective sense of victimization shared across the Islamic world.

Against this backdrop, the drumbeat for war against Iraq emanating from Washington after 9/11 fell on deaf Muslim ears. Despite the public relations blitz launched by the American and British governments, few Muslims as well as non-Muslims were convinced that the war against Iraq was justified. As the leader of this campaign, the United States was largely isolated, with even close allies like France and Germany declining to sign up.

The Turkish response to an American request to use its territory to launch an attack on Iraq is particularly instructive. Here was a Cold War ally, a major member of NATO, and a rare Muslim friend of Israel's. The country's powerful generals had traditionally maintained close links with the Pentagon. When asked to provide logistical support and right of passage to the United States, to Washington's surprise and horror, Turkey said no. When the American request was placed before the Turkish parliament, members overwhelmingly voted against it.

I first went to Turkey as a student at the Middle East Technical University in Ankara nearly fifty years ago. This institution had been established with American assistance, and the campus was self-consciously modelled on American universities. The public sound system blared out Western pop songs during the lunch break, and it was unthinkable for a girl to wear a headscarf on campus. In those days, downtown Ankara was faintly rustic, but aspirations to copy American fashions were everywhere. On campus in those days, there were no calls to prayer and no mosque, even though the overwhelming majority of the student body was Muslim. Istanbul was even more Westernized, with night clubs, bars, and girls in skimpy skirts in evidence across the city.

Over the years, I have seen Turkey change into an increasingly conservative country. On successive visits, growing evidence of an Islamic revival has become apparent, ranging from an amplified call to prayer at the Blue Mosque to restrictions on the sale of alcohol in certain places. The Justice and Development Party (AKP) is mildly Islamist and has held power since 2002. During this period, it has turned the economy into a powerhouse, and has steadily steered Turkey toward a more independent position in the region. From toeing the American line and being Israel's most (and only) steadfast Muslim friend, Turkey is now widely seen as an independent and important player in the Islamic world. Thus, the country's rejection of the American request to use its Incirlik base to conduct operations against Iraq in 2003 came as no great shock to those familiar with the country's gradual transformation and ultimately raised Turkey's standing in the Muslim world. Rebuffed time and again by the European Union in its attempt to obtain membership, Turkey has increasingly perceived its place as squarely within the Muslim world. This shift has been propelled by the country's rising middle class, which is neither secular nor Westernized. The AKP's support comes from an increasingly religious majority that sees their country as having drifted a long way from its Islamic moorings and now insists that it return to its traditional roots.

Meanwhile, in Pakistan, violent demonstrations broke out to protest the American-led attack on Iraq. Indeed, the public reaction was so hostile that even a military dictator like General Musharraf could not think of sending Pakistani troops to become members of the coalition. No Muslim troops joined the fighting despite Bush's entreaties and blandishments.

When the first missiles and bombs were launched against targets in Baghdad on 24 March 2003, their effect was electrifying. Although 'shock and awe'—the US military's description of its aerial campaign—was seen as an exciting but bloodless video game by most Americans from the perspective of pilots flying high over their targets, it was viewed from ground zero in millions of Muslim homes. Camera teams from Al Jazeera beamed images of dead and bleeding victims of the assault as flames engulfed their homes. Exhausted doctors spoke into the cameras, complaining that they had no medicines to treat the wounded as their stocks had been depleted by years of sanctions. Muslims across the Islamic world were glued to their TV sets around the clock as the tragedy went on in real time. The upbeat note evident in the voices of CNN and BBC announcers was in stark contrast with the sombre expressions on the faces of their counterparts on news channels in the Muslim world.

As the short, one-sided battle progressed, and Iraqi resistance crumbled in the face of a mobile, high-tech onslaught, Muslim viewers mourned and seethed with rage. During the first Gulf War, trucks adorned with paintings of Saddam Hussein on a white steed could be seen across Pakistan. At that point in time, he was widely viewed as a modern Saladin, the Kurdish commander who defeated the Crusaders. During this attack, Saddam was seen as a tragic figure being targeted by a vengeful and implacable United States. Although the Muslim street did not explode in the paroxysm of anger that had been anticipated, a deep bitterness took hold. In even the most liberal, Westernized Muslim household, people passionately believed that America had invaded Iraq for its oil, and to take a major supporter of the Palestinian people out of the equation. Thus, as the underground Iraqi resistance grew and mounting numbers of American soldiers began returning home in body bags, a widespread feeling of quiet rejoicing continued to grow.

This short excerpt from an article by Said Al-Naggar, writing in the Egyptian newspaper *Al-Wafd* shortly after the attack on Iraq, gives a flavour of how most Arabs saw the one-sided conflict:

> The invasion might bring material dividends such as benefiting the 'oil interests' of Bush and his Vice President Dick Cheney. It will

> bring profit to the American military industrial complex and satisfy Israel's aim of redrawing the Middle East and attaining hegemony. But it will also entail a loss of credibility and respect for America in the world, which cannot be compensated for.

If the invasion of Iraq infuriated millions of Muslims, the images of torture from the prison camp at Abu Ghraib radicalized thousands. Here was the clearest evidence that the Americans were out not just to defeat the Iraqis, but also to grind their faces into the dust. The photographs of Iraqi prisoners being stripped and humiliated by a female American soldier seared the consciousness of Muslims everywhere. Neither official denials from the Pentagon, nor the trial of lower-level soldiers, succeeded in convincing Muslims that the treatment of prisoners at this notorious prison camp was not part of a deliberate policy.

However, the element of hypocrisy in this outrage should be noted. For years, Saddam Hussein tortured prisoners in far worse ways without provoking protests in his own country—or anywhere else in the Muslim world. He was certainly not alone in his efforts. Year after year, Amnesty International as well as other human rights organizations have documented numerous cases of torture in most Muslim countries. Indeed, physical abuse is the standard operating procedure during police investigations and is a routine tool used to exercise political repression. Even in relatively open Muslim societies, such as Pakistan and Turkey, torture is common. The Human Rights Commission of Pakistan has detailed hundreds of such cases in its annual reports.

Nevertheless, America could no longer claim the moral high ground after its invasion of Iraq and the widespread pattern of prisoner abuse that emerged during the occupation. Neo-conservative talk of introducing democracy in the region fell on deaf ears. Isolated and out on a limb, Bush could not afford to antagonize his Arab friends in the region like Saudi Arabia, Egypt, and Jordan by pressing them to reform their authoritarian political systems. Indeed, conservative Islamic ideology gained ground, partly as a reaction to the invasion of Iraq, as evident in the electoral success of Hamas in Gaza and the West Bank and Hezbollah in Lebanon. In the 2002 elections in Pakistan, Islamic parties did better than ever before—albeit with more than a little help from General Musharraf and the ISI, the country's powerful military intelligence service.

Muslims were increasingly seeing the American-led wars in Afghanistan and Iraq as part of a wider assault on them. Suddenly, bin Laden's long-standing demand for foreign troops to leave Muslim lands began making sense. So virulent did this anti-American sentiment become that Muslims have closed their eyes to the many positive humanitarian gestures Washington has made in the last few years toward them. In a talk I gave to post-grad students at the Area Studies Centre for Africa, North and South America at Islamabad University, I asked them to name a few pro-Muslim initiatives launched by Washington in the recent past. Not getting a single response, I mentioned several, including the intervention in Bosnia to halt the genocide of Bosnian Muslims, a similar policy to prevent Serbs from killing Muslims in Kosovo, the generous American medical and financial aid that poured into north Pakistan in the wake of a devastating earthquake in 2004 that killed around 60,000, and the help in providing food and shelter to a million displaced people when the Taliban took over Pakistan's Swat Valley.

Another fallout of the American response to 9/11 in Afghanistan and Iraq was other states' grateful embrace of the policy of preemptive attack when faced with even the remotest terrorist threat. In addition, national struggles that were not religious in any sense except that freedom fighters happened to be Muslims were dubbed extremist conflicts, thereby justifying the most repressive measures. Suddenly, even justifiable struggles for independence, autonomy, or a share in power became terrorist movements. From Chechnya to Kashmir, local and national conflicts were tagged as Muslim uprisings. This became a self-fulfilling prophecy as these movements began forming links with global jihadist outfits and soon developed agendas that outgrew their original, limited goals. To an increasing extent, they energized each other and received moral and material support from larger Muslim groups. Ultimately, some of them developed local franchises of the Al Qaeda brand.

However, few Americans were aware of the termites eating away at the woodwork. They focused on Iraq and the bloody uprising gaining momentum there, taking their eyes off the ball in Afghanistan. Considered a minor sideshow compared to the increasingly bloody occupation of Iraq, Afghanistan began seeing a steady resurgence of the Taliban. Once down and out following the initial American-led assault, Mullah Omar's forces took advantage of the shift in Bush's focus to the Middle East. This irrational diversion of attention to Iraq has cost the United States dearly—and not just in terms of dollars and lives. As we have noted, the unjustified and illegal war against Iraq has unnecessarily alienated millions of Muslims and lost America all the sympathy and goodwill it had immediately following 9/11.

For Muslims who had settled in the United States and Europe, the invasion of Iraq posed an intolerable dilemma. They could not bring themselves to rationalize the killing of innocent Iraqi civilians; as such, they could hardly 'support the troops.' At the same time, many of them felt they were the targets of suspicion as part of a Fifth Column in an increasingly hostile America after 9/11, and in Britain after the terror attacks on London transport on 7/7. Many young Muslims sought to resolve this inner conflict by joining the ranks of those waging jihad as mujahideen.

Thousands of Muslims made their way to Iraq to join the insurgency, with hundreds volunteering as suicide bombers. Paying large sums to people smugglers to lead them across the porous Iraqi border with Syria, these young jihadis were taken to safe houses across the occupied country, where they were indoctrinated and instructed. Most of them could not even fire a gun, but pulling the cord on a suicide vest is not a very complicated task. A newly formed franchise of Al Qaeda in Iraq used this cannon fodder to launch a series of lethal attacks against occupation forces, those Iraqis seen to be collaborating with them, and Shi'ites who began to flex their muscles for the first time after being dominated by the Sunni minority under Saddam Hussein. Casualties among allied forces mounted rapidly. Young Saudis began crossing into neighbouring Iraq to join the fray. Although the Pentagon barred the media from broadcasting footage of bodies returning home in coffins in an effort to downplay its losses, the numbers began to escalate to alarming levels, raising the spectre of Vietnam.

Considerable evidence suggests that fighters travelled to Afghanistan from Iraq to instruct the Taliban in the successful techniques they had developed to make improvised explosive devices (IEDs), which continue to be used to devastating effect against Western forces. Suicide bombing—a new weapon for Afghans—made its appearance on the battlefield and has been used to deadly effect. This cross-fertilization of tactics and ideas between jihadi groups is having far-reaching effects. Of course, the Internet has had a profound impact on recruitment and motivation, a phenomenon we will discuss in a later chapter.

Even as American troops are pulling out of Iraq, the legacy of the war is a potent one. The country was always a fragile entity held together by a succession of strongmen. For centuries, the Ottoman Empire ruled over Basra, Baghdad, and Mosul, the three provinces that constitute modern Iraq. Only after the defeat of the Turks in World War I did the British cobble together a state that comprised all three provinces. Now, after the fall of Hussein and the withdrawal of American forces, it is entirely possible that Sunnis, Shi'ites, and Kurds might decide to go their own way once more. Should this happen, the fallout of this new reality across the region will be vast. Rather than ushering in a new era of democracy and freedom, the American invasion of Iraq might be the precursor of the Balkanization of the country, together with all the attendant risks and violence a secession brings in its wake. As we know all too well, extremist forces thrive in confusion and chaos. Presently, the prospects for cohesion do not look good as Iraqi leaders continue to squabble. The presence of US forces is acting as a glue, but once they pull out, it is possible that Kurds, Shi'ites and Sunnis will revert to the Ottoman model of three separate states.

American and British cheerleaders for the war in Iraq—from Bush and Blair downwards—have long insisted that the attack and occupation had little to do with the wave of anti-West sentiment that has gained ground in the Muslim world. This flies in the face of my personal experience as well as the polling numbers. It also contradicts the reality of the increased poison being spewed from hundreds of Muslim websites.

I got to know Latif, a successful Moroccan businessman who has travelled widely and is perfectly bilingual in Arabic and French, a few years ago in Morocco, and caught up with him again in Canada on a short visit in 2010. Inevitably, the conversation turned to the state of the Muslim world and the rise of extremist violence.

'You know, Irfan,' he said to me one evening. 'I was so pro-American when I was young that I even made a plan to run away from home and hide on a ship sailing to New York. I was fourteen then, and James Dean was my hero. My dream was to get on a motorcycle and travel across the country. I even sent my son to the American School in Rabat and then to a university in the States. But even I was totally opposed to the invasion of Iraq. Of course Saddam Hussein was a vicious dictator, but we all know there are others like him in the region. And I certainly didn't believe for a moment that he had any WMDs left after the first Gulf War. It's this insane war that has inflamed and radicalized so many in the Muslim world, and turned them against America.'

This view has been echoed time and again in conversations in drawing rooms as well as in cyberspace. The theme of the Americans wanting to grab Iraqi oil and eliminate a leader who stood up to them repeatedly recurs. Some American readers have asked me why Iraqis aren't grateful for being freed from Saddam Hussein's cruel yoke. It is certainly true that Western troops were not welcomed by cheering crowds and garlands of flowers. Nevertheless, a majority of Iraqis were genuinely happy to be rid of a leader who had oppressed them for years. However, when the occupation began going wrong, their hope turned to despair. Security broke down, electricity and supplies became even more erratic, unemployment soared, and above all ordinary Iraqis were often subjected to daily violence and humiliation by foreign occupation troops. Civilian casualties mounted as many were caught in the crossfire between insurgents and American soldiers. As the Shi'ite–Sunni warfare reached a crescendo, entire neighbourhoods were subjected to ethnic cleansing.

Americans tend to forget that for all of Hussein's authoritarian ways, he ran an essentially secular dictatorship in which religion did not figure as a major factor in policy-making. Thus, the country's substantial Christian minority was completely integrated into mainstream society—so much so that Tariq Aziz, a Christian, served as foreign minister for years. Others did well in business and the professions. However, following the American-led invasion, Islamists suddenly found themselves in a position of power and turned against their Christian neighbours, forcing tens of thousands to flee the country and find refuge in Syria and Jordan; those who could escaped to Europe and America. According to estimates, some 400,000 of a million Christians have been forced to leave Iraq. Churches have been attacked, and scores of Christians have been killed by extremists.

By the same measure, pre-invasion Iraq provided women with greater protection and opportunities than just about any other Arab country. They were represented in the bureaucracy, universities, and professional fields and were free to move around and dress pretty much as they pleased. Certainly they were not forced to remain cloistered at home or to cover themselves up in burqas or even headscarves. This changed abruptly in the wake of the invasion. Again, Sunni and Shi'ite clerics imposed the same backward vision of Islam on women as their counterparts do in Iran and Saudi Arabia. Thus, while all Iraqis bore the brunt of the war and the occupation, Christians and women were persecuted and marginalized much as they are in other Muslim countries.

It is also important to remember that for all the many flaws of Iraq's leaders over the last fifty years, they did achieve nearly universal education. Moreover, before a decade of sanctions gutted it, they had an excellent public health system. So when Americans want to know why the people of Iraq are so ungrateful for being rid of Saddam Hussein, it should be noted that their expectations had been raised only to be quickly dashed by the grim reality of the occupation. Across the region, Muslims recognized the Iraqis as a sophisticated, educated people; although they saw Saddam Hussein as an aggressive dictator, for them he had the redeeming quality of standing up to America and Israel.

To see this country and its people being subjected to unprecedented violence and humiliation was a painful experience, even for the most moderate Muslims. Iraqis' daily tribulations prominently featured on TV screens across the Muslim world thanks to Al Jazeera. Not surprisingly, the Doha-based TV channel drew the wrath of American generals and politicians alike. When its offices were targeted by American troops earlier in Kabul and then in Baghdad, few Muslims bought the explanation that the attacks had been accidental.

As the insurgency intensified and Al Qaeda became more entrenched, its computer-savvy cyber-warriors began putting out a powerful message of resistance, invoking the obligation of jihad to defend a Muslim nation occupied by foreign forces. Adult male Muslims are indeed under an Islamic injunction to come to the defense of fellow Muslims being oppressed by non-believers. Many answered this call while the millions who did not or could not harboured a deep resentment bordering on hatred for the occupying forces. Some young men plotted vengeance in their apartments in New York or the suburbs of London. Clerics leading the prayers in mosques around the world amplified the message of resistance and jihad. From Morocco to Indonesia, Muslims exulted as allied casualties mounted. Indeed, the insurgents restored a measure of pride among the *ummah*: At last, the Americans were getting a taste of their own medicine.

This must make unpleasant reading for most Americans, but the reality is that the path from the Twin Towers to Kabul to Baghdad now goes through some very hostile territory. Much of this anger has built up since 2003, when Bush—for his own bizarre reasons—decided to attack a country that had nothing to do with either 9/11 or WMDs. Unfortunately for the United States and the rest of the world, the American Congress and the media rolled over before Bush and his cabal of neocons, ultimately failing to exercise due diligence on the flimsy and doctored evidence presented to them. Blair eagerly clambered on board the war party's bandwagon instead of urging restraint, as France and Germany did. There are times when an ally can and should risk unpopularity and counsel caution instead of joining the pack. Blair, to his everlasting discredit, found the proximity to imperial power too beguiling to resist.

Thus, the die was cast, and the world has changed forever. We are left to wonder how things would have turned out had the United States and its allies focused on Afghanistan and not been diverted by the misadventure in Iraq. With a stronger military presence in Afghanistan, the Taliban would not have been able to regroup and stage the comeback they have, and NATO forces would not be groping for an exit strategy that will see their foes back in power as soon as they leave. The year 2002 was a pivotal moment in history, when things could have gone either way: By invading Iraq, the United States energized political Islam and served as a recruiting agency for extremists. A Taliban victory in Afghanistan will electrify the Muslim world, sending out a signal of American vulnerability and the power of political Islam. When the Afghan mujahideen forced the mighty Red Army from their country, millions of Muslims cheered. An American defeat would bring many new recruits to the extremist cause while destabilizing pro-West governments from Islamabad to Riyadh. An Indian official, Y.K. Sinha, confirmed this view during a discussion with US Political Counselor Uzra Zeya in New Delhi, according to State

Department cable ID 250219 dated 23 February 2010, released by Wikileaks:

> Sinha closed the discussion on Afghanistan by asserting that a precipitate exit would embolden 'fanatics' to feel they had defeated both the USSR and the US, and the result would be very bad for the region.

The fallout would not stop there. As young Muslims become further radicalized, their host communities in the West will become more suspicious and hostile. Across the Muslim world, American interests will be increasingly targeted. In short, the tragic events of 9/11 will haunt us for years to come as Bush's 'war on terror' morphs into a war without end. The Twin Towers have indeed cast a very long shadow.

Mercifully, the rapid and dramatic changes taking place in the Middle East and North Africa offer a glimmer of hope. As we will discuss later on, the Arab Spring has suddenly opened up possibilities that simply did not exist a year ago. How the United States responds to them will determine the shape of things to come. Will it seize this opportunity or will it stay behind the curve? Only time will tell.

3

The Caliphate Versus the Great Satan

Often, non-Muslim friends ask me what militant groups really *want*? Given the thousands dead, the suicide bombings and other wanton acts of terrorism that have claimed so many innocent victims in America and elsewhere, this is a fair question. The answer, in a word, is power. The following quote from *Milestones*, a seminal work by Sayyid Qutb, Islam's most influential thinker of the twentieth century, gives a sense of the drive that propels and sustains the ongoing Islamic resurgence:

> Conditions change, the Muslim loses his physical power and is conquered; yet the consciousness does not depart from him that he is the most superior. If he remains a Believer, he looks upon his conqueror from a superior position. He remains certain that this is a temporary condition which will pass away and that faith will turn the tide from which there is no escape. Even if death is his portion, he will never bow his head. Death comes to all, but for him there is martyrdom. He will proceed to the Garden, while his conquerors go to the fire. What a difference!

Thus, the ongoing conflict can be seen as a struggle to regain the power the Islamic world once wielded, but was lost long ago to the West. Starting in the seventeenth century, as modern learning, science and technology empowered Europe, the mighty Muslim empires of Turkey, Iran and Moghul India went into a terminal decline. Conquered and colonized, much of the Muslim world sank into a torpor of defeat and despair. However, the resentment at being displaced in the global pecking order simmered away just below the surface, inspiring revivalist movements from time to time. Perhaps the most enduring of these was the Muslim Brotherhood, an organization formed by Hassan al-Bannah in Egypt in 1928. The inspiration to many Islamist movements, the Muslim Brotherhood gave birth to Hamas and Al Qaeda, among other militant groups. Although it proclaims itself to be a non-violent movement, many accuse it of being involved in a terrorist campaign against the Egyptian state, especially in the overthrow of the Egyptian monarchy in 1952. Over the years, many extreme, violent sub-groups have splintered off from the Brotherhood to carve out their own bloody identity. Long banned in Egypt, the Brothers have been subjected to decades of imprisonment, torture and execution. Although some curbs have been relaxed in recent years, the Brothers were still subject to frequent crackdowns under Mubarak. In its earlier phase, the Brotherhood grew at a phenomenal rate: From a mere 800 members in 1936, it swiftly spanned the Arab world with an estimated 2 million members in 1948. Clearly, the Brotherhood had tapped into a deep undercurrent of frustration with the post-colonial, secular power structures that emerged after World War II. Above all, the creation of Israel in 1948, and the humiliating military defeat the Arabs suffered in its immediate aftermath, contributed to the Brotherhood's popularity. The message from its leaders at this critical juncture was that the Arabs had been defeated by non-believers because they had turned away from the faith and had been indulging in hedonistic, un-Islamic practices.

The organization's motto is revealing: 'Allah is our objective. The Prophet is our leader. The Qur'an is our constitution. Jihad is our way. Dying in the way of Allah is our highest aspiration.' Its stated objective is to reorder Muslim society along the precepts of the Qur'an and the Sunnah (the words and the traditions of the Prophet) as they constitute 'the perfect way of life,' according to the Brotherhood. Once Islamic governments come into being, they must be unified under a Caliphate in a *Dar el-Islam*, the Domain of Islam that would reclaim lost Muslim lands and stretch from Spain to Indonesia.

A return to the Caliphate is a recurring theme in the demands proclaimed by almost every militant group as well as in the writings of Muslim thinkers and in many sermons after the Friday prayers in mosques across the world. One reason is that this institution is at the heart of Islamic scriptures and forms the lynchpin of Muslim society. As such, it is even more crucial than the pivotal role the Papacy plays in Catholicism. When Western troops invaded Turkey after World War I, thousands of Indian Muslims donated money—and women gave their jewelry—to help Turkey because the Caliph had been resident in Istanbul for centuries. A political movement to save the Caliphate was launched in India to influence the British, although it was the new ultra-secular Turkish government of Mustafa Kemal Pasha that ultimately abolished this ancient institution in 1924 and exiled the incumbent to Italy.

In 2010, I saw an elegant self-portrait of the last Caliph, Abdul Mejid, in Istanbul's Modern Art Gallery. It revealed a sensitive, elderly man with a sad, slightly quizzical expression, wearing full Ottoman regalia. An accomplished painter, two of his skilfully executed seascapes are also on display in the gallery. Shortly before being removed from his exalted rank, he wrote to the new president's office, asking that his allowance be increased. This incensed Mustafa Kemal, who was already looking for ways to abolish the Caliphate. He wrote an angry response, accusing the Caliph of 'impertinence.' Finally, the Turkish leader found an excuse when two Indian Muslim politicians wrote to him, requesting that the Caliphate be preserved. Denouncing this initiative as interference in Turkey's internal affairs, he finally ended an institution that had survived since the advent of Islam, albeit in a much debased form.

This constant refrain to revive the Caliphate recurs time and again. For example, on a Pakistan defence website, an exchange on the institution appeared not long ago. One blogger wrote:

> The entire Muslim world fell into ruin when the Khilafat [Caliphate] ended. We've been in a deep hole ever since for many decades now. Muslims, now numbering more than 1.3 billion, have no power or say in the world. We're just a bunch of pathetic heaps who whine and complain about our condition...I pray that I live to see the day when the Khilafat returns. Muslims have ruled this world many times, we can do it again. The hidden beast that is the *ummah* will shake the world.

The blogger forgets that Islam had been in decline long before the end of the Caliphate. Nevertheless, this dream ripples through the echo chamber that is the World Wide Web. Islamic websites and chat rooms make constant reference to the return of the Caliphate in much the same way Christian evangelists talk about the Second Coming. The difference, of course, is that the former event will signal the return of the Muslims to their rightful place on the global stage, whereas the latter will usher in the end of the world.

At this point, an American reader could be excused for asking what all this has to do with him or her. After all, Muslim aspirations, beliefs, and traditions are remote from modern American society. Why shouldn't people living far from Muslim lands be allowed to get on with their lives? The problem lies in the fact that—for good or ill—the leadership of the Western, Judeo-Christian world has passed on to America; with this mantle goes the poisoned chalice.

At the end of World War II, an exhausted and bankrupt Europe was in no mood or shape to harbour any dreams of resurrecting its colonial empires. Colonies rapidly declared independence, and a new, post-colonial era began. Meanwhile, the post-war Soviet Union started flexing its muscles and exerted a strong pull among newly liberated countries whose leaders often had socialist leanings. To counter Soviet influence, Washington began an aggressive policy of buying friends and reinforcing right-wing governments, irrespective of their lack of democratic credentials and legitimacy. In fact, the pragmatic State Department seemed to prefer dealing with strongmen who could and did crush left-wing and liberal democratic movements and leaders. Had US-supported leadership in the Third World been able to provide reasonably decent governance, it is likely that the siren song of socialism would have lost some of its appeal. However, in country after country, the corruption and incompetence of governments enjoying American support caused an increase in the mass appeal of left-wing parties.

In much of the Muslim world, a motley crew of kings, despots, and generals have held sway since the end of World War II. In the few democracies that have managed to emerge in the region, elected politicians have struggled to keep powerful generals in their barracks. Almost invariably, Washington has tended to support the most dictatorial regimes, consequently becoming widely viewed as backing the ruling elites against the interests of ordinary people. More often than not, the bulk of American aid has gone to the armed forces that use their new weapons to maintain an unjust status quo and persecute nascent democratic movements to keep despots in power. Thus, Americans have become hate figures among ordinary Muslims for propping up rotten, repressive governments. In Washington's calculus, populist leaders tend to assert their independence and balk at taking orders. During the Cold War, they were as likely as not to play both sides in order to get aid from Moscow and Washington.

Thus, for tactical but short-sighted reasons, America has ended up on the wrong side of history. Although the Cold War might have been won, the battle for the hearts and minds of most of the world's 1.3 billion Muslims has been lost. Today, the overriding narrative is about the widespread perception that America pursues anti-Muslim policies either directly (as in Iraq and Afghanistan) or indirectly by giving Israel a blank check to dispossess and oppress the Palestinians, and by supporting corrupt and inept despots who exploit their people. There is enough truth in these charges to make them seem part of a larger pattern.

Many Americans cannot understand why they are so hated in

Iran, for example. When Ayatollah Khomeini dubbed the United States the Great Satan, he may have provoked some superior smirks in the West, but he was articulating a deeply shared hatred for a country widely perceived to have done so much to harm the interests of Iran. For much of the nineteenth and twentieth centuries, a weak and backward Persia was dominated by the rivalry between Britain and Russia, with both great powers trampling over Persian dignity and sovereignty at will.

After World War II, Iran was ruled by a young and inexperienced king, Reza Shah Pahelvi, under British tutelage. When his democratically elected prime minister, Dr Mohammed Mosaddegh, nationalized the British-controlled Anglo-Iranian Oil Company (AIOC) in 1951, the stage was set for a CIA-led coup against an elected government. Although this might have seemed a good idea at the time, it ultimately changed the course of Iranian history and poisoned relations with the United States for decades to come. The AIOC continued to violate its 1933 treaty with Iran, yet it refused to renegotiate prices or the living conditions of its Iranian workers. After the company was nationalized, the British attempted to destabilize the Mosaddegh government by hiring agitators and demonstrators. With Eisenhower's election in the United States in 1952, Britain's Prime Minister Winston Churchill found an ally who was willing to mount a full-blown coup to topple Mosaddegh. Demonstrations (paid for by the CIA) broke out, and on August 19, 1953, Mosaddegh was arrested and sentenced to life imprisonment. Many of his supporters were executed or jailed. The Shah had fled before the coup, but now returned in triumph and ordered the execution of many army officers.

It is interesting to speculate on Iran's trajectory had its nascent democracy been allowed to flourish instead of being strangled at birth by the United States and Britain. Here was a key, non-Arab Muslim country with a rich, ancient, and sophisticated civilization. Blessed with large oil and gas reserves, there is every possibility that it might have emerged as a modern, progressive state instead of following the course it so tragically did. The CIA coup led directly to a repressive dictatorship under the Shah that lasted nearly three decades. The Shah's cruel rule subsequently created the conditions that spawned another three decades of theocratic oppression under the ayatollahs. Thus, in a short-sighted search for a pliable, pro-western regime in Iran, the United States ended up with probably the most anti-American government in the world. There is some irony in this demonstration of the law of unintended consequences, but for the people of Iran and the region, the elevation of a benighted cabal of clerics to power in Tehran is a nightmare they have been living with for more than thirty years. The region has also faced the challenge of Iran's attempts to export its Islamic revolution.

As it was, the 1953 coup ushered in a quarter century of brutal dictatorship. All opposition was systematically crushed. Savak, the Shah's hated and feared intelligence agency, was trained by the CIA and Israel's Mossad, and relentlessly pursued the Shah's opponents at home and abroad. My father was the UNESCO representative in Iran in the late 1960s, and I travelled to Iran for a couple of vacations during this time. While I enjoyed exploring Iran's rich and ancient cultural heritage, I was aware of the tight control the government exercised. For instance, the local police had to be informed if more than six guests were being invited to a private function. *Kayhan*, the English-language newspaper, was utterly devoid of any critical comment about the government. Iranians leaving the country had to get special exit permits, which were refused to anybody suspected of harbouring anti-Shah sentiments.

A few years later, in 1973, my then-wife and I were travelling overland to Turkey from Pakistan, and met a young man and woman in our compartment on the Tehran–Istanbul train. As the journey took three days, we tried to get to know them. Initially, they were quite guarded, which we attributed to shyness. However, as soon as we crossed the Turkish border, they opened up and told us about the reality of life in Iran under the Shah. They were brother and sister, and both knew university students who had been picked up by Savak, never to reappear. Their parents were afraid to press their inquiries out of fear that they too would be arrested. They told us about police raids on student hostels and the beatings inflicted on student activists in public places.

While most of his countrymen lived in poverty and fear, the Shah enjoyed a life of obscene luxury. Tehran put forth an impression of wealth and sophistication, yet the vast hinterland was deprived of the most basic amenities. When I drove to Pakistan from Germany with friends as a university student in 1963, our car was often stopped in east Iran by road workers begging for matchboxes. The oil embargo of 1973 brought a bonanza for Iran and other OPEC countries. Suddenly, the Shah was Washington's poster boy as he went on a shopping spree for the latest American arms. The United States saw him as a lynchpin in its Middle East anti-Soviet coalition. Even as the Shah was teetering on the brink in 1979, shortly before his ouster, US President Jimmy Carter called Iran an 'island of stability in one of the most troubled areas of the world.'

Thus, an entire generation of Iranians grew up under the oppressive regime presided over by a Shah who was very visibly propped up by successive American administrations. For young, idealistic Iranians, the lack of any democratic space was intensely frustrating. Many joined the underground Communist party Tudeh. Others gravitated toward the Muslim-Marxist Mujahedin-e-Khalq (MEK), or the People's Mujahideen (plural form of mujahid, one following the path of jihad). Both were hunted by Savak for their fierce opposition to the Shah. Ironically, while they fought with the ayatollahs for the overthrow of the Iranian monarch in 1979, they were early victims of the Islamic Republic's refusal to accommodate any left-wing groups in its ranks. The ruthless purge that was carried out by the ayatollahs and their security forces was a precursor of the savage clampdown imposed on dissenters who took to the streets in protest against President Ahmedinejad's apparently rigged reelection in 2009.

Given the long and bitter history of American involvement in the overthrow of an elected government and the subsequent support for the Shah, the occupation of the American embassy by young Islamist activists in Tehran in 1980 should have surprised nobody. The long drawn-out confrontation dragged on for 444 days, dooming Carter's reelection chances. Most Americans were rightly outraged by the storming of their embassy and the capture of 66 American hostages; however, they failed to appreciate what drove a group of students, egged on by the ayatollahs, to commit this breach of international law and diplomatic norms. These young zealots had grown up during the Shah's despotic rule and were convinced that their ordeal had been caused by the American-led coup against Mosaddegh, and Washington's subsequent support for the king and the security apparatus that underpinned his throne. Nor were these perceptions far off the mark: A substantial body of documents, articles and books has since been published to establish the close links between America and Iran under the Shah. This relationship spanned the spectrum from arms sales to economic cooperation to collaboration between the CIA and Savak. The CIA's hand behind the Mosaddegh coup is equally well documented. Thus, although the rest of the world watched the hostage crisis with alarm and disapproval, for Iranians and many in the wider Muslim world, the embassy takeover represented payback for American policies. The botched rescue attempt ordered by President Carter handed the ayatollahs' revolutionary government a propaganda victory: For many believers, the sandstorm that brought down several American helicopters was a sign of Allah's approval of the Islamic revolution in Iran.

The crippling economic sanctions imposed on Iran following the hostage crisis included a freeze on Iranian assets and bank accounts held in the United States. Billions of dollars of Iranian funds remain tied up in court cases in America to this day, adding to the lingering bitterness that continues to mark US-Iranian relations.

While Iran's agony has continued under the ayatollahs for the last three decades, the older generation of revolutionaries remains locked in an anti-American stance. The good news is that younger Iranians are only dimly aware of the Shah's despotism and the role the United States played in those bad old days to subvert democratic aspirations. For them, the goal is to throw out the ayatollahs and their theocratic rule. American efforts to nurture the democratic Green movement that sprang up spontaneously in response to President Ahmedinejad's rigged reelection have had mixed results. Young protestors have been branded (and often jailed and tortured) as American stooges. US-led attempts to neuter the Iranian nuclear programme have run into the patriotism of a proud and ancient nation that views them as unjust efforts to block its legitimate rights to nuclear technology.

Consider the world through Iranian eyes. To the east lie Pakistan and India, both nuclear powers that built up their atomic arsenals in defiance of American-led non-proliferation efforts; to the west is Israel, a covert and hostile nuclear power that has accumulated a sizeable stockpile of atomic warheads with a wink and a nod from Washington and is now threatening to attack Iran; to the north is Russia, with its huge nuclear arsenal; and to the south is the Gulf, where a large and threatening American naval presence is on permanent deployment. Afghanistan to the east and Iraq to the west have large bases with tens of thousands of American soldiers and hundreds of military aircraft. It is a small wonder that many Iranians feel surrounded and besieged, and therefore want their own nuclear deterrent. For them, American-led UN sanctions are a continuation of the anti-Iran policies Washington has been pursuing for nearly six decades. They have good reason to ask why Iranian nuclear ambitions should be so strenuously opposed when other neighbouring states have been allowed to attain nuclear status.

Despite Ahmedinejad's undignified posturing and his hateful anti-Semitic rhetoric, many Iranians see American double standards at work here. Although Shi'ite Iran is viewed with suspicion by many Sunni states, there is considerable sympathy for it at the street level. Many Muslims around the world see it as a victim of American bullying. Publicly, they cite Saddam Hussein's non-existent WMDs as an analogy: A similar drumbeat was heard in Western capitals and the media before the second Gulf War.

Among themselves, they ask why Israel should be allowed to have a monopoly on nuclear arms in the region.

These are legitimate concerns and questions, but thus far, Washington has failed to address them. Given the power of its military—the United States spends nearly as much as the rest of the world combined on its armed forces—it is inevitable that it has assumed the role of world policeman. Another reason, of course, is that its economic and financial interests are so far-flung that it needs to maintain a global military presence. However, the cop on the beat is often resented and disliked, even by law-abiding citizens.

This brief Iranian case study serves as a reminder of how events in the distant past can haunt us decades later. It also underscores the fact that those at the receiving end of history often live in the past, unable to let go of ancient wrongs. Many Iranians have speculated about how different their country would be today but for the CIA coup against Mosaddegh in 1953. Few Americans would be aware of or interested in this bit of history, yet it plays a central part in how Iranians perceive the United States sixty years after the event.

Similarly, millions of Muslims hark back to a warm, fuzzy memory of early Islam, when the first four Caliphs ruled a nascent Islamic empire in its early years. Although three of them met violent ends, their rule is seen as an idyllic period. For almost all Muslims, this was the golden period of Islam, when harmony and equality reigned, and exploitation and injustice did not exist. This powerful myth now inspires many to seek a return to that utopian state and drives the agenda of political Islam. Only the restoration of the Caliphate can bring Islam back to its pure, unsullied roots. The West, led by America, is seen to be blocking the attainment of this dream through its support of pro-West, un-Islamic despots and its perceived anti-Muslim policies.

This is an important strand in the anti-American narrative that has taken hold among extremist Islamist groups as well as among many everyday Muslims around the world. However, it's not the only one, as we will see in subsequent chapters.

4

Past Tense, Future Imperfect

If we take the historical perspective, the ongoing confrontation between Islam and Christendom began long before either faith was born. One person who took this long view was Osama bin Laden. In an audiotape delivered to Al Jazeera on 4 January 2004, the Al Qaeda chief made clear his thoughts about the conflict in the context of the American occupation of Iraq:

> There can be no dialogue with occupiers except with weapons. If we look at the nature of the conflict between us and the West, we find that when they invaded our countries more than 2,500 years ago they did not have a sound religion or ethics. Their motive was to steal and plunder. Our ancestors in Bilad al-Sham [Greater Syria] remained under occupation for more than ten decades. We defeated them only after the mission of our Prophet Mohammed. It was the true commitment to Islam that reshaped the Arab character, liberated it from pre-Islamic concepts, enlightened hearts and minds, and released energies. At that time, neither the Arabs nor anybody else could stand in the way of the battalions of faith. The Persians, Tartars, Turks, Romans, and Berbers collapsed in front of the shouts of 'God is great....
>
> When our adherence to our religion weakened, and our rulers became corrupt, we became weak and the Romans returned, waging their infamous Crusader wars. They occupied the al-Aqsa Mosque[1], but after 90 years we regained our strength when we

[1] The famous mosque in the Dome of the Rock in Jerusalem.

> returned to our religion. Thus, with the help of God, we regained the al-Aqsa Mosque at the hands of a wise leader who pursued a sound approach. The leader was Salah-al-Din[2] ...Islamic countries in the past century were not liberated from the Crusaders' military occupation except through jihad in the name of God....[3]

Most Americans are unburdened by this version of history and could be excused for dismissing bin Laden's tirades as the ravings of a deluded madman. Nevertheless, his words on perceived historic wrongs resonate deeply among many Muslims. This sense of collective victimhood—and of recurring Western aggression—runs deep in the *ummah*'s psyche. By constantly conflating the Western presence in, and domination of, Muslim nations with the Crusades that took place a thousand years ago, ideologues as well as terrorists seek to tap into a historic narrative that continues to evoke strong emotions among millions across the Muslim world. Islamic websites and terrorist groups often use the term 'crusaders' to denote both Israelis and Americans.

Thus, we can view the ongoing conflict as yet another chapter in the long struggle between the East and West. For centuries, the Persian Empire was locked in battle with the Greek city-states for control of the gateway to the West. This war ebbed and flowed, with periods of uneasy peace. However, much of the area that today constitutes modern Turkey was contested territory. After the demise of Greece as a military power in the region, the Roman Empire extended its sway to Byzantium and beyond, colonizing large swaths of North Africa. After the fall of Rome to Germanic tribes, Constantinople became the seat of the Christian power in the East. From here, mercenary armies and vassal tribes dominated much of the Middle East. Priests spread the faith, and merchants traded with most of the known world.

---

[2] Saladin.

[3] Lawrence, Bruce (ed.), *Messages to the World: The Statements of Osama bin Laden*, Verso, 2005.

Christian Rome might have replaced Greece as the dominant power in the region, yet the Persian Empire continued to exert pressure on its neighbour. Wars weakened both empires at a time when a new force was stirring in the harsh Arabian desert. Unknown to either Byzantium or Persia, warring and divided Arab tribes were coalescing into a mighty army under the banner of Islam. They had fought each other for centuries, posing little threat to their powerful neighbours. Within a decade of Mohammed's death in 632 AD, Muslim armies boiled out of the desert like a hurricane, flattening everything in their path. In a series of lightning manoeuvres, they crushed their conventional, slow-moving opponents, who were unused to facing the highly mobile, lightly armed and tough Arab tribesmen who were completely adapted to the hardships of the desert.

Another factor that facilitated this succession of Muslim victories was that both Persians and Byzantines were exhausted after years of unrelenting warfare. One reason the Byzantines were so unprepared to face this new threat is that they had lost the services of their Ghassanid allies—a powerful Christian tribe of Arabs who had kept watch on the eastern fringes of the empire for their Byzantine overlords. The reason for this break is not clear, but by a quirk of history, this screening force abandoned Constantinople at a time the Romans needed them most. This tribe and its role were mentioned by bin Laden in his January 4 recording:

> We would also be like our forefathers, the Al-Ghasasinah. The concern of their elders was to be appointed officers for the Byzantines and to be named kings in order to safeguard the interests of the Byzantines by killing their brothers of the peninsula's Arabs. Such is the case of the new Al-Ghasasinahs; namely, Arab rulers.

When the Muslim army faced the Ghassanids at the battle of Yarmuk in 642 AD, thousands crossed over to the green banner of Islam. The Ghassanids were defeated, and their separate identity erased forever.

It is important to remember that Mohammed did not consider Islam to be a new faith. He repeatedly stated that he was renewing the message of God first revealed to Abraham, then to Moses, and repeated to a succession of prophets, including Jesus. Thus, as far as he was concerned, he was the latest in a chain of messengers. For Muslims, what was fundamentally different about him is that he was the last prophet as Islam was considered the perfect version of a faith many Jews and Christians had drifted away from. According to the early Muslims, Judaism and Christianity had become diluted over time, and their followers had gone astray. Richard Fletcher emphasizes this point in his book, *The Cross and the Crescent*[4]:

> ...it is reasonably clear that Muhammed did not think that he was 'founding a new religion'. The phrase would probably not have made any sense to him. He had been chosen by the one true God as the Messenger who might bring the fullness of divine revelation, partially granted to earlier prophets such as Abraham, Moses or Jesus, to the Arabs of the Arabian Peninsula, and thereby coax them away from their traditional polytheism and idolatry. The Messenger was essentially a Reminder:
>
> '...it is a Reminder
> (and whoso wills, shall remember it)
> upon pages, high-honored,
> uplifted, purified,
> by the hands of scribes noble, pious.'[5]

Thus the Prophet and his followers were both perplexed and angered when neither Jews nor Christians rushed to embrace Islam. On the contrary, clerics of the older faiths were scornful of this upstart religion and rejected it out of hand. Mohammed was dismissed as a mountebank and the Antichrist. Jewish tribes who lived alongside early Muslims in Medina sniggered at what they

---

[4] Allen Lane, 2003.

[5] The Qur'an, 80:11-16, translated by A.J. Arberry.

considered an ignorant and heretical imitation of their ancient faith. For their opposition to Mohammed and Islam, they were mostly expelled or killed. This early rejection set the stage for centuries of confrontation between followers of the Abrahamic faiths.

In the Qur'an itself, there is considerable ambiguity regarding 'the People of the Book,' or *ahle-kitab*, the Arabic term used to describe Jews and Christians. According to verse 29:46, Muslims are directed thus: 'Dispute not with the People of the Book, except in the fairer manner....' However, in verse 9:30, the tone changes: 'The Jews say, 'Ezra is the son of God'; the Christians say, 'The Messiah is the son of God'. That is the utterance of their mouths, conforming with the unbelievers before them. God assail them. How they are perverted!'

The concept of the Holy Trinity was another cause for the Muslim rejection of Christianity. How, they argued, could the same deity be the Son, the Father, and the Holy Ghost? Clearly, God's message to Jesus had been corrupted and misunderstood by his followers. The simple clarity of one all-powerful God was in stark contrast to the subtle ambiguities of Christianity that set the stage for centuries of theological hair-splitting. One reason so many uneducated people—both Arab and non-Arab alike—flocked to Islam's banner was that they could easily comprehend the direct message contained in the Qur'an. As the Muslim holy book was also a code of conduct for the individual and for the government that was in keeping with the social mores of the times, it was relatively simple to follow without making many drastic changes in attitudes and lifestyle. The Bible, on the other hand, called for turning the other cheek, a concept completely at odds with normal human behaviour, then and now.

As a schoolboy at St Patrick's High School in Karachi (a school run by Catholic missionaries established 150 years ago) in the early 1960s, I had to attend Islamic studies classes off campus while my Christian classmates studied the Bible. Our teacher, a Muslim cleric, would regularly bombard us with a comparison of doctrinal points of difference between the two faiths. The concept of the Holy Trinity came in for especially robust criticism. The good priests in charge of our education at St. Patrick's had no idea that their students were being so crudely brainwashed. Now, of course, officially prescribed and produced textbooks used by state schools indoctrinate students in considering all non-Muslims to be misguided, and Islam to be the only faith leading to salvation.

In his magisterial account of this long conflict, Andrew Wheatcroft traces the complex interaction between Islam and Christendom. Specifically, he focuses on how words and images were employed to describe the Other, serving to harden hearts and attitudes. As an example of the enduring impact of past events on the collective psyche, he cites the key battle of Lepanto in which an Ottoman fleet was destroyed by the combined navies of a Christian coalition in 1571. This event was celebrated for centuries across the Christian world, and was the subject of songs, stories, paintings, and plays. To underline the difference of attitudes toward victory and defeat among Christians and Muslims, Wheatcroft writes:

> This cycle of celebration and the memory of victory had no direct counterpart in the Islamic world. There the catastrophe at Lepanto was mourned as an act of Divine Will. The contemporary chronicle of the battle laconically recorded that 'the Imperial fleet encountered the fleet of the wretched infidels and the will of God turned another way'.... It was not the Ottoman tradition to make a lasting memorial out of victory or to chasten themselves with the remembrance of defeat....
>
> Of all the great victories won by Ottoman arms, only the capture of Constantinople by Mehmed II was remembered and commemorated in the manner of the West celebrating Lepanto, and then without the pictorial and textual effusion that the Christian victory generated. As a result, it embedded itself less firmly into the domain of history and memory.[6]

---

[6] Wheatcroft, Andrew. *Infidels: The conflict between Christendom and Islam 638–2002*, Viking, 2003.

Wheatcroft further points out that whereas images were central to Christianity, Islam was a 'calligraphic' civilization as representations of human figures were generally forbidden among Sunni Muslims. Thus, while Muslims were demonized as dark, ferocious, turbaned figures with bloody scimitars in one hand and helpless, semi-dressed white Christian women in the other, there were no comparable images in the Muslim world to depict European soldiers. Wheatcroft elaborates his thesis thus:

> The Christian preoccupation with 'Islam', if we judge it by the volume of written texts—books, exegeses, descriptions, polemics, odes and epics—far exceed any Muslim interest in western Christendom. We should distinguish Islam or Christianity, which are the faiths their adherents would recognize, from 'Islam' or 'Christianity', which are images constructed by their enemies. From the mid-seventh century, 'Islam' was seen as the prime external challenge to the True Christian Faith. Only the enemy within, heresy, came close to this deadly menace. The image of 'Islam' as enemy, competitor, and arch-adversary grew more complex and more potent over time. The initial crudity of the image was made more subtle both by adding new dimensions as circumstances altered, and by jettisoning those no longer relevant. So, the crude parodies of the Prophet Mohammed tended to diminish while ever more baroque descriptions of Islamic virulence multiplied.

Over time, these powerful images of marauding, bloodthirsty Muslims sank deep into the Western consciousness. Mothers in Christian countries frightened their children into obedience by threatening that 'the Turk will get you if you don't listen.' Even when the expansionist impulse of early Islam had abated and trade replaced warfare, Muslims were always the Other. In *Infidels*, Wheatcroft elaborates upon the lasting effects of Western Christian iconography on the popular psyche:

> Over the centuries, under Western eyes, the Muslim infidel had assumed many different guises. They had been *Agarenes*,

> *Ishmaelites, Saracens, Moors, Turks, Tartars, Bedouins, Arabs.* With each iteration the image of the infidel became more precise. Visually speaking, an Agarene or an Ishmaelite or even a Saracen has no particular shape. It is just a name. But Moors, Turks or Bedouins have a very precise and definite visual image. They have become fixed, in the sense that a photographic image is chemically 'fixed' and made permanent, by printed images and by works of art.

For their part, Muslims made virtually no attempt to understand the West, and learn about its culture and language. On the contrary, Europeans were considered uncouth barbarians unworthy of social intercourse. A major exception to this lack of curiosity was the Moorish occupation of Spain, which lasted some eight centuries. This extended Muslim presence in a major European country produced a dazzling, eclectic culture that influenced the West in ways that endure to this day. In Muslim Spain, Jews and Christians were often accorded honour and power in a multi-faith society. Scholars and students flocked to Seville and Granada to learn from teachers who revived old Greek and Roman texts though translation into Arabic and charted new paths in the sciences, from mathematics to medicine. Although there were aberrations when zealous rulers held sway, by and large, Moorish Spain was a model of religious harmony far ahead of its time. Obviously, Muslims were a small minority in Spain and realized the importance of tolerance if they were to continue their rule. However, the rest of the Muslim world harboured little desire to learn from or about the Christian world. Explorers like Ibne Batuta travelled east rather than west. There was no attempt to translate and study Christian texts in the manner the Qur'an was rendered into European languages.

Still, knowledge of the Muslim holy book was not without its own risks, as John of Damascus learned. Wheatcroft refers to his calling Mohammed the Antichrist. John of Damascus knew Arabic and had read the Qur'an, and he was considered 'excessively moderate' by his fellow clerics. Indeed, a synod condemned him in 754 for being 'Saracen minded' and 'too sympathetic to

Islam.' Wheatcroft quotes Nicetas Byzantios' work on John of Dasmascus's declaration that Islam is 'a step backwards, a retrogression,' 'a destruction and a ruin,' and 'a bad and noxious religion.' The cleric concluded his condemnation by stating, 'Thus I do not hesitate to pronounce [my judgment] on Mohammed: he is the very Antichrist.'

John of Damascus's views about Islam were widespread among the Christian clergy. He condemned Islam as 'a people-deceiving cult of the Ishmaelites, the forerunner of the Antichrist....It derives from Ishmael, who was born to Abraham of Hagar, wherefore they are called Hagarenes or Ishmaelites. And they call them Saracens, inasmuch as they were sent away empty-handed by Sarah....These were idolaters and worshippers of the morning-star...and until the time of Heraclius they were plain idolaters. From that time till now a false prophet appeared among them, surnamed Muhammad, who, having happened upon the Old and the New Testament and apparently having conversed with an Arian monk, put together his own heresy.'[7]

These early insults must have stung the followers of a young religion seeking acceptance and legitimacy among the adherents of more established faiths. Much of the ferocity of the early conflicts between the armies of Islam and Christendom can be traced to the insults heaped on the Prophet of Islam. Indeed, this resentment lingers to this day, as evident in the violent reaction to the cartoons of the Prophet that appeared in the Danish newspaper *Jyllands-Posten* in 2005. In the backlash, more than one hundred people were killed in several Muslim countries as mobs attacked Danish embassies and consulates.

Still, it was not until the Crusades that the differences between Islam and Christendom hardened into the state of conflict that endures to this day. Jerusalem was holy to Christians, Jews, and Muslims alike. For the latter, it was the third most holy city (after Mecca and Medina), as they believed that the Prophet Mohammed

---

[7] Karabell, Zachary, *People of the Book*, John Murray, 2007.

made his miraculous ascent into the heavens from the Dome of the Rock, the site of the historic shrine. For Jews and Christians, Jerusalem was the spiritual and physical home of their faiths. Shi'ite Muslim Fatimid rulers in Cairo generally allowed Christian pilgrims access to the holy city, earning hefty fees in the process. However, constant warfare in Palestine between the Fatimids and the Abbasids of Baghdad to the east as well as the Fatimids and the Byzantines of Constantinople to the west made the region dangerous for travellers.

In the midst of this turmoil, the accession of the Fatimid Caliph Al-Hakim in 996 AD made things even worse. This capricious ruler soon issued a series of edicts forcing Jewish and Christian inhabitants of Jerusalem to wear distinctive garb, and numerous synagogues and churches were razed to the ground. This persecution culminated in the destruction of the shrine of the Holy Sepulcher in 1009. In 1021, Al-Hakim rode out alone from Cairo, never to return. With the end of his reign, the harsh intolerance that marked Al-Hakim's rule came to an end, but the indignities and destruction of Christian holy sites caused a strong reaction in Rome. Wheatcroft cites a papal encyclical issued by Pope Sergius IV:

> Let all Christians know that news has come from the east to the seat of the apostles that the church of the Holy Sepulcher has been destroyed from roof to foundations by the impious hands of the pagans. This destruction has plunged the entire church and the city of Rome into deep grief and distress. The whole world is in mourning and the people tremble, breathing deep sighs....
>
> With the Lord's help we intend to kill all these enemies and restore the Redeemer's Holy Sepulcher. Nor, my sons, are you to fear the sea's turbulence, nor dread the fury of war, for God has promised that whoever loses the present life for the sake of Christ will gain another life which he will never lose. For this is not a battle for an earthly kingdom, but for the eternal Lord.[8]

---

[8] Wheatcroft, Andrew, *Infidels*; op cit.

This call to arms resonated slowly but powerfully. Although the Holy Sepulcher had been destroyed nearly a century earlier, anger among Christians in Europe continued to fester and was reinforced by pilgrims who returned with stories of ill treatment along the way. Peter the Hermit, a French monk, tapped into this popular fury and gathered thousands to his 'war for Christ.' Despite his poverty and his gaunt appearance, he was a charismatic figure; by the time he arrived in Cologne in 1096, he had an army of 15,000 enthusiastic volunteers behind him. Marching off on this quixotic quest, this ragtag army grew to around 25,000 by the time it reached Constantinople, where Byzantine rulers refused admission to the city. Proceeding toward Jerusalem, it was ambushed by Seljuk Turks and decimated, thereby ending the First Crusade. Several more were to follow, and Christian knights were successful in establishing a few toeholds along the coast of the Holy Land, apart from capturing Jerusalem itself, slaughtering its Jewish, Christian, and Muslim inhabitants in a bloodbath that shocked people even in those violent days.

However, the occupation of Jerusalem lasted less than a century. The end came with Saladin's defeat of the Crusader army in the Battle of Hattin and their expulsion from Jerusalem in 1187. The Third Crusade was led by Richard I of England, but despite some successes, it failed to recapture Jerusalem. Several other expeditions were mounted over the next century or so, but none made lasting gains.

Given the transient nature of this enterprise, it is hard for Americans to understand why the Crusades represent such a powerful symbol for Muslims. After all, Christian control over Jerusalem and the coastal belt of present-day Israel, Lebanon, and Palestine was fleeting. Even the word 'crusade' was a much later invention and was never used for the military expeditions that set off at the time. So why do many Muslims—especially extremists and terrorist groups—continue to call Israelis and Western forces in Muslim lands 'crusaders'? Obviously, the term has huge historic connotations.

Similarly, Saladin remains an iconic figure to this day. Many Muslims continue to await the return of a Saladin to lead them to glory again. In the first Gulf War in 1990, I recall seeing Saddam Hussein, the Iraqi dictator, being depicted on painted Pakistani trucks as the heroic liberator of Jerusalem, riding on a white horse with a sword in one hand and the green banner of Islam in the other.

The crusader analogy was reinforced by the creation of Israel in the ancient Biblical lands that are still so bitterly contested. Here were large numbers of European Jews, vilely persecuted and made homeless by Nazi Germany—a European country—who were taking over the same area that had drawn the crusaders nearly a thousand years ago. Never mind that the creation of the Jewish state had been authorized by the United Nations—a body dominated by the West and in which Muslims have little say. Thus, the birth of Israel was (and still is) widely viewed as a Western colonial enterprise that simply continued what the crusaders had started centuries ago. To this day, few Muslims are willing to accept the fact that Arabs had wrested Jerusalem from Christians soon after the appearance of Islam. Going back even further, the city had been Jewish, then Roman, and next Christian. Clearly, a city holy to all three Abrahamic faiths will continue to excite passions until better sense prevails and a means to share it is defined.

Just how deeply the thousand-year-old Crusades continue to resonate in many Muslim minds was apparent in the October 2010 plot to send an explosive device from Yemen to Chicago on an American cargo plane. The name of the addressee on one package was Reynald Krak (i.e., Reynald of Chatillon), a French knight of the Second Crusade whose claim to fame was his brutal murders of Muslim pilgrims to Jerusalem. He was in turn beheaded by Saladin.[9]

Another longer Muslim–Christian conflict occurred in Spain, where the Muslim occupation lasted more than eight centuries. As previously noted, the Muslim presence was not simply a

[9] As reported by the *New York Times*, 11/4/2010.

military enterprise, but an extended period of colonization and cooperation as well. Indeed, Muslim extremists include Spain—the fabled Al-Andalus—as one of the lands they want Christians to vacate. Significantly, the other package sent to Chicago from Yemen in the terrorist plot was addressed to Diego Deza, a Spanish Grand Inquisitor infamous for his torture of Muslims suspected of concealing their faith under the guise of conversion to Christianity.[10]

This ancient rivalry resurfaced in the controversy surrounding the famous 'mosque-cathedral' of Cordoba. This stunning Moorish structure was built as a mosque in the eighth century, but consecrated as a cathedral after the Spanish *reconquista* in the thirteenth century. A UNESCO world heritage site, the building has long served as a magnet for tourists. When Bishop Demetrio Fernandez called for the monument to be renamed a cathedral in October 2010, he provoked an immediate backlash. One reason for his request was what he cited as the attempt by several Muslims to pray inside the 'mosque-cathedral'.[11]

These anecdotes give us a sense of how powerfully past events shape ideas and perceptions in the present. Although most Americans would tend to dismiss past conflicts between Muslims and Europeans as none of their concern, the reality is that they do influence the ongoing ferment in the Muslim world. Whether we like it or not, bin Laden and his ilk are driven at least partially by events that happened a millennium or more ago.

The lengthy domination of the Balkans by Ottoman Turks provides us with yet another example of the long shadow cast by the Muslim presence in Europe. The vicious anti-Muslim pogroms run by the Serbs in the 1990s, the siege of Sarajevo, and the massacre of nearly 8,000 Muslims at Srebrenica in 1995 serve as a painful reminder of the power of religious animosity based on perceptions of past wrongs. Ironically, although US President Bill Clinton

[10] As reported by the *New York Times*, 11/4/2010.

[11] As reported by the *New York Times*, 11/6/2010.

prodded his European allies to finally get off the fence and join American forces in halting the conflict, the United States was never given due credit in the Islamic world for intervening on the side of the Bosnian Muslims and later rescuing the Muslims of Kosovo. In both conflicts, the United States overcame the pusillanimity of other NATO members and prevented a possible genocide. However, Serbian atrocities did serve to radicalize thousands of young Muslims who watched the horrors of the Balkans on TV and blamed their governments for doing nothing to help their co-religionists. Until the conflict erupted after the break-up of socialist Yugoslavia, few Muslims were even aware that millions of their brethren were Europeans. Many foreign Muslim volunteers who managed to reach Bosnia to fight were amazed to see blond, blue-eyed Muslim women in skirts. For their part, the Bosnian army had little use for the newly arrived bearded partisans who could speak no European language.

To a great extent, Ottoman rule over what had been part of the Byzantine Empire for centuries shaped European perceptions about Muslims. The Balkans were conquered by the Ottomans in a series of battles that culminated with the defeat of the Serbs in the Battle of Kosovo Polje (the Field of Blackbirds) in 1389. For the next five centuries, most of the Balkans were ruled by the Ottomans, and stories of their brutality became part of Western folklore. Yet the Ottomans did not rule directly or seek to incorporate the region into a single political entity; rather, they governed a system of 'millets', or religious communities, using local churches and nobility to impose a loose hegemony.

Apart from the burden placed on the largely non-Muslim communities by rapacious tax-collectors, the system of 'devshirme' or 'blood tax' most enraged the subjected people. This was the obligation of mostly Christian families to contribute a son each to the Ottoman Empire. Far from enslaving these children, the Turks educated them to become janissaries, civil servants and diplomats. Many rose to positions of authority and eminence. Meanwhile, Western travel writers and journalists depicted this system as a cruel enslavement of Christian children by the 'wicked Turk'. Few other forms of formal discrimination against their non-Muslim subjects were evident, although Ottoman governors and their underlings did tend to favour Muslim subjects in court cases and civil disputes.

Ottoman rule over Greece, the cradle of the Hellenic civilization that continues to be a central part of the Western heritage, outraged much of Europe. In particular, the Greek Revolt of 1821 became a trigger for an outpouring of anti-Ottoman, pro-Greek propaganda. Wheatcroft writes in *Infidels*:

> The French press presented highly colored accounts of Ottoman atrocities. On May 27, 1821, *Le Constitutionnel* reported that it had been officially decided in Constantinople to 'slaughter all Christian subjects of the Ottoman empire'; by July 24, this had become a plan of the Ottomans to wipe Christianity from the face of the earth. The *Gazette de France* of May 25, 1821, had compared the Turks to bloodthirsty wild beasts, a 'mob attacking every Christian without any distinction'. Ironically, at that time, in the Peleponnese[12], the Greeks fitted this stereotype better than the Turks....

The rise of nationalism in the Balkans coincided with the decline of the Ottoman Empire in the nineteenth century, yet even after the collapse of the empire and the emergence of a mosaic of nation states in the region, past resentments ran deep. Once Yugoslavia fragmented in 1990, a vicious civil war based on virulent Serb nationalism and a visceral hatred of Muslims seen as descendants of the Turkish overlords broke out. In particular, Ratko Mladic, the commander of Serb forces, reportedly instructed his soldiers to 'destroy all that bears a Turkish sign.' After the massacre of 8,000 unarmed Muslim boys and men at Srebrenica, he was quoted as saying: 'We have evened the score with the Turks.'[13] The fact that

---

[12] Where 20,000 Muslim men, women and children were slaughtered by the Greeks.

[13] Somun, Hajrudin, 'Turks in the Balkans,' *Today's Zaman*, 4/25/2010.

the Dutch contingent of UN peacekeepers did nothing to protect the Muslims under their care was widely perceived in the Islamic world as a sign of Western animus towards their faith. The refusal of European nations to intervene in the one-sided conflict, thereby allowing the bloodletting to continue, confirmed this impression. Day after day, images of the siege of Sarajevo and horrors like Srebrenica were beamed into Muslim homes around the world.

It took Serb authorities sixteen years to capture Mladic from a village where he lived peacefully among relatives, further indicating the degree of support he enjoyed. A large number of Serb nationalists demonstrated over his arrest and transfer to the International Court of Justice at The Hague for his trial for genocide and crimes against humanity. This is another reminder of the hatred many Serbs continue to harbour towards their Muslim neighbours in Bosnia.

Other historical events and their impact on hardening stereotypes abound. When Indian troops mutinied against their British officers in 1857, they killed many together with their families. Exaggerated accounts of the extent and manner of the deaths soon reverberated in England through a hysterical British press. A virulent jingoism led to demands for vengeance. Articles, poems, polemics, and paintings reinforced the image of the vicious oriental. No less a figure than Charles Dickens has been quoted as saying 'I wish I were Commander in Chief in India. I should do my utmost to exterminate the Race upon whom the stain of the late cruelties rested...and raze it off the face of the Earth.'[14]

In this event, those who bore the brunt of this vengeful British bloodlust were the Muslims of India. Although the uprising was launched by Hindus, Bahadur Shah Zafar was then the Mughal emperor of India. A forlorn, powerless figurehead, he was thrust into the fray by the rebels, who demanded his blessings for their

---

[14] Nayder, Lillian. *Dickens and Empire: Discourses of Class, Race and Colonialism in the works of Charles Dickens—Victorian Studies*, edited by Grace Moore, Aldershot and Burlington, 2005.

enterprise. Unable or unwilling to refuse, he paid a heavy price when the British defeated the Indian rebels. His sons were arrested and killed out of hand, while he was tried and exiled to Burma, where he died in Rangoon in poverty and solitude. Meanwhile, thousands of his Muslim subjects were killed, imprisoned, or exiled. Much of the old city of Delhi was razed to the ground. The Muslim aristocracy was most closely identified with the rebellion and was ruthlessly decimated. Henceforth, Muslims would be marginalized by the British rulers of India, who gave Hindus prominence. This reaction had the long-term effect of pushing the two communities apart. Muslim clerics blamed the disaster on the Mughal court that had created communal harmony through an eclectic blend of Hindu and Muslim cultures and rituals. When Muslims suffered the bloodbath, they were told by religious leaders that their plight was the result of leaving the righteous path laid down by the Qur'an and the Sunnah. Religious extremism replaced tolerance. The Muslims of the subcontinent withdrew into a sullen and angry seclusion that boded ill for unity in a post-colonial India a century later. Indeed, the emergence of Pakistan in 1947, and the anti-Hindu, anti-India, posture it has adopted, can be traced back to the violent events of 1857.

The colonial era provides many examples of Muslim-Christian tension. Priests, soldiers, and traders from the West took advantage of the weakness and backwardness they found in the East. Centuries of racism and brutality marked this interaction, and even today remain deeply embedded in the psyche of the ruled. Although this global land grab included many non-Muslim nations and peoples, the Muslims felt they had been displaced in the international pecking order by rapacious and conniving Europeans.

After this brief overview of the long war between East and West, I can sympathize with American readers who might want to know what all these old conflicts have to do with them. Many of these readers are descendants of migrants who fled the Old World to escape precisely these ancient religious conflicts. Although they retain many aspects of their cultural identities, they have put distant disputes behind them. The problem is that for the rest of the world, history continues to mark their sense of who they are. For Muslims, in particular, the past weighs heavily on their collective psyche. Being relegated from their preeminent position in world affairs to the status of losers has not been easy to accept, especially as they continue to languish near the bottom of world rankings. Even the vast oil wealth of several Muslim countries has not enabled them to translate their black gold into serious political power.

Still, it is possible to read too much into past conflicts as we seek to delve into the causes of present attitudes and tensions. Zachary Karabell makes this point in the introduction of his book *People of the Book: The forgotten history of Islam and the West*[15]:

> I studied Arabic, travelled throughout the Middle East, and began to teach the history of the region and the history of Islam. I found that my students usually viewed Islam through a dark prism of Muslim hordes threatening to deluge Christendom. The actual stories might have been blurry in their minds, but each time they saw a picture of a mosque or an imam leading prayer, it struck a deep negative chord: Islam is a religion of war and violence, and Muslims have clashed with Christians and Jews forever. These beliefs were hardly limited to my students. They are part of our culture.
>
> Throughout the Middle East and North Africa, I encountered a similar prejudice towards the West. Well before the events of September 11, 2001, there was an entrenched belief that the West is the enemy of Islam. That has only intensified in recent years. Images of an aggressive, imperialist West from the time of the Crusades through the twentieth century animate angry Pakistani preachers in Peshawar, indignant Saudi clerics in Medina, and of course Osama bin Laden. Not only is the court of Harun al-Rashid [the fifth Abbasid caliph renowned for his justice and culture, he ruled from 786 AD to 809 AD] forgotten, but so too is medieval

[15] John Murray, 2007.

> [Muslim] Iberia, where the Jewish polymath Maimonides, the Sufi mystic Ibn 'Arabi, and a phalanx of Christian monks helped one another unravel the meaning of God and the universe; so too is the twelfth-century Levant, where the inhabitants of Crusader city-states and Muslim emirates traded, bartered and intermarried; so is the Ottoman Empire, where each religious community, whether Greek Orthodox, Jewish, or Maronite Christian, was allowed almost complete religious autonomy save for the payment of annual taxes....

Certainly, it is easy to overlook the long periods of peaceful interaction between Islamic communities and Western ones. My European and American friends are constantly and pleasantly surprised by the hospitality they experience in Pakistan. Despite the recent rise of anti-Western sentiments in much of the Muslim world, little evidence of such sentiments exists in most streets and bazaars. My wife and stepdaughters are English and have been regular visitors to Pakistan over the years, where they go shopping, visit the beach, and eat at restaurants. Apart from the occasional curious stare, they have never encountered any hostility. There are certainly some areas of Karachi I would not take them to, but by the same token, there are neighbourhoods of London that would be unsafe for me to visit.

Thus, while a long history of conflict may shape the agenda for extremists and clerics, most Muslims remain largely unaffected by it. They certainly don't hold individual Europeans and Americans responsible for the real or perceived sins of their fathers. Moderate Muslims never tire of maintaining that Islam is a religion of peace and that the vast majority of Muslims are peaceful people. Although this has become something of a cliché, it is nevertheless an accurate assertion: Just as everyday Christians and Jews are not violent, Muslims too want nothing more than to get on with their lives. However, just as ordinary folk can be motivated to commit violent acts under certain circumstances, Muslims react reflexively and emotionally to some specific stimuli. As the episode with the cartoons about the Prophet Mohammed in a Danish newspaper demonstrated, their religious sentiments can be easily exploited by clerics, politicians and extremists.

Unfortunately, what has lingered in the collective memories of both Muslims and the West are the wars, conquests, and mutual contempt that have marked their long and bitter rivalry. For the West, bad things come from the East; for the Muslims, nothing good has come from the West.

5

Mutual Misunderstandings in the Middle East

Ever since I began reading newspapers, no region in the world has monopolized the headlines to the same extent as the Middle East. Specifically, the Israeli-Arab conflict has claimed our attention insistently and without letting up. Wars, invasions, and occupation have dominated the print and broadcast media around the world. Why this preoccupation with the region? Why does this issue raise such passion in supporters and detractors of Israel alike? Can we somehow get a break from this never-ending crisis?

Whatever our position on the conflict, none of us is neutral. Even for the most objective observers and students of history, there are two divergent narratives that reflect virtually opposite interpretations of the same set of facts. Who the good and the bad guys are depends on your perspective, but this black-and-white picture of the Israel-Palestinian dispute only has room for moral absolutes, not ambiguity or doubt.

Supporters of Israel have questioned the double standards at work here. A single Palestinian casualty will make the news around the world whereas the media often ignore far more serious Muslim-on-Muslim killings. Equally ignored are other Muslim nationalistic uprisings in Kashmir, Chechnya, the Philippines and Thailand. Similarly, the murderous internecine turf battles between Hamas and the Palestinian Authority are glossed over. As a result,

Israelis and their supporters ask—with some justification—why their actions are placed under the microscope while others escape international censure.

I suspect that this preoccupation with the Israeli-Palestinian dispute has a lot to do with the larger, longer Muslim-Christian conflict examined in the previous chapter. Although Israel is obviously a Jewish state, the fact that Israelis are associated with the crusaders in the extremist lexicon reveals that the country is in fact considered a Western outpost by many Muslims, much as the crusader kingdoms were a thousand years ago. Its vociferous support from right-wing American evangelists would suggest that—whether consciously or unconsciously—it is seen in much the same light by many Americans. Another source of Israel's support (albeit dwindling now) derives from liberal Americans who see it as an island of democracy and Western values in a sea of (Arab) despotism. Many of these prejudices are subliminal and are fuelled by the iconography and historic myth-making discussed in the previous chapter. However, these views feed into the rigid mindset that has come to characterize attitudes in both camps.

Thus, the Israeli–Palestinian conflict has become yet another clash in the long war between Islam and Christendom, regardless of how much Israelis see themselves as citizens of a Jewish state. Like it or not, Muslims and Christians alike have taken rigid positions on the rights and wrongs of the dispute. Of course, millions of people who do not subscribe to either faith have strong views on the conflict as well, but are seldom as passionately committed as Muslim, Jewish, and Christian partisans of Israel and Palestine.

The long struggle to create Israel, its many wars with its neighbours, and the legal disputes surrounding its occupation of the West Bank have been written about at length by scholars and journalists. Understandably, all Muslims and many non-Muslims reject the notion of Israel being created on 'the Promised Land' for the 'Chosen People'. They argue that, if such a formula becomes the basis for creating a state, others could well put forward similar claims based on passages from other holy books.

The Balfour Declaration of 1917 containing the British government's intention of creating a homeland for the Jews is dismissed by most Muslims as a colonial instrument of no moral or legal validity. The post-World-War-I carve-up of the Middle East that took place at Versailles in 1919 is also viewed as a purely colonial arrangement witnessed by a handful of Arab Quislings. Finally, the UN resolution establishing the state of Israel in 1948 is rejected as a decision taken over the heads of neighbouring Arab countries as well as the Palestinians themselves. Regardless of the historic and legal rights and wrongs underlying the creation of Israel, I have long argued in my newspaper columns that—given the UN's blessings and the now more than six decades of turbulent existence—Muslims should become reconciled to its presence and recognize the Zionist state. I have maintained that recognition does not imply approval of its policies; indeed, if it did, many Muslim states would not be recognized by the international community, given their appalling human rights record. However, I feel strongly that, while Israel has the right to exist and prosper within its legal boundaries, it does not have the right to occupy and annex Palestinian land captured in the 1967 war.

To understand how deeply the issue is seared into the Muslim consciousness, consider the following open letter Osama bin Laden wrote under the umbrella of the Advice and Reform Committee, an organization he set up in London in 1994, to bin Baz, the late Chief Mufti of Saudi Arabia, and then the most senior juridical authority in the kingdom. The context is bin Baz's *fatwa* supporting the stationing of Western forces in Saudi Arabia before and during the first Gulf War in 1990, as well as his blessings for the Oslo accords containing the Arab recognition of Israel in exchange for the creation of a Palestinian state. Bin Laden writes:

> You issued a juridical decree wholly endorsing this peace[1], which was praised and lauded by the prime minister of the Zionist enemy

---

[1] A reference to the Oslo accords.

and his parliament, after which the Saudi government announced its intent for more normalization with the Jews.

And it seemed as if you were not satisfied with abandoning Saudi Arabia, home of the two Holy Sanctuaries[2], to the Crusader-Jewish forces of occupation[3], until you had brought another disaster on Jerusalem, the third of the Sanctuaries, by conferring legitimacy on the contracts of surrender to the Jews that were signed by the traitorous and cowardly Arab tyrants. These contracts constitute a serious and dangerous calamity containing deceit and deception from a number of different perspectives....

The current Jewish enemy is not an enemy settled in his own original country fighting in its defense until he gains a peace agreement, but an attacking enemy and a corrupter of religion and the world, for whom the words of the Sheikh of Islam ibn Taimiya[4] apply: 'There is no greater duty after faith than unconditionally fighting the attacking enemy who corrupts religion and the world. He must be resisted as hard as possible....'

The legal duty regarding Palestine and our brothers there—these poor men, women and children who have nowhere to go—is to wage jihad for the sake of God, and to motivate our umma to jihad so that Palestine may be completely liberated and returned to Islamic sovereignty....[5]

Bin Laden has been quoted at some length here because his views broadly reflect those of millions of conservative Muslims who remain opposed to the existence of Israel. But bin Laden and other extremist groups also realize that a peace deal would rob them of a powerful recruitment tool; hence, they have rejected any compromise on the issue.

---

[2] Mecca and Medina.

[3] Western forces stationed in the kingdom.

[4] A fourteenth-century scholar who first advanced a religious justification for *jihad* against fellow Muslims.

[5] Lawrence, Bruce (editor), *Messages to the World: The Statements of Osama Bin Laden*, Verso, 2005, pp. 9-10.

Meanwhile, by its open-ended support of Israel and its occupation of Palestinian lands, America has put itself in the firing line. I was a student at Karachi University during the Six Day War of 1967. As the full extent of the military disaster that had befallen the Arab armies became apparent, the Arab students on the university campus went into mourning. Stunned and bewildered, they huddled in small groups, discussing the implications of the sweeping Israeli victory. When defending the pathetic performance of the Arab forces, they frequently blamed America for the debacle.

It is human nature to deny that you were beaten by a smaller adversary, blaming your defeat on some more powerful figure in the background instead. To rationalize a military debacle of such proportions, the Arabs constructed the mystique of a powerful American foe who helped the Israelis with its superior technology and through its agents among the Arabs. This narrative was accepted across the Islamic world and today is part of the Muslim narrative surrounding the conflict.

To get a sense of how deeply the Arab defeat was felt by Muslims everywhere, I asked a Sri Lankan Muslim friend how his community reacted at the time. Isfahani Anver is an urbane Colombo lawyer who is also a keen student of history. He told me how his father, also a lawyer and a sophisticated, Westernized Muslim, responded to the shattering news: 'For days, my father was very upset. As there weren't any other grownups around, he kept telling me that the Arabs must prepare for another round, but it would take them twenty-five years to get ready, given the American support for Israel.'

The reality is that US President Lyndon Johnson resisted calls to airlift arms to Israel during the Six Day War, partly because the CIA had forecast a sweeping Israeli victory. In the Yom Kippur War of 1973, this myth of American intervention became reality when Israel suffered a series of stunning setbacks in the initial phase of the war. US President Richard Nixon ordered a massive airlift of American arms that enabled Israel to make up its heavy losses. In addition, US satellite imagery helped the Israeli Defence

Forces (IDF) identify gaps and weaknesses in the Egyptian lines. These were then exploited by daring Israeli armoured thrusts that isolated a large Egyptian force in the Sinai. This open and effective assistance for Israel, while helping its ally stave off a major military disaster, caused a wave of anger directed at the United States. The immediate reaction was a boycott of oil exports to the United States and several other Western nations by the major producers in the region. The price of oil shot up, quadrupling from $3 a barrel to $12 overnight. Western economies were hard hit, with stock markets crashing and inflation soaring. This caused an immediate backlash—especially in America, where anti-Arab and anti-Iranian sentiments soared.

The Muslim world, revelling in the news of early Arab successes, cheered at reports of scores of Israeli planes shot down and hundreds of tanks destroyed. Soon this jubilation turned to frustration as the IDF counterattacked. Sullenly, Egypt and Syria accepted an American-brokered ceasefire. Extremists like the Muslim Brotherhood had a field day, excoriating the United States and reminding Muslims around the world that Israel was being kept afloat by its American benefactor to continue its occupation of the West Bank and Gaza. This one-sided approach to the conflict ensured that, henceforth, the United States would be regarded with deep suspicion in the region.

Egypt subsequently reached a separate peace with Israel at Camp David in 1978, recovering the Sinai in the process. However, the Golan Heights continues to be under Israeli occupation, as does the West Bank. Inevitably, military occupation breeds repression, which in turn stiffens resistance. Over time, the nature of the Palestinian freedom struggle has been transformed from a secular one led by Yasser Arafat's PLO to a purely Islamic response spearheaded by Hamas. Although the PLO accepted the right of Israel to exist years ago, Hamas has adopted a hard line: It is willing to accept an indefinite ceasefire with Israel in exchange for an end to the occupation, but it remains reluctant to follow the PLO example. Its Islamist charter, as well as the support it gets from Syria and Iran, has contributed to this maximalist position.

Regardless of whether secular or extremist, Muslim or Christian, all Palestinians are united in their hatred of Israel for the onerous occupation of their lands. Enduring hours at Israeli security checkpoints, putting up with the daily humiliations of searches and identity checks, and suffering from years of deprivation, two generations have grown up under the occupation. When they see American arms in the hands of their oppressors and are subjected to bombardment from American-made jets firing American-made rockets, they blame the Americans equally for their predicament. Their pain and suffering resonates across the Muslim world, radicalizing thousands as they, for example, watch the Israeli assault on Gaza in 2008, in which more than 1,300 Palestinians—most of them non-combatants, including hundreds of children—were killed compared to thirteen Israeli casualties.

The Israeli narrative, of course, diverges sharply from this Palestinian one. Successive governments have maintained that they are ready for peace, provided they have a partner with whom they can negotiate and that the Palestinians renounce terrorism. They also demand recognition from Arab countries and insist on retaining control over Jerusalem, the 'eternal capital of Jews'. Israeli negotiators also demand continued control over the Palestinian–Jordan border. Furthermore, they reject the notion that Palestinians who fled Israel during the fighting at the state's birth—or those who were driven out—have the right to return to their homes. Part of the Israeli narrative is that they have been forced to impose harsh security measures to prevent acts of terrorism against its people in Israel and in the settlements it has built in the occupied territories.

American support for Israel has not always been as solid and uncritical as it is now. Although the United States threw its weight behind the UN resolution creating the state in 1948 and was the first country to recognize it, the massive economic, diplomatic and military aid that now flows from Washington to Tel Aviv was slow in reaching its present level. During the 1956 Suez crisis, when Britain, France, and Israel invaded Egypt following Egyptian President Nasser's nationalization of the Suez Canal, US President Eisenhower took a very tough line, virtually issuing an ultimatum to France and Britain to pull out their forces. This demarche was successful, but their new neighbour's role in the attack confirmed Israel's status as a colonial, Western outpost in Arab eyes.

Uncritical support for Israel was not part of American foreign policy until the 1970s. Even then, the United States did not support Israel's settlement policies in the occupied territories, seeing them as an obstacle to peace. Indeed, nothing is as contentious in this tangled conflict as the continuous construction activity Israel has been carrying on in the occupied territories—virtually since it captured them in 1967. Although, during the first decade of the occupation, settlements were mostly limited to scarcely populated areas under Labor governments, the scenario changed dramatically under the post-1977 Likud government. On the Peace Now website, Mark Rosenblum and Gideon D. Remba posted an article entitled 'How Israel's Settlements Dilemma Arose,' in which they write:

> The Likud party's 1977 election platform clearly stated its aims to gain a firm grip and eventual sovereignty over the territories so as to reconstitute the Biblical Land of Israel: 'The right of the Jewish people to the Land of Israel is eternal and is an integral part of its right to security and peace. Judea and Samaria will therefore not to be turned over to any foreign rule; between the sea and Jordan will only be Israeli sovereignty. Any plan that involves surrender of part of the Western Eretz Yisrael[6] militates against our right to the Land [and] will inevitably lead to a Palestinian state...' Accordingly, Prime Minster Begin radically increased settlement efforts in these territories, launching a massive, heavily subsidized program of settlement construction in the West Bank....
>
> Post-Oslo Labor governments sought to channel most settlement construction into blocs, mostly closer to the 1967 border, which

[6] Greater Israel.

> Israel expected to annex under a future peace agreement. But Labor leaders failed to take into account the extent to which the ongoing settlement campaign—and the military occupation that supported it and Labor's tolerance for ongoing settlement expansion and bypass road building in other parts of Gaza and the West Bank—undermined Palestinian trust in Israeli intentions for the territory, sabotaging the prospects for a negotiated two-state solution to the Palestinian-Israeli conflict. Nor was Labor's expansive definition of the settlement blocs to be annexed under an agreement acceptable to even the most moderate Palestinians, as some of the settlements... extended deep into the West Bank, making a territorially contiguous and viable Palestinian state impossible.[7]

Given Israel's continuing efforts to create 'facts on the ground' in the shape of settlements deemed illegal under international law, Palestinian disillusionment with the stuttering peace process is understandable. Apart from expressing its 'disappointment' with this hectic construction activity, the United States has done little to actually use its clout with Tel Aviv to halt it. Thus from the Palestinian perspective, America is complicit in the land grab taking place before their eyes. They ask—with considerable justification—how they can be expected to sit down and negotiate a two-state solution when the land that will make up the future state of Palestine is steadily being annexed.

When US President Barack Obama addressed the Muslim world from Cairo in 2009, he raised hopes of a more even-handed approach toward the Palestinian–Israeli conflict. In his eloquent speech, heard live by millions of Muslims across the world, the American president said:

> Israelis must recognize that, just as Israel's right to exist cannot be denied, neither can Palestine's. The US does not accept the legitimacy of continued Israeli settlements. This construction

[7] www.chicagopeacenow.org

> violates previous agreements and undermines efforts to achieve peace. It is time for these settlements to stop.
>
> And Israel must also live up to its obligations to ensure that Palestinians can live and work and develop their society. Just as it devastates Palestinian families, the continuing humanitarian crisis in Gaza does not serve Israel's security, neither does the continuing lack of opportunity in the West Bank.
>
> Progress in the daily lives of the Palestinian people must be a critical part of a road to peace. And Israel must take concrete steps to enable such progress.

Such words had never been publicly spoken by any serving American president in the past, and they electrified the Muslim world. Finally, millions of Muslims thought, there would be some American pressure on Israel that would end the hated occupation and lead to the emergence of an independent and viable Palestinian state. However, as the weeks turned into months, nothing changed despite a flurry of American diplomatic activity. A succession of American officials, from Secretary of State Hillary Clinton downward, has shuttled in and out of Tel Aviv to little avail. After a brief pause, construction activity continues at an even faster rate. In a bid to breathe life into the moribund peace process, the United States offered Israel a multi-billion dollar sweetener that included a gift of twenty F-35 jet fighters to persuade it to halt construction on occupied territory. The offer was spurned by the Israeli government. Indeed, given Palestinian reluctance to negotiate with an adversary that continues to usurp more and more of their lands, and Israeli determination to hold firm to the annexation policy announced by Likud more than three decades ago, the only momentum behind the peace process appears to come from Washington.

So why does the United States seem more eager than the two adversaries to achieve a breakthrough? In a perceptive article[8], Ethan Bronner writes:

---

[8] 'Why America Chases an Israeli-Palestinian Peace.' *New York Times*, 11/20/2010.

> Lt. General Keith W. Dayton, who left Israel last month after overseeing the training of Palestinian security forces for five years, liked to tell the story of his first assignment in the Middle East. Charged with locating Iraq's elusive weapons of mass destruction after Saddam Hussein was deposed in 2003, General Dayton found no weapons but kept coming across something else inside Iraqi military barracks—drawings of Al Aqsa Mosque in Jerusalem being squeezed by a serpent labeled Israel. He was amazed to see that hundreds of miles from the Holy Land, the Arab-Israeli dispute felt so immediate and significant.

Bronner quotes General Jones, the former National Security Adviser, as saying that, if he could 'pick one foreign policy issue to tackle, it would be the Israeli-Palestinian conflict, because its resolution would help with all the others.' Appearing before Congress, General David Petraeus said that the lack of progress in the peace talks endangered American lives in the region. Bronner asks why the United States is pushing so hard for a resolution to the conflict, and explains that:

> The answer has a number of levels, but the most important is this: The United States believes that if it can end the Israeli-Palestinian conflict, its fraught relationship with the Muslim world will greatly improve, thereby allowing America to accomplish much that is currently eluding it in places like Iraq, Iran and Afghanistan, not to mention easing its role as the prime guarantor of Israel's own security.

Given the obvious American interest in achieving a settlement based on the two-state formula, Muslims (and many non-Muslims) cannot understand why the conflict still has not been resolved after the passage of so many years and so much bloodshed and misery. Most Muslims attribute Israeli foot-dragging to the hold the Zionist lobby has over the American establishment. They simply do not understand the cultural and strategic ties that have developed between Israel and the United States over the years.

Nor can they grasp the American political dynamics that promote unquestioning backing for Israel in Congress and the mainstream media.

The truth is that most Muslims live in autocratically governed countries and have little understanding of the way democracies function. They are used to their leaders issuing orders with little concern for how they are accepted by their people. In this model, where citizens are not represented and thus have no role in decision-making, public opinion plays a minor role in formulating foreign policy. Conspiracy theories bridge the gap between reality and perception. It is certainly true that American supporters of Israel—Jews and Christians alike—are highly organized and create a formidable political lobby; yet while they exercise their clout to protect Israeli interests, America has its own strategic reasons for maintaining Israeli military superiority in the region.

However, for most Muslims following the daily stories of Palestinian suffering carried by TV channels like Al Jazeera and Al Arabiya, among other media outlets, the conflict is seen in black and white: Israel is oppressing the Palestinians, and America is lending it open-ended and unquestioning support. This equation—oversimplified though it might be—is at the centre of the Muslim perception of the US–Israeli relationship. In this worldview, the oppression of the Palestinian people is part of a broader anti-Muslim conspiracy orchestrated from Washington. It would be no exaggeration to say that this single conflict has done more to poison Muslim attitudes toward America than any other.

Given their highly emotional support for Palestinians, it is hard for any Muslim to step back and look at the Israeli narrative. In an article entitled 'A clash of narratives' published in *Dawn* in 2003, I urged my mostly Pakistani readers to look at the conflict through Israeli eyes:

> To get an idea of the power of their [Israeli] attachment to their land, one has to travel back in time and space for two millennia across much of Europe and the Middle East. Jews have been

dispersed, persecuted and hounded from one country to another. In much of this period they have been prevented from owning land and farming, hence their focus on banking and finance. This long history of pain and suffering culminated in the Holocaust when millions of Jews were killed by the Nazis. No other people have been so reviled and abused: Christians, Muslims and Hindus have had their own territories, and have no experience of living in a diaspora for centuries.

None of this is meant to excuse or condone the way Israelis are behaving towards the Palestinians. However, it is important to understand why they do not view the creation of Israel as a colonial presence: most of them genuinely see their return to the 'Promised Land' as the redemption of a Biblical promise made to their forefathers by God.

This is diametrically opposed to the Palestinian narrative of dispossession and oppression, and in all clashes of conflicting nationalisms, there are winners and losers. Israelis want to know why the displaced Palestinians can't be absorbed by Arab states with vast territories, while Palestinians want to know why they are being asked to pay for the suffering of the Jews.

Muslims across the world see the creation of Israel as well as the subsequent financial, military and diplomatic support it has received from the West as an extension of the Crusades, and further evidence of Western hostility towards Islam. Washington's open-ended approval of Israeli actions is especially viewed as encouraging Tel Aviv's refusal to withdraw from occupied territory, and is therefore the object of Muslim rage and extremist violence.

In this unending cycle of real and perceived wrongs, the history of the region continues to be written in blood. It is clear that the Israeli experiment will not be ended with Jews migrating to different parts of the globe yet again. No matter how much many Muslims wish for such an outcome, this is not about to happen. Similarly, Palestinians are going to continue to lash out against their occupation and oppression, often with lethal results.

The only way out of this quagmire is for Palestinians to accept the presence of Israel, and for Israelis to withdraw to their legal frontiers. Jerusalem could be the capital of both nations. Israelis argue that the presence of an independent Palestinian state would be a threat to their security. But given the fact that they are the dominant power in the region, this perception cannot be taken seriously.

Avraham Burg, until recently speaker of the Israeli Knesset, wrote in Al-Quds of Jerusalem: 'Through thousands of years of exile we were weak. The Christian world loved our weakness; it symbolised their strength. But at a certain historic moment the Zionist movement arose, the movement of Jewish national rebirth. A brave and honest leadership led this downtrodden people to nearly unimaginable accomplishments. In one historic moment, we decided to stop being weak, and the nature of our dialogue with other nations was utterly changed....'

'Until Muslims arrive at this 'historic moment' and get 'a brave and honest leadership', they are likely to suffer humiliation and defeat.

I was braced for a storm of abusive emails from readers when this article appeared in Pakistan; in the event, I received mostly supportive letters. Thus, it would seem that a degree of reluctant admiration exists for Israel's undeniable achievements among many Muslims. Still, the perceived collusion between Israel and America in the occupation of Palestine rankles many. Inevitably, these sentiments spike during times of tension, such as the 2009 Israeli assault on Gaza, or the crude interception of the flotilla that killed nine Turkish activists in 2010. Time and again, the United States has blocked or watered down UN Security Council resolutions seeking to censure Israel. This, to Muslims, is yet another example of blatant American favouritism.

What Muslims fail to grasp is why, when faced with choosing between the two sides, many Americans instinctively side with Israel. The lack of democratic institutions, the treatment of women, the backward attitudes and the many cultural differences that separate the West from the Islamic world are in sharp contrast to the similarities between Israel and America. The surge in pro-Israel and anti-Muslim sentiments in the United States coincided with the oil embargo of 1973 that followed the Yom Kippur War.

Fred Halliday, professor of international relations at the London School of Economics and a prolific author, has coined the term 'anti-Muslimism' to distinguish between prejudice against Islam and negative feelings toward Muslims. He maintains that rising Islamophobia in the West has little to with Islam; it is more racist than being directed against the teachings of a faith. In *Islam and the Myth of Confrontation*, he writes:

> Strategic anti-Muslimism dates from the early 1970s, and is above all, a result of the 1973 OPEC oil price rises: even though these were not the result of a uniquely Muslim coalition (OPEC includes Venezuela), the 1973 rises provoked a reaction that included anti-Muslim and associated racial hostility to Arabs and Iranians. This was particularly so in the USA where, for the first time, what had hitherto been experienced as an independent economic system was exposed to a form of foreign pressure, conceived of as blackmail or threat. Then came the Iranian revolution, and for the USA in particular, the hostage crisis, which confirmed the image of the Islamic fanatic and terrorist: this rhetoric did not distinguish Persians from Arabs. Side by side with this alarm, related to oil and the hostages, was a set of anti-Arab prejudices emanating from the Arab-Israeli dispute. These had been identifiable since the 1940s, but became more evident from the 1960s onwards, partly as a result of the 1967 war, and then as a result of the rise of a terrorist faction within the Palestinian movement. These stereotypes were played up by the press, but were reinforced by novels such as Leon Uris's *Exodus* and *The Hajj*, and by films. In the USA in particular the composite of Arab-Persian-Muslim-terrorist was established through the intersection of these influences....[9]

Since then, 9/11, two Gulf wars, and the war in Afghanistan have served to solidify this composite image of Muslims in mainstream America.

---

[9] Halliday, Fred, *Islam and the Myth of Confrontation*, op cit.

In their demand for an even-handed approach from America in the Israel-Palestinian conflict, Muslims generally overlook how Americans see them. They merely perceive the pro-Israel tilt without analyzing what underlies the anti-Muslim side of the equation. This lack of understanding feeds into anti-American sentiment that permeates the Muslim world; thus, one set of prejudices among Americans feeds a reaction in Muslims. Many Muslims who have little idea of internal American political compulsions are outraged at what they see as blatant favouritism toward Israel and discrimination against Muslims. Thus, when Hillary Clinton refused a campaign contribution from an Arab donor in her 2000 campaign for a New York Senate seat, Muslims everywhere were outraged at what seemed a gratuitous snub. They simply did not realize how crucial the Jewish vote is for anybody running for public office in New York.

Muslims around the world are repeatedly outraged by what they view as unfair pro-Israeli rhetoric that so frequently figures into American politics. As far back as 1976, then-presidential candidate Jimmy Carter said that he saw American support for Israel as more of a 'moral imperative' than a political issue. Since Jews make up less than 3 per cent of the American population, foreigners often cannot understand how they can wield so much influence over US foreign policy. As a result, Muslims attribute Israeli/Zionist clout within America to a Jewish conspiracy involving shadowy figures in banks, the media, and government who shape and manipulate policies to serve Israeli interests.

In a lucid explanation of the role played by Jews in American politics, Jeffrey S. Helmreich writes in an article entitled 'The Israel Swing Factor: How the American Jewish Vote Influences U.S. Elections,' published on the Jerusalem Centre for Public Affairs website (15 January 2001):

> There are two clashing myths on the political power of American Jewry. One claims that the community is too small to affect national elections; Jews make up less than 3 per cent of the US population.

> A contrasting view holds that US Jews play a disproportionately large role in national politics thanks to their campaign donations and media influence.
>
> According to evidence confirmed in the most recent [2000] elections, however, American Jewish voters maintain the potential to be *the* decisive factor in national election results. Yet, this ability does not emanate from any financial or public relations clout, which is overestimated. Rather, American Jews wield power through their high concentration in key states, and their tendency to behave as a swing vote in ways that set them apart from virtually all other groups in American politics....
>
> But the greatest political strength of American Jewry lies in the fact that it is a *uniquely swayable bloc*. The issue of support for Israel has proven capable of spurring a sizeable portion of Jews to switch parties in large enough numbers to tip the scale in national or statewide elections. Moreover, the 'Israel swing vote' is especially open to political courtship because, unlike the interests of other minority groups, support for Israel has long been compatible with traditional Republican and Democratic agendas. By contrast, most other issues (abortion, affirmative action, etc.) cannot be embraced by Republicans or Democrats without alienating certain support bases. A pro-Israel stance runs no such risk. On the other hand, being distinctly unsupportive of Israel can hurt a candidate's chances....

This explains why candidates running in national and state elections adopt such extreme pro-Israel, anti-Arab postures. Muslims abroad following these contests hear the words without knowing the true context and are understandably angry with America for its pro-Israel slant. Much of this fury manifests itself in the anti-American slogans and the ritual burning of the Stars and Stripes in Muslim streets across the Muslim world whenever Israel undertakes yet more 'security operations' against the Palestinians or against its neighbours. Since the electoral cycle in America is virtually unending, with few gaps between presidential, congressional, and gubernatorial elections, the global media echo the words of the candidates virtually around the year. Cherry-picking the statements that are likely to resound the loudest, newspapers and TV news broadcasts in the Islamic world are likely to focus on pro-Israel and anti-Muslim words from public speeches in America.

Another aspect to the conundrum that most Muslims do not grasp is the messy nature of Israeli politics. The country's system of proportionate representation is geared to produce coalition governments that hang together not through any ideological congruence, but due to political expediency. This fractious arrangement is subject to constant blackmail by small right-wing parties like Shas, the ultra-orthodox party that vehemently opposes any concessions to the Palestinians. In addition to Israel's often dysfunctional system, which makes it even more difficult to make tough political choices, many Israelis currently have a low desire to reach out to Palestinians. In their view, Arabs are being unreasonable by not accepting the deals offered in the past. In particular, they point to the continuing resistance led by Hamas despite the fact that Israel handed back Gaza to them. The largely ineffective homemade rockets fired from Gaza at Israeli targets and the stone-throwing children of the *intifada*[10] have convinced most Israelis that there is little point in negotiating with Palestinians. Thus, pacifists like members of Peace Now have been reduced to a marginalized, largely irrelevant fringe group.

Many Americans would be surprised to see how closely their elections are followed around the world, but given their country's large footprint in international affairs, they shouldn't be. Just because few of them bother to follow political developments abroad does not stop the rest of the world from having an almost unhealthy interest in American politics. The Muslim world, in particular, is obsessed with sporadic US attempts to settle the Israel-Palestine dispute. Although expectations are low, the feelings of bitterness and disappointment are palpable every time peace talks

---

[10] Uprising.

fail. Each time, the perception that America is favouring Israel is strengthened, as is the feeling that it is against Muslims.

Most mainstream politicians in the United States and Israel deny any linkage between the Middle East conflict and the sense of injustice and anger the continued occupation of Palestinian lands provokes in the Muslim world. This rage is directed toward Israel, America, and the Muslim governments that are perceived to be colluding with Washington. None of this is meant to suggest that, if this dispute were to be resolved, Muslims would immediately sign up for a love fest with America. Issues like Iraq and Afghanistan would continue to pose problems in the relationship with Muslim nations. In many parts of the Muslim world, America would still be seen as propping up illegitimate, oppressive regimes. Among certain groups of Muslims fighting for a separate identity, America would still be viewed as the superpower standing with the governments that deny them freedom. However, these are all separate issues that—while causing local anti-American grievances—do not unite the Muslim *ummah* in the same way the Palestinian struggle does. The reality is that this single issue has radicalized a generation of young Muslims around the world. Palestinian resistance leaders are touted as heroes, not the terrorists the Western media portray them to be. For instance, my brother and his wife—he trained as an architect in London and she in San Francisco—named their daughter Leila after Leila Khaled, the Palestinian heroine who hijacked a TWA plane in 1969. She was also the subject of a recent award-winning film.

Despite the clear advantages that would flow from the resolution of this decades-long conflict, it is not clear how any American administration will find the will to press its Israeli ally to make the necessary compromises, given the realities of electoral politics. It is equally obvious that, left to themselves, Israeli politicians will not wish to take on the hard right, and the hundreds of thousands of settlers, by giving up occupied land. Indeed, after creating its so-called security barrier, Israel no longer fears a recurrence of the wave of suicide bombers that shook the country earlier. Thus, as far as many Israelis are concerned, they can live with the status quo as long as their American ally is solidly behind them. The problem with this standoff is that it will continue being the focal point of anti-American sentiment, thereby reinforcing the image of America as a country that has no sympathy for the suffering of Muslims.

6

The Pakistani Paradox

Survey after survey shows Pakistan—a country created in 1947 in the name of Islam that has become increasingly obsessed with religiosity—to be one of the most anti-American Muslim states in the world, yet there was a time when it was considered among America's staunchest allies. What happened to so radically transform Pakistan's attitude toward the United States? The answer lies in the Pakistani paradox.

In 1979, Dr Abdus Salam of Pakistan became the first Muslim to win the Nobel Prize in physics for his pioneering work in uniting the 'weak' and electromagnetic forces. That same year, he was prevented from speaking at Islamabad University by extremist students who carried out a violent demonstration to protest his presence. These two events encapsulate the Pakistani paradox: On the one hand, the country produces doctors, scientists, bankers, and engineers who compete successfully with the best in the world. On the other, mindless fundamentalists rampage across Pakistan, killing and maiming in the name of Islam. More insidiously, their supporters have come to infiltrate the media, the military, the bureaucracy, and the judiciary, thereby obtaining a foothold in every organ of the state.

Dr Salam was ostracized because he was a follower of the Ahmadi sect, a nineteenth-century belief rejected by many Muslims due to certain unorthodox ideas introduced by its founder, Mirza Ghulam Ahmad. In 1974, Ahmadis were declared to be non-Muslims in

Pakistan; since then, they have been persecuted relentlessly and their freedom to worship severely curtailed. Scores are in jail for the so-called crime of using the Islamic salutation '*Asalam Walaikum*' ('peace be upon you') because they are deemed to be usurping a Muslim greeting. Meanwhile, most Pakistanis are delighted if a non-Muslim foreigner makes the effort to use the expression. Such contradictions expose the hypocrisy rampant in Pakistani society today. They also spring from the idea of Pakistan itself: When a state is carved out in the name of a religion, we should hardly be surprised when that faith comes to dominate the public discourse and influence individual thinking and social behaviour.

The other paradox that often confuses foreigners is that—despite their shrill pronouncements of piety and street power—religious parties do very poorly at the polls. In most general elections, they struggle to achieve 5 per cent of the votes cast, which rarely translates into even 10 seats in the 342-seat National Assembly. The reason for this apparent contradiction between the Islamic image of the country and its electoral realities is fairly straightforward: In Pakistan, as in most countries, politics are local, with people using the ballot for tactical reasons. In most constituencies, the main issues are jobs, running water, roads and electricity. Seeing elections as their chance to improve their lives, people vote for candidates and parties who, in their opinion, can deliver. In this calculus, clerics are considered unworldly folk whose intercession might be useful in the afterlife, but not in this one.

This tension between fundamentalism and moderation lies at the heart of the seemingly endless cycle of violence the country is experiencing. In fact, it is built into Pakistan's DNA. Conceived as a homeland for the Muslims of the Subcontinent, rather than as an Islamic state, by its founder, Muhammed Ali Jinnah, his dream of a modern, secular nation has been steadily subverted. Indeed, it is hard to reconcile the religious violence that wracks present-day Pakistan with its founding father's vision. Speaking to the yet-to-be-born state's Constituent Assembly on August 11, 1947 (three days before Pakistan came into being), Jinnah said:

> You are free; you are free to go to your temples; you are free to go to your mosques or any other place of worship in this State of Pakistan. You may belong to any religion or caste or creed: that has nothing to do with the business of the state....
>
> We are starting with this fundamental principle that we are all citizens and equal citizens of one State. .. Now I think we should keep this in front of us as our ideal and you will find that in course of time Hindus will cease to be Hindus and Muslims would cease to be Muslims, not in the religious sense, because that is the personal faith of each individual, but in the political sense as citizens of the State....

This is as clear a declaration of the secular ideal as any statesman has made, yet Pakistan continues to move away from the liberal goal Jinnah set for the new state he created virtually single-handedly. One reason for this divergence between dream and reality is that Jinnah died barely a year after making this ringing pronouncement. His successors had neither his political stature nor his vision to stand up to the Islamists led by the influential scholar Maulana Maudoodi. During its first three decades, a Westernized elite ruled the post-colonial state, entering into several American-led alliances. Although these pacts were aimed at countering the Communist threat, for Pakistani leaders they produced a flood of modern American arms to match India's far larger arsenal.

From its very creation, Pakistan has been obsessed with the perceived threat from India; indeed, most of its internal and external policies can be understood only in this context. The two countries fought a war over Kashmir within a year of independence in 1947; sixty-four years and three wars later, the dispute continues to poison relations. When fighting broke out in September 1965 after a Pakistani military gamble in Kashmir, the United States slapped an arms embargo on both countries. Although seemingly even-handed, the embargo in fact affected only Pakistan as its military was almost totally dependent on American arms. India, on the other hand, imported its military hardware from different sources, albeit predominantly from the Soviet Union. Thus, when Pakistan was quickly forced to agree to a ceasefire following a military stalemate, millions of Pakistanis were deeply disillusioned. They had been told by their country's propaganda machine that their military had the upper hand, so the ceasefire came as an unpleasant shock. General Ayub Khan, the army dictator at the time, was accused by his opponents of toeing the American line. He was indeed pro-American, but his acceptance of the Soviet-brokered ceasefire was dictated partly by the fact that his troops were running low on spare parts and ammunition.

Unwilling to publicly accept responsibility for its many blunders and miscalculations in its planning and execution of strategy and tactics, the Pakistani military high command sought to blame the Americans for cutting off supplies in the middle of the war. To this day, most Pakistanis are ignorant of the fact that the military pacts under which Pakistan received American supplies specifically included provisions restricting their use for defensive purposes and stipulated that they could only be used against a Communist threat. Clearly, instigating a war against India to wrest Kashmir from its control was not a part of the understanding between the United States and Pakistan. Nevertheless, two generations of Pakistanis have grown up with the conviction that their country was let down in its hour of need by a perfidious and unreliable American ally.

This sense of betrayal was reinforced during the 1971 war with India, in which Pakistan's distant eastern wing broke away to form Bangladesh. The brutal civil war that erupted when the Pakistani army tried to suppress the Bangladeshi freedom movement drew condemnation from around the world, including from the United States. Most people in West Pakistan (the home of the army units used in the unsuccessful attempt to crush the insurgents) were unaware of—or in denial of—the sheer scale of the slaughter taking place a thousand miles away. Whereas India was supported by a range of countries, including its close friend, the Soviet Union, Pakistan was isolated, with only China and some Muslim countries desisting from public condemnation. When India launched an attack in December 1971, Pakistani units, cut off in East Pakistan, surrendered within days. The United States sought to prevent India from invading West Pakistan by announcing that it was sending the Seventh Fleet to the Bay of Bengal. Many Pakistanis assumed this intervention would rescue their forces and save the day. The ultimate result was the establishment of Bangladesh and more than 90,000 Pakistani troops being interned in Indian prisoner of war camps. Most Pakistanis were more humiliated by the defeat than concerned by the hundreds of thousands of civilian deaths that tragically accompanied the birth of Bangladesh. Apart from Indian perfidy, many blamed the United States for not coming to Pakistan's aid.

The next chapter in this litany of perceived betrayals came when Pakistan, under the populist leader Zulfikar Ali Bhutto, announced its intention to launch a nuclear programme following the Indian test of a nuclear device in 1974. Bhutto persuaded Dr A.Q. Khan, a metallurgist working in a Dutch nuclear facility at the time, to return to Pakistan to lead the country's efforts to achieve parity with India. This is the same scientist who later attained international notoriety with his clandestine proliferation activities. When Bhutto was ousted by a military coup in 1977 following weeks of street protests, his followers widely believed his removal had been orchestrated by the United States to cripple Pakistan's nuclear programme.

General Zia, the army chief who toppled and executed Bhutto, continued supporting Pakistan's covert nuclear programme and was saved from international censure and American sanctions by the Soviet invasion of Afghanistan in December 1979. Suddenly, the world's attention was focused on one of the poorest regions on the globe. American policymakers were presented with an opportunity to turn Afghanistan into the Soviet Union's own Vietnam. However, this could only happen with Pakistan's support. For the time being, any thoughts of applying sanctions against the country for its covert nuclear programme would have to be shelved. The CIA and Pakistan's military intelligence agency, the Inter-Services Intelligence (ISI), developed and pursued a highly effective operation to train and arm Afghan insurgents to fight the Soviets. These fighters were aided by thousands of Arabs who flocked to Pakistan to join the jihad against the infidels who had invaded a Muslim country. Although the military effectiveness of these foreigners is questionable, they brought in cash and—in Osama bin Laden's case—engineering equipment and expertise.

From the very beginning of this clandestine enterprise, Zia had insisted on retaining control over which Afghan groups were to get funds and arms. The ISI froze the Americans out of the loop despite the billions they had pumped into the efforts. Zia made sure that hard-line Islamic outfits would get the lion's share of the cash and the arms, which was in line with his personal ideological leaning. He had previously declared Pakistan to be 'the laboratory of Islam.' In this case, the experiment went horribly wrong, as we can see from the rabid extremism ravaging the country today. Zia's fundamentalism also had the effect of creating armed and dangerous militant groups in Pakistan's border badlands, known as the Federally Administered Tribal Areas (FATA). Traditionally and constitutionally, these regions had enjoyed a great deal of autonomy, with law and order being maintained under tribal law and by tribal leaders. Almost overnight, these deeply conservative and backward areas were playing host to millions of Afghan refugees and thousands of Afghan, Pakistani, and foreign fighters.

As long as the Soviets were in Afghanistan and American and Saudi money was flowing into Pakistan, the focus was on fighting the common foe. Once the Red Army—drained by years of fighting and waning support at home—pulled out in 1988, American interest in the region flagged, and funds dried up. Pakistan's nuclear programme once again came under American scrutiny. Thus far, the US president had used his authority to certify once a year that—in his judgement—Pakistan did not possess a nuclear device. This waiver staved off the automatic trigger written into foreign aid legislation aimed at countries pursuing the development of nuclear weapons. Introduced by Congressman Stephen Solarz and Senator

Larry Pressler, the amendments called for halting assistance to countries like Pakistan. Following the Soviet defeat, these legislative provisions were invoked, and military and economic aid was cut off in 1990.

Even worse in Pakistani eyes was the decision to block the release of the twenty-eight F-16 fighters for which Pakistan had paid $470 million. The Pakistani Air Force deemed these high-performance aircraft to be crucial for obtaining an edge over the far larger Indian Air Force. Lockheed, the manufacturer of the aircraft, refused to refund the money on the grounds that the planes had been manufactured according to the contract, and it was not responsible for the US government's decision to block their transfer to Pakistan. For millions of Pakistanis, the retention of both the F-16s and the cash was an act of highway robbery. The fact that the country was saddled with a huge Afghan refugee population while simultaneously being deprived of American assistance was played up by an increasingly anti-American media.

During the Afghan war, hundreds of Pakistani military officers had been sponsored for training in the United States, often returning with fond memories of their stay at American training facilities. They also forged professional and personal links with the American officers with whom they had trained. Abruptly, all this changed. Deprived of American arms and training, the mood in Pakistani officers' messes turned ugly. The phrase most commonly used to describe the American attitude was that, after having served Washington's interests in Afghanistan, Pakistan was discarded 'like a used condom.' This increasingly bitter view made its way into the media and into the living rooms of the intelligentsia. At a party in Karachi in the mid-1990s, I recall a senior air force officer arguing passionately that, to make up for the budgetary hole caused by the American sanctions, Pakistan should sell its nuclear technology to countries hostile to the United States. Thus, for almost a decade, Pakistan was 'America's most sanctioned ally.'

Just as aid to certain sectors (e.g. agriculture) was being restored toward the end of the 1990s, Pakistan's nuclear tests in

1998 following India's triggered another round of sanctions. In 1999, General Musharraf's coup further confirmed Pakistan's pariah status. Had it not been for 9/11, it is likely that Pakistan would have continued to remain isolated and mired in its own contradictions and state of denial, blaming the world for its woes. Al Qaeda's terror attacks against the United States on that fateful day in September proved to be a bonanza for Pakistan. From being a country on the verge of bankruptcy and default, Pakistan was again vaulted into a frontline status, with the world led by the United States showering largesse on it. However, this infusion of cash into a sickly economy and the restoration of military assistance did little to restore America's image: In July 2010, a Pew Research Center study showed that nearly two thirds of Pakistanis viewed America as an enemy, placing it lower than India—the country's traditional foe—in terms of popularity.

This must be deeply depressing to American diplomats, especially as Pakistan is now the recipient of the largest US aid package in the world. The furor in Pakistan over the passage of the Kerry-Lugar Bill in the US Congress in 2009 provides a stark reminder of how testy relations between the two countries have become. The bill aimed to enhance US economic assistance to Pakistan by providing $7.5 billion over the next five years. One would think such a bill would be widely welcomed. On the contrary, a maelstrom was whipped up in the Pakistani media, attacking certain provisions in the bill as interference in the country's internal matters. Indeed, the draft legislation (and later, the approved act) contains strictures about the supremacy of the elected government as well as the independence of the judiciary—pointed reminders to Pakistan's powerful, coup-prone military to stop meddling in politics. According to many observers, the media campaign was orchestrated by the army in an effort to pressure the American administration to make changes in the Kerry-Lugar Bill.

Reporting on the controversy, Omar Waraich, *Time* magazine correspondent in Pakistan, wrote: 'The furor over the aid package has left President Asif Ali Zardari increasingly isolated as normally fractious opposition parties unite against the 'humiliating' conditions, with even the junior partners in Zardari's ruling coalition expressing misgivings. Public opinion ranges from suspicion to hostility, and the army high command broke with its recent habit of remaining quiet on political matters to issue an ominous statement. Following a meeting of its corps commanders, the army—the country's most powerful institution, long accustomed to keeping the political class in line—expressed 'serious concern' over what it said were the 'national security' implications of the aid package....'[1]

On its AfPak website, the American journal *Foreign Policy* ran an article by Katherine Tiedemann entitled 'Sound and Fury, Signifying Nothing'[2], in which she wrote:

> The Pakistani Army, according to reports last week, has written a strong 'non-paper' to Pakistan's leadership regarding unacceptable elements in the new Kerry-Lugar Bill (KLB), which will provide $1.5 billion in economic assistance annually to Pakistan with some conditions regarding accountability. The military was joined, perhaps unsurprisingly, by the political opposition...in condemning terms that were described as 'insulting and unacceptable'....
>
> The Pakistan Army's corps commanders and leadership expressed concern, according to Pakistani reports, over the bill's 'clauses about the country's nuclear program, suggestions of Pakistan's support for cross-border militancy and civilian government's [sic] role in military promotions and appointments.'[3]

However, when I asked a senior serving army general why he and his colleagues were so upset about the proposed aid package, his answer was very revealing of the military's mindset. According

[1] *Time*, October 8, 2009.

[2] October 13, 2009.

[3] http://afpak.foreignpolicy.com/posts/2009/10/13/sound_and_fury_signifying_nothing

to him, what the army really objected to were provisions in the act that restricted the reallocation of funds to the country's nuclear programme, which he said was aimed at limiting the number of nuclear warheads in the Pakistani arsenal. 'Surely,' I replied, 'you have more than enough to deter India. In any case, given the long common borders, no sane person would ever actually use these weapons without causing catastrophic fallout damage in his own country.' His answer was chilling: 'Actually, evidence from the atom bombs dropped on Hiroshima and Nagasaki by the United States in World War II does not prove your point as the soil near these cities was not contaminated for very long.'

Whatever the real cause for the army's ire, the firestorm around the Kerry-Lugar Bill lasted weeks, with one talking head after another solemnly asserting on Pakistan's many TV channels that the legislation somehow violated the nation's sovereignty. In my column, I frequently lambasted this self-defeating attitude and argued that, if Pakistanis felt so strongly about it, they should refuse to accept the aid package being offered. I was accused of being unpatriotic by many readers, with several charging me with being on the US payroll.

America's trampling of Pakistan's national sovereignty has been a constant refrain in the current phase of the contentious relations between the two countries. As American drone attacks in Pakistan's tribal areas have increased exponentially, so have the protests in the country's cities and its influential TV chat shows. Paradoxically, the left and the right have joined hands in condemning the attacks, with op-ed articles in liberal newspapers and magazines—as well as clerics in their Friday sermons—holding forth against this brazen flouting of Pakistan's sovereignty.

Yet there is more to this campaign than meets the eye. It is official US policy to deny knowledge of these attacks; each time they target militants, the Pakistani government lodges a pro-forma protest. However, the reality is that a tacit understanding exists between the two countries permitting these attacks. Indeed, some of these drones operate from Shamsie, a secret airfield in Pakistan's

Balochistan province. Senator Dianne Feinstein, chairwoman of the Senate Intelligence Committee, was quoted as asserting that the unmanned aircraft operated from a base located in Pakistan[4]. Despite this information being in the public domain, Pakistani commentators continue to attack Washington for the drone campaign, and religious parties regularly burn effigies of Uncle Sam as well as the Stars and Stripes in cities across Pakistan. Apart from the sovereignty issue, the collateral damage caused by the Hellfire missiles fired from Reaper and Predator drones drives a lot of the acrimonious, anti-American comment in the media. Asif Haroon Raja, a retired brigadier general, wrote the following in the *Asian Tribune*:

> The drones hit suspected Al-Qaeda and pro-Pakistan Taliban disregarding collateral damage incurred and ignores anti-army militants. Each attack by the deadly flying machines kill majority of civilians including women and children and very few noted militants get targeted. In this year [2008] so far 24 missile attacks have taken place killing 344 civilians. The number of so-called militants does not exceed ten.[5]

Since publication of this article, the number of drone attacks has risen sharply, and anger toward America has increased proportionately. A survey conducted by the Pew Research Center in spring 2010 found that only 17 per cent of the Pakistanis questioned had a favourable view of America. Thus, despite the passage of the Kerry-Lugar Bill and the fresh infusion of US assistance, the country's unpopularity remains alarmingly high.

Interestingly, those in the firing line of the drones do not appear to share the views of the majority of Pakistanis or human rights activists abroad Farhat Taj is an academic from the northwest area of Pakistan near the Afghan border. A research fellow at the Centre

---

[4] *Los Angeles Times*, 02/13/2009.

[5] http://www.asiantribune.com/comment/reply/14327

for Gender Research at the University of Oslo and a member of the Aryana Institute for Regional Research and Advocacy (AIRRA), she speaks Pushto, the language of the majority of the people in the region. She is a regular contributor to the Pakistani media, writing the following in *The News* on 5 March 2009:

> Between last November and January AIRRA sent five teams, each made up of five researchers, to the parts of FATA[6] that are often hit by American drones, to conduct a survey of public opinion about the attacks. The teams visited Wana (South Waziristan), Ladda (South Waziristan), Miranshah (North Waziristan), Razmak (North Waziristan) and Parachinar (Khurram Agency). The teams handed out 650 questionnaires to people in the areas.... The 550 respondents (100 declined to answer) were from professions related to business, education, health and transport. Following are the questions and responses of the people of FATA:
>
> Do you see the drone attacks bringing about fear and terror in the common people? (Yes 45 per cent; No 55 per cent)
>
> Do you think the drones are accurate in their strikes? (Yes 52 per cent; No 48 per cent)
>
> Do you think anti-American feelings in the area increased due to drone attacks recently? (Yes 42 per cent; No 58 per cent)
>
> Should Pakistan military carry out targeted strikes at the militant organizations? (Yes 70 per cent; No 30 per cent)
>
> Do the militant organizations get damaged due to drone attacks? (Yes 60 per cent; No 40 per cent)
>
> A group of researchers at AIRRA draw these conclusions from the survey: The popular notion outside the Pakhtun belt[7] that a large majority of the local population supports the Taliban movement lacks substance. The notion that anti-Americanism in the region has increased due to drone attacks is rejected....
>
> The survey also reinforces my own ethnographic interactions with the people of FATA, both inside FATA and the FATA

[6] Federally Administered Tribal Areas.

[7] The area encompassing FATA.

IDP's[8]....This includes people I personally met and those I am in contact with through telephone calls and emails....The number is well over 2,000. I asked almost all these people if they see the US drone attacks on FATA as a violation of Pakistan's sovereignty. More than two thirds said they did not. Pakistan's sovereignty, they argued, was insulted and annihilated by Al-Qaeda and the Taliban, whose territory FATA is after Pakistan lost it to them.... Many people laughed when I mentioned the word sovereignty with respect to Pakistan.

Over two thirds of the people viewed Al-Qaeda and the Taliban as enemy number one, and wanted the Pakistani army to clear the area of the militants. A little under two thirds want the Americans to continue the drone attacks because the Pakistani army is unwilling or unable to retake the territory from the Taliban.

The people I asked about civilian casualties in the drone attacks said most of the attacks had hit their targets, which include Arab, Chechen, Uzbek and Tajik terrorists of Al-Qaeda, Pakistani Taliban (Pakhtun and Punjabi) and training camps of the terrorists. There has been some collateral damage.

The drones hit *hujras* [compounds] or houses which the Taliban forced people to rent to them. There is collateral damage when the family forced to rent out the property is living in an adjacent house or a portion of the property rented out.

The Taliban and Al-Qaeda have unleashed a reign of terror on the people of FATA. People are afraid that the Taliban will suspect their loyalty and behead them. Thus, in order to prove their loyalty to the Taliban and Al-Qaeda, they offer them to rent their houses and *hujras* for residential purposes....

People told me that typically what happens after every drone attack is that the Taliban and Al-Qaeda terrorists cordon off the area. No one from the local population is allowed to access the site, even if there are local people killed or injured.... The Taliban and Al-Qaeda remove everything they want from the site....

The survey conducted by ARRIA and my ethnographic interactions contradict the mantra of violation of the sovereignty of Pakistan perpetuated by the armchair analysts in the media....

[8] Internally Displaced Persons.

> What is happening in FATA is destroying the lives and culture of the FATA people, threatening the integrity of Pakistan and world peace. Fantasies of armchair analysts are helping no one but Al-Qaeda and the Taliban—enemies of the land and culture I love, and our state....[9]
>
> I have quoted Ms. Taj at some length because her findings and conclusions are so diametrically opposed to the constant refrain one finds in the Pakistani and the foreign media. The argument that the drone attacks are destabilizing Pakistan and breaking international law is echoed in the West as well. Yet, Ms Taj's forthright rejection of this view was corroborated by a very senior civil servant who worked in Peshawar until 2010, when he told me that, 'the further people are from FATA, the more strident they are in their denunciation of the drone attacks.'

The whole issue of sovereignty has inflamed Pakistani public opinion as few other debates have done. The anger over the perception that national dignity and honour are being trampled underfoot by the Americans unites right and left as well as liberals and mullahs. The army—a fiercely nationalistic institution—is prickly and defensive as it is viewed as being unable to fend off the drone attacks. Instead of blaming the army for having created many of the jihadi outfits active in Pakistan and Afghanistan and for helping the Taliban take over much of Afghanistan before 9/11, most Pakistanis hold the Americans responsible for the sharp rise of terrorist attacks within the country. Indeed, as the terrorists flee to other areas to escape the drones, they seek to destabilize the Pakistani state through devastating suicide attacks, many of which are directed against the army, the police, and the intelligence services.

When floods devastated a huge swath of Pakistan in 2010, destroying crops worth billions and displacing millions of people living along the Indus, the country launched a worldwide appeal for help. The United States was the biggest donor, sending a large

[9] *The News*, Karachi, March 5, 2009.

fleet of helicopters to rescue thousands of stranded farmers as well as deliver food and medicine to isolated pockets of displaced persons. Despite this rapid and generous assistance, the Internet was soon buzzing with rumors of a mysterious American plot to harm Pakistan through something called HAARP technology, which allegedly has the ability to alter the weather. No sensible reason was ever suggested why America would wish to weaken a country that was its ally in the anti-Taliban campaign.

A recent episode that roiled relations between the two countries shows the depth of the suspicion and tension. On 28 January 2011, Raymond Davis, an American CIA contract employee, was driving in Lahore when—according to him—two young men on a motorbike tried to rob him at gunpoint. He shot them dead. A support vehicle that raced in to help him accidentally killed a man on a bicycle. When the police arrested Davis, he claimed diplomatic immunity, insisting that he had fired in self-defence. The Pakistani media immediately went into overdrive, with pundits claiming that Davis should be tried under Pakistani law and hanged. Demonstrators from Islamic parties chanted slogans against the government's failure to protect its citizens. The police registered a case of murder, and Davis was remanded into their custody for questioning. The weak civilian government was forced into trying to placate both the Americans and an increasingly hysterical Pakistani public. The blogosphere was full of rants against 'American imperialism.'

A few sensible voices pointed out that this was clearly a case of self-defence and, in any case, the Vienna Convention that guaranteed immunity to diplomats required Davis to be handed over to the American embassy. The issue was further clouded by the fact that Davis was employed by the CIA on contract and was armed when, under Pakistani law, diplomats are forbidden from carrying firearms. Whatever the diplomatic and legal niceties of the case, the sound and fury it generated provide an accurate indicator of the deep antagonism that has come to mark relations between the two allies.

The case was finally closed after weeks of heated controversy and legal and diplomatic manoeuvring between Islamabad and Washington. Ultimately, the families of the two Pakistanis killed by Davis agreed to accept blood money totalling more than two million dollars in order to withdraw their case from court. This Islamic provision, introduced into Pakistan's criminal code by General Zia in the 1980s, was invoked to break the intractable deadlock over the case.

However, this incident paled into insignificance by the killing of bin Laden just three months later. Once his presence was suspected in Abbottabad (home to Pakistan's equivalent of the West Point military academy) in September 2010, the CIA rented a house close to his to keep him under close observation. Meanwhile, an elite team of US Navy SEAL commandos began training for a secret mission into Pakistan to attack the elusive Al Qaeda chief. In total darkness, three Black Hawk helicopters and two Chinooks flew in below the Pakistani radar to Abbottabad, approximately 60 miles north of Islamabad, and carried out the daring raid that resulted in bin Laden's death. His body was removed by the SEAL team and later buried at sea.

When news of the operation broke, it provoked opposite reactions in America and Pakistan. Americans were understandably delighted over the long-delayed success in tracking down the man responsible for 9/11. Meanwhile, most Pakistanis were furious with their intelligence services and their defence forces for not knowing about bin Laden's presence so close to the capital for more than five years, and for not detecting or preventing American forces from crossing the border to conduct a military operation deep within the country. Newspaper editorials and TV chat show hosts and guests went into overdrive to castigate the Pakistani government for its ignorance and its impotence. However, most of the public rage was reserved for America for not sharing its information about bin Laden and leaving it to the Pakistani authorities to arrest him. Yet, as American officials made clear, they have serious doubts about sharing critical information with

ISI, the Pakistani military intelligence service, because of fears that it would be leaked by pro-jihadi elements within the agency. Indeed, the CIA and the Pentagon have complained of instances when information supplied to the ISI was passed on to insurgents. In one specific instance in June 2011, aerial surveillance videos of two busy bomb-making factories in the tribal areas were handed over to the ISI; when Pakistani troops arrived there 24 hours later, the factories were deserted.

These are just two examples of the kind of visceral anti-Americanism that has taken root in Pakistan. In fact, they are part of a larger paranoid perception that the rest of the world is out to 'get' Pakistan. Whether it is adverse umpiring decisions in cricket or the international anti-proliferation regime that puts the country in the spotlight, there is a feeling that somehow foreigners want to damage Pakistan. Currently, this paranoia is being driven by Western (particularly American) unease about the possibility of Pakistan's nuclear weapons falling into extremist hands. Thus, there are constant suspicions and rumours of American plots to neutralize Pakistan's nuclear arsenal. As the nuclear programme is a major source of national pride, such perceptions reinforce anti-Americanism at every level.

Another area of contention is that, by fighting 'America's war' against the Taliban, Pakistan is being subjected not only to drone attacks, but also to suicide bombings. People are not willing to take a hard look at the mushroom growth of *madressas*, where little more than Islamic texts are taught, or the steady march of the hard-line Wahabi version of Islam that has spread with active Saudi support since the 1970s. Above all, many Pakistanis close their eyes to the arms, training, and financing extremist militants have received from Pakistan's army and intelligence services over the years. These heavily armed groups have now trained their guns and their suicide bombers on the state of Pakistan after it decided to support America and curtail the infiltration of these terrorists into Afghanistan and Kashmir. Despite the clear evidence that it is largely Pakistan's own fault that these dangerous groups are now out of control—indeed, that they exist at all—millions of Pakistanis insist on blaming America for much of its increasing problems. Whether it's a military coup or administrative bungling, many so-called media analysts and bloggers point the finger at Washington.

So how did things get so bad? Growing up in Karachi in the 1950s, I remember having American neighbours who worked in the US embassy. On our street, we played cricket in an empty lot, and our American friends quickly learned the game. We were in and out of each other's homes, exchanging comics and records and raiding each other's fridges. Americans were very much part of the city's cultural and social scene, with the American Center organizing frequent concerts and movies. I read voraciously, borrowing hundreds of books from the USIS library as well as the British Council. Later, working in Lahore and Islamabad, I had a number of American friends, some of them diplomats who entertained and went to parties without a second thought for their security. In Islamabad, foreigners went trekking up the nearby Margalla hills and cycled on the capital's wide roads. The city's few good restaurants were full of diplomats, as were the handicraft shops. An artificially created modern city, Islamabad might not have been the most amusing place for an overseas posting for diplomats, but it provided a scenic setting far removed from the country's teeming millions and its everyday squalor. As many have noted, the real Pakistan starts ten miles away from its capital city. Although it has been described as boring, nobody considered it especially dangerous.

Things began changing in 1979, when the American Embassy was burned down by a mob in the wake of the seizure of the Grand Mosque in Mecca on November 20 by a large group of Muslim (mostly Saudi) insurgents. Claiming that they were led by the *mahdi*, the promised redeemer who would restore Islam to its glory, the well-armed band locked the gates and took hundreds of hostages. In the fortnight that followed, scores were killed, with insurgents picking off Saudi soldiers from their vantage points in the mosque's high minarets. As non-Muslims are forbidden to enter Islam's holy of holies, Pakistani commandos of the Special Services Group were called in to finally end the standoff. They used tanks to batter the massive gates down and went into the basement complex to flush the insurgents out. Virtually all of them were killed in the battle, with the survivors being executed by the Saudi government. The only one to escape was Osama bin Laden's half-brother Mahrous, who had joined the extremists. It is widely believed that trucks belonging to the bin Laden engineering firm, then renovating the mosque, were employed to bring in the automatic weapons used by the insurgents. Due to the close links between the bin Ladens and the Saudi royal family, young Mahrous was spared. (It should be noted that, according to some sources, the Saudis asked French commandos to clear the mosque of the militants).

The shock wave from this unimaginable act spread throughout the Muslim world. Demonstrations took place from Indonesia to Egypt. Most Muslims were convinced that the Americans were somehow behind the seizure. Indeed, Iran's Ayatollah Khomeini charged 'the Americans and the Zionists' of organizing the plot. In Pakistan, a small left-wing student protest against American policies on November 21 was suddenly hijacked by busloads of members of the youth wing of the Jamaat-e-Islami, a large Islamist political party. Later reports are confused about who fired first, but the protestors claim that an American marine opened fire on the crowd. Whatever the truth, in the ensuing battle, two Americans—including a marine—were killed and the embassy building burned to the ground. The remaining embassy staff were saved by retreating into an underground safe room with steel doors. Five hours later, Pakistani soldiers battled their way to the basement to rescue the diplomats and support staff. Interestingly, for much of the time this drama was being played out, General Zia ul Haq, the dictator who had seized power two years earlier, was bicycling from his official house to his office for a photo opportunity just a few miles from Islamabad.

The attack on the US embassy was seen as an aberration. Nobody at the time thought individual Americans were at risk. Life went on in Islamabad and elsewhere in Pakistan. In the late 1980s, I was living in Islamabad and often went to parties in American homes. Until it was attacked in 1988 by a mob of extremists following the furor surrounding the *Satanic Verses*, the American Center was the focal point for many cultural events. The *fatwa* issued by Ayatollah Khomeini, calling for Salman Rushdie's death, ignored the fact that the Indian-born British author had nothing to do with the United States. Unfortunately, facts carry little weight with zealots whose worldview is shaped by a rigid ideology and ignorance in equal measure.

Even after this attack, there was little anti-American sentiment on a personal level. Foreigners, including Americans, went about their business in Pakistan without any serious worries about their security. It was not until the first Gulf War in 1990 that hostility toward Americans became rampant. Although Saddam Hussein was a secular dictator who had invaded and occupied Kuwait, a Muslim neighbour, he was regarded as a hero for standing up to America. Conspiracy theories did the rounds about how he had been tricked by the American ambassador into launching his suicidal adventure. When images of the death and destruction caused by American bombs and missiles started beaming into homes across the Muslim world, the outrage was palpable. In Pakistan, the mood was sullen. As the vaunted Iraqi Republican Guard was pulverized by daisy-cutter and bunker-buster bombs dropped by B-52s, the humiliation of yet another Muslim military defeat was channelled into an anti-American frenzy.

The first Gulf War coincided roughly with the retreat of the Red Army from Afghanistan and the consequent drawdown of the American presence and interest in the region. The period also saw Pakistan-specific anti-proliferation sanctions kicking in. All these factors combined to produce a toxic anti-Americanism that has since grown steadily, being sustained and heightened over the last two decades by the Israeli crackdown on Palestinians in the West

Bank and Gaza as well as its invasion of Lebanon in 2004, the Serb massacre of thousands of Bosnian Muslims, the Russian assault on Chechnya, and the growing friendship between arch-foe India and America. Above all, the invasion of Iraq in the second Gulf War on the pretext of nonexistent weapons of mass destruction triggered a flood of anger that lingers to this day. Even the attack on neighbouring Afghanistan in the aftermath of 9/11 did not cause so much rage as many saw the link between the Al Qaeda terror strike against the United States and the American response.

In Pakistan, these events and perceptions feed into an anti-American narrative that now informs public debate on just about every topic. Whether it is corruption and mismanagement by a pro-American Pakistani government—possibly the last one for years to come—or terrorist attacks against Pakistani targets, the Americans somehow get blamed. Understandably, the Obama administration is at a loss on how to change these deeply ingrained attitudes. On the one hand, it is now committed to giving its ally $1.5 billion a year in economic assistance over the next five years; on the other, Pakistan's principal benefactor is made the scapegoat for all the country's problems—many of its own creation. Cracking the Pakistani paradox is the cause of recurring headaches for the US State Department. More importantly, it is threatening the long-term stability of the deeply troubled state.

7

The Virtual Ummah and Online Jihad

It is ironic and instructive that an ideology that opposes most forms of modernism should make such effective use of cutting-edge communications tools. An even greater irony is that the tools invented and popularized by Americans should be turned against them by the same extremists who hate and despise much of what America stands for. Indeed, the spread of global jihad overlaps the mushroom growth of the Internet, cell phone use and the popularity of home videos. Since the early Nineties, these ubiquitous instruments of mass communication have driven the globalization of the jihad. To an ever-increasing extent, the Internet has become the backbone of extremist propaganda, motivation and training. Given the pressure the jihadists are under from governments around the world, it could be argued that without the Internet they would be unable to function. Cyberspace provides them with a cloak of anonymity, and a sanctuary from drone attacks, covert action and an increasingly effective counter-terrorism machinery.

In a report produced for the Quilliam Foundation, a counter-extremist think-tank based in the UK, Mohammed Ali Musawi writes:

> Jihadists began using the Internet almost as soon as it became accessible to the public in the 1990s. As with many other terrorist groups and movements seeking to communicate their cause and demands to a local, regional or global audience, the Internet presented

> obvious opportunities...In addition to offering an uncensored channel of communication, websites can also be maintained from any location that has an Internet connection, they are cheap to run and can be tailored to reach specific audiences. These features, together with perceived anonymity and invulnerability, made the Internet a playground for jihadists from the late 1990s onwards, becoming in many ways the cyber equivalent of Afghanistan or Yemen; ungoverned, de-territorialised spaces where transnational networks of militants could operate with impunity [1]

When I typed 'Jihadist websites in English' into Google, I got 363,000 results. But to put this figure in perspective, I found 392,000 websites listed in a Google search for 'right-wing militant groups.' So clearly, there are lots of people in cyberspace, with lots of time on their hands, who seek to remake the world in their vision of utopia, and never mind the collateral damage. And there are lots of nuts out there too, spewing hate at anybody who does not share their warped worldview. The one common theme running through these sites is a lack of tolerance and humanity. Clearly, cyberspace has become the battleground for conflicting ideologies, and the global jihad has gone digital. To get an idea of how dependent cyber-jihadists are on the Web, here is an excerpt from a brief article called Cyber Jihad posted on the Global Jihad website:

> The implementation of the Global Jihad leans on two pillars: the suicide attackers or bombers on the operational side and the Internet or cyber space on the management aspect. The three components Command, Control and Communication, necessary for any successful operation, including terror attacks, are carried out almost inclusively [sic] through the Internet. The cyber space is also the main Islamic militancy tool for propaganda, distributing ideas, recruiting volunteers and raising money...[2]

---

[1] 'Cheering for Osama: How Jihadists use Internet Discussion Forums.' www.quilliamfoundation.org

[2] http://www.globaljihad.net/view_page.asp?id=399

Often, jihadist sites are hacked into and shut down, forcing them to migrate to other sites, or to open mirror sites. And frequently, cyber warriors counter-attack to swamp sites with denial of service techniques involving multiple servers and computers. There is thus a low-intensity battle going in cyberspace that most of us are unaware of. At times of crisis, the intensity of this digital warfare increases, as it did when Israel attacked Gaza in January 2008. Supporters of Israel and the Palestinians went into battle across the Internet in an attempt to shut each other's sites down. In a sense, this is an echo from earlier attempts to broadcast and jam propaganda across the ether by radio and TV.

But before we jump to the conclusion that millions of Muslims are hunched over their computers, accessing the dysfunctional ravings of demented mullahs, let me suggest that most people across the Islamic world are too busy with their lives to spend much time in cyberspace. Obviously, many young Muslims are influenced by what they read and see on extremist websites: after all, Major Nidal Hasan, the Fort Hood shooter who killed thirteen people at the US army base, was motivated to go on this shooting spree by Anwar Al-Awlaki, the American cleric who, before his death in a CIA drone attack, blogged his hate-filled message from Yemen. He was also a major influence on Umar Farouk, the Nigerian Muslim student who tried to blow up a plane over Chicago, and only failed because his explosive-laced underwear did not ignite properly. Faisal Shahzad, the Times Square bomber, also spent time watching webcasts of Al-Awlaki's sermons. Similarly, Roshanara Begum, a British Muslim, attacked a member of Parliament because he had voted for the war on Iraq. She, too, had read Al-Awlaki's messages in cyberspace, and listened to his sermons.

So clearly, the Internet provides a forum to preachers and ideologues to spread their messages of hate from sanctuaries around the world. In cyberspace, the voices of extremism are amplified and transmitted instantly across the globe at minimal cost. Quick to realize the potential of this technology, jihadists became some of the most tech-savvy exponents of cyber warfare. A good example of the increasingly sophisticated use of the Internet is *Inspire*, a webzine produced for Al Qaeda in the Arabian Peninsula (AQAP). Slick and well edited, the publication is largely the brainchild of Samir Khan, a young American of Pakistani origin who lived undercover in Yemen until he too met his end in the drone attack that killed his mentor, Al-Awlaki, in October 2011. In the January 2011 edition of *Inspire*, Anwar Al-Awlaki argued that Muslims have the right and the duty to rob Westerners to support the jihad:

> Every Muslim who lives in *dar al-harb* [literally, the Land of War in contrast to *dar al-Islam*, but in today's context, the term refers to countries at war with Muslims, i.e., the USA, Britain, etc.] should avoid paying any of his wealth to the disbelievers whether it be in the form of taxes, duties, or fines...
>
> In the case of the United States, both the government and private citizens should be targeted. America and Americans are the Imams [prayer leaders] of *kufr* [disbelief] in this day and age. The American people who vote for war-mongering governments are intent on no good. Anyone who inflicts harm on them in any form is doing a favour to the *ummah* [the nation of Islam]...
>
> Since *jihad* around the world is in dire need of financial support, we urge our brothers in the West to take it upon themselves to give this issue a priority in their plans. Rather than Muslims financing the *jihad* from their own pockets, they should finance it from the pockets of their enemies...

The article is laced with quotes from the Qur'an as well as opinions from religious scholars. Although Al-Awlaki did not receive any formal training in Islamic theology, he was widely admired for his inspiring sermons, many of them being available online. A dual US and Yemeni citizen, he was born in the US, and spent his early childhood there while his father completed his master's and doctoral studies. He grew up in Yemen before returning to America to get a B.S. in civil engineering, and a Master's degree in education. He was alleged to be in contact with two of the 9/11 bombers, and was later accused of being involved in a number of high-profile terror plots. He left the US in 2002, and then spent two years in Britain, where he preached in a number of mosques and delivered several motivational lectures to British Muslims. While he was the target of an American-led manhunt, he was sheltered by his tribe in a remote corner of Yemen. Despite his isolation, he was very active on the Internet, maintaining a blog and a high-profile presence on Facebook. He collaborated with Samir Khan to produce *Inspire*, the webzine that had a large following among young Muslim radicals in the West, but was also widely read by the Western anti-terrorist community.

Samir Khan was another US citizen who lived in Yemen until his death. Born in Saudi Arabia to Pakistani parents in 1986, he moved to Charlotte, North Carolina, with his family as a child. At 15, he was running a pro-Osama bin Laden blog after attending a summer programme organized by a Washington mosque. After setting up a string of Islamist websites, he moved to Yemen, from where he edited and wrote a large portion of *Inspire*. In an article in the January 2011 issue, he described how to bring down buildings by carefully locating explosives at key points in the structure, and how to buy and maintain AK-47 assault rifles. In an earlier article, he boasted about how proud he was of being a traitor to America.

Both Al-Awlaki and Khan demonstrated the problems of controlling extremism in an open society like the USA. But at the same time, the fact that so few Muslims have chosen to go down this route is also a source of hope. Despite the thousands of websites seeking volunteers and funds for the jihad, only a handful of Muslims have paid much attention. Even slick webzines like *Inspire* cause more of a stir in the intelligence community than among ordinary Muslims. Indeed, I had to trawl through several websites before I could download the latest edition of the magazine. None of my many Muslim friends have even heard of it. Although several public agencies, private groups and individuals attempt to monitor and block extremist sites, the Internet still remains the anarchic space its creators intended it to be.

The dependence of the modern generation of jihadists on digital tools was best captured by Hamid Mir, the Pakistani journalist and biographer of Osama bin Laden, as he watched al Qaeda fighters fleeing the caves of Tora Bora in the aftermath of the US bombing in November 2001. According to Mir, 'every second Al Qaeda member carried a laptop computer along with a Kalashnikov'.

This graphic image was cited by Steve Coll and Susan B. Glasser in an article[3] in the *Washington Post* Both are staffers with the paper, and Coll is the author of *Ghost Wars*, an authoritative account of CIA operations in Afghanistan and Pakistan. The authors write:

> Nearly four years later, al Qaeda has become the first guerrilla movement in history to migrate from physical space to cyberspace. With laptops and DVDs, in secret hideouts and at neighborhood Internet cafes, young code-writing jihadists have sought to replicate the training, communication, planning and preaching facilities they lost in Afghanistan with countless new locations on the Internet...
>
> Among other things, al Qaeda and its offshoots are building a massive and dynamic online library of training materials—some supported by experts who answer questions on message boards or in chat rooms—covering such varied subjects as how to mix ricin poison, how to make a bomb from commercial chemicals, how to pose as a fisherman and sneak through Syria into Iraq, how to shoot at a U.S. soldier, and how to navigate by the stars while running through a night-shrouded desert. These materials are cascading across the Web in Arabic, Urdu, Pashto and other first languages of jihadist volunteers...
>
> Jihadists seek to overcome in cyberspace specific obstacles they face from armies and police forces in the physical world. In planning attacks, radical operatives are often at risk when they congregate at a mosque or cross a border with false documents. They are safer working on the Web. Al Qaeda and its offshoots 'have understood

[3] 'Terrorists Turn to the Web as Base of Operations,' *The Washington Post*, 7 August 2005

> that space and time in many ways have been conquered by the Internet', said John Arquilla, a professor at the Naval Postgraduate School...
>
> The Web's shapeless disregard for national boundaries and ethnic markers fits exactly with bin Laden's original vision for al Qaeda, which he founded to stimulate revolt among the worldwide Muslim *ummah*, or community of believers. Bin Laden's appeal among some Muslims has long flowed in part from his rare willingness among Arab leaders to surround himself with racially and ethnically diverse followers, to ignore ancient prejudices and national borders. In this sense of utopian ambition, the Web has become a gathering place for a rainbow coalition of jihadists. It offers al Qaeda a 'virtual sanctuary' on a global scale, Rand Corp. terrorism specialist Bruce Hoffman said. 'The Internet is the ideal medium for terrorism today: anonymous but pervasive.'

Even though relatively few Muslims actually spend much time on the Internet, downloading hate-filled sermons and jihadist training manuals, the ones who do can get very obsessive. For a trained psychiatrist like Major Nidal Hasan, the Fort Hood shooter, to turn his gun on his army colleagues must have required some powerful motivation. It is doubtful that a medical professional could be easily convinced to do what he did on that fateful November day in 2009. His email exchanges with the Yemeni al Qaeda ideologue Anwar Al-Awlaki might provide a clue. Many observers ascribe his attack to a deep dread of his impending deployment to Iraq. In other parts of the world, where young Muslims have been radicalized on the Internet, the initial trigger appears to lie closer at hand in the shape of resentments, frustration and a feeling of isolation. Often, maladjusted kids from immigrant families are alienated from the mainstream. Frequently, they are at the receiving end of real or imagined slights because of their faith; this is a trend that has become more marked since 9/11. But other religious and ethnic groups also face some degree of prejudice without taking up arms against the West. It would appear that alienation, combined with the presence of a large network of extremist websites that exploit these feelings of persecution to radicalize young people, makes the online jihad so lethal.

Just as the Internet is used as a sanctuary by jihadists, it serves to link ordinary Muslims together in a network of believers. Here, Muslims discuss their everyday issues with each other and with clerics who advise them on how to interpret Islamic injunctions on a host of matters ranging from marriage to jobs. The development of this virtual *ummah*, or nation of believers, is especially helpful to Muslims living in isolated communities in non-Muslim lands. In cyberspace, they can get guidance and support from *alims*, or theologians, in how to conduct themselves among the *kuffar* (a mildly pejorative Arabic term for non-believers). But this advice has a downside: it insulates migrant Muslims from their non-Muslim neighbours, and makes integration a slower process. While an earlier generation of Muslim migrants, often cut off from their fellow believers, made an effort to get along with the host community, now many are encouraged to stand apart. For instance, here is a student writing to an Islamic guidance website:[4]

> Question: I am a student in a school in the west. Praise be to Allah, I spend most of my time with Muslims, but I am suffering because of my own laziness and the laziness of the Muslims here. Hence I have started working with non-Muslims here in the field of study only. Is that regarded as taking the *kuffar* as close friends? What are the conditions of working with them in this case?
>
> Answer: ... before you think about working with non-Muslims, why don't you think about how to ward off laziness from yourself and your Muslim brothers?
>
> But if it is the matter of choosing between working hard with the *kuffar* or sleeping among the Muslims, then you should work and strive hard...And pay attention to the following:
>
> 1) Do not take women as study companions, because you know about their attitudes and you know what will result

[4] www.islamqa.com/en/ref/islamqa/46453

> from keeping company with them and mixing with them. Moreover you know that such relationships are forbidden in Islam.
>
> 2) Limit these relationships to that which is required for work and study...

This is hardly sound advice to a young man starting life in the west. But this exhortation to live separately from non-Muslims is the staple fare for conservative Muslims. Another example of this exclusiveness is contained in this question and answer at the same website:

> Question: Is it permissible for a Muslim to stay in the house of a non-Muslim and pray there?
> Answer: With regard to staying in a non-Muslim's house as a matter of hospitality and friendship between them, that should not be done except in cases of necessity when there is no alternative...

Instead of building bridges between Muslims and non-Muslims, such websites are busy erecting walls.

Apart from promoting separateness instead of bringing people closer together, the Internet also amplifies messages of hate. Incidents involving Americans, in particular, seem to resonate more deeply in the *ummah* than those involving other nationalities. For instance, when Raymond Davis, the American CIA contractor we met in an earlier chapter, shot dead two young Pakistanis in Lahore on January 27, 2011, the Pakistani media as well as the Internet were immediately flooded with calls for his hanging. Despite claiming self-defence and diplomatic immunity, Davis was jailed for several weeks while a court deliberated over whether he was indeed entitled to immunity under the Vienna Convention. Meanwhile, anti-American sentiment reached a peak on the streets, TV studios and, above all, on the Internet. Demonstrators demanded Davis's hanging. Pakistan's sovereignty and honour were invoked ad nauseam by TV talking heads and by bloggers on the Internet. And when I argued for restraint and sanity in a column, I was flooded with emails accusing me of having sold out to the Americans. Fortunately, many readers supported my position. A reader identifying himself as Farjaad Khan unleashed this tirade in an email regarding my column about the Davis case:

> Raymond Davis or any other national of the world has NO RIGHT[5] to come to Pakistan and KILL her citizens EVEN in self-defence... You are a pathetic, annoying son of a bitch who deserves to be chased out of Pakistan in a humiliating way. You are a disgrace to the nation for INTENTIONALLY hiding the fact and playing for your masters.... You think Pakistanis are FOOL [sic]. Thank God for the Internet, alternate media, and loyal human-being-loving local and international media who tell us the truth which all make [sic] sense... *(This email concluded with some choice expletives in Urdu.)*

Pakistanis living in and out of the country joined in this hysterical debate about Raymond Davis. This is just one example of how the Internet acts as an amplifier in promoting extreme views. Articles and blogs—often without a shred of evidence or logic—drive an extreme anti-West agenda. Indeed, this is becoming the default position for populist bloggers as well as supposedly serious journalists whose words now reach across the Web to computer screens thousands of miles away. TV chat shows containing virulent anti-American diatribes are instantly uploaded on YouTube and are viewed by people around the world. Other social networking sites provide readily available platforms for targeting America for its real and perceived anti-Muslim positions.

While such views do not necessarily turn Muslim web citizens into jihadists, they do help create a xenophobic environment where hatred for the 'other'—in this case America—is legitimized. As we have noted earlier, this phenomenon is hardly exclusive to Muslims: unfortunately, there is a lot of hatred out there, and the Internet has made it easier to channelize and direct this rage. But in the Muslim

[5] Caps as in the original email.

psyche, the anger feeds into the larger feeling of frustration over the decline of the Islamic world, and the perception of victimhood so many Muslims appear to share. Thus, cyberspace is a place where thousands of Muslims around the world can connect and share their real or imaginary grievances against America. This, in turn, creates an environment where jihadists like Osama bin Laden are vigorously defended and accorded legitimacy and iconic status.

Here, too, gullible young people connect with cynical ideologues of the jihad and become radicalized. While only a tiny handful actually take the next step and begin plotting terror attacks, the Internet does provide an enabling space where vague resentments harden into hate, and then into a resolve to do harm. The next stage is the search for like-minded wannabe jihadists to form a cell that connects to a charismatic ideological godfather like Al-Awlaki who will talk young disciples over any moral scruples they might have over attacks that target the innocent. Where Westerners are concerned, extremists often argue that there are no innocents because citizens elect governments that undertake anti-Muslim policies. Thus, terrorist attacks are equated with self-defence. The killing of children below voting age is justified by the argument that Muslim children are being killed by Western forces in drone attacks in the tribal areas of Pakistan, and by soldiers and helicopters in Iraq and Afghanistan. The indiscriminate slaughter of Muslims in these countries by jihadists is rationalized by invoking the doctrine of *takfir*, or apostasy. While this extremist philosophy will be discussed in a later chapter, it is being increasingly deployed as an ideological weapon by jihadists against other Muslims as a means of de-legitimizing governments, and of justifying killing fellow Muslims.

Islamic websites resound with ideological splits and doctrinaire conflict. Esoteric arguments are marshalled to declare other points of view un-Islamic, and therefore falling in the category of *takfir*. Lengthy posts examine the finer points of *fiqh*, or Islamic jurisprudence. One writer dwells at length on Lenin's influence on Sayyid Qutb, the ideological godfather of political Islam. Another scholar examines the Quranic injunctions against music when a blogger asks for the ruling on organizing a fund-raising concert at a Muslim school to raise money for a new toilet block. (The conclusion is that such an activity would be un-Islamic.) Skimming over some of these blogs, one is left bemused by how much energy is being expended on these fine points of doctrine. Indeed, some of the exchanges are not dissimilar to the medieval exercise of counting the number of angels that could fit on the point of a needle.

Thus, the Internet has also become a marketplace for pushing various strands of Islamic thought. Bloggers argue just as fiercely with other Muslims in cyberspace as they do with non-Muslims. While the traffic to these sites is not startling, a steady stream of believers log in regularly to participate in these chat sessions, with many starting their own threads with questions and comments. In a sense, this corner of cyberspace resembles a virtual seminary echoing with arguments and debate. Except, of course, a real seminary would not tolerate the kind of dissent seen on these websites. However, some discussions are killed off by the webmasters for using abusive or threatening language.

For millions of Internet users, the Web is an unlimited space for exchanging ideas, information and insults. The vast majority surf the Internet to enrich themselves intellectually, even though many are left more confused than informed. Some explore websites that confirm their beliefs and prejudices. Others get hooked to conspiracy theories that are in line with their particular paranoid mindset. In short, the Web is all things to all people, and you can find whatever you are looking for. Occasionally, by a stroke of serendipity, you discover things you weren't looking for. Many Muslims log on to touch base with other Muslims, and find answers to questions about their faith. In the process, they come across—or are directed to—websites where they discover extremist views that arouse their curiosity. In wishing to find out more, they are influenced to discard their own straightforward belief system, and to sign up to more extreme philosophies that emphasize exclusiveness and a contempt for other faiths and their followers. Young people who feel ghettoized in foreign lands are more vulnerable to such influences. The entire process has more to do with alienation than with religion: the fact of belonging to an exclusive community of believers who are convinced they have a monopoly on the truth can be an empowering experience.

Those who spend hours obsessively on their computers, scouring the Web for sites that coincide or conflict with their ideas, arguing endlessly, and conducting cyber jihad, are very often sad losers without much of a life. For them, cyberspace represents an opportunity to carve out their own destiny in a way they are unable to in the real world. For many, this digital world is the one they connect with in ways they are unable to with reality. In a sense, they are similar to the millions who spend a large proportion of their waking hours playing web-based video games. The real world morphs seamlessly into the cyber world, and in time, the distinction between the two becomes blurred.

Just as young gamers are often unable to make a distinction between the pixelated violence on their computer screens and real blood and pain, so too do many would-be cyber jihadists attempt to transpose their extremist fantasies onto real life.

In 2004, a rap artist called Digihad Sheikh Terra loaded a song called Dirty Kuffar onto YouTube. Viewed by over 30,000, it is a compilation of violent images transposed onto hate figures of the period like George Bush, Dick Cheney, Donald Rumsfeld, Hosni Mubarak of Egypt, and General Pervez Musharraf of Pakistan. The lyrics are simple, rhyming words like 'kuffar' and 'khalifa' (caliph), and the message of hate and violence comes through loud and clear. As we noted earlier, digital tools created and popularized in the United States are increasingly being used against it to drum up support for the global jihad. Mercifully, few Muslims are taking much notice.

But others are: when I typed 'anti-jihadist websites' into Google, I was confronted with no less than 1.6 million sites. The ones I checked out were full of anti-Muslim tirades with highly selective quotes from Islamic texts and websites. If one were to believe these overwrought right-wing bloggers, America is on the verge of a Muslim takeover, and Shariah is poised to replace the US Constitution. One of them, www.jihadwatch.org, carries an ad for a book titled *Barack Obama and Islam: How he is flirting with Disaster*. Another book offered at a special rate is *Stealth Jihad*. So clearly, overreaction to the extremist threat is not confined to Washington and the security establishment.

However, there are many serious sites dedicated to keeping tabs on news and views posted on jihadist blogs. Jihadica.com is probably one of the best, offering translations, analyses and updates. One article on the site ('Entering a new dimension—Jihad via Bluetooth') details the extent to which the new media plays a part in the global jihad. According to the article, there is a special data package for mobile phones available that aims at 'sympathizers and adherents of jihadist principles'. This software allows users to access documents or watch jihadist videos on their phones, and can be used to transmit these 'highly indoctrinating and radicalizing sources' to other Bluetooth-enabled devices. The data offered on this service includes a vast body of jihadist material. Encryption software is also available. Videos, audio recordings and images glorifying jihadist 'martyrs' and terrorist operations can be easily downloaded and shared widely. Text messages in a variety of formats are also available to download a wide variety of jihadist literature. These range from a biography of Shamil Basayev, the Chechen warlord who was the planner of the Moscow theatre siege that ended in hundreds of deaths following a bungled Russian rescue attempt, to an article titled 'And Incite the Believers' by an Al Qaeda member called Abdullah bin Muhammad al-Rushud.

Clearly, jihadists are adept at using every new communication tool that rolls out of Silicon Valley or the factories producing the new generation of cell phones. Young, high-tech zealots sharpen their computer skills across the Islamic world, and pick up on new technologies as soon as they emerge. The November 2010 edition of *Inspire* contains extensive and jaw-dropping coverage of the attempt to bring down two cargo planes in the Middle East belonging to UPS and DHL by filling the toner cartridges of laser printers with PETN high explosive. The knowledge of how airport X-ray machines work to detect explosive materials is incredibly detailed, and the design of the device is very sophisticated. The only reason the plot failed was because of a tip-off from Saudi intelligence. It is obvious that however much they may be wedded to a medieval mindset, the younger generation of jihadists are no slouches when it comes to cutting-edge technology.

Although the Twin Towers remain powerful symbols of the anti-Americanism prevalent in much of the Muslim world, the war has largely moved from Ground Zero to cyberspace in the decade after the iconic structures were brought down by Al Qaeda. This is where minds are moulded and radicalized, funds are raised, poisonous propaganda spread, websites hacked, and counterattacks launched. Sustaining this low-level digital warfare is an environment created by hundreds of websites that preach a message of hatred for Western values and a return to a harsh, literal vision of Islam. Ranged against these voices are mostly right-wing bloggers who have seized upon the widespread suspicion and hostility toward political Islam to express the most outrageous racism and xenophobia.

The Internet, with its absence of censorship and societal constraints, provides an ideal soapbox. At London's Speaker's Corner in Hyde Park, every Sunday draws dozens of people with causes to promote or attack. They set up their small platforms or tables, and hold forth on topics as diverse as the Palestinian conflict to the need to arrest the decline in the number of songbirds. Sunday morning strollers amble around to listen to the speakers. Some are full of anger, some of humor, and almost all of them are eccentric. Public figures from the Queen to the Pope are subjected to barbs and insults, and government policies are roundly abused. No attempt is made to curb this ultimate example of free speech. I suppose political correctness prevents the most outrageous expression of racism, but that's just about the only self-imposed restriction in evidence.

However, there are no PC police patrolling the Internet. Here, bloggers post the vilest rants against those who dare to question their beliefs. Exaggeration and abuse are the staple of thousands of websites. The most extraordinary accusations are made based on total fabrications. For example, The Protocols of the Elders of Zion, a fraudulent defamation of Jewry produced in Czarist Russia at the start of the twentieth century, is presented as a blueprint for world conquest on both extremist Muslim and Christian websites. A gullible young person coming across the document on the Internet would probably accept its authenticity. Others who have heard about it would have their anti-Semitism legitimized by reading the contents. I know many people who insist on its veracity, despite the fact that the Protocols have long been exposed as a fraudulent document created by the Russian secret police.

This is just one example of how the most blatant lies are amplified and perpetrated in cyberspace. The most bizarre conspiracy theories go viral on the Internet, with the United States figuring in most of them. In the last chapter, we noted how many bloggers latched onto an experimental weather-changing technology called HAARP to explain the devastating floods that hit Pakistan in 2010, rendering millions homeless and causing billions of dollars of damage. Unsurprisingly, the United States was the sinister power behind the HAARP attack. None of these bloggers explained why it should also have been the biggest donor to the emergency flood relief effort.

Mining extremist websites has become a highly specialized skill in the world of security and intelligence. Some experts and scholars provide analyses and translations to subscribers, others work for governments. Over the last decade, tracking extremist websites has become big business. For my part, I would not like to spend any more time reading these unpleasant and often poorly written blogs.

8

Muslims in the West: A Fifth Column?

For many of my European and American friends, I am the only Muslim they have ever met socially. So I am accustomed to—if slightly bored of—being faced with questions about Islam and Muslim countries and traditions. One frequently asked question focused on why Muslims in Britain tend to cluster together in ghettos in industrial towns. These areas have become flashpoints for violence and have produced most of those plotting terror attacks in the country and abroad. I point out the tendency of ethnic groups to gravitate toward each other when living in a foreign land. This was equally true of the British when they colonized much of the world in the nineteenth century. Another question is why so few Muslims seek to learn about the society in which they have chosen to live—if they don't like it, why don't they simply go back? Most second-generation Muslim migrants are torn between the seductive materialism of the West and the deeply conservative values they are taught at home and in the mosque. To a great extent, their identity crisis sets them apart and makes it difficult to assimilate. Yet despite their confusion about who they are, their Western environment is the only home they know.

Over the last decade, survey after survey has tracked the growing suspicion and mistrust Muslims in the West face. In early 2011, Britain's Searchlight Education Foundation released a report it had commissioned called *Fear and Hope*. Based on interviews with 5,000 Britons across the country, its conclusions were, according to the *Guardian*, 'stark, brutal, and unequivocal'. Among other insights, the survey found that 52 per cent of the large survey sample agreed with the proposition that 'Muslims caused problems in the UK'.

These feelings are echoed across Europe and America. Politicians and the public are increasingly discarding notions of political correctness to express their strong reservations and outright dislike for Muslim customs, culture, and mores. Although many of these sentiments were once limited to the privacy of homes, they are now evident across a broad spectrum of the media as well as in parliaments, where some European countries have passed legislation banning the public use of Islamic garb for women. Much of this rhetoric appears in the public discourse as opposition to immigration, and *migrants* is now widely recognized as a code word for 'Muslims'. Thus, while newly enacted French laws bar the display of religious symbols in state schools and the wearing of garments that conceal the face in public, they are seen as targeting the *hijab* and the *niqab* some Muslim women wear when outside their homes. Indeed, these laws sparked a huge debate about the right to wear whatever clothes one chooses in a liberal democracy. However, French legislators—supported by many Frenchmen and women and the media—have argued that in a secular country, there is no place for the public display of religious symbols. Other nations, while they have not yet taken such extreme steps, are now openly discussing the place of Islamic rituals and practices in Western society in a way that would have been unthinkable just a few years ago.

In Germany, a massive controversy broke out when Thilo Sarrazin's book *Germany Is Doing Away with Itself*[1] was published in 2010. Sarrazin, a board member of the Bundesbank and a Social Democrat, was forced to resign, but his book remains a runaway bestseller. The author argued that, in time, the Turkish community in Germany—presently accounting for 6 per cent of the total

---

[1] *Deutschland Schafft Sich Ab.*

population—would compete to outnumber the Germans, thereby 'dumbing down' the country with its inferior gene pool. Sarrazin accuses Turks and Kurds of inbreeding, thus causing 'congenital disabilities.' He goes on to claim that migrants from the Middle East are a 'genetic minus' for Germany. Sarrazin writes: 'But the subject is usually hushed up. Perish the thought that genetic factors could be partially responsible for the failure of the Turkish populations in the German school system.'

More appalling than this thesis was the public reaction to the book in Germany. A *Focus* magazine poll indicates that 31 per cent of respondents agreed that Germany is 'becoming dumber' because of immigrants, while 62 per cent said that Sarrazin's views were justified. Turks have traditionally been the targets of German xenophobia and racism. After 9/11, this anti-Turk sentiment morphed into Islamophobia. In a thoughtful article on the subject for the *Guardian*[2], Gary Younge writes:

> Nationalist mythologies, compounded by poverty and discrimination, underpin a widespread anxiety that has shifted its focus from race to religion and colour to culture. People of Turkish descent make up about 6 per cent of the population. Two-thirds of them have German citizenship. They were once the scapegoats, but now it is the Muslims.

He goes on to quote Barbara John, Berlin's former migration and integration commissioner: 'After 9/11, religion became the determining explanation for everything Turkish people did.'

In short, many in the West now stigmatize all Muslims for the real and perceived threat from extremists. From bin Laden to the Times Square bomber, the jihadist menace is—consciously or unconsciously—blamed on Muslims in general, who are increasingly viewed as a fifth column who produce and shelter home-grown terrorists involved in a number of plots and successful

[2] 15 March 2011.

attacks in the West since 9/11. In addition to these domestic security concerns, growing numbers of casualties among Western forces fighting in Iraq and Afghanistan have contributed to this rising tide of anger and intolerance. Although ordinary Muslims obviously had nothing to do with the decision to go to war, they find themselves at the receiving end of resentment over the rising cost of these overseas adventures in terms of blood and money. Many soldiers have returned with terrible injuries, while others have brought back internal scars and traumas. All these experiences feed into the zeitgeist.

Then, of course, there is the resentment over rising oil prices, especially in the wake of any wars or political instability in the Middle East. People in Europe and America forget that very often, their own governments make more money in taxes from oil than OPEC members do. A breakup of the price of a gallon of gas at the pump shows that in many countries, more money goes to oil companies, tanker operators, and governments than into the coffers of the producers. Nevertheless, this money is seen as unearned income, especially when it is squandered on the luxurious lifestyle of oil-rich rulers and their families.

Intolerance among Muslims of any criticism of their faith or its symbols is another red flag to most people in Europe and America. Thus, when the Islamic world—including Muslims in the West—exploded in a paroxysm of rage over the publication of cartoons of the Prophet Mohammed depicted in an unflattering light in a Danish newspaper, Westerners were puzzled. They simply could not understand the reason behind the fury. Having grown up in a culture where the most sacrosanct icons are regularly pilloried in the media, on the screen, and on the stage, they could not grasp that people would kill and burn to protest the perceived disrespect toward their Prophet. From the Salman Rushdie affair to the *Jyllands-Posten* cartoons, the West increasingly views Muslims as intolerant, violent, humourless people with alien, unattractive values and traditions who refuse to blend in. Their rejection of

Western culture and lifestyle provokes the question: If they don't like us, why don't they just go back home?

To repeat a cliché, Muslims have become the new African-Americans. In Europe, perhaps more than in America, many Muslims remain in their ghettos and have been slow to learn the local languages and adapt to local customs. Their desire to maintain their separate identity has often caused misunderstandings and conflict with their neighbours. From food to dress, they have generally insisted on sticking to the old ways that set them apart.

It is quite natural for the indigenous population to resent newcomers, especially when they become highly visible by living together in tight-knit communities and sticking to traditions and customs vastly different from the mainstream culture. In human society, suspicion of the 'other' is a throwback to prehistoric times, when tribes guarded their turf and resources very jealously. Over time, especially in the last century, a deliberate effort has been made—more so in the West than elsewhere—to eliminate racism, at least from the public discourse. Many countries have enacted legislation to ensure equality across gender, race, and religion. After World War II and the horrors it spawned—the worst being the Holocaust—people of good will and conscience recoiled from the ugliness and ignorance that lie at the heart of racism. After the end of segregation in the United States and of apartheid in South Africa, it was hoped that racism had finally been routed from the public sphere.

Although laws have been changed, deep-rooted feelings remain, especially among poorly educated and economically deprived people. Many continue nursing atavistic suspicions of those who look and act differently, although such people have come to terms with changing public norms and generally keep their racism to themselves or voice their feelings to like-minded individuals in private. Fascist and racist groups attract members who subscribe to their socially unacceptable theories of racial superiority. Yet these are marginal elements with little support from the wider public. This process is still a work in progress, but received a major setback on 9/11. Suddenly, the 'war on terror' provided people with a licence to openly denigrate millions of followers of another faith. Although Islam has adherents from every race and continent, the targets of this vilification campaign were virtually all non-white. Thus, by attacking Muslims and Islam for being behind extremist terrorism, patriots can invoke national security to vindicate their racism. Indeed, they claim that racism has nothing to do with their Islamophobia.

Feeding this rising tide of anti-Islam sentiment is the growing anti-Americanism that is so evident across the Muslim world. Many Muslims living in the West prefer not to voice their true feelings to pollsters and journalists, yet they are privately critical not just of government policies toward the Muslim world, but of the society in which they live. They are fearful that values they see as being completely opposed to theirs will infect their children, who will lose their Muslim identity. All too often, binge drinking and promiscuity make them want to protect their kids from activities seen as sinful. Parents are scared that their children might marry a non-Muslim, causing a loss of face within the community. These are just some of the fears that promote a ghetto mentality that continues to separate Muslims from their hosts.

Islam unites Muslims in the Western diaspora in a way that other faiths do not. The experience of praying together at local mosques, shopping for halal meat in the local neighbourhood stores, and being part of a worldwide nation of Islam strengthens a sense of identity among people who are otherwise deprived and often disoriented in an alien and seemingly hostile culture. Although Muslim countries share little but a common religion and are all too often at daggers drawn, migrant Muslims in the West cling to their faith and to each other in a strange and threatening setting. Almost inevitably, all these elements feed into a 'them versus us' syndrome that sets up barriers between migrant Muslims in the West and their host communities.

I was given a striking example of the strength of the bonds Muslims share at a personal level by Eqbal Ahmed, a highly respected Pakistani thinker, political activist and academic and a dear friend until his death in 1999. In 1971, at the height of the Vietnam War, he was a member of a group of anti-war radicals who discussed a citizens' arrest of Henry Kissinger, US President Richard Nixon's secretary of state, and demand a cessation of the war as the price for his release. This quixotic plot was in the talking stages when the FBI arrested seven of the activists. Eqbal, then a fellow at the Adlai Stevenson Institute in Chicago, was jailed for a few weeks before the case was dismissed. Years later, he told me of his nervousness as he first walked into a prison that was full of hardened criminals, most of whom towered threateningly over the frail young Pakistani. A huge African-American prisoner approached him and demanded to know where he was from. When Eqbal said Pakistan, the prisoner uttered the Islamic greeting '*Assalam Walaikum*,' and Eqbal answered with the traditional response '*Walaikum Assalam*' ('Peace be upon you' and 'Upon you, peace'). From that moment until he was released, Eqbal was protected by the prison's Black Muslims, who engaged him in long conversations about Islam and his experiences in Algeria when he had joined the FLN, an anti-colonial group, in their war of liberation against France.

The downside of this bonding is that it delays the process of integration. Whereas most other migrant communities do their best to blend in with the majority by adapting to the mainstream modes of behaviour, Muslims tend to cling to their own dress, customs, and traditions. This makes them stand out and, in the post-9/11 climate of suspicion and hostility, makes them targets of selective profiling.

Christopher Caldwell is an American journalist who has undertaken a careful, hard-headed analysis of the Muslim phenomenon in Europe in his book *Reflections on the Revolution in Europe: Immigration, Islam, and the West*. He starts by pointing out that, in the middle of the twentieth century, there were virtually no Muslims in Western Europe; today, there are between 15 and 17 million. At the start of this wave of immigration, no public discussion or debate was conducted: The migrants came to man the factories, transport systems, and civic amenities of a Europe hard hit by labour shortages in the wake of World War II. The post-war economic boom demanded workers, and few questions were asked when young men from across the world arrived to sign up for the lowest-paying jobs available. Many of them were Muslims from Africa and Asia. Once they were installed, they saved whatever they could, transferring a large portion of their wages to their families. Gradually, they sent home for their wives and children. Over time, the next generation also married young men and women from back home. Indeed, few sought spouses from the host (European) community, thus perpetuating the gulf between the two. Whereas the original immigrants were often self-effacing, law-abiding folk, their children—born and raised in Europe—were conflicted by the conservative, Islamic values taught at home and the more permissive cultural norms prevailing in school and on the streets. Struggling for an identity, many latched onto the extremist philosophy that began to percolate through the Muslim diaspora in mosques and on the Internet. Rejecting the more submissive attitude of their parents, many in the younger generation of Muslims insist on flaunting their faith: the girls often wearing the head-scarf or the all-encompassing *niqab*, and the young men sporting long, unkempt beards and the *kiffaya*. Their parents, by contrast, have often turned their backs on this traditional attire. Indeed, the irony is that the younger generation is much more likely to make their faith a badge of identity than their elders, even though their understanding of religious texts is often quite superficial.

Such militancy has pushed Muslims further apart from their host communities in the West. As previously noted, the advice Muslims receive from clerics in many mosques and on the Internet often exacerbates the problem. From Washington to Warsaw, politicians urge moderate Muslims to stand up and denounce extremism. This is now the mantra for editorial writers and talking heads on TV chat shows. The reality is that any Muslim who criticizes extremism and militancy is immediately written off as an Uncle Tom. Moderate Muslims simply have no street cred with the younger generation of Islamic militants. Muslim parents I know are appalled when their children adopt the garb of traditional Islam, but just have to put up with it, much as Western parents wearily accept their kids piercing their lips or sporting Mohawk haircuts. Both sets of parents hope their children are going through a passing fad and pray that it will soon pass. More often than not, it does. Ironically, an unkempt Islamic beard is more threatening to an American than a weird hairdo, while a full *niqab* is more repellent to a liberal European than full body tattoos.

What is the extent of the perceived 'Islamic threat' in the United States? Estimates of the number of Muslims in America vary from 1.35 million[3] to 7 million[4]. In between these extremes, we have 4.7 million (*Encyclopedia Britannica*), 2.5 million (Pew Research Center), and 5 million (*US News & World Report*). The reason for this wide disparity in estimates is, of course, the absence of a column for religion in the US census forms. Whatever the exact number, Muslims account for a tiny fraction of the American population of around 310 million. How many of them stand accused of terrorism? According to the Triangle Center on Terrorism and Homeland Security, a think-tank, the number of Muslims actually arrested for planning or carrying out acts of terrorism in the United States was twenty-one in 2010. Given these numbers, it is hard to imagine hordes of wild-eyed, bearded Muslims threatening the foundations of American society.

In this context, the hearings on Muslims in America[5] called by Peter King, chairman of the House Committee on Homeland Security, in March 2011 prompted charges of a McCarthyite witch-hunt. Liberal Americans and Muslims alike blasted the

---

[3] The American Religious Identification Survey.

[4] Council for American Islamic Relations.

[5] The Extent of Radicalization in the American Muslim Community and that Community's Response.

congressman for using the issue to grab headlines. Many critics view the congressional hearings as the wrong forum in which to discuss the issue; some insist that the matter has been blown out of all proportion to the real threat. Perhaps the one positive thing to emerge from the acrimonious initial hearings was the knowledge, provided by law enforcement officers, that 40 per cent of all known terror plots had been thwarted through information provided by Muslims.

As the hearings opened on 9 March 2011, Gallup released a poll revealing the expanding gap between Americans and Muslims as well as Islam in general. Only 53 per cent of respondents agreed with the suggestion that Muslims in America were supportive of the United States. More striking was the finding that 52 per cent of all Americans considered the King hearings to be appropriate, compared with 38 per cent who said they were inappropriate.

As these hearings show, the presence of Muslims in America—small though it might be—has become a highly contentious issue. Muslims argue that many of the so-called terrorist plots are no more than idle talk among young men, with some of them being entrapped by undercover agents who have penetrated their groups. In a number of high-profile cases, young Muslims have been approached by federal agents who have allegedly made all the running in concocting bizarre terror plots. For instance, in 2006, two Muslims in Albany were contacted by a Muslim FBI informant who offered to lend Mohammed Hossain $50,000 to renovate his pizzeria. According to the agent, the confusingly named Shahed Hussain (who introduced himself as 'Malik'), the money for the loan came from the sale of a shoulder-fired missile that was to be used to kill a Pakistani diplomat[6].

During the trial, many details surfaced that smacked of deliberate entrapment. Nevertheless, the accused were convicted of 'conspiring to aid a terrorist group and provide support for a

---

[6] http://www.nytimes.com/2006/10/11/nyregion/11plot.html?scp=1&sq=10/11/2006 per cent202 per cent20Albany per cent20Men&st=cse

weapon of mass destruction'. The terrorist group in question was the Jaish-e-Mohammed (JEM), a banned Pakistani outfit that 'Malik' said he supported. Mohammed Hossain's repayment of the loan to 'Malik' in instalments was equated with a deliberate effort to support JEM. The other accused was an Iraqi Kurdish refugee who was an imam at the local mosque. He was roped in to witness the loan and was also convicted; he faces deportation on his release. The case reveals the murky nature of undercover work, with agents being under pressure to justify the time they are putting into surveillance and penetration. All too often, law enforcement agencies and prosecutors are tempted into questionable means to make a case and get a conviction. Once an arrest has been announced, it makes headlines across America and much of the world. Such intense media coverage in turn reinforces the public image of Muslims as violent extremists.

Incidentally, Shahed Hussain—the same FBI informer—was involved in another sting operation in which four penniless and barely functional African-Americans were convicted of a supposed attempt to bomb two synagogues in New York. Hussain, this time calling himself Maqsood, recruited the 'Newburgh Four' at the Masjid al-Ikhlas mosque in the run-down suburb of Newburgh. Promising them cash and a new BMW, he persuaded them to place fake bombs at a synagogue and a Jewish centre. Almost immediately, this unlikely group of conspirators were scooped up by the police and—despite clear evidence of entrapment produced by the defence—all four were convicted. According to *Slate*[7], Shahed Hussain was paid approximately $100,000 by the FBI for his role in this operation.

None of this is to suggest that all terror plots are the result of entrapment. Far from it. There are dangerous terrorists out there who are scheming to wreak death and destruction in the United States given any opportunity. They tirelessly seek to influence young and vulnerable Muslims to do their bidding. Terrorists like

---

[7] In Ted Conover's piece 'The Pathetic Newburgh Four', 11/23/2010.

Faisal Shahzad (the Times Square bomber), Richard Reid (the shoe bomber), and Umar Farouk Abdulmuttalab (the Nigerian Christmas bomber) all serve to remind us that the United States is under very real threat from Islamist groups. Still, the reality is that, since 9/11, very few attacks have been successful. Through luck, good intelligence, and tight security measures, the few really dangerous plots have been detected and successfully neutralized.

Muslims in America complain that, whenever there is a real or suspected plot involving their fellow believers, the media go to town trumpeting the news. Meanwhile when cases are dropped for lack of evidence and the suspects released, no public apology is made to them; rather, they are eternally stigmatized. Indeed, their innocence is barely reported, leaving an impression that somehow they are still under suspicion. On the other hand, American Muslims assert that, when extremists of other persuasions are involved in terror plots, their crimes go virtually unreported. Thus, when Roger Stockham was arrested in Detroit in 2011 with a truckload of explosives that he intended to use to blow up a mosque, there was scarcely a ripple in the American media. This, many Muslims maintain, is a reflection on the rising tide of Islamophobia in the country.

The Council on American-Islamic Relations (CAIR) is an advocacy body not entirely free of controversy. Indeed, Congressman Peter King, Chairman of the House Committee on Home Security, has branded it an extremist organization. Yet King has long been a supporter of the IRA, even when it was carrying out a string of lethal attacks in the United Kingdom, so his views must be taken with a grain of salt. In an article on its website CAIR[8] defines Islamophobia thus:

> 'Islamophobia refers to unfounded fear of and hostility towards Islam. Such fear and hostility leads to discriminations [sic] against Muslims, exclusion of Muslims from mainstream political or social

---

[8] http://www.cair.com

> process, stereotyping, the presumption of guilt by association, and finally hate crimes. In twenty-first century America, all of these evils are present and in some quarters tolerated.

The article goes on to cite findings from a survey among American Muslim voters that CAIR conducted in 2006. According to the poll, 62 per cent have a bachelor's degree or higher—twice the national average for registered voters; more than half are professionals; 43 per cent have a household income of $50,000 or higher; 89 per cent vote regularly; 64 per cent fly the American flag; and 77 per cent said they worship the same God that Christians and Jews do. Although the survey covers only Muslim voters, not all American Muslims, these findings suggest that Muslims in the United States are not as disengaged from the mainstream as many pundits and politicians suggest.

The same survey indicates differences, too: Only 12 per cent think the war against Iraq was worthwhile; 69 per cent say that a just resolution of the Palestinian conflict would improve America's standing in the Muslim world; 55 per cent feel the 'war on terror' morphed into a war on Islam; and only 10 per cent support the use of the military to spread democracy in other countries.

Despite these generally positive findings, the unnamed author of the CAIR article sees many negative perceptions among Americans toward Muslims, citing various surveys that report rising suspicion and hostility toward Muslims in America. According to the 2004 Pew Forum on Religion and Public Life Poll, four out of ten Americans have an unfavorable view of Islam, and 46 per cent believe that Islam 'is more likely than other religions to encourage violence among its believers.' ABC News found that, although only 14 per cent of Americans believed that Islam encouraged violence four months after 9/11, this number had risen to 34 per cent in 2005. The article also cites a Cornell University survey from December 2004 that found that 44 per cent of all Americans believe that 'some curtailment of civil liberties is necessary for American Muslims'; 26 per cent agreed that mosques should be closely monitored while

29 per cent agreed that undercover agents should infiltrate Muslim civic and voluntary organizations.

A full reading of the Cornell University poll findings[9] reveals a more nuanced conclusion. For instance, 65 per cent of Christian respondents who described themselves as highly religious viewed Islam as encouraging violence more than other religions do, while only 42 per cent of those who said they were not very religious saw Islam in the same light. Furthermore, the highly religious respondents viewed Islamic countries as violent (64 per cent), fanatical (61 per cent), and dangerous (64 per cent). The less religious group saw Muslim countries in a less unfavourable light, with 49 per cent saying they were violent, 46 per cent perceiving them as fanatical, and 44 per cent thinking they were dangerous. Finally, 80 per cent of all respondents said they saw Islamic countries 'as being oppressive toward women.'

Just as the Cornell survey found wide variations in opinions depending on the degree of religiosity among its respondents, differences in political affiliations also produced varying perceptions. Although 40 per cent of Republican respondents agreed that Muslims should be required to register their whereabouts, only 24 per cent of Democrats and 17 per cent of the independent respondents were of the same view. Even more interesting—although not entirely unexpected—is the finding that TV viewing was important in shaping opinions. Respondents who watched a lot of TV news were more likely to favour the curtailment of civil liberties, such as official monitoring of Internet use among Muslims. Erik Nisbet, a Cornell senior research associate and one of those responsible for commissioning this study, observed: 'The more attention paid to television news, the more you fear terrorism, and you are more likely to favour restrictions on civil liberties.'

Another Muslim advocacy outfit in the United States is the Islamic Society of North America (ISNA). In its written testimony to the Peter King hearings on American Muslims, the society observed:

[9] http://www.news.cornell.edu/releases/Dec04/Muslim.Poll.bpf.html

> The hearing as it is currently structured proposes holding a public scrutiny of one specific community on the basis of religion; such institutionalized generalizations have not been seen since the internment of Japanese Americans in World War II. We all shared in the suffering of 9/11 as one American family. American Muslims died in the Twin Towers that day, and we mourned their loss just as we mourned the loss of all the victims of that day's brutal attacks. Since then, we too have felt the fear of potential terror attacks, and many in our community have spoken out when they suspected dangers to their communities. In Times Square, for example, it was a Muslim vendor who notified authorities when he saw a parked van that seemed suspicious, and on many occasions, Muslim parents have turned in their own children.

Should we take these words at face value? The reality is that Muslims in America—or anywhere else, for that matter—are scarcely unanimous in their views. ISNA's claim to represent Muslims in the United States is fiercely disputed (as, indeed, is CAIR's). The organization is accused of speaking only for a fringe group of deeply conservative Arabs, of relegating women to a secondary position, and of virtually ignoring Muslims of African origin. In a scathing attack, Umbreen Shah writes:

> Run mostly by first-generation immigrant Muslims with cultural baggage from their homeland, ISNA management has been unable to relate to their American-born Muslim constituency which is the future of Islam in America.
>
> African Americans are the most underrepresented of all groups in ISNA....Given that African Americans make [up] the largest percentage of American Muslims, the fact that they don't have a sizeable stake raises a lot of questions about the validity of ISNA as an American Muslim organization.
>
> There is a tendency in ISNA to enforce a particular religiously conservative philosophy without adapting to the people it serves. Women presenters at ISNA have been routinely asked to wear hijab during presentation even though they don't normally wear

> the headscarf. This has promoted hypocrisy and contention when presenters have refused to wear it.
>
> Women in ISNA's board of directors are limited to a sample space of one, and she too expressed her elitism on the topic of mixed gender prayers by saying 'Most Muslim women are content with separate prayer space in the mosque', echoing white supremacists who said blacks have an innate preference for segregation.[10]

These divergent and often diametrically opposing voices represent the diversity of Muslim opinion in America. While some groups and individuals harbour a deep-rooted resentment against western values like gender equality and individual freedom, others have embraced them. Contrary to the general perception of Muslims as a monolithic mass of threatening would-be terrorists, there are many shades of opinions, just as there are within followers of any faith. One crucial difference exists: Extremist followers from other religions generally do not turn into suicide bombers.

Tarek Fatah is a Canadian Muslim of Pakistani origin who has often stirred controversy among Islam's large online community through his robust defense of secularism and his sharp, solidly argued attacks on Islamists seeking to impose their dystopian vision of Islam on the world. Author of two books[11], Fatah set up the Muslim Canadian Congress as a platform for liberal Muslims. While in Canada, Fatah has interacted with Muslim groups and individuals across North America in addition to engaging in vigorous debates in cyberspace. He has consistently tackled the thorny issues of the Islamic world's refusal to come to grips with the reality of the modern world and its state of denial.

In extended telephone conversations with me in 2010 from his home in Toronto, Fatah expressed his dismay about the attitudes of some of the wealthiest Muslims who have made Canada and

---

[10] 'ISNA Thugs', www.chowk.com, September 8, 2005.

[11] *Chasing a Mirage: The Tragic Illusion of an Islamic State*, Ontario: John Wiley & Sons Canada, Ltd, 2008 and *The Jew Is Not My Enemy: Unveiling the Myths that Fuel Muslim Anti-Semitism*, McClelland & Stewart, 2010

the United States their home. According to him, even young professional Muslims born, educated and now working in North America privately express their disdain for the values of their host communities. When he has attended gatherings of Muslim organizations, he has constantly been struck by how insulated their members remain from western culture, except at the very superficial level.

Before moving to Canada, Fatah lived in Saudi Arabia for a few years; he spoke bitterly about the rampant racism there. According to him, while Saudis tend to kowtow to Europeans and Americans, they behave with arrogance and downright cruelty toward Asian and African workers. Indeed, despite its egalitarian doctrine, Arabs claim a special place in Islam. Among Arabs, descendents of the Quraish[12] continue to declare their primacy. One reason African Muslims are not accorded a position of equality in many Islamic organizations is that they were once slaves in Arabia. It is significant that, upon Barack Obama's election as America's first black president, Ayman al-Zawahiri, Al Qaeda's leader after long being bin Laden's deputy, issued a video in which he called Obama, Colin Powell, and Condoleezza Rice 'house negroes', implying that they did the bidding of their white masters.

Clearly, opinion among Muslims in America is widely divided. Contrary to what many in the West think, Muslims do not represent an ethnic group; virtually every race on the globe is represented in the colorful mosaic that is the world of Islam. For many of them, Islam is the only common factor they share. Although, as we have seen, it is a powerful bond, it does not entirely define the identities of Muslims. Different ethnicities, languages, histories and cultures divide Muslims, just as they do the followers of other faiths. Whereas some Muslims hate America, they get on with their lives as law-abiding citizens. A handful actively seek to lash out against the West; fortunately, they represent a tiny minority of a tiny minority.

---

[12] The tribe of the Prophet Mohammed.

9

A Licence to Kill?

Many Muslims, especially those uncomfortably poised between their societies and the West, defensively utter the mantra 'Islam is a religion of peace' when accused of being followers of a violent religion. Their growing number of detractors, spooked by the real and perceived threats emanating from the Islamic world as well as from Muslim communities in the West, are convinced that the teachings of Islam urge its followers to kill non-Muslims in the name of the faith.

So who's right? Actually, both are—and both are wrong.

As with the texts of any dogma, believers can cherry pick sections of the Qur'an to support whatever point of view they have chosen. Thus, feminists can prove that Islam's holy book clearly encourages the oppression of women, while Muslims (many women included) point out that, when it was revealed, the Qur'an was a revolutionary message that liberated women. Again, both would be perfectly correct. Similarly, socialists can find verses that call for an equitable distribution of wealth, while champions of free enterprise point to sections that declare private property to be sacrosanct, and that trade and commerce are perfectly kosher, or halal.

All these seeming contradictions underscore the difficulties involved in seeking a single, consistent message in any ancient texts underpinning a faith. After all, how do Christians reconcile the Old Testament doctrine of 'an eye for an eye' with Christ's advice to turn the other cheek? The Qur'an, like all holy scriptures, is all things to all men. The same book that provides spiritual sustenance to peaceful Sufis who often—to the deep disapproval of fundamentalists—sing and dance at their festivals also gives terrorists material they construe as a licence to kill.

Throughout history, a major function of religion has been to explain a complex world in a simple way and to teach people a set of rules intended to lead to peace and harmony. Above all, followers of all faiths are urged to accept life as it is, and to look to their reward in the afterlife for following the decreed moral code. Almost universally—at least in monotheist faiths—deviation from the established path is punishable by everlasting damnation. The follower of each religion is convinced that his/her belief is superior to all others and is the only one that promises true salvation. Over the centuries, this sense of righteousness has led to endless warfare as believers have attempted to plant the flag of their faith in other lands and in other souls. Kings and generals have cynically used religion to further their political and military agendas. Rulers and priests have acted in concert to exploit religion to maintain their grip on power. For millennia, ordinary people have put up with the excesses of this alliance between state and church because they have been indoctrinated with the notion that their temporal ruler has God's blessings and that they will be rewarded in heaven for their patience and their suffering.

In this sense, the Muslim world's history has paralleled Christendom's. Theoretically, there is no religious hierarchy in Islam, but one quickly sprang up in the early days of the faith. While it lacked the cohesion and power represented by the Papacy, the Caliphate in its early days wielded huge moral authority across the Muslim world. However, the institution was weakened by the rapid subordination of its spiritual aspect to temporal power. Over time, it became a handmaiden to the Sultan of the day, whether in Baghdad, Damascus, Cairo, or Constantinople. Across the Muslim world, imams led the prayers in mosques, conducted marriages, and prayed for the dead, serving an important social function yet wielding little political power. This was the domain of hereditary rulers and their satraps. *Imams* and other religious scholars were tasked with giving leaders legitimacy in the eyes of the ruled and imposing a uniform moral code that included respect for authority.

In Islam, there is a clear historical line between the point at which the Qur'an was revealed to the Prophet Mohammed and the preceding period known as *Jahilyah*. This translates roughly as the Time of Ignorance. Descriptions of this period depict Arabs as loutish, idol-worshipping tribesmen continuously at war. In depictions of this pre-Islamic era, female babies were often abandoned, and drunken debauchery was the norm. Muslims maintain that Islam lifted the tribes of Arabia out of this benighted state and united them into a cohesive social structure, with the Caliph as their temporal and spiritual leader.

Since then, as subsequent Caliphs focused more on political and military power as well as on their personal gratification, they drifted away from the tenets of Islam—at least in the eyes of their critics. Time and again, religious scholars and priests raised their voices in protest. Military setbacks as well as natural disasters were blamed on rulers who had deviated from the Prophet's path. Such discontent often triggered local revolts, encouraged by rivals to power. Islamic history is a saga of fratricidal warfare in the name of the faith, with claimants fighting for the throne and all boasting divine support. In the absence of clear guidelines for succession, brother battled brother for the crown across the Islamic world and throughout Islamic history.

Western pundits often wonder when Islam will follow Christianity's example and have its own Reformation. They forget that Martin Luther was motivated by the Catholic Church's excesses and its rampant corruption. His remedy was to call for a return to the earlier, purer days of the Christian faith. In Islam, this is a recurrent theme best represented by the teachings of Abdul Wahab, the eighteenth-century reformer. His doctrine of insisting on the observance of the literal commandments of Allah, as revealed to the Prophet Mohammed and recorded in the Qur'an, is now the official dogma in Saudi Arabia. Wahabism is the austere, extremist form of Islam that has been propagated across the world with virtually unlimited Saudi funding. In *madressas* throughout much of the Muslim world and in the form of chairs of Islamic studies in the West, this harsh version of the faith has done much to radicalize young Muslims. It is no coincidence that most of the suicide bombers who flew their planes into the Twin Towers and the Pentagon were Saudis.

The belief that Islam is the final version of God's message—first revealed to Moses and then to Jesus—sustains a sense of spiritual superiority among many Muslims. Indeed, verse 5:3 of the Qur'an categorically states: 'Today I have perfected your religion for you.' Supporting this idea is the conviction that the Qur'an is the literal word of God and that the words it contains are identical to those uttered by the Archangel Gabriel to the Prophet Mohammed over a period of two decades. These interlinked beliefs make it very difficult to reinterpret any portion of the Qur'an without being accused of heresy. Although early Islam allowed the practice of *ijtihad*, or arriving at decisions independently of established schools of thought, this approach was discouraged and fell into disuse a thousand years ago. Many scholars attribute the Muslim world's stagnation in the sciences and philosophy to this closing of doors to *ijtihad*.

Many Muslims today follow the letter of their faith while often forgetting its spirit. Thus, they are content with observing the five pillars of Islam: the belief in the oneness of God, and that Mohammed is his prophet; prayers; fasting during Ramadan; paying *zakat*, or a tax to help the poor; and the performance of Hajj, the pilgrimage to Mecca. A pious Muslim is convinced that, by observing these commandments, his place in heaven is assured. All too often, he overlooks the more difficult, more spiritual requirements of his faith. In their literal interpretation, most Muslims have a checklist of things to do and things to avoid. The ultra-conservative Wahabi version is a singularly austere and joyless rendering of Islam, with strict punishments for any infringement.

Whenever I have written about the need to interpret Islamic injunctions in light of the many changes that have taken place in the world since Islam appeared, I have received many emails from outraged Muslim readers. Fortunately, many have supported me as well. The problem lies in the belief that the Qur'an contains the literal word of God and, therefore, cannot be altered or reinterpreted. However, many scholars of the Qur'an have proved that the holy book cannot possibly be exactly the same as the words spoken by Gabriel to Mohammed. For one, Arabic was in a state of development when the word of God was revealed to Mohammed, and the verses were dictated to scribes by the Prophet over a period of twenty years. These were never compiled in the form of a single volume during his lifetime. When the Caliph Omar decided to order the exercise of unification of the scattered texts, he was initially reluctant as he was undertaking something even the Prophet never had.

In his book *In Search of the Original Koran: the True History of the Revealed Text*[1], Mondher Sfar, a Tunisian scholar, digs deeply into the origins of the Muslim holy book. He begins his exploration by reminding us that the Qur'an, as revealed to Mohammed, is only a part of the master text closely guarded by God:

> The transmission of the divine message to Muhammed took place in a particular mode that is more complex than the one represented in orthodox Muslim doctrine. According to the latter, God literally dictated his message. Thus, Muhammed is meant to have reproduced in the Koran the words that were created for all eternity by Allah.
>
> In fact, the text revealed to the Prophet comes from another text kept close to God. This is the famous tablet, in Arabic *lawh*, the exclusive property of God, and to which he is the only one to have access....It was only on the basis of this original that the Koranic text was transmitted to Muhammed and then to mankind. From

[1] Prometheus Books; New York, 2008, translated from the French by Emilia Lanier.

> the start, then, the Koran establishes a distinction of decisive importance within the process of revelation.
>
> Here in effect lies a question central to our inquiry into the authenticity of the revealed text. Consequently, Koranic doctrine is clear: The revealed Koranic text represents merely a supposed copy that cannot be confused with the heavenly original, and in this sense, it could not possibly pretend to be authentic. Here, the Koranic text is free from ambiguity: The heavenly original text is designated by the term *kitab*, which signifies 'writing,' while the text that derives from it by means of revelation is called *qur'an*, an entity that is essentially liturgical and designates recitation.

Safr quotes from the Qur'an to expand on the theme of a heavenly master text: 'This original, moreover, is designated as the "Mother of the Book" (*umm al-kitab*): "By the Book that makes these things plain [...] in the Mother of the Book, in Our Keeping." (43:2-4) This notion of "Mother" signifies in the Arabic language the "source", or else the "centre", as in the Koranic expression "the mother of cities" (*umm al-qura*), referring to Mecca as the Arab capital. It is the very function of the original to play the role of matrix or kernel from which the copy is drawn. Thus we see appearing a genetic relation, or rather the *precedence* of an immutable original over a copy exposed to all dangers.'

One reason most Muslims are reluctant to accept the notion that their holy book has undergone changes is that this would bring their belief at par with other faiths, with all the mutations their holy texts have been subjected to. Such a supposition would, in their eyes, strip their belief of its uniqueness. The other element of exclusivity in Islam is the Qur'anic revelation that the Prophet Mohammed is the last of a long line of prophets, making Islam God's final message to mankind and the Qur'an the last divine revelation. Earlier versions conveyed through Moses and Jesus and recorded in the Torah and the Bible, respectively, had become distorted, and their message ignored by much of mankind, resulting in the need to renew it through the Qur'an as revealed to the Prophet Mohammed.

These interlinked beliefs in the finality of Mohammed's prophethood and the Qur'an as the unaltered, literal word of God imbue Muslims with a sense of being the chosen of God. Clearly, the final message must supersede the previous ones. Although Jews and Christians are to be respected as 'people of the book,' they obviously cannot be placed on the same pedestal as the faithful. Indeed, there is a thread of ambiguity toward Christians and Jews running through the Qur'an: They are to be protected, but they should not be befriended and may even be killed. An explanation for these contradictory injunctions lies in the political context of the revelations. In the early, Meccan phase, Islam was weak and vulnerable, and Muslims needed all the alliances with neighbouring tribes they could muster. In the later, Medina, phase, Islam was on the ascendant, and adopted a more robust, aggressive posture. This change in political and military fortune is reflected in the tone of the verses revealed to the Prophet Mohammed over two decades.

For fundamentalists, one of the most influential Muslim thinkers of the last millennium was Ibn Taimiya, a fourteenth-century theologian and logician who wrote extensively about the un-Islamic practices he discerned had crept into the everyday practices of many Muslims. Specifically, he inveighed against many Sufi traditions and Jewish and Christian festivals that, according to him, were tainting the purity of Islamic belief. In his annotated translation of the *Kitab iqtida as-sirat al mustaqim mukhalafat ashab al-jahm*[2], Muhammed Umar Memon introduces us to the puritanical ideas that led to Ibn Taimiya's frequent imprisonment and ultimate death in prison in 1328. Regarding the need to differentiate Muslims from Jews, Ibn Taimiya wrote:

[2] *Ibn Taimiya's Struggle Against Popular Religion*, Mouton Publishers, 1976.

From this it clearly emerges that whatever imitation of the Jews was effected in the early part of the *hijra*[3], to be abrogated subsequently for the reason that in those days the Jews could not be told apart from the Muslims in either their hair style or garb or sign.

Thus it is established from the Koran, *Sunna*[4] and the Consensus... that according to divine legislation unbelievers should be opposed and Muslims should be different from them in ritual, symbol, and practice.

The reason is that the non-Muslims could not have been effectively opposed till after the emergence and rise of Islam as reflected in the jihad and the imposition and humiliation of *jizya*[5] upon the non-Muslims.

Thus, at first, when Muslims were weak they were not enjoined to oppose the non-Muslims, but once the faith was fully formulated, proclaimed and made victorious the opposition was prescribed.

The same holds even for the present [italics added]. Were a Muslim to find himself in *dar al-harb*[6] or *dar al-kufr*[7] without a war going on, he is no longer under injunction to oppose them [the unbelievers] in their external mode of life lest it should prove harmful....As to *dar al-Islam*[8] and the glorious Islamic period, the poll tax[9] and the humiliation were imposed upon non-Muslims while Muslims were enjoined to differ from them. Thus conforming with and differing from non-Muslims depends on circumstances of a given time, which demonstrates the wisdom of these Traditions[10].

---

[3] The migration of Mohammed and his small band of followers from Mecca where they were under threat to Medina in 622 AD.

[4] Sayings and habits of the Prophet.

[5] A discriminatory tax.

[6] The abode of war.

[7] The abode of non-belief.

[8] The abode of Islam.

[9] *Jaziya*.

[10] pp. 189-190

This permission to dissimulate according to circumstances prevails to this day. Thus, a Muslim living in the West is encouraged to hide his contempt for the lifestyle of his neighbours whereas, in his own country, he will denounce similar demeanour from a non-Muslim. In part, this also explains how a Muslim can reconcile the wide range of Qur'anic injunctions about non-Muslims contained in the holy book. For example, believers are exhorted not to befriend Jews and Christians in the following verse from the Qur'an:

> 'O ye who believe! Take not the Jews and Christians as Auliya[11], they are but Auliya to one another. And if any amongst you takes them as Auliya, then surely he is one of them. Verily, Allah guides not those people who are the Zalimun[12] (5:51)

Yet the following two verses appear to contradict this injunction:

> Allah forbids you not, respecting those who have not fought against you on account of your religion, and who have not driven you forth from your homes, that you be kind to them and act equitably towards them; surely Allah loves those who are equitable. (60:8)
>
> Allah only forbids you, respecting those who have fought against you on account of your religion, and have driven you out of your homes, and have helped others in driving you out, that you make friends with them, and whoever makes friends with them—it is those that are the transgressors. (60:9)

Another factor feeding into these and other contradictions in the Muslim holy book is the presence of thousands of narratives concerning the words and deeds of the Prophet Mohammed. Mostly recorded in the eighth and ninth centuries, these *ahadith*[13] cast

---

[11] Friends, protectors, helpers, etc.

[12] Polytheists, wrong-doers, unjust.

[13] Singular: *hadith*.

light on the Prophet's life and times and serve to illustrate various aspects of the Qur'an. However, as they were gathered together decades after Mohammed's death in 632 AD, their authenticity in many cases has been questioned by scholars. Although various schools of Islamic jurisprudence have scrutinized and attested to the claims of accuracy, the contradictory nature of some of the *ahadith* render them unreliable. The very fact that they were passed along orally for well over a century after the Prophet's death before being recorded make some Islamic scholars wary of accepting them as historic facts. In addition, many Muslims accept the Qur'an as the sole source of their faith.

This long preamble explains, for example, why Muslims in Afghanistan were enraged when the Baptist pastor Terry Jones supervised the burning of a copy of the Qur'an before his tiny congregation in Florida on March 20, 2011. In Afghanistan's Mazar-e-Sharif, a hitherto peaceful town, mullahs whipped up a crowd with lurid tales of a mass burning of the holy book and stormed a UN compound, ultimately killing a dozen UN staff members. This also explains why many Muslims are so quickly incensed when they see their Prophet Mohammed belittled in any way, as evident in the furore across the Islamic world over the Salman Rushdie affair as well as the cartoons published by a Danish newspaper. Above all, the conviction that the Qur'an is the final and literal message God revealed to his Messenger makes it virtually impossible for pious Muslims to admit to any need for revising or reinterpreting any of the injunctions it contains.

Much of the confusion over how Muslims should interact with non-Muslims stems from the multiplicity of contradictory verses regarding the subject in the Qur'an. Apologists have attempted to contextualize these verses in order to explain away the contradictions that a lay reader encounters so frequently. However, such theological contortions do little to dispel the overall impression of a faith where non-believers are at best tolerated and at worst persecuted.

Muslims point to the acceptance of non-Muslims under

Islamic rule in different countries in different eras. For instance, Moorish Spain is held up as an example of tolerance of Jews and Christians in a dark period of European history, during which the persecution of anybody not adhering closely to Catholicism was institutionalized under the Vatican. Compared to the horrors of the Inquisition, Muslim rule over Spain was undoubtedly far more benign for centuries than any other in Europe. Jews and Christians rose to great heights under Muslim rulers, and the arts and sciences flourished as never before. Still, we should keep in mind that Muslims were the minority and therefore needed the acquiescence—if not the support—of their non-Muslim subjects. The truth is that neither in Spain nor in any other country ruled by Muslims were non-believers accorded equal rights. Tolerance of Jews and Christians varied from ruler to ruler. They were occasionally the targets of pogroms and persecution in the later stages of Muslim rule over the Iberian peninsula.

In India, the other great empire in which Muslims governed over a largely non-Muslim population, the Moghuls were generally tolerant of the Hindu beliefs of the majority of their subjects. Whereas pre-Moghul Muslim invaders carried out massacres of Hindus and the destruction of many temples, once the Moghuls put down roots in the Indian subcontinent, they absorbed local influences and intermarried with their Indian subjects. Indeed, several of the emperors evolved an eclectic culture, with Akbar flirting dangerously with apostasy by creating a composite religion that incorporated features of various beliefs. Aurangzeb's fundamentalism ultimately led to the downfall of the Moghul dynasty. However, although many Hindus attained high station within the empire, it was the Muslim aristocracy that held ultimate power.

It is clear that it was usually the dictates of statecraft rather than the demands of Islamic belief that determined the interaction between Muslims and non-Muslims. Where Muslims were in a minority and governed largely non-Muslim subjects, pragmatism trumped piety, and Islamic injunctions were frequently suspended in the interest of harmony. However, infidels in Muslim-majority territories did not fare as well, often being forced to pay *jaziya*, a levy imposed on non-Muslims, and subjected to petty humiliations. Nevertheless, when compared with the intolerance that prevailed in Europe during the Dark Ages, Muslim rule over non-Muslim subjects was generally far more benign.

The European conquest and colonization of many Muslim lands in the nineteenth and twentieth centuries saw the displacement of Islamic *sharia* law by secular, manmade codes that introduced the notion of equal rights. The concept of non-Muslims being the *ahl al-dhimma*[14] was no longer acceptable and, under western colonial rule, Christian subjects were often given preference in state jobs. When the tide of colonialism turned after World War II, the departing European rulers left their legal systems and the equality they accorded all religions intact. However, in Islamic countries like Pakistan, minorities suffered a steady erosion of civil rights, despite the fact that they retained notional legal protection.

The second half of the twentieth century witnessed a sharp increase in the number of Muslims migrating to the West. Whereas barely any lived in West Europe or America before World War II, numbers soared as Muslims from the Middle East, North Africa, Sub-Saharan Africa, and South Asia sailed to former colonial capitals to find work in countries ravaged by the war that were desperately short of labour. Soon, they sent for their families; within a generation, millions were installed in urban centres from Berlin to Birmingham. The United States and Canada also opened their doors to large numbers of immigrants, and mosques rapidly sprang up across North America.

This huge influx of Muslims in the lands of non-believers had no precedence in Islamic history. For centuries, Muslims had been advised against living and travelling in Europe for fear of defilement. Other than during the period between the defeat of the last Moorish kingdom in Cordoba and their expulsion from Spain,

---

[14] The people under protection.

large numbers of Muslims had never lived under non-believers by choice. Suddenly, these communities had to adjust to neighbours eating pork, drinking alcohol and indulging in extramarital sex. A grudging accommodation developed between the host and guest communities, yet strong reservations remained on both sides. For pious Muslims strongly anchored to their faith, life in the West was a minefield of unintended sins. It was their duty to shield their children from the temptations of what they saw as a licentious, debauched lifestyle. Parents and prayer leaders at mosques joined hands to warn the younger generation of the evils of the Western culture.

As we have seen, the post-World War II era also witnessed the rise of Islamic radicalism, partly due to the rise of despotism in much of the Muslim world. Resentment of both religious pro-West dictators and nationalistic, secular rulers grew steadily, especially in the face of rampant corruption and mismanagement. This anger was often channelled by pan-Islamic movements like the Muslim Brotherhood. However, Islamic tradition calls for accepting the political order, provided the ruler does not actively flout the teachings of Islam. *Fitna*, or discord, is frowned upon, and the Qur'an contains explicit warnings against taking the life of fellow Muslims: 'And whoever kills a believer intentionally, his recompense is Hell to abide therein, and the Wrath and the Curse of Allah are upon him, and a great punishment is prepared for him' (4:93).

How could Muslims circumvent these specific injunctions against overthrowing Muslim rulers? Influential hard-line scholars like Syed Qutb pointed out that Muslim rulers at the time had led their people into *jahilya*, the pre-Islamic pagan era; thus, they must be resisted. Furthermore, according to him, Western society never emerged from this state. By conflating the two, he made it the task of the true believer to resist both. In his chapter entitled 'Islam is the Real Civilization' in *Milestones*, his seminal work, Qutb issues this call to arms:

> But the movement which is a natural outgrowth of the Islamic belief and which is the essence of the Islamic society does not let

> any individual hide himself, every individual of this society must move! There should be a movement in his belief, a movement in his blood, a movement in his community, and in the structure of this organic society, and as the *Jahilyah* is all around him, and its residual influences in his mind and in the minds in those around him, the struggle goes on and the *Jihad* continues until the Day of Redemption.[15]

Thus, just as Bush's 'war on terror' is a war without end, so is the jihad. By conflating the *jahilyah* with modern western civilization as well as with secular or pro-West Muslim leaders, extremists have targeted most of the world for their holy war. In the following quote, Qutb describes his perception of the immorality from which Western society suffers:

> In all modern *jahili* societies, the meaning of 'morality' is limited to such an extent that all those aspects which distinguish man from animal are considered beyond its sphere. In these societies, illegitimate sexual relationships, even homosexuality, are not considered immoral. The meaning of ethics is limited to economic affairs or sometimes to political affairs which fall into the category of 'government interests'....
>
> Among *jahili* societies, writers, journalists and editors advise both married and unmarried people that free sexual relationships are not immoral. However, it is immoral if a boy uses his partner, or a girl uses her partner for sex, while feeling no love in his or her heart. It is bad if a wife continues to guard her chastity while her love for her husband has vanished; it is admirable if she finds another lover. Dozens of stories are written about this theme; many newspaper editorials, articles, cartoons, serious and light columns all invite to this way of life.
>
> From the point of view of 'human' progress, all such societies are not civilised but are backward.[16]

[15] Islamic Book Service, New Delhi, 2009, pp 102-103.

[16] Ibid., pp 98-99.

This, then, forms an integral part of the discourse of militant Islam today. Expanding on the theme of the irreconcilable differences between the Islamic world and the areas under *jahilyah*, Qutb writes in his chapter entitled 'A Muslim's Nationality and His Belief':

> 'There is only one place on earth which can be called the home of Islam[17], and it is the place where the Islamic state is established and the Shari'ah[18] is the authority and God's limits are observed, and where all the Muslims administer the affairs of the state with mutual consultation. The rest of the world is the home of hostility[19]. Muslims can have only two possible relations with *Dar ul-Harb*: peace with a contractual agreement, or war . . .
>
> A Muslim has no country except that part of the earth where the *Shari'ah* of God is established and human relationships are based on the foundation of relationship with God; a Muslim has no nationality except his belief, which makes him a member of the Muslim community in *Dar ul-Islam*....

Qutb thus negates the concept of the nation-state and reaffirms the existence of the wider Muslim nation—namely, the *ummah*. Since only a Caliph can lead the *ummah*, all other leaders who hold sway over Muslim lands must be usurpers who are to be opposed and toppled. What emerges from this discourse is that all non-Muslim societies are *jahili*, or backward and benighted, and that Muslim rulers have no legal or moral authority to govern. Feeding into this worldview is the widespread perception in the Muslim world (and elsewhere) that western society is decadent and morally bankrupt. Qutb repeatedly assails the cult of the individual he sees as dominating western culture.

The second strand in the extremist take on the prevailing situation is the corruption and the poor governance that have long

[17] Dar-ul-Islam.

[18] Islamic law.

[19] Dar-ul-Harb.

been the hallmark of Muslim states. Whether secular or Islamic, leaders of these countries have fuelled extremism through their repeated failure to provide their people with decent education and employment opportunities. Often, these crooked despots are propped up by the United States for its own political and economic interests. Hatred for their rulers is thus also directed by Muslims toward America and Americans.

In order to justify violence against fellow Muslims, extremists have resorted to the doctrine of *takfir*, or the denouncement of a believer as an apostate. Apostasy is punishable by death; thus, Muslims accused of *takfir* (i.e., deviating from their faith) can be legitimately executed. Traditionally, only the authority of the religious hierarchy of an Islamic state could meticulously consider a case before declaring a Muslim a *kafir*, or non-believer.[20] However, a group of fundamentalists known as Takfiris—an offshoot of the Salafi movement—have taken it upon themselves to excommunicate Muslims, thereby subjecting them to the death penalty. The Salafis believe in a literalist interpretation of Islam and were not originally a violent group. However, the Takfiris have arrogated to themselves the right to declare any Muslim an apostate and, thus, subject to the death penalty. For this radical departure from orthodoxy, they have the theological support of Ibn Taimiya, the medieval scholar previously discussed.

The following text provides part of the Wikipedia entry on Takfiris:[21]

> Takfiris also reject the traditional Muslim duty to obey one's legitimate rulers in all manners that do not contradict Sharia, as sedition is viewed as a great danger to a nation. However Takfiris consider all political authority that does not abide by their interpretation of Islam as illegitimate and apostate; a view which

[20] The Arabic root of both *kafir* and *takfir* is *kufr*, or disbelief.

[21] http://en.wikipedia.org/w/index.php?title=Takfiri

> closely mirrors Qutb's views on *jahiliyah*. As such, violence against such regimes is considered legitimate.
>
> Takfiri views on suicide also differ significantly from that of orthodox Islam. Takfiris believe that one who deliberately kills himself whilst attempting to kill enemies is a martyr (*Shahid*) and therefore goes straight to heaven. As such all sin is absolved when a person is martyred, allowing carte blanche for the indiscriminate killing of non-combatants, for example.[22]

Here then is the 'licence to kill' that allows and even encourages extremist terrorists to slaughter Muslims, non-Muslims, women, and children in the name of their faith. By invoking the doctrine of *takfir*, they have set themselves up as judge, jury, and hangman. Whether flying planes into the Twin Towers or sending waves of suicide bombers against their fellow Muslims in Pakistan, Saudi Arabia, and Afghanistan, Al Qaeda, drawing its inspiration from the Takfiri theology we have discussed, and its ideological partners consider their bloody acts to be perfectly righteous and legitimate. However, Takfiris are clearly a tiny sect; the foot soldiers of the jihad do not get into the finer points of theology to arrive at these murderous conclusions. Nevertheless, once they have been told their acts of terrorism are not only sanctioned by Islam, but also lead straight to heaven, they are quickly brainwashed into becoming human bombs.

In the January 2011 issue of *Inspire*, the slick online mouthpiece of Al Qaeda in the Arabian Peninsula (AQAP), Samir Khan gives a detailed moral justification behind the war against Muslim rulers. In an article entitled 'The Central Issue,' the young American co-editor of *Inspire* writes:

---

[22] This entry is based on John Esposito's *Unholy War: Terror in the name of Islam* (OUP, 2002), and Vincenzo Oliveti's *Terror's Source. The Ideology of Wahhabi-Salafism and its Consequences*; Amadeus Books, 2002.

The idea of defending the Muslim lands from the disbelieving occupation forces had taken on a new meaning. It was an idea that paved the way for the Al Qaeda Organization.

Mujahidin jurists and thinkers from Egypt who had the lengthiest and toughest experience in working for the re-establishment of an Islamic state in Egypt, exported the idea that the so-called Muslim governments in the Islamic lands are in fact occupation forces. Unless and until they are removed physically, the Muslims would be living in the same state of sin similar to that of a foreign army occupying a Muslim land.

This idea was derived from the jurisprudence on how to deal with an apostate. Islamic law gives the death sentence to those who leave the religion. An apostate is determined by the action he had done publicly. For instance, if he were to become a Christian, or spy on the Muslim for the disbelievers, or join the ranks of the enemy to fight the Muslims and such, he would have committed major disbelief (*kufr akbar*) as is recognized by our classical scholars in consent. Islamic scholars have given a little more than ten major acts that would lead one to apostasy...The *khawaraji*[23] had an extreme creed that included all sinners in the category of apostasy. Praise be to Allah, the *mujahidin*[24] are nothing like this.

Khan continues:

The Egyptian *mujahidin* claimed that the rulers of the Muslim lands were apostate due to two main reasons. These included not ruling by *shari'ah*, and taking the disbelievers as helpers and guardians[25] against the Muslims...Additionally it signals that they are ruling by man-made laws that include elements of Democracy, Jahillyah and other borrowed forms of laws.

The second reason implies spying on the Muslims for the sake of the disbelievers, giving the disbelievers military and spy bases in their respective countries to fight the Muslims, actively participating

[23] A seventh-century extremist sect.

[24] Warriors of the jihad.

[25] *Awliya*.

> in the murdering of Muslims for the sake of disbelievers, torturing, mistreating and even raping Muslims for the sake of gaining confidence from the disbelievers....
>
> All of this spells apostasy of a very high degree. The question then comes: within a modern government structure, just exactly who are the apostates? This ruling applies to all those within the government sectors that carry out the acts of disbelief....
>
> Today the Saudi monarchy is the prime example of this ugly apostasy. Their monarchy can be likened to dog dung wrapped in gold silk....
>
> Then comes Saudi's [sic] romantic relationship with America that includes military aid to fight Muslims in the Arabian Peninsula and in return the Crusaders are given military bases to launch wars against the Muslims around the world that go beyond the boundaries of their own laws in killing and weapons deployments; their protection of Israel from the Muslims; ... their use of magic and communication with vile *jinns* to locate positions of the mujahidin; and finally their torture dungeons that don't even spare the elderly scholars.

This, then, is the modern jihadi charge sheet against America and those Muslim rulers who support it. By lumping them together and accusing them of apostasy, Khan and other Takfiris justify the use of wholesale murder.

The whole concept of apostasy is one that troubles many Muslims. On the one hand, the Qur'an clearly and unequivocally asserts that there should be no compulsion in matters of religion. On the other, many *ahadith* say that Muslims who turn away from their faith should be killed. Perhaps the most complete study of apostasy in Islam was undertaken by Maulana Abul Ala Mawdudi, one of the most influential thinkers in the Muslim world in the twentieth century. He founded the Jamaat-e-Islami, a political party and movement that has been a major factor in determining Pakistan's path toward fundamentalism and that continues to shape the public discourse there. In a long article in Urdu that was serialized in the Indian monthly magazine *Tarjuman al*

Qur'an between October 1942 and June 1943, Mawdudi brought his impressive scholarship and erudition to bear on the question of apostasy and its punishment under Islamic law. Translated into English by Syed Silas Husain and Ernest Hahn in 1994 from the 1963 edition published as a book by Islamic Publishers Ltd., Lahore, the article sheds light on the fate of those who leave the fold of Islam. Mawdudi quotes this verse from the Qur'an:

> But if they repent and establish worship and pay the poor-due, then are they your brethren in religion. We detail our revelations for a people who have knowledge. And if they break their pledges after their treaty (hath been made with you) and assail your religion, then fight the heads of disbelief—Lo! They have no binding oaths that they might desist (9:11-12).

To support this Qur'anic directive, Mawdudi cites this *hadith* or Tradition of the Prophet (and several similar ones):

> The Messenger of God stated: In no way is it permitted to shed the blood of a Muslim other than the following reasons: a) although married, he commits adultery; b) after being a Muslim he chooses *kufr*[26]; and c) he takes someone's life.

The historical context of this Islamic injunction lies in the immediate aftermath of the Prophet's death in 632 AD. Abu Bakr, the first Caliph, was faced with an uprising of many Arabs who, while accepting Islam, refused to pay *zakat*[27]. Others rejected Mohammed's prophethood on the grounds that—had he been a true prophet—he would not have died; some proclaimed their own prophets. Still others refused to acknowledge Abu Bakr as their leader. Faced with this rebellion, Abu Bakr waged fierce war, dubbing the rebels apostates. For the young religion, this was a battle for survival. Had Abu Bakr ignored this widespread

---

[26] Disbelief.

[27] The obligatory poor tax.

rejection of Mohammed's faith by several Arabian tribes Islam undoubtedly would have never emerged as the dominant power in the region. Most likely, it would have dwindled into insignificance as a marginal sect. That so many of the warnings and sanctions against apostasy subsequently found their way into the *ahadith* should come as no surprise. In all probability, they served as a post-facto rationalization for the harshness of the suppression of apostasy.

But in this day and age, it baffles and shocks the world that people should be condemned to death for opting out of their faith. In recent years, three Muslim Afghans have been arrested for the 'sin' of converting to Christianity. After international outcry, Abdul Rehman was released after he was convicted in 2005, but he had to leave his country to escape attacks by outraged clerics. In 2010, Said Musa and Shoaib Abdullah were also arrested for the same so-called crime. The former has been released and has found asylum in the United Kingdom, but Abdullah remains in jail and is likely to receive the death penalty. His only hope lies in international indignation and pressure on the government.

How can any Muslim resolve the contradiction between actively evangelizing across the world and converting thousands of non-Muslims to their faith while killing those who leave Islam? In truth, many Muslims—especially those living in the West—squirm when asked to justify the belief that their religion does not allow followers to leave it. More often than not, they grasp for historical explanations and repeat the Qur'anic declaration that there should be no compulsion in religion. However, as we have seen from Mawdudi's detailed exposition, it seems clear that apostasy is indeed punishable by death according to one interpretation.

Over the years, Muslim societies have quietly put away harsh Islamic injunctions and practices as they are in direct conflict with modern customs. For instance, while slavery is permitted in Islam, there are no slave markets anywhere in the Muslim world today. Furthermore, only Saudi Arabia—and possibly the Taliban—decapitates prisoners for a range of crimes or chop off hands for theft in public. Iran is the only country in which women are condemned to death by stoning for adultery. Thus, even deeply conservative Muslim societies can shed archaic, cruel practices because they no longer make sense.

The other thing to remember is that the theological terrain we have traversed here remains the domain of a small handful of Muslims. The vast majority is content with the religious instruction they received from their parents and in their local mosques. The whole debate over the Takfiri ideology has passed most Muslims by, and few would even be familiar with the term and its implications. While it might be an indispensable justification for terrorists, it is hardly something taught in schools and in homes. Nevertheless, the shift to a greater public display of Islamic symbols and dogma that has taken place in Muslim societies in recent years has given extremism greater acceptability among moderates. As a result, there is less public condemnation of Islamic terrorism and threatening speech than there ought to be.

I would like to end this chapter with a possibly apocryphal story to illustrate the moral minefield that the whole debate over apostasy has become. A few years ago, a German aid worker fell in love with a Muslim girl in Peshawar, a generally conservative city in northwest Pakistan. Her family insisted that he convert to Islam before permitting their daughter to marry him. Deeply in love, he did so, even undergoing a painful circumcision in the process. A couple of years later, the couple broke up, and the German decided to revert to his Christian faith. He was told that if he did so, he could be killed for apostasy. This might well be an urban legend, but it does demonstrate the pitfalls of clinging blindly to traditions that come to us from the ancient past.

10

Jason, Jihad, and Jobs

In the ancient Greek myth about Jason's quest for the Golden Fleece, the hero was given a bag of dragon's teeth and told to plant them in a field. As soon as he did so, an armed warrior sprang up at each spot where a tooth had been planted; this fierce army then turned on Jason.

In its fight against global jihad, America has seemed a bit like Jason: Every time it cuts down an enemy, more spring up to attack it. In one version of the legend, Medea—a princess in love with Jason—gives him a pebble to throw at the soldiers. When one of them is hit, he thinks it was thrown by one of his comrades and attacks him. Soon, the soldiers are too busy fighting each other to worry about Jason. Alas, there is no such pebble for America to throw. Instead, it's making do with Hellfire missiles fired from remotely piloted aircraft like the Reaper and the Predator. Such strikes, in addition to killing Al Qaeda and Taliban leaders and their foot soldiers, also cause casualties among the civilians they shelter, simultaneously generating huge waves of anger across Pakistan, thereby serving as a powerful recruitment tool for jihadis.

Similarly, American military action in Iraq, Afghanistan, Yemen, and Somalia is causing a host of dragon's teeth to sprout and produce fanatical young jihadis. Many Muslims supported (or at least accepted) America's invasion of Afghanistan in the wake of the 9/11 attacks. However, the subsequent decade of escalating US-led violence in Muslim countries has led to a sharp rise in anti-Americanism. It has also radicalized an entire generation of young Muslims, some of whom have signed up for the global jihad. Another effect of this reflexive resort to military action is the increasing Islamization of previously secular Muslim societies under the pressure of anti-American public opinion.

As we have seen, much of the momentum for the Muslim resurgence comes from ideas and ideals. Whether we like it or not, the fact is that many of those engaged in the jihad against America and the West are idealists. They genuinely believe that the triumph of Islam and the rebirth of the Caliphate will lead to a better world. Just as many Americans and Europeans are convinced that democracy and globalization are forces for good, a significant number of Muslims are of the firm belief that the imposition of Islamic law will produce a world where peace, equality, and brotherhood will prevail. These utopian dreams fuel much of the fervour and ferment among young Muslims. The ideal Islamic world fundamentalists want to usher in would be akin to the brief period of the rule of the four caliphs who followed the Prophet Mohammed after his death in 632 AD. According to the myth-making surrounding this short era, this was a time in which the poor were equal to the rich, the weak received justice, and rulers made sure that nobody went hungry.

Hamid Gul, a retired Pakistani general, provided a modern take on this utopia while speaking to Roger Hardy, a British journalist, in 2002:

> [In an Islamic state] there will be justice across the board. The courts will be free: they will be interpreting the Qur'an, and it will put all anxieties at rest. Number two, the education system will be equal, not class-based—right now it is class-based—and *madressas* will automatically disappear; but so will some of the public schools [that] are accessible only to the rich and mighty.
>
> The economic system will change. There will be interest-free banking. The taxation will be direct—there will be no indirect taxation. And minorities will be free to practise their religion, their

> way of life, their culture—whatever they wish to. And feudalism will be no more—that I can assure you. In Islam there is no place for feudalism.... And, incidentally, the clerics will have no place, because Islam is not for the clerics....
>
> And of course Pakistan will be a perfect democracy, because the sovereignty of Allah has to be practised through the people of Pakistan. There is no room for dictatorship, there is no room for usurpers, there is no room for people who want to perpetrate their own vested interest; none whatsoever.[1]

Gul is not some callow, uneducated boy from the hills. As a three-star general, he was head of Pakistan's powerful Inter-Services Intelligence (ISI) agency in the late 1980s and was instrumental in supporting jihadi insurgents in Afghanistan as well as during the Kashmir uprising. After he was fired by Benazir Bhutto in 1989, he became active in Islamist circles, tirelessly supporting extremist views in the Pakistani and foreign media. Of great concern is the fact that many serving and retired officers in Pakistan's military share his extreme views.

A fortnight after 9/11, Gul was interviewed by Arnaud de Borchgrave, an American journalist. Insisting that the terror attacks on the Twin Towers and the Pentagon had been an Israeli operation, Gul went on to spell out his take on what Allah's sovereignty would entail:

> Democracy does not work. Politicians are constantly thinking of their next election, not the public good ...The Qur'an calls a spade a spade. It is the supreme law and tells right from wrong. There is no notion of 'my country, right or wrong' under divine law. The creator's will predominates. All is subservient to Allah's will.... The Prophet's last sermon was a universal document of human rights for everyone that surpasses everything that came since, including

---

[1] Hardy, Roger, *The Muslim Revolt*, C. Hurst and Co. Ltd., 2010, pp. 77-78.

> America's declaration of independence and the UN charter...divine law should supersede man-made law.[2]

If an educated, widely travelled army general—and far too many of his colleagues for comfort—could so eagerly embrace this utopian scenario of a perfect world under an Islamic dispensation, think of the appeal it must hold for immature boys at *madressas*, where the bulk of the curriculum is the rote learning of the Qur'an. In badly governed, corrupt and usually poor countries (sadly, a description of much of the Islamic world), those at the bottom of the pecking order are strongly attracted to the vision of a society that would give them dignity and equality of opportunity. Since childhood, they are reassured that such a society did indeed exist under the four divinely guided caliphs in Islam's infancy. They are further told that only if the current corrupt, pro-western leaders are overthrown can the golden era be recreated. From here, it is but a short step to agree that such an Islamic utopia is worth fighting and dying for.

In a sense, this heaven on earth is more attractive than Marx's workers' paradise for it caters to the spirit as well as to man's material well-being. On the one hand, it has features of socialist equality; on the other, it provides for private capital and commerce. Unlike the godless philosophy incorporated into Marxist doctrine, Islam has a rich description of the sensual rewards that await a good Muslim in heaven. So, for most Muslims, what's not to like?

Against the appeal of socialism and the state capitalism of the Soviet Union, America deployed the siren song of consumerism and the proven efficiency of capitalism. Compared to the repressive dictatorships that held sway over socialist states, the attractions of democracy were self-evident. Hollywood movies and TV shows promoted the whole package, making them ideal marketing tools for an increasingly affluent American way of life. Many in the

---

[2] Ibid., pp. 78-79.

socialist world living under Stalinist tyrannies stared hungrily and enviously at the West, with its freedom and wealth. When the USSR finally collapsed under the weight of its own contradictions, few tears were shed—except by those who benefited directly from being members of the Communist Party.

Meanwhile, against the ideology that spawned 9/11 and other extremist terrorist activities, the only response the United States was able to deploy was force. The attack on Afghanistan did not initially cause any great outrage; the invasion of Iraq did. For reasons still unclear, George W. Bush decided to unleash 'shock and awe' against the Iraqi state and people. This misadventure gave jihadis around the world an unexpected boost. To counter a narrative made up in equal parts of the attractions of an Islamic state and the need to defend the *ummah* against a western power seemingly bent on killing and humiliating Muslims, Bush's immediate response was to exclaim 'Bring 'em on!'

Reinforcing this triumphant stance were hawks like Donald Rumsfeld, Dick Cheney and Paul Wolfowitz. President Bush was careful to distinguish between Islam and the extremist ideology of Al Qaeda, whereas the neocon cabal that surrounded him made no secret of their contempt and hostility toward Muslims. Much of the US strategy towards winning Muslim hearts and minds seemed to be initially based solely on former US President Lyndon Johnson's famous dictum: 'If you've got 'em by the balls, their hearts and minds will follow.'

However, as resistance to America hardened and broadened in Iraq, Afghanistan and elsewhere in the Muslim world, the realization that extremism has to be countered with a more nuanced approach began to sink in. In a paper entitled 'What's The Big Idea? Confronting the Ideology of Islamist Extremism'[3] produced for the Homeland Security Policy Institute and the Washington

---

[3] http://www.gwumc.edu/hspi/policy/issuebrief080_confrontingideology.cfm

Institute for Near East Policy in February 2011, Frank Cillufo, J. Scott Carpenter, and Matthew Levitt write:

> The fact is that addressing specific outbreaks of violent extremism will not prevent its virulent spread unless the underlying extremist ideology is exposed, unpacked, dissected and combated. Although al-Qaeda's leadership has to an extent been weakened and its global reach attenuated, the underlying ideology continues to spread and gain traction among vulnerable populations....Al-Qaeda's ideology is thriving and other, arguably smarter, adversaries continue to exploit the group's ideological package by tapping into growing unrest and parasitically manipulating local grievances. This phenomenon is further amplified by the ballooning youth bulge in Muslim-majority countries.
>
> The administration's global engagement and public diplomacy approach may be effective in significant ways, but it has done demonstrably little to impact the spread and appeal of radical Islamist extremism....
>
> A narrowly defined, traditional counterterrorism approach, coupled with a broad engagement policy, even if aggressively implemented, can only achieve so much. Such an approach hampers efforts to intervene early in the radicalization process, either domestically or abroad, to prevent individuals or sub-communities from becoming violent. After a person becomes violent, they have entered the domain of law-enforcement or military action. This reactive policy combination does little to empower those in the trenches seeking to defend their communities from extremist subversion. In short, kinetic responses are important but not sufficient.

Thus, the authors argue that it is not sufficient to fight insurgents and terrorists in Iraq or Afghanistan; the real challenge lies in confronting and neutralizing the ideology that gave rise to this violence in the first place. They call for a deeper understanding of and a more nuanced approach to Muslim communities, emphasizing the need to avoid stereotypes:

> The reasons the extremist narrative finds fertile soil in diverse Muslim communities across the globe are as varied as the societies themselves. Some respond to a radicalizer's message because they feel excluded from their societies, trapped in poverty or hopelessness by authoritarian regimes. Others living in liberal democratic Western nations, though well-off and well-educated, struggle with issues of belonging and identity; for them, the Islamist message resonates deeply. Radicalizers enjoy great success by connecting a recruit's local grievance to a radical global narrative that combines Islamist extremism with 'clash of civilizations' rhetoric, pitting the monolithic West against the monolithic Muslim *ummah*. In nearly all cases, radicalizers suggest a person's identity can be—indeed must be—reduced solely to being 'Muslim. And what it means to be Muslim, of course, is defined by the radicalizer. This has profound policy and programmatic implications, since emphasizing other aspects of a potential recruit's identity or constructing alternative narratives is critical to short-circuiting the radicalization process.

As the anti-extremism think tank, the Quilliam Foundation, picturesquely notes in a 2008 paper entitled 'Pulling Together to Defeat Terror:'[4] 'At the very least, the rhetoric of radicals provides the mood music to which suicide bombers dance.'

Having diagnosed the fundamental problem accurately, what do the authors of 'What's The Big Idea?' recommend as a remedy? Sadly, their recommendations fall far short of what's genuinely needed:

> Elements of a cohesive national strategy could incorporate a range of approaches that have proven effective in other contexts. The power of negative imagery, as in a political campaign, could be harnessed to hurt our adversaries and further chip away at their appeal and credibility in the eyes of their peers, followers and sympathizers. A sustained and systematic strategic communications effort aimed at exposing the hypocrisy of Islamists' words versus their deeds could also knock them off balance, as could embarrassing their leadership

---

[4] posted on its website http://www.quilliamfoundation.org

> by bringing to light their seamy connections to criminal enterprises and drug trafficking organizations.

The truth is that, currently, America has little credibility in the Muslim world or in Muslim communities in the West. When George W. Bush invaded Iraq on the pretext of Saddam Hussein's nonexistent WMDs, he instantly lost his country the trust of virtually all Muslims everywhere. 'It's all about the oil,' remarked the cynics. 'This is yet another Western attack against a Muslim country,' said others. Nobody believed the American administration then (and few do now) that the attack ultimately resulted from a misreading of intelligence reports.

The subsequently published appalling images of humiliated and tortured Iraqi prisoners from Abu Ghraib, followed by the lingering incarceration of hundreds of Muslims at Guantanamo Bay, led to dark tales of the extraordinary rendition and torture of scores of Muslim suspects doing the rounds. All this fed into a narrative of sustained American hostility toward Muslims and Islam. Against this daily diet of animosity and ongoing violence reported by the media across the world, the trigger of 9/11 faded from Muslim memory. People in several Muslim countries whose daily experience of terror attacks has hardened them to random violence simply could not understand why Americans could not put 9/11 behind them and move on.

Such perceptions shape the attitudes of many Muslims toward America today. One small example of the lack of American credibility in many Muslims' eyes struck me when I was watching Pakistani and international TV coverage in the immediate aftermath of bin Laden's killing in the daring raid carried out by US SEAL commandos in May 2011. Many Pakistanis interviewed by the media had bizarre ideas about the event. Some said the Al Qaeda leader had died in Afghanistan years ago and his body had been brought to the house in Abbottabad to discredit Pakistan. Others doubted that the terrorist mastermind had been killed at all. Still others insisted that Pakistan's ISI had played a pivotal role in the operation, when it had clearly been cut out of the loop. The blogosphere was also humming with conspiracy theories that whirled around bin Laden's death. One example was posted by a someone identifying himself as a retired brigadier-general of the Pakistan army, Farooq Hameed Khan, on the discussion group Pakistanpress[5] two days after the American raid:

> Where is the proof or evidence that it was the real OBL and not his decoy, lookalike or dummy who was killed in the Abbottabad raid by US Special Forces? Was it the real OBL in the white shroud that was consigned to the Arabian Sea? What prevented the US raiders to capture [sic] OBL alive? An alive or wounded Osama shown to the world would have justified Obama's claim of victory against Osama and Al Qaeda. Why did Obama not reveal that a US helicopter was lost in the operation?
>
> The Americans are masters in the art of strategic deception. Was this operation staged to tell the world that OBL was killed in the operation while hiding in a city not far from Islamabad? Was this operation engineered to be Pakistan's 9/11 to embarrass Pakistan Army/ISI? Or did the Pakistani security services call the US bluff? Will the real and smiling Osama emerge in a video shortly? Will the US or Pakistan have the last laugh?

This bizarre rant reflects the mindset of far too many in Pakistan's security and defense services for it to be funny.

In addition, in Afghanistan, a decade of American-led occupation and accompanying violence has made the people weary and cynical. Whenever innocent Afghans have accidentally been killed due to poor targeting or faulty intelligence, the relatives of the victims have been paid compensation. Yet it is not easy to accept payment for the death of a son or a daughter. The residual pain turns to bitterness and hate. In Pakistan's tribal areas, where drone attacks have killed many terrorists, they have also inflicted much collateral damage among the men, women, and children behind whom local

[5] pakistanpress@googlegroups.com

and foreign jihadis sought shelter. The ripple effect of these deaths cascades through the media and into the streets and homes across the countries that this remotely waged warfare infects.

In this context of generalized violence attributed to the United States, to talk about 'the power of negative imagery, as in political campaigns' as the authors of 'What's The Big Idea?' suggest is fairly meaningless. Currently, negative imagery is far too often the exclusive preserve of the United States, at least in Muslim eyes. The problem is not so much with the message as with the messenger: Anything emanating from Washington is automatically suspect in today's toxic environment of distrust and suspicion.

Nearly fifty years ago, at the height of the Cold War, the United States was actively engaged in a struggle to seize the ideological high ground against its Soviet foe. In the frontline of this propaganda battle was the United States Information Agency (USIA), an organization absorbed by the State Department in 1999 because it was deemed not to have an independent role or clear goal following the collapse of the Soviet Union. Edward R. Murrow, who served as the director of the USIA between 1961 and 1964, stated in 1963:

> American traditions and the American ethic require us to be truthful...truth is the best propaganda and lies are the worst. To be persuasive we must be believable; to be believable we must be credible; to be credible we must be truthful. It is as simple as that.[6]

Alas, it's not so simple. As we know all too well, in war, truth is the first casualty. Take the hugely unpopular drone attacks in Pakistan as an example. Despite their increasingly frequent use under the Obama administration, the United States refuses to admit that the CIA is behind such attacks. Such refusal stems partly from the need to spare the Pakistani government the embarrassment of

---

[6] Epstein, Susan B, "U.S. Public Diplomacy: Background and the 9/11 Commission Recommendations," 2006

officially admitting that it is either complicit in the drone campaign or incapable of stopping them, and partly from the fact that they are illegal under international law as targeted attacks on alleged terrorists amount to extrajudicial killing.

Whatever the reasons, it is American policy not to comment officially on drone attacks. Whenever there are casualties among non-combatants—a frequent occurrence—no apologies are made. Nor is compensation offered. Pakistan lodges a pro forma protest after each attack, but the general consensus is that the country's rulers are complicit. The result of this policy of dissembling is that both governments have lost credibility. Neither has made any effort to explain to Pakistanis and to the outside world why drone attacks are necessary and effective.

The last decade has witnessed a huge proliferation of private media outlets across the world. Muslim countries have not been exempt from this trend. In areas where the airwaves and the print media were under the tight control of despots, many TV channels have sprung up to challenge official censorship. The Internet has now become a dominant provider of news, views, rumour, and gossip. Social networks like Twitter and Facebook, combined with the incessant text messaging that takes place around the world, have made it impossible for autocrats to block subversive news and information. However, as these new media erode the power of dictators, they also hasten the spread of conspiracy theories and anti-American propaganda.

Cyberspace is where extremists gather to exchange views and radicalize new recruits to the jihad. As discussed earlier, Islamist websites effortlessly reach across the globe to create networks of supporters and influence impressionable young Muslims who might be struggling with issues of isolation and identity in the West. Invariably, these extreme (often violent) interpretations of Islam go unchallenged. Discussion threads carrying a warped and dangerous worldview are accepted as gospel. Although many anti-terrorist websites oppose these voices, they have little credibility with Muslim web users. Indeed, they are too often singing to the choir. Knowledgeable, credible voices are needed on Islamic sites to challenge and deconstruct the extremist narrative.

The Takfiri ideology, whose evolution we examined in an earlier chapter, provides much of the justification for violent jihad and terrorism. Mercifully, it is an interpretation of Islam that is not widely prevalent. Nevertheless, it continues to be a rallying cry for global jihad.

Another place radicalization occurs and anti-West opinions harden is the mosque. Here, barely educated clerics hold forth against the evils of modernity, especially in their Friday sermons. America is invariably singled out for its alleged atrocities against Muslims around the world. Control over mosques traditionally rested with Muslim rulers who supported them financially. Today, this control has slipped to religious parties or militant groups in many countries. In Turkey, the Friday sermon is written in the Religious Affairs Ministry in Ankara and faxed to *mullahs* across the country. These prayer leaders are on the state payroll, and thus have little choice in toeing the official line. In secular dictatorships like Hussein's Iraq a decade ago and Bashar al Assad's Syria today, mosques are tightly controlled and the Friday sermons monitored by the ubiquitous secret services. Since 9/11, in many Western countries, the activities centred around mosques have been closely watched by intelligence agents.

Yet in dysfunctional countries like Somalia, Afghanistan, and Pakistan, where control over large swaths of territory is tenuous at best, clerics are free to encourage their congregants to commit violence against anybody who follows a slightly different interpretation of Islam. *Madressas* also often serve as breeding grounds for extremism. All too often, they are funded by Saudi official and private largesse to propagate the extreme Wahabi interpretation followed by the majority in the kingdom.

These, then, are the spaces where extremist ideology needs to be countered and controlled. Governments can crack down on mosques and *madressas*—in theory at least. However, the Internet remains anarchic and mostly unmonitored. Many governments keep tabs on the sites suspected users log on to, but the content of jihadi websites remains available at the click of a mouse. Although many are often hacked into, tech-savvy extremists have become adept at creating mirror sites and taking other evasive measures.

Thus far, America and its allies have made little effort—in public, at least—to drain the extremist swamp of its Wahabi/Salafi/Takfiri content. As previously discussed, Saudi Arabia has been instrumental in exporting a harsh, literalist interpretation of Islam to much of the Muslim world by financing *madressas* and mosques. In addition, it has funded mosques across Europe and America, from where preachers on the Saudi payroll indoctrinate Muslim migrants from around the world. Many chairs of Islamic studies in western universities are similarly financed by Saudi Arabia to provide an intellectual framework for extremism. Since the oil embargo of 1973 and the resulting bonanza it received in its aftermath, the Saudi capital of Riyadh has become the epicentre of an extremist ideology that has spread across the world. As Tarek Fatah, the well-known Canadian Muslim author and opponent of Islamic extremism, writes:

> Muslims today cannot deny the fact that a brutal and oppressive regime rules Saudi Arabia, one that occupies the cities of Mecca and Medina, yet across the world, Saudi-funded organizations ensure that any criticism of the Saudi regime and state is seen as an attack on Islam.
>
> The Saudis can do anything they wish and yet face no scrutiny. Take, for example, the case of the Prophet's 1,400-year-old home in Mecca. The Saudis plan to demolish it. What makes this planned demolition worse is the fact that the home of the Prophet is to make way for a parking lot, two fifty-storey hotel towers and seven thirty-five-storey apartment blocks—a project known as the Jabal Omar Scheme—all within a stone's throw of the Grand Mosque. Had the site been destroyed by non-Muslims or some occupying western army, the entire Muslim world would have seethed with outrage. But the news of the demolition was met with a deafening silence. By November 2007, not a single Muslim country, no ayatollah, no

> mufti, no king, not even an American or Canadian imam had dared utter a word in protest. Such is the power of Saudi influence on the Muslim narrative.[7]

Ironically, one of the two main contractors listed on the project profile website is Binladen Construction, the family business of the bin Ladens.

Most Muslim governments defer to the Saudi royal family because of their wealth and the prestige they enjoy as custodians of Mecca and Medina, the two holiest sites in Islam. Yet there is no reason why the United States and other Western countries should not lean hard on the Saudis to put a halt to their proselytizing activities. Of course, this is easier said than done; the West is too heavily reliant on Saudi oil to wish to alienate the government. In addition, America and Britain sell billions of dollars' worth of arms to the Saudis. These sales go a long way in providing employment and keeping the price of their weapons systems lower than it would have been with shorter production runs. Spare parts and training contracts are other lucrative sources of revenue. Thus, Western countries have little incentive to push the Saudi royal family to curb the export of its Wahabi version of Islam around the world.

Nevertheless, a strong case can be made for a serious rethinking of the present American policy toward Saudi Arabia. The reality is that, given the high cost of maintaining literally thousands of members of the royal family as well providing billions of dollars in subsidies to placate its population, Saudi Arabia has to sell its oil. It simply does not have the option of significantly reducing output. Moreover, with millions of young Arabs demanding democratic rights across the Middle East today, Washington has more leverage with the Saudi kingdom, should President Obama choose to use it. The Saudi royal family needs the Americans to stay in power now more than ever before.

---

[7] Fatah, Tarek, *Chasing a Mirage: The Tragic Illusion of an Islamic State*, John Wiley & Sons Canada Ltd, 2008, pp. 51-52.

In the battle for hearts and minds in the Muslim world, everything else is peripheral when compared with education. In its recommendations, the 9/11 Commission accorded American assistance for education a high priority, placing particular emphasis on textbooks. Public diplomacy has also been recommended as an area in which the United States needs to increase resources.

Growing up in Karachi in the 1950s, I recall making extensive use of the USIS library to borrow books. Initially, adventure stories like the Hardy Boys series absorbed my attention, although I soon graduated to Steinbeck, Hemingway, and Faulkner. The British Council also offered a good library and was another favourite haunt. Both centres often had visiting music and theatre groups performing before full houses in a city starved of cultural activities. Now, given security concerns and budget cuts, neither country supports these basic services in Pakistan. Perhaps the biggest casualty in these fraught post-9/11 days is the virtual halt in the interaction between diplomats and the citizens of the Muslim countries to which they are accredited. Fear of terrorism has confined diplomats to their homes and compounds; as a result, very few social exchanges of the sort that were so common until the 1990s take place. Thus, the most effective kind of public diplomacy is now moribund. Journalists, artists, and bureaucrats once visited Western diplomats and invited them to their homes, enabling both sides to learn about different cultures and lifestyles. The absence of these casual social exchanges has denied both sides a deeper understanding of how their respective societies function.

Understandably, tourism has also declined in many Muslim countries. Many Western travellers once visited places like Tehran, Kabul, and Lahore to see the sites, but today foreigners are rare due to the fear of random violence. In addition to the loss of revenue this drop in traffic has caused, it has also sharply reduced chance encounters between people of different cultures, ultimately leading to growing xenophobia, with all the attendant possibilities of misunderstandings through a lack of direct communication. Young

Muslims with no direct contact with Westerners increasingly form their impressions of America and Europe from trashy TV shows and B-grade, soft porn movies. This one-dimensional view confirms the fulminations of *mullahs* and *jihadis* about the decadence of the West. Sadly, with a virtual end to normal social interaction, libraries, and cultural exchanges, there is very little space in which public diplomacy can come into its own.

Meanwhile, in the West, the growing tendency is to tar all Muslims with the same extremist brush. For many in America, Islam has become an ethnicity rather than a religion, and all Muslims are lumped together into a vast collective 'Other' that is perpetually hostile and dangerous. This view of Muslims as a monolithic, implacable horde rather than as millions of individuals living in dozens of countries with their own languages, history and culture greatly reduces the possibility of promoting understanding and meaningful social discourse.

When we demonize a people, we strip them of their identities and impose an artificial mask that's easy to hate. Indeed, the Japanese and Germans in World War II were depicted as caricatures, their supposedly evil nature exaggerated beyond all recognition. No doubt the allies were similarly demonized by Nazi Germany and the wartime Japanese government. This is the nature of propaganda in times of conflict. However, in a battle for hearts and minds, such oversimplification becomes counter-productive. For example, when an extremist can point to clear instances of Islamophobia, it becomes easier to convince a young Muslim that his negative view of the West is justified. Similarly, anti-Islamic websites are replete with imagery and words aimed at convincing visitors of the violence supposedly inherent in Islam. Both approaches trivialize and demonize the other, making rapprochement and mutual understanding more difficult.

Perhaps education is the only long-term way forward. As I write this chapter, I am struck by the fact that the brave young demonstrators carrying the banner of democracy against dictators across the Middle East have hardly voiced any anti-America slogans and have not, to the best of my knowledge, burned the Stars and Stripes anywhere from Tripoli to Bahrain. This observation finds an echo in Henry Porter's column in *The Observer*:

> There are incredible changes going on in the Arab world, with millions reaching for democracy and the values of a free society. Sacrifices are being made in Syria in the cause of freedom, which in their heroism, mock al-Qaeda's bloodthirsty ramblings and claims for martyrdom. In Tunis earlier this year, I was moved to hear young people talk about parliamentary democracy, a bicameral system, rights, freedom from random arrest and abuse, equity and transparency, fair elections.... There was absolutely no mention of the 'evil influence' of America and Israel or Bin Laden's cause.[8]

Yet, the United States and Israel have long been whipping boys across the Muslim world. So what has changed in the ongoing movement? One answer lies in the increased outlay on education in most countries experiencing the current political ferment. According to a World Bank report entitled 'The Road Not Traveled: Educational Reform in the Middle East and North Africa,'[9] countries of the region increased expenditures on education to more than 5 per cent of GDP on average between 1965 and 2003—more than almost any grouping of developing countries—which ultimately resulted in high literacy rates across the region and produced greater gender parity in education as well as a declining birth rate. To a considerable extent, what has caused the ongoing revolt is the fact that most of these countries are poorly governed, and their economies have not generated the jobs needed to absorb the growing number of educated young people entering the employment market. Thus, clearly, an educated population has higher aspirations and a lower acceptance of authoritarian rule. Families tend to be smaller, more equality exists between men and

---

[8] 'Can we ever condone the notion of state-sponsored assassination?', *The Observer*, 5/9/2011.

[9] MENA Development Report, World Bank, 2008.

women, and people are less prone to extremism and violence. As such, it is evident that the returns on investment in education are high in economic, political, and social terms.

Other predominantly Muslim countries like Bangladesh, Malaysia, and Indonesia have undergone a similar experience. Iran has more women enrolled in universities than men and has a literacy rate of over 96 per cent among those between fifteen and twenty-four. Sadly, Pakistan and Afghanistan lag far behind; whereas the Afghan government, with the help of the occupying coalition, has been making a significant investment in education, Pakistan's lack of progress remains deeply worrying and depressing. According to a UNESCO report entitled 'On the Road to Resilience: Capacity development with the Ministry of Education in Afghanistan,'[10] there are grounds for optimism in Afghanistan based on the success of the last few years. For instance, between 2001 and 2009, enrolment in primary education has increased from 0.9 million to 7 million, with the number of girls increasing from virtually zero to 37 per cent; since 2003, 5,000 schools have been built or rehabilitated. Nevertheless, much remains to be done. Indeed, 42 per cent of the school-age population remains out of school, and only 50 per cent of the schools are in usable buildings, with the rest in tents or outdoors. In addition, the Taliban conducted an average of two attacks a day on schools, teachers, and/or pupils in 2008.

Pakistan shares these physical dangers to educational institutions in its Federally Administered Tribal Areas along the border with Afghanistan. In recent years, extremists have destroyed scores of educational facilities, with special attention being paid to girls' schools and colleges. However, the similarities with Afghanistan end there: Whereas its war-ravaged neighbour is trying to educate its children, Pakistan's efforts in this crucial field are embarrassingly inadequate. For instance, its budgetary allocation for education has fallen to around 2 per cent of its GDP, and even this sum is

[10] UNESCO International Institute for Educational Planning, 2011.

not fully utilized. According to a recent report entitled 'Education Emergency Pakistan,' prepared by the Pakistan Education Task Force (2011)[11], one out of every 10 children of school-going age around the world not in a classroom is in Pakistan. The report is a damning indictment of the low priority given to education by successive governments—both military and civilian. Those who wonder at the dysfunctional nature of the Pakistani state and its endemic violence and chaos need look no further. With 7 million children out of primary school (3 million of whom will never enter a classroom), what else can we expect but poverty, crime and militancy? In a country with deep social and economic divisions, the children of the 20 per cent richest Pakistanis receive seven years more of schooling than the poorest. The poor clearly recognize the value of education. In a rural survey cited by Education Emergency, more than 85 per cent of the respondents believed that education made people better citizens, helped citizens elect better leaders, and reduced extremism, and more than 90 per cent thought education made people 'better human beings'.

Despite these well-known benefits, Pakistan's education system remains grossly under-resourced, and those staffing it are unmotivated and indifferent. For example, the Education Emergency report informs us that on any given day, 15 per cent-20 per cent of all schoolteachers are absent. 31 per cent of all men and 41 per cent of all women between the ages of fifteen and twenty-four are illiterate. Only 65 per cent of all Pakistani state schools have drinking water; 62 per cent have toilets; 61 per cent have boundary walls; and a pathetic 39 per cent have electricity.

Clearly, this is where focus is needed if the country's trajectory is to be changed. The Kerry-Lugar Act commits $1.5 billion annually to socio-economic development for five years until 2015, with the possibility of extending it for an additional five years. This is not sufficient for the task at hand, but it does give Washington leverage

---

[11] http://www.dawn.com/2011/03/09/education-emeregency-pakistan.html

with Islamabad to improve and expand the country's ramshackle educational system.

In the struggle for hearts and minds in this ideological war, education may seem a very long-term objective and irrelevant to the needs of the battlefield, but consider the fallout from a poorly educated region where an entire generation is out of step with the rest of the world. With few educational and employment opportunities, millions of young men have no option but to turn to crime or militancy to survive. Countries in Southeast Asia have shown that, given political will and resources, great progress can be made in a single generation. Both are lacking in Pakistan. The donor community, led by the United States, could link aid disbursement to specific educational goals such as school places created, teachers trained, curricula modernized, etc. Progress could be monitored by international institutions like UNESCO.

Currently, some 5 per cent of Pakistani children are educated in *madressas*, and their future is bleak. With few of these religious schools offering instruction in science, math, or English, graduates have no job prospects beyond leading the prayers in mosques. Alternatively, they join one of the large number of militant groups that have proliferated in many parts of the country. Thus far, successive Pakistani governments have avoided confronting the religious parties who run these medieval institutions and have failed to regulate what they teach. Many are hotbeds of extremism that brainwash students to hate the West and everything it stands for. Any educational reform in Pakistan would need to address this problem.

Some argue that education does not necessarily lead to a diminishing of the extremist threat, citing the example of 9/11, as most of those involved were highly educated young men. Indeed, many high-profile terrorists either killed or captured in recent years have been extremely qualified individuals, often with professional degrees. For example, Faisal Shahzad, the Times Square bomber, had an MBA and worked as a financial analyst. But for every highly educated terrorist like him, there are hundreds of poor, illiterate young men in Pakistan and Afghanistan who gladly join up to fight against the coalition and the state for as little as five dollars a day. Teenagers are recruited to become suicide bombers, with some of them being as young as thirteen. These are the foot soldiers of the jihad, and if their numbers are to be reduced, youngsters have to be given an education that opens doors other than those leading to the jihadist paradise.

In addition to the armed militancy, there is a need to reduce the rampant religiosity that informs the public narrative in many Muslim countries. In his thoughtful examination of the sources and strands of extremism, the French scholar Olivier Roy observes:

> For the Taliban, religion should have the monopoly of the symbolic sphere. Life should be entirely devoted to preparing oneself for the hereafter, and this can be done only through abiding by a strict code of conduct and ritual.[12]

Despite the emphasis in the Muslim scriptures about the need to seek knowledge, many literalists insist that the only learning we should spend our time on is available in the Qur'an, the *ahadith*, and various commentaries on the holy texts. These are some of the attitudes that need to be confronted through a modern education that addresses the issues of the twenty-first century.

To sum up, the broader war against obscurantism and global jihad needs more than a robust military response. In a sense, this is probably the easier part of the struggle. The ideological battle for hearts and minds is more complex and demands a nuanced and multidimensional response. Thus far, it is not evident that we have a handle on this aspect of the struggle that lies ahead.

---

[12] Roy, Olivier, *Globalised Islam: The Search for a New Ummah*, Pakistan edition published by Alhamra Publishing through an agreement with Hurst & Co. Ltd, 2004, p. 261. First published in France as *L'Islam mondialise*, Editions du Soleil, 2002.

11

Pakistan's Red Lines

One morning in June 2011, a little girl jumped out of a car and ran desperately toward a security check post in Darra Islam in Pakistan's remote northwest district of Lower Dir. Suhana was nine years old, and had been kidnapped the day before by two burqa-clad women and two armed men on her way to school and drugged. When she came to, she was told she would be taken near a check post where she was to detonate a suicide vest. When the car parked a hundred yards or so from the target, the kidnappers struggled to fit on the explosive vest to Suhana's frail body. In the confusion, she jumped out and ran towards the security staff, who took her into custody. The kidnappers drove off, no doubt to launch other similar attacks.

Even in Pakistan, a country wracked by years of escalating terror attacks, this attempt was a new low. But children have been used repeatedly in suicide attacks because they are more likely to avoid suspicion.

Indeed, recruiting children to act as suicide bombers has become something of a cottage industry. Baitullah Mehsud, a Pakistani Taliban leader killed in a drone attack in 2009, boasted that suicide bombers were his 'atom bombs' that could counter the American nuclear arsenal. He is reputed to have trained many children in a school run in his area, and sold them to other terrorist groups for prices ranging between $6,000 and $12,000.

In 2008, the Pakistan army launched an offensive against Mehsud's stronghold in South Waziristan. Major General Tariq

Khan, the officer commanding the operation, told journalists that a school in the village was 'like a factory and it had been recruiting nine-to twelve-year old boys and turning them into suicide bombers...' The troops also found a DVD showing children being trained.[1]

Gul goes on to recount one specific case:

> "One young suicide bomber from Dera Ismail Khan who collapsed as he approached a paramilitary camp on the outskirts of Swat in September [2008], recounted the kind of fairy tales the trainers spun to entice children into becoming suicide bombers. 'My ustad [teacher] told me I would rocket into paradise once I pressed the button', the boy explained, pointing to the trigger of the suicide jacket he had wrapped around his waist. A security official recalled that when the boy was taken to a military hospital for a check-up, he was visibly moved by the sight of the nurses dressed in white. He blurted out: 'My ustad had promised me *hoors* [the lovely virgins promised to good Muslims in heaven] like these once I reached paradise'.[2]

This story would have been laughable if it hadn't been so pathetic: teenaged boys with little or no education, no prospects and no money, being promised a sensual, eternal paradise by hardened, cynical killers. And apart from the simple kids who fall for these promises of everlasting bliss, there are many others who are either kidnapped or persuaded by stirring tales of daring battles against the hated American invaders and their Pakistani toadies.

These, then, are the human bombs devastating targets across Pakistan. Increasingly, they are used to attack security forces manning check posts which they approach unsuspected before blowing themselves up. Over the last decade, some 5,000 Pakistani

---

[1] Cited by Ijaz Gul in *The Al Qaeda Connection*, by Penguin India, 2009, p. 137.

[2] Ijaz Gul, op. cit.

security personnel have been killed by terrorists, together with over 30,000 civilians.

Generally, more experienced and battle-hardened militants are used to attack well-guarded military targets. In October 2009, an assault took place that shocked even a country that had witnessed a decade of bloodletting committed by jihadists. Gunmen in army uniforms in a van with military markings passed unchallenged through one check post guarding the Pakistani army's General Headquarters, or GHQ, in a busy, commercial part of Rawalpindi, about fifteen miles from Islamabad. As it neared the gates, several armed gunmen jumped out, and shot the guards. Soldiers manning watchtowers opened fire, killing three of the terrorists, and wounding one. Other gunmen, also in army uniforms, followed and killed their injured companion. This confused the guards who assumed that the newcomers were army reinforcements, and they stopped firing as the militants ran through the open gate.

Inside, the assailants quickly took thirty-nine officers and civilians hostage, dividing them into two groups guarded by militants wearing suicide vests. Zahid Hussain, the veteran Pakistani journalist who has pieced together a detailed account of the attack in his meticulously researched book *The Scorpion's Tail*, writes:

> The gunmen verbally abused the hostages and accused them of fighting America's war and killing its own people. They spoke partly in English, indicating that they were well educated.[3]

The attackers presented a list of demands for the release of the hostages that included freeing a hundred or so Pakistani and Afghan militants being held by security forces. Negotiations dragged on until commandos stormed the building and killed the assailants, but not before one of them managed to detonate his

---

[3] Hussain, Zahid, *The Scorpion's Tail*, Free Press, 2010, p. 164.

suicide belt. Nineteen people were killed in this incident, including nine soldiers and eight assailants.

This audacious assault on the army's holy of holies was deeply embarrassing for Pakistan's powerful generals. But it was also very disturbing on another level: it revealed that the attackers had more than a passing knowledge of military procedures as well as their target's layout. The planning and execution of the attack bore the hallmark of a highly trained commando unit. Here was clear evidence that some serving or retired military personnel had passed on information to the jihadists. Another troubling aspect of the operation surfaced when investigators established that it had been carried out by different groups from different parts of the country who were coordinating their attacks in an unprecedented manner.

One of the international community's worst nightmares is that nuclear weapons might fall into the hands of terrorists. Nowhere is this scenario more likely than in Pakistan. Although the army has a sophisticated command and control system in place, and components of Pakistan's nuclear arsenal are widely and secretly dispersed, many still fret about terrorists breaching security with the help of sympathizers within the armed forces. These fears were re-awakened when on May 20, 2011, less than three weeks after the Abbottabad operation that killed Osama bin Laden, the Mehran naval base in Karachi, Pakistan's biggest city, was attacked by six terrorists. With military precision, they scaled the wall, cutting through the barbed wire at a blind spot between security cameras. Once inside the perimeter, they made their way to where two new US-supplied Orion P3C maritime surveillance aircraft worth $36 million each were parked. There, they destroyed the planes with rocket-propelled grenades, and then took cover in nearby buildings. From here, they held off security forces for over sixteen hours, killing a dozen before they were finally cut down. During the fighting, they refused to accept several offers to surrender. Reportedly, two of the assailants escaped.

During a briefing to Pakistan's National Assembly, the deputy naval chief confirmed what the whole world suspected: the attackers had inside help. In a startling exclusive story carried by *Asia Times Online* on May 27, investigative reporter Saleem Shahzad disclosed that the attack had been in retaliation for a number of arrests of suspected extremists within the navy's ranks. Shahzad wrote:

> Within a week [of Osama bin Laden's death], insiders at PNS Mehran [naval base] provided maps, pictures of different exit and entry routes taken in daylight and at night, the location of hangers and details of likely reaction from external security forces.
> As a result, the militants were able to enter the heavily guarded facility where one group targeted the aircraft, a second group took on the first strike force and the third finally escaped with the others providing covering fire. Those who stayed behind were killed.

Shahzad promised a follow-up story, but tragically, he was killed within days of the appearance of this report. His murder is a telling comment on the nexus between extremists and Pakistan's armed forces that Shahzad had reported on. Picked up in Islamabad in the early evening while on his way to a TV studio where he was due for a chat show, his body was discovered two days later 60 miles from Islamabad. A few days before his disappearance and death, he had emailed Ali Dayan Hassan, senior researcher for Human Rights Watch in Pakistan, asking him to release the contents of his letter in case anything happened to him. He mentioned a veiled threat he had received when summoned to the ISI, Pakistan's notorious military intelligence agency, where he was asked to reveal his sources for an earlier story.

When his body was found, it bore bruises and torture marks. It is possible that his kidnappers wanted to work him over as a warning, but the beating got out of hand. In any case, the crime bore the fingerprints of spooks who have carried out similar acts of thuggery in the past. Within days of the murder, Admiral Mullen, the US joint chief of staff, said the US government had credible information that Shahzad's killing had been officially sanctioned. This serious charge was strongly denied by the Pakistani government, but grave suspicions about its involvement linger.

Just a few days later, Waqar Kayani, a journalist working for the *Guardian*, was beaten up in broad daylight in Islamabad by men wearing police uniforms. Two days previously, he had revealed in his London-based newspaper how he had been kidnapped and tortured by operatives from the Intelligence Bureau a year earlier. Umar Cheema, a reporter for *The News*, went public on how he had been abducted in Islamabad, tortured and sodomized in 2010, blaming the ISI. While the government has denied any involvement, these acts of violence have made Pakistan one of the most dangerous countries in the world for journalists.

Daniel Pearl, the American *Wall Street Journal* reporter who was kidnapped and brutally murdered by a jihadist group in Karachi in 2002, was investigating possible links between Richard Reid, the so-called Shoe Bomber, and militant Islamist groups in Pakistan with ties to the ISI. After his death, the French writer Bernard-Henri Levy travelled to Pakistan to research the crime, and wrote the book *Who Killed Daniel Pearl?* His conclusion was that Pearl had stumbled across ties between the ISI and certain terrorist groups, and that's why he was silenced. While there is no hard evidence to back this claim, it only adds to the growing body of allegations, made by foreigners and Pakistanis alike, of a nexus between certain militant groups, including the notorious Haqqani group active in Afghanistan, and elements within the ISI. (As an aside, I corresponded with Pearl's father shortly after his tragic death, and was deeply touched to learn that the Pearl family had set up a foundation in the journalist's name. One of the aims of the Daniel Pearl Foundation is to sponsor young Pakistani journalists for training in the US.)

This alleged link between the ISI and various extremist groups gained widespread currency and credibility with the discovery of Osama bin Laden in Abbottabad, a military town less than a hundred miles from Islamabad. When it emerged that the Al Qaeda chief and mastermind behind the 9/11 attacks had been living in his large, scruffy compound for over five years, many in America and elsewhere asked how it was possible for a powerful intelligence agency like the ISI to be unaware of his presence for such a long time when he lived a few hundred yards from Pakistan's elite military academy. Deeply humiliated not just by bin Laden's extended presence on Pakistani soil, but also by the undetected and unchallenged SEAL raid, the country's military high command went into deep denial. In the event, they pleaded ignorance rather than connivance, and suffered the unaccustomed ignominy of scorn and abuse heaped on them by millions of Pakistanis.

This was something new for Pakistan's all-powerful military that, as the country's most organized and disciplined institution, is used to calling the shots, whether ruling directly or not. In his perceptive and penetrating exploration of Pakistan, its history, institutions and society, Anatol Lieven writes about the army:

> Commitment to the army, and to the unity and discipline of the army, is drilled into every officer and soldier from the first hour of their joining the military. Together with the material rewards of loyal service, it constitutes a very powerful obstacle to any thought of a coup from below, which would by definition...destroy it and the country altogether. Every military coup in Pakistan has therefore been carried out by the chief of the army staff of the time...Islamist conspiracies by junior officers against their superiors (of which there have been two over the past generation) have been penetrated and smashed by Military Intelligence.
>
> Military morale has come under unprecedented strain from the war in Afghanistan and the very widespread feeling among ordinary Pakistanis that the military have become servants of the Americans. So far, however, discipline has held, and in my view will continue to do so unless the US does something that ordinary soldiers would see as a direct affront to their honour.[4]

Immediately following the Abbottabad raid, the army launched a damage-control exercise to distance itself from the United States.

---

[4] Lieven, Anatol, *Pakistan: A Hard Country*, Penguin Books, 2010, p. 163

It demanded that American instructors teaching anti-insurgency tactics to the Frontier Corps be withdrawn, and insisted on the pull-out of a number of CIA operatives from Pakistan. Publicly, it complained that the Americans were not sharing intelligence with their Pakistani counterparts. After the militant raid launched against the naval base in Karachi just weeks after Abbottabad, there were more red faces among the powerful military establishment. Things did not improve when leaked stories in the American media accused the ISI of alerting militants when the CIA passed on photographs of two bomb-making factories in the tribal areas. When Pakistani troops arrived there twenty-four hours later, they found the factories had been abandoned very recently.

The perception in Pakistan and among many of its soldiers that the high command is toeing the American line to the detriment of national interest is damaging the army's reluctantly pro-American leadership. We may indeed be heading toward the point of no return Lieven wrote about when the highly disciplined Pakistani army might crack. In retaliation for the expulsion of US army trainers and CIA operatives, Washington announced that it was withholding $800 million out of its annual military assistance. This merely confirmed the widely-held view in broad sections of the Pakistan military and the media that the Americans are fickle allies. However, it is unlikely that the tipping point in US-Pak relations has arrived yet. As Simon Tisdall writes in the *Guardian*:

> Like some long-married couples, the US and Pakistan are chronic bickerers. Their latest spat, over Washington's decision to withhold $800 million in military aid, is more serious than usual, but will blow over in time. The bottom line for both partners is they need each other more than they dislike each other.
>
> ...Two basic faultlines underlie frictions. One is the American perception that Pakistan is not co-operating fully in its 'war on terror' and is playing a double game by maintaining links to selected Afghan Taliban and home-grown terror groups.

> The other is the Pakistani perception that Pakistan has been placed in the invidious position of fighting America's wars for it, and has suffered disproportionately as a result.[5]

Many Americans in and out of the administration simply do not understand that Pakistan and the United States do not have identical priorities and perceptions in the Afghan conflict. American generals and politicians, understandably enough, want the Pakistan army to go after elements, including the Haqqani network, that conduct cross-border incursions to attack NATO troops in Afghanistan. But Pakistani generals already have their hands full dealing with home-grown militant outfits that are spreading murder and mayhem across the country. The last thing they need is fierce retaliation from the powerful Haqqani group. From Pakistan's perspective, these militants do not pose a threat to Pakistan, and might well prove to be a trump card when western forces pull out in 2014, as announced by President Obama. The biggest nightmare facing Pakistan's defense planners is an alliance between India and a pro-India Afghanistan in the aftermath of NATO's withdrawal from the region. In the eyes of the country's defense establishment, this encirclement would put Pakistan in an untenable situation. Of course, this threat perception is based on the premise that India is Pakistan's eternal and existential enemy, forever plotting to destabilize and disintegrate its smaller neighbour. This conviction has been drummed into successive generations of Pakistan's officers and soldiers, and is an integral part of Pakistan's strategic doctrine.

This mindset among Pakistan's military explains the decades of Islamization of its rank and file. When I joined the civil service, our training included a two-month stint with an army regiment. In their wisdom, Pakistan's ruling generals in the late 1960s decided that a dose of military discipline would make us better civil servants. On a field exercise in Balochistan one evening, I was chatting with

---

[5] *Guardian*; 12 July 2011

the commanding officer, an intelligent, well-read colonel. At the time, tensions with India were high, as they so often are. I asked the officer how the Pakistan army could take on a much bigger Indian army. I will never forget his reply: in all seriousness, he said that one Muslim was equal to five Hindu soldiers, and this would redress the military imbalance between the two countries. This religious zeal has only grown with time. Under General Zia's military rule between 1977 and 1988, not only the army but all of Pakistani society was subjected to an intense Islamization that has created the country's deeply conservative mindset. In both the military and the civil service, promotions have been made contingent on an officer's outward display of Islamic belief.

But it's not just the army in Pakistan that's being deeply Islamized: in January 2011, Salman Taseer, Governor of Punjab, the country's biggest province, was gunned down in broad daylight in Islamabad. His cold-blooded killer was Mumtaz Qadri, a police constable who was on the governor's security team. Apparently, he told his colleagues he was going to commit the murder before he fired thirty shots at Taseer as he emerged from a coffee shop. Salman Taseer was an old friend, and I mourned his death. But I was even more shocked by the widespread reaction: lawyers at the courtroom where the murderer was charged showered him with rose petals, and offered to defend him free of charge. A couple of years ago, these same lawyers had led street protests for judicial independence that toppled General Musharraf. Many people in Pakistan justified Qadri's crime because Salman Taseer had openly supported a Christian victim of Pakistan's draconian blasphemy laws that have terrorized so many non-Muslims.

Arabic and Islamic studies were made compulsory in all state and private schools under Zia. So much so that years ago, my son Shakir, then eight years old, returned from school one day and announced he had been punished in his Islamic studies class. The reason turned out to be that when asked what Islam taught us, Shakir had innocently answered: 'Arabic.'

The Pakistan military today remains deeply devout. Thus, it had little difficulty using religion as a recruitment tool to rally Muslims around the world to fight the Soviets in Afghanistan during the 1980s. After the Red Army was defeated, many Pakistani officers from the ISI and the regular army retained their ties with the mujahideen they had armed and trained. The Haqqani group was one such outfit. Today, it is one of the most powerful elements in the Afghan insurgency.

After the Soviet pullout from Afghanistan in 1988, the ISI turned its sights toward Kashmir, where a popular uprising had broken out against Indian rule. Trained terrorists were soon being infiltrated into Indian Kashmir to join the fight. A few years later in Afghanistan, the Pakistan military began advising and arming a hitherto unknown group who called themselves the Taliban. The Arabic word is the plural of 'talib,' or student. Normally, it is used for students at religious seminaries, and in this case described a group of idealistic young Afghans who had studied in Pakistani *madressas* and many had fought the Soviets. Now they sought to end the state of anarchy that was further destroying their war-torn country caught up in a vicious civil war in which rival warlords battled for power. In Pakistan's military calculation, such a group might restore peace, and would be amenable to dictation from Islamabad.

But the Pakistan military's game of footsies with Islamic militant groups, including the Taliban, ended after 9/11 following George W. Bush's famous ultimatum of 'Either you are with us, or you are against us.' Outwardly, at least, Pakistan severed its links with these groups, but doubts have lingered whether the ISI has indeed cut off its relationship with the militants it had armed and nurtured. Foreign generals and politicians whose troops are fighting in Afghanistan have repeatedly alleged that the ISI continues to maintain ties with several terrorist groups. Recently, a *New York Times*[6] report quoted an unnamed militant commander as

[6] 4 July 2011

asserting unequivocally that retired army and intelligence officers were continuing to support jihadist groups. Carlotta Gall, quoting a prominent former militant commander, says:

> The Pakistani military continues to nurture a broad range of militant groups as part of a three-decade strategy of using proxies against its neighbors and American forces in Afghanistan...The former commander said he was supported by the Pakistani military for 15 years as a fighter, leader and trainer of insurgents until he quit a few years ago....Militant groups like Lashkar-e-Taiba, Harkat-ul-Mujahideen and Hizbul Mujahideen, are run by religious leaders, with the Pakistani military providing training, strategic planning and protection. The system was still functioning, he said.

The ex-militant commander alleged that the Pakistani military and the ISI continue to support groups they could use against its arch-enemy, India, especially over the disputed Kashmir valley. He went on to say: 'Although the military has lost control of many of the firebrand fighters, and has little control over the foreign fighters in the tribal areas who belong to Al Qaeda...it was reluctant to move against them...'

This seeming contradiction between harbouring certain terrorists, and yet suffering thousands of casualties fighting others, brings us to the heart of the contradiction in which Pakistan's military establishment finds itself. By attempting to cherry-pick between jihadis who are fighting exclusively in Afghanistan, and the ones who are seeking to destabilize the Pakistani state, defence planners overlook the fact that all too often these groups are operating under a loose but common umbrella, and frequently cooperate.

As we have seen, the military has been extensively and deeply Islamized, and now has many officers and soldiers sympathetic to the Taliban among its ranks. For the high command, it is becoming increasingly difficult to balance the demands of fighting as an American ally, and the institutional and ideological constraints of waging war against fellow Muslims on Washington's behest. But the tricky compromise of fighting some extremists and not others is angering both the Americans and the jihadists. Hence the constant American refrain to 'do more,' as well as the unrelenting militant attacks against Pakistani security forces. Having suffered more casualties in the ongoing war than the combined NATO forces in Afghanistan, Pakistani soldiers are understandably annoyed when they are taunted with the charge that they aren't doing enough. But these frictions will continue as long as there is so little understanding of each other's strategic and political positions.

In the toxic mix of paranoia, denial and extremism that prevails across Pakistan today, it is not easy to promote clarity and objectivity. In an interview with *Newsline*, a trail-blazing Pakistani investigative monthly magazine, Hamid Gul, the retired lieutenant-general we have met before, captures this confusion in all its absurdity. Responding to a question about the safety of Pakistan's nuclear arsenal in the wake of the militant attack on a naval base in Karachi, Gul replied:

> I am convinced the war on terror is meant to destabilise Pakistan, destroy it economically and then achieve the objective of giving India the role of regional superpower. Washington successfully managed to install the rulers of its choice in Pakistan at a stage when Pakistan was at the crossroads. [Pakistani president] Asif Zardari and company are working for completing the US agenda at Pakistan's cost. When Asif Zardari pronounces India is not Pakistan's enemy, he actually furthers the US agenda of changing the Pakistani mindset...[7]

Apart from not saying a single word about the security of Pakistan's nuclear arsenal, Gul proceeds to mouth the same conspiracy theory that is often repeated in drawing rooms as well as military messes across Pakistan. Fortunately, the same issue of *Newsline* also gives us the views of an eminently rational and well-informed scholar. Stephen Cohen, senior fellow at the Brookings

---

[7] *Newsline*; Karachi; June 2011

Institution, and author of a ground-breaking study of the Pakistan army, was interviewed by the magazine's Sairah Irshad Khan. According to him, 'some sections of the army are even more anti-American than they are anti-India.' Cohen went on to say that the army's use of militant Islam dates back to 1971 when it formed Islamist paramilitary groups in East Pakistan to counter freedom fighters struggling for independence. He concluded by saying: 'This collaboration became more specialised during [General] Zia's government, both in Kashmir and Afghanistan. Now it is a full-fledged strategic alliance for the Pakistan military.'[8]

This, then, is the deeply Islamized but highly professional army that the US-led coalition in Afghanistan is relying on to guard its flanks. And as we have seen, the Pakistan army has its own agenda based on its own threat perceptions. Over the years, it has expanded its role from being the protector of the country's physical borders to the guardianship of Pakistan's ideology. Of course, nobody has been able to agree on exactly what this ideology actually is. But just as the Turkish army was sucked into politics by insisting on enforcing Mustafa Kemal Pasha's secular vision on the country, so too has the Pakistani army come to play an ever-expanding role in the country's murky politics. This, in turn, has led it into becoming a major player in industry, real estate and finance. Through its pension funds and welfare trusts, it now occupies the strategic heights of Pakistan's economy. These political and economic activities have, over time, eroded the professional edge of senior officers, apart from bringing them into disrepute for repeatedly interfering in the political process, and not allowing institutions to take root.

For all its flaws, however, the Pakistani army is the only game in town. Whether it likes it or not, the United States has little choice but to engage with it, and eliminate as much friction from the relationship as it can. For Pakistan's military establishment, modern American military equipment is essential to maintain even

[8] *Newsline*; Karachi; op cit.

a degree of credibility against India's giant war machine. And US engagement in the region is viewed as crucial to ward off the perceived Indian threat. So the two countries and the two militaries are stuck: unable to live with each other, but equally unable to live apart.

Nothing has shaken the trust between the Pakistan and US militaries as the death of 24 Pakistani soldiers at two security check-posts on the unmarked Pak-Afghan border on 27 November 2011. On a dark night, a joint US-Afghan patrol was conducting an operation in a village in Kunar province a hundred yards or so inside Afghanistan. When Pakistani troops at the small camp saw muzzle flashes and heard gunfire, they apparently assumed they were under attack from militants, and opened fire according to a US enquiry report. The Americans on the other side of the border assumed they were being attacked and responded. They also called in air support. During the ensuing firefight – which spread to a near-by border post – 24 Pakistani soldiers were killed and several others wounded.

As news of the incident broke the next day, there was a firestorm in the Pakistani media. While the American government expressed its regrets, it stopped short of an apology, promising an enquiry. The Pakistani reaction was less measured: almost immediately, the Pakistan army claimed its soldiers had been deliberately targeted. The government halted the hundreds of container trucks carrying supplies to NATO forces from Pakistani ports, causing a huge backlog with vehicles being stranded at the border as well as other points close to Karachi. Furthermore, Islamabad declared it would not send a delegation to the Afghan security conference being held in Bonn the following week. Finally, the army announced that it would not participate in the American enquiry into the deadly incident.

The American report that was leaked to the press in December revealed a string of errors of judgment and procedures. But the most glaring cause it revealed was the lack of trust on both sides. The Americans, fearing their patrol's movement would be leaked to the Taliban if they informed their Pakistani counterparts along the border, kept Pakistan in the dark. And the Pakistani side had apparently not revealed the exact location of their border posts while reporting the initial attack. Even when the Americans became aware that they were firing on Pakistani troops, it took 45 minutes for word to reach higher command, and for orders to halt firing to filter down to the units involved. The report concluded that the American firing was initially triggered by firing from the Pakistani side, a charge Islamabad denies.

Whatever happened that night, one thing is clear: the entire incident was caused by a lack of trust that has bedevilled relations between the two sides almost since the beginning of the war. Indeed, 2011 has been a terrible year for Pak-US relations, beginning with the Raymond Davis affair in January when the CIA contractor gunned down two young Pakistanis in broad daylight on a Lahore street. In this case, the two governments were at loggerhead for weeks as the American claimed diplomatic immunity. Finally, he was released after the payment of blood money to the families of the deceased, much to the fury of the Pakistani public and the media who were baying for his blood. Then came the 2 May SEAL raid that killed Osama bin Laden, and raised serious questions about the Pakistan military's complicity or incompetence. For the first time in years, Pakistani generals were publicly accused of not protecting the country's borders, and failing to stop the Americans. People also asked how it was possible that the Al-Qaeda leader had lived fairly openly in Abbotabad, a garrison town deep inside Pakistan, without the army being aware of his presence for five years. Stung and humiliated, Pakistani generals lashed out at the Americans for keeping them out of the loop. Cooperation with the CIA and the Pentagon was sharply reduced, and scores of US intelligence and military personnel were sent packing.

The November incident was the third body blow to an already fragile relationship in one year. Although both sides need each other as the Afghan endgame approaches, there is an increasing degree of prickliness evident. The US Congress has passed a bill making the release of $700 million in military support payment conditional on certification from the secretaries of state and defense that Pakistan is acting to deny the availability of chemical fertilizer to the Taliban. This nitrogen-based substance has been widely used in Afghanistan to make simple but deadly Improvised Explosive Devices (IEDs), and the Americans have been pressing Pakistan to restrict sales. However, as it is used by thousands of farmers, there is no quick fix to the problem.

The reaction to the incident among senior levels of the Pakistan army indicates the almost pathological hatred for America that has taken root in an institution that is simultaneously dependent on Washington for much of its military hardware. Even though there has been some diversification of arms procurement, the reality is that only American weapons systems have the technological edge Pakistan needs. Despite this, anti-Americanism is rife in military messes across the country. And given the number of journalists on the ISI and MI (Military Intelligence) payroll, this sentiment has been widely disseminated through the media. But thus far, hotheads in uniform are not in charge, a danger that has figured widely in the western media.

In his long, detailed study of the Pakistan army, Shuja Nawaz, a Washington-based writer, concludes:

> While the army remains a conservative institution at heart, it is not yet a breeding ground for large numbers of radical Islamists that many fear...[9]

But it doesn't take more than a handful of officers with extremist views to cause havoc. All too often, junior officers have used their training and knowledge of weapons and tactics to attack the Pakistani state. Saleem Shahzad, the slain journalist, had won worldwide respect for his coverage of some of the most notorious jihadist groups. In his posthumously published book

---

[9] Nawaz, Shuja; *Crossed Swords: Pakistan, its army, and the wars within*; Oxford University Press; 2008, p. 585

Inside Al-Qaeda and the Taliban, he tracks the activities of two brothers, Khurram and Haroon, the former a captain and the latter a major in the Pakistan army, who resigned their commissions after 9/11 to join militant groups. Khurram was killed in Afghanistan's Helmand province, but Haroon was soon advising Al Qaeda and the Taliban on strategy. After researching the tactics used by the Vietcong against US forces in Vietnam, as well as the methods employed by the Tamil Tigers in Sri Lanka, Haroon gave a presentation to Al Qaeda commanders in North Waziristan, in Pakistan's tribal areas:

> He advocated that a start be made in the Afghan provinces of Khost, Paktia, and Paktika, with a three-pronged...offensive strategy, similar to the one that General Giap had used in North Vietnam in the 1960s to defeat the United States...Haroon emphasized that the central idea of General Giap's strategy was to catch the enemy by surprise, and he placed emphasis on the training of select warriors for special operations...[10]

Whether this advice had any impact on the battlefield or not, the fact that an experienced Pakistani officer was giving it at all is a matter for concern. According to Shahzad, Haroon was the brains behind the Mumbai attack in November 2008, when a handful of militants from the Pakistan-based Lashkar-e-Taiba (LeT), attacked a number of hotels and public places in India's commercial capital, and killed over 160 innocent civilians in a bloody operation lasting some 68 hours.

Over the years, Washington has repeatedly accused Pakistan's ISI of supporting extremists in Pakistan and Afghanistan, a charge that has been strongly refuted by Islamabad. However, there is now considerable evidence to suggest that a number of retired officers continue to play an active role in advising various terrorist groups. After years of working closely with jihadis, many have

---

[10] Shahzad, Syed Saleem, *Inside Al-Qaeda and the Taliban: Beyond Bin Laden and 9/11*, Pluto Press, 2011, p. 88.

been converted to their extremist ideology. As they retain links with colleagues still in their old outfit, they get information from sympathizers that they then pass on to their jihadi friends. This gives the Pakistan military deniability, while allowing them to continue maintaining unofficial links with the militant groups that are fighting western forces in Afghanistan.

These shadowy links between serving and retired officers are virtually impossible to trace or break. Tying them together is the extremist salafist branch of Islam that connects them to the anti-American jihad. In the preface to his book, Shahzad wrote:

> After meeting them [three Pakistan army officers who had resigned their commissions to join the jihad] I began to see the world of Al-Qaeda from an entirely new perspective—that of unmeasured energy emerging purely on the strength of conviction and human ingenuity against the sophisticated might of advanced technology to provoke the United States...with 9/11. The aim was to draw the United States to fight in a region where people live in the stone age...
>
> Al-Qaeda's first objective was to win the war against the West in Afghanistan. Its next objective was to move on to have the fighting extend all the way from Central Asia to Bangladesh to exhaust the superpower's resources, before bringing it to the field in the Middle East for the final battles to revive the Muslim political order under the Caliphate, which would then lead to the liberation of all Muslim territories.
>
> This book is written at the critical juncture when the defeat of the western coalition is imminent. Some commentators have painted the dreaded picture of a nuclear-armed Al-Qaeda supported by Muslim states threatening the world, but after many years of fighting, what stands out above all else is Al-Qaeda's arsenal is not its weaponry, but its uncanny ability to exploit unfolding events to engineer the collapse of its high-tech enemies.[11]

---

[11] Shahzad, Syed Saleem, op cit

While Shahzad was a remarkably well-informed journalist with unrivalled contacts among the Taliban and Al Qaeda, he was perhaps too close to the combatants to see the wider picture. His book, while an incisive study of the war in the AfPak theatre, does not factor in the changes taking place in the Middle East and North Africa. His nostrils were too full of the whiff of cordite to catch the sweeter smell of the Arab Spring.

In the killing fields of Pakistan's tribal areas and the badlands of Afghanistan, the war is going badly for the American-led coalition. Despite its huge technological edge, NATO has been fought to a draw, and one that is basically unsustainable. Ten years and hundreds of billions of dollars after the start of the war, the best the United States can do is to seek an exit from a country that has been a graveyard of other empires. Any exit will do for a proud nation that is exhausted from fighting a war whose purpose is increasingly unclear. A battered economy adds impetus to the increasingly popular call to bring the troops back home.

For any hope of leaving behind an Afghanistan where the Taliban do not sweep back to power within weeks of NATO's departure, Pakistan's cooperation is crucial. As we have seen, Pakistan's help is neither unconditional nor free of deception. While US troops can withdraw from Afghanistan at will, Pakistan has no such option: geography, history and culture bind the two neighbours together. The best Washington and Islamabad can do is to see how far their interests overlap, and cooperate to this extent without having unrealistic expectations of each other. Many in the American administration and the media complain that Pakistan is not doing enough to justify the billions in military aid it has received. But the Pakistan army deeply resents the implication that it is a mercenary army that would act against the national interest for the sake of American military assistance. These perceptions continue to cause ructions in the relationship, threatening to lead to outright rupture.

Many observers have made the point that, in global terms, Pakistan is far more important than Afghanistan. With a population of around 180 million and a substantial nuclear arsenal, the country is vital to regional and international stability. As Anatol Lieven writes:

> In the short-term, of course, western policy towards Pakistan will be shaped by developments in Afghanistan, but this policy should not be dictated by those developments. For Pakistan is in the end a great deal more important and potentially dangerous than Afghanistan. Whatever strategy the US ends up adopting in Afghanistan, Pakistan will be critical to its success. Quite apart from Islamabad's strategic calculations, this is made inevitable by the fact that more than half of the Pathan ethnicity [the group that the vast majority of the Taliban are drawn from] lives in Pakistan, while maintaining a strong interest in what happens to the Pathans on the other side of the Durand Line.[12]
>
> Whatever happens, Pakistan will therefore insist both that Pathans are strongly represented in any Afghan regime, and that Islamabad has a share of influence in Afghanistan, at least to the point where other countries – meaning above all India – cannot use Afghanistan as a base from which to threaten Pakistan.[13]

So it is important to see Pakistan's red lines, and understand the limits of its army's cooperation. It is also essential to view the country's defence and intelligence services in the context of the larger, increasingly Islamized Pakistani society. Only a nuanced understanding will lead to a more mature, substantive relationship.

---

[12] The boundary drawn by the British to separate Afghanistan and British India in 1892

[13] Lieven, Anatol, *Pakistan: A Hard Country*, p. 477.

12

Grounds for Hope in the Arab Spring

When I began writing this book in the summer of 2010, I was deeply pessimistic about the future of the relations between the Muslim world and the West. Osama bin Laden was very much alive, supposedly plotting more mayhem from his hideout in Pakistan's tribal areas. The Taliban were inflicting increasing casualties on the American-led coalition in Afghanistan. Iraq's internal power struggle seemed unending. Arab dictators and assorted kings had an iron grip on their peoples' jugulars. And the poisonous deadlock between Israel and the Palestinians seemed no closer to a solution. If anything, the situation across much of the Muslim world was frozen in a time warp

With no good news in sight, I was expecting to conclude this book on a rather gloomy note. Looking ahead at the time, I could only see a steady increase in support for the forces of darkness as more and more unemployed young Muslims—disenchanted with American policies that supported the rulers who oppressed them—answered the call of global jihad. I could foresee a backlash building up in America and Europe against Islam and Muslim immigrants as terrorist attacks provoked increasing hostility among the host communities. This Islamophobia (which is already evident in some Western cities) would feed into the anti-West narrative that had taken hold in many Muslims. This mutual animosity would ratchet up the sense of sullen bitterness and anger that, according to many opinion polls, characterized Muslim attitudes toward the West.

This, broadly speaking, was how I saw the future of the interaction between the West and the Islamic world. Indeed, I was perilously close to echoing aspects of Samuel Huntington's Clash of Civilizations thesis. Then, something totally unexpected and almost miraculous happened. On 17 December 2010, a Tunisian vegetable peddler named Mohamed Bouazizi in the town of Sidi Bouzid set himself on fire to protest against official highhandedness. The 26-year-old man's self-immolation was the spark that lit the fuse to the widespread revolt that broke out across North Africa and the Middle East. Four weeks later, President Zine al-Abidine Ben Ali, the dictator who had ruled Tunisia for twenty-three years, fled to exile in Saudi Arabia. The country's Jasmine Revolution had succeeded in getting rid of a despot who had enriched himself while ruling with an iron hand. Scenes of exultant crowds were beamed across the world, inspiring millions of Muslims across the region.

Egypt was the next country to get rid of a dictator who had ruled for decades. Hosni Mubarak, long Washington's man in Cairo, seemed as permanently installed as the Sphinx. Having assumed power after the assassination of Anwar Sadat in 1981, Egypt's strongman was set to transfer power to his son as his health worsened. Throughout his long career as president, Mubarak had rigged elections while giving his Western supporters the semblance of running a democracy. But this sham was wearing thin. Opponents at home and abroad regularly exposed the massive human rights violations that were a feature of Mubarak's rule. Many suspected terrorists were allegedly rendered to Egypt's intelligence services by the CIA for interrogation, a euphemism for torture.

When hundreds of thousands of demonstrators flooded Cairo's famous Tahrir Square, few expected them to succeed against a well-entrenched dictatorship that had successfully crushed all dissent. But as the world watched in awe and admiration, young men and women kept coming to the square, or just camped there in unprecedented numbers. Unarmed and disorganized, they faced police bullets and batons every day. Arab dictators—as well as the rest of the world—expected a bloodbath, with the army cracking down to preserve its power. But in the event, for reasons of self-preservation, the generals maintained a strict neutrality, and left the police to respond to the challenge. Demoralized and poorly directed, the police proved ineffective when faced with thousands of peaceful Egyptians. Finally prodded by the US, Mubarak resigned and is now being tried, along with his two sons.

If the changes in Tunisia were a portent of things to come, Cairo's Tahrir Square became a beacon for Arabs across the region. Demonstrators poured into the streets of Yemen, Libya, Bahrain and Syria. Morocco, Jordan and Saudi Arabia witnessed crowds protesting in unprecedented numbers. Generally peaceful, these young Arabs were fed up with living under dictators who allowed no individual freedoms and who were both corrupt and incompetent. With high unemployment and constant bullying from the minions of the state, people had little to lose and, inspired by the successes of uprisings in Tunisia and Egypt, they decided to go for broke in a mass rebellion that threatens to transform the political landscape of the Middle East and North Africa. In Libya, a full-fledged civil war has ended with the demise of Colonel Gaddafi's tyrannical 42-year-old rule with NATO's help.

In Syria, nearly 3,000 unarmed protesters have been gunned down during daily protests against Bashar al-Assad's despotic regime. Thousands have escaped Syrian troops by crossing the border into Turkey. The regime is increasingly isolated as even Syria's closest supporters are revolted by the brutal crackdown. It is only a matter of time before Bashar al-Assad succumbs to internal opposition and external sanctions.

In the context of our examination of Muslim attitudes toward the West, what do these changes portend? The Arab kaleidoscope has been severely shaken, and the bits of coloured glass will never return to their earlier stasis. There are fears in the West that Islamist groups will take advantage of the opportunity arising from the ongoing turmoil to seize power. Given the lack of organization apparent in the protest movements in the region, these are legitimate concerns as the Muslim Brotherhood and its offshoots are the only organized and disciplined parties currently in the field. However, the fact that few protestors appear to be pushing an anti-American, pro-Islam agenda would indicate that the Islamists were as taken aback by these spontaneous protests as the rulers now trying to hold back the tide. The American State Department and the CIA were caught just as flat-footed as the rest of the world.

In Egypt, which has the oldest and the most entrenched Islamic opposition in the form of the Muslim Brotherhood, the Brothers were late in joining the fray. After years of repression in which thousands of their members were jailed, tortured and executed, they were understandably wary of exposing themselves to yet another crackdown should the democracy movement have failed. Over the years, the Brotherhood has mellowed as many of its more militant members formed extremist splinter groups and went their way. One indication of the organization's move toward political legitimacy and acceptance is its announcement that it will not field candidates for all the seats up for election in July, and is not interested in nominating a candidate for the presidency from among its ranks. Nevertheless, the Brothers were very active in ensuring a victory in the referendum over changes in the constitution. Secular activists, recognizing their lack of preparation for an early election, would have preferred more time to form and organize political parties. We must remember that dictators like Mubarak simply did not permit the opposition to undertake normal political activities such as recruiting members and raising funds.

At the time of writing, the Muslim Brotherhood is poised to form the next government in Egypt, having won the early rounds of the general elections. The hardline Salafists have the second biggest number of seats, with secular groups being too divided and disorganized to figure significantly. The results have rung alarm bells in western capitals, but the groundswell of support for the Brothers is hard to ignore, given their long and honourable resistance to autocratic rule in Egypt. The Brothers have also been active at grassroot mobilization in a way secular opponents of Mubarak were not.

The situation in Tunisia is somewhat analogous, with the religious party Ennhada gaining a clear electoral victory over its secular rivals. According to an article by Scott Sayare in the *New York Times*,[1] the country is deeply divided about the direction it might take in the event of an Ennhada victory:

> With crucial elections scheduled for July 24, Ennhada's popularity and organizational strength are of growing concern to many activists and politicians, who worry that the secular revolution in this moderate state—the revolt that galvanized the Arab Spring—might see the birth of a conservative Islamic government.

But the fact that other Islamist parties have condemned Ennhada for being 'too secular' would seem to dispel fears of a Khomeini-like takeover. The party has supported a rule that makes it mandatory to field as many women as men in the July elections. Ennhada leaders have likened themselves to Turkey's mildly Islamist AK Party, and have denied that they would force women to wear veils if they come to power.

In the other countries where the Arab Spring has manifested itself, there are few indications to suggest that hard-line extremists are poised to take over. Dictators like Bashar al-Assad of Syria and Muammar Gaddafi of Libya raised the spectre of Al Qaeda in a desperate bid for western support and understanding as they used brutal force to crush the popular movements against them. But at the time of writing, there is little evidence to suggest that armed terrorists are waiting in the wings to take over the pro-democracy movement. In Libya, many questions have been raised about the presence of Islamists in the forefront of the anti-Gaddafi uprising. Qaddafi's death and the emergence of an interim coalition government has not raised the threat of an Islamist takeover.

However, it is highly unlikely that an Iran-like theocracy will seize power in the aftermath of the Arab spring. Islamists have

---

[1] 16 May 2011

consistently declared that they have no intention of grabbing power through undemocratic means and then imposing Shariah law. The reality is that many secular Arabs have fought in the trenches against despots, and have made many sacrifices. It is hard to see them now succumbing to a religious dictatorship that would erase all the freedoms they have sacrificed so much for. The presence of large numbers of women at the forefront of the protests is another reason to hope that the Arab Spring will retain its early secular promise. Nevertheless, if some of the newly liberated countries do choose an Islamic path, this is not necessarily a cause for alarm. Libya, for example, is a deeply conservative country where Islamic values are bound to influence lawmakers as they draft a new constitution. This does not mean that the country will be anti-West.

So given the mixed secular and Islamist shades of the Arab Spring, what is the future of the relationship between the Muslim world and the West? The answer is—as so often when gazing into the crystal ball—it depends. If the West (and more specifically, Washington) throws its weight behind the rapacious ruling classes of Arab countries in a bid to prop them up, the crowds agitating in the streets, and getting killed, jailed and beaten up in the process, will feel understandably angry and betrayed. And if this Western support effectively aborts the nascent democracy movements, anti-American sentiments will multiply and harden. On the other hand, if Washington and its partners come out in favour of the protestors, the governments that emerge from the present turmoil will be grateful for the support. Thus far, the US has clearly shown that it will cherry-pick from these separate uprisings: backing change in hostile countries like Libya and Syria, while implicitly supporting friends like the ruling Saudi royal family, President Saleh of Yemen, and the Al Khalifas of Bahrain. However, there were hopeful signs that the United States is reconsidering its policy toward the region in President Obama's speech at the State Department on 19 May 2011, when he said:

> So we face an historic opportunity. We have embraced the chance to show that America values the dignity of a street vendor in Tunisia more than the raw power of the dictator... After decades of accepting the world as it is in the region, we have a chance to pursue the world as it should be...
>
> For six months, we have witnessed an extraordinary change take place in the Middle East and North Africa. Square by square, town by town, country by country, the people have risen up to demand their basic human rights. Two leaders have stepped aside. More may follow.

About the festering Israel-Palestine conflict, President Obama signalled a shift in US policy when he demanded a return to the 1967 borders:

> The status quo is unsustainable...The dream of a Jewish and democratic state cannot be fulfilled with permanent occupation... The United States believes that negotiations should result in two states, with permanent Palestinian borders with Israel, Jordan and Egypt, and permanent Israeli borders with Palestine. The borders of Israel and Palestine should be based on the 1967 lines with mutually agreed swaps, so that secure and recognized borders are established for both states.

As I write this, the jury's still out on whether a deal that caters to legitimate Palestinian demands and Israel's stated security concerns is possible. But the fact that President Obama has reaffirmed American commitment to the 1967 border raises hopes that he would like the United States to be more even-handed in the dispute than it has thus far. However, the American reaction to Palestine's bid for statehood were dashed with a threat to veto any such resolution at the UN.

After seeing the fate of the dictators of Egypt, Libya and Tunisia, the other strongmen in the region have dug in their heels. In Bahrain, Syria and Yemen, security forces have exacted a bloody toll among the unarmed protestors who heroically take to the streets day after day. And while we look on in admiration, it is easy to ignore the differences in the freedom struggles across the region, and lump them all together in a single, vast pro-democracy movement. The fact is that there are sectarian and tribal forces fuelling these struggles, and each will play out differently. And if one sect or tribe wins out, there is no guarantee that the losing side will be accorded their full democratic rights. For example, in Bahrain, a Shiite majority is ruled by a Sunni minority. After years of being locked out of the power structure, the persecuted Shiites have finally risen in revolt. They have been subjected to the most horrendous crackdown with Saudi assistance. Should they win, however, we cannot be sure that they will not seek retribution. In Syria, the situation is reversed, with the minority Alewites ruling over a majority Sunni population.

Despite these crosscurrents and doubts surrounding the final outcome of the Arab Spring, the fact that it has shaken a moribund and vicious bunch of dictators and kings should be reason enough to celebrate. Whatever happens, there is no going back. The movement might face reverses here and there, but the victory of democracy in a crucial country like Egypt could well ensure there is no return to the dark days of dictatorship in the entire region. Thus far, despots had clung to power by diverting popular anger toward America and Israel. Like the dog that didn't bark, the most significant element in the ongoing uprising is the absence of both hate figures from the slogans chanted in Tahrir Square and other centers of protest. Judging by what we have witnessed thus far, it would appear that Arab youth have become relatively immune to the anti-West virus that had poisoned the older generation. Indeed, much of this hate appears to have been the result of repressive rule propped up by Western policies. In the case of anti-American regimes, government propaganda was largely responsible for shaping public attitudes. Once these dictatorships have been swept away and replaced with representative governments, there is good reason to expect that people will have little reason to blame the

West for their problems, as they have been encouraged by their leaders to do for decades.

Another major positive outcome of the Arab Spring could be a solution of the festering Palestinian dispute. As we have noted, this contentious issue has helped radicalize two generations of Muslims around the world, and its resolution would go a long way in drawing the venom from the vexed ties between the Muslim world and the West. Thus far, thanks to its overwhelming military superiority over any combination of Arab armies, and its iron grip over the occupied Palestinian territories, Israel has not had to make the tough choices needed for a negotiated settlement. The resultant deadlock has produced a steady rise in extremist militancy within the West Bank and Gaza as young Palestinians fed up with living in a prison that denies them dignity and opportunities, are in a constant state of frustration and rebellion.

Peace treaties with Egypt and Jordan, combined with an armed truce with Syria, have been instrumental in allowing Israel a free hand in effectively colonizing large swaths of the West Bank. Suddenly, changes in the neighbourhood hold out the possibility of producing governments that reflect greater concern for the Palestinian right to statehood than ousted dictators ever did. And as we saw during the 63rd anniversary of Israel's birth on May 15—a day mourned as the *Nakba*, or the Catastrophe, by Palestinians—thousands of unarmed Palestinian refugees staged an unprecedented protest. This took the form of simultaneous marches toward the Israeli border from Syria, Egypt, Lebanon and Jordan. In an effort to halt the unarmed demonstrators, Israeli guards opened fire, killing at least a dozen, and injuring many others. There is a real concern in Tel Aviv that this form of protest might catch on.

Another chink in Israel's armour was exposed recently when Turkey, the Zionist state's sole Muslim ally, distanced itself. Ruled by a popular, mildly Islamist AK Party, Turkey was infuriated by the death of nine of its citizens when the flotilla trying to reach

Gaza with food and medicines in 2010 was boarded by Israeli troops. In the ensuing violence, several unarmed volunteers from around the world were shot.

All these changes have eroded Israel's strategic position, and this shift in regional tectonic plates might motivate its leaders to be a little more flexible in their approach to peace talks. Thus far, both Israel and the US have bemoaned the absence of democracies in the region. So they should welcome the emergence of freely elected governments in the place of repressive regimes. In reality, of course, nothing fills Israeli politicians and generals with greater horror than this prospect. And yet, there is every reason for Israelis to welcome this development, and seize the opportunity to break the cycle of occupation and violence.

Another wild card that focused minds in Tel Aviv was the real possibility of the state of Palestine being recognized by an overwhelming majority of the United Nations General Assembly in September 2011. While such a resolution would have been largely symbolic, it could have exerted considerable moral pressure on Israel. Occupying a member state of the UN would create considerable legal and political problems for Tel Aviv. Even though the US effectively killed this move through the threat to veto the move in the Security Council, this step has alienated significant numbers of Muslims around the world. It also confirmed that President Obama did not mean what he said in Cairo in 2009 when he voiced his support for a state for Palestinians, and opposed settlement building by Israel.

Despite Israeli and US opposition, several factors are converging toward a possible two-state solution to this unending conflict. If and when such a deal is signed, a major irritant in the relationship between America and the Muslim world will have been removed. President Obama, recognizing the sudden opportunity that has opened up, said in Washington on 17 May 2011, during King Abdullah of Jordan's visit:

> Despite the many changes—or perhaps because of the many changes that are taking place in the region—it's more vital than ever that both Israelis and Palestinians find a way to get back to the table...

Obama went on to expand on this theme in a speech to AIPAC, the powerful Israeli lobbying group, on May 22, 2011:

> Here are the facts we must all confront. First, the number of Palestinians living west of the Jordan River is growing rapidly and fundamentally reshaping the demographic realities of both Israel and the Palestinian Territories. This will make it harder and harder—without a peace deal—to maintain Israel as both a Jewish state and a democratic state.
>
> Second, technology will make it harder for Israel to defend itself in the absence of a genuine peace.
>
> Third, a new generation of Arabs is reshaping the region. A just and lasting peace can no longer be forged with one or two Arab leaders. Going forward, millions of Arab citizens have to see that peace is possible for that peace to be sustained.
>
> And just as the context has changed in the Middle East, so too has it been changing in the international community over the last several years. There's a reason why the Palestinians are pursuing their interests at the United Nations. They recognize that there is an impatience with the peace process, or the absence of one, not just in the Arab world—in Latin America, in Asia, and in Europe. And that impatience is growing, and it's already manifesting itself in capitals around the world.

Sadly, President Obama has not lived up to his soaring rhetoric thus far. Perhaps he will show more spine if he wins a second term.

Already, the Arab Spring has shown young Palestinians that they can be in charge of their own destiny. Israel's leaders would be foolish to try and thwart their aspirations any longer. And America would be unwise to support Israel in such a doomed enterprise.

My optimistic take on the Arab Spring should not be misunderstood: I do not see it as an instant panacea to cure all the ills of the region. Nor is it a quick fix for the animosity that has built up over the centuries between the Muslim world and the West. Nevertheless, the democracy movement has unleashed a myriad of possibilities. And while the march toward representative rule will encounter many hurdles, and progress will be uneven, we need to welcome these changes, while bracing ourselves for the occasional wobble.

Apart from these recent explosive changes in the political scenario of the Arab world, are there other grounds to expect an improvement in the relations between the West and the Muslim world? Fred Halliday, the well-known British academic and writer, certainly thinks so:

> The rise of Islamist movements and the invocation of Islam as a justification for political action do not represent some general, transhistorical phenomena; they reflect particular forces within specific societies in the contemporary world. In other words, they are a response to current problems, often of a social and political nature. Where Islamist movements arise, or where particular groups identify themselves as primarily 'Muslims,' they are responding not to a timeless influence, but to the issues their societies and communities face today. Such issues include the intrusion of the state into everyday life, the evolution of legal codes, the fact of external domination (or the belief that this is a major factor), rapid urbanization, competition for education and employment positions, cultural and social changes, not least in relation to the position of women. None of these problems is specific to the Islamic world; each, to a considerable degree, has come as a result of recent changes in these societies. If one tries to explain the rise of Islamist movements in Iran, Algeria, Afghanistan, Palestine and elsewhere, one can start by examining the problems facing the population of these countries. If, in Western Europe, communities from Islamic countries increasingly define themselves in Islamic terms, this may not be so much a reassertion of some already existing Muslim identity, as a response to the problems of immigration and status, racist prejudice, employment discrimination and alienation that

> they face where they now are. It is, of course, part of the self-image involved in expressing such allegations, that they claim their Muslim identity as an eternal given and a universal, pan-Islamic, adhesion. However, such claims are part of the ideology, not of the explanation.[2]

Basically, Professor Halliday has argued that the Muslim identity is neither static nor monolithic. As does any community, Muslims respond to changing circumstances within their own societies, as well as to external stimuli. Indeed, this argument goes a long way in explaining the Arab Spring: educated young men and women, deprived for years of basic freedoms and opportunities, rise up in revolt against ossified systems and leaders. There is reason to expect, therefore, that these emerging democracies will shun the extremism that appealed earlier as an attractive alternative to repressive dictatorships. Anti-Americanism will, in this scenario, drain away as Washington will no longer be seen as propping up despots and dictators. In countries that were historically anti-West partly because of western support for Israel, a fair settlement of the Palestinian conflict would go a long way in resetting relationships.

The very fact that extremist groups calling for global jihad have been completely marginalized in the ongoing struggle gives us reason to hope that, over time, they will shrivel and die from a lack of fresh recruits. However, to inject a note of caution, it should be kept in mind that many nationalist movements engaged in freedom struggles—such as those in Chechnya and Kashmir—have a strong Islamist ideology underpinning them. These will not disappear until the issues that caused them are addressed. But these movements have local agendas, and are not part of the global jihad.

In his book *Jihad versus McWorld*, Benjamin Barber uses the 'jihad' in his title as a metaphor for tribalism and a pre-modern

---

[2] Halliday, Fred, *Islam and the Myth of Confrontation*, first edition 1996, reprinted by I.B. Tauris & Co, 2003, pp. 118-119.

ethos, while 'McWorld' represents consumerism and globalization. Barber argues that both forces are undermining democracy, but concludes on this possibility:

> With mediating civic institutions firmly in place and democracy once again the sovereign preserver of our plural worlds, Jihad can yield to healthy forms of cultural differences and group identity while McWorld can take its rightful and delimited place as the economic engine of a world in which economics is only one crucial dimension. With McWorld's excess in control, communities of blood and spirit will not have to make war on it and, beyond the homogeneous theme parks of commerce, we may rediscover free spaces in which it is possible to live not only as consumers but as citizens.[3]

When questioning and criticizing literal interpretations of Islam that strike people as violent and barbaric, we tend to forget what Christendom was like when it was the same age as Islam is today. Imagine, for a moment, that it is the year 1400 in Europe. This would be the Dark Ages, before the Reformation, and well before the Enlightenment. The Hundred Years War was still being fought until Joan of Arc ended the siege of Orleans to turn the tide. Heretics were burned at the stake with sickening regularity. The Spanish, Portuguese, and Ottoman empires were being formed and the Byzantine Empire ended with the capture of Constantinople by the Turks in 1453. The Jews were expelled from Spain in 1492 and the Spanish Inquisition was cleansing souls at a furious rate.

Obviously, the rest of the world isn't going to wait for centuries for Muslims to catch up and enter the 21st century. Nonetheless, history teaches us that revolutions and religions need time to round off the rough edges and move on from dogma and literalism. In the crucible of reality, extremism seldom retains its sharp-edged clarity and its self-righteous utopian militancy forever. Given the

---

[3] Barber, Benjamin R., *Jihad versus McWorld*, Random House, 1995, p. 300.

history of the antagonism between Islam and Christendom that we briefly examined earlier, we should not forget that in between bouts of conflict there have been long periods of cooperation and fruitful commercial intercourse.

Reflecting on the long history of interaction between the three Abrahamic faiths, Zachary Karabell writes in the introduction to his *People of the Book*:

> Reclaiming the legacy of coexistence may not make the world whole, but it does show that Islam and Christianity need not be locked in a death dance. To the degree that each creed holds that it alone has the key to truth and salvation, there will always be a degree of tension. But rivalry and competition do not lead inexorably towards war and violence. Christians, Jews, and Muslims have lived constructively with one another. They have taught one another and they have learned from one another. Judaism was central to the formation of Islam, and for a millennium and a half, until the end of the Second World War, Jews under Muslim rule enjoyed more safety, freedom and autonomy than they ever did under Christian rule. Muslim states over the course of fourteen centuries have allowed for religious diversity and not insisted on trying to convert those who follow a different creed. From the beginning of Islam, Christian and Muslim states traded with one another…
>
> Focusing only on conflict is like skipping every other page while reading a book. It isn't just incomplete; it is misleading to the point of incoherence. At the same time, it is important to avoid the opposite temptation and not replace one distorted reading of the past with another. Too often, those who attempt to rectify the imbalance provide the missing pages, but delete the others. The result is just as skewed. The tolerance of Muslim society is praised and moments of concord are highlighted, but the violence and animosity are downplayed. Coexistence is treated as the norm and conflict as the anomaly, when in truth, both are threaded through the past and our present…[4]

---

[4] Karabell, Zachary, *People of the Book*, op cit.

For those who believe in the inevitability of an unending conflict between Islam and the West, Karabell has these words of comfort:

> ...Muslim societies have been their most tolerant when they have been secure. That is hardly unusual in human affairs, but for most of the last century, few Muslim communities have felt secure. One of the results of September 11 is that western societies have also become insecure, rationally or not. The result is a rise in intolerance on all sides. Increasingly, more people throughout the world believe that Muslim and western societies are destined to clash and that they will always clash until one or another triumphs. That belief is poisonous, and one antidote is the rich historical tradition that says other paths are not only possible. But have been taken time and again.[5]

While the centuries of Muslim rule in Moorish Spain remain the high-water mark of coexistence and religious tolerance, the Ottomans were also remarkably open in their approach to ruling a multi-faith empire. Jews and Christians rose to positions of power, wealth, and eminence. The Ottoman bureaucracy was far ahead of its times in terms of its recognition of, and respect for, merit. Muslim rule in India, too, was largely tolerant, and intermarriage with Hindus was common. Of course, the fortunes of non-Muslims—and indeed, of Muslim citizens—were subject to fluctuations with a change of the incumbent ruler. Some were less tolerant than others, and more than one was certifiably insane. But it would be fair to say that in those times, a person not of the dominant creed would have done better under Muslim rule than in any country in Christendom.

Toward the end of *People of the Book*, Karabell writes:

---

[5] Karabell, Zachary, *People of the Book*, John Murray; 2007, pp. 8-9.

> Indeed, in the past few decades, polemics about the coming war between Islam and the West have proliferated...We are told of new *madressas* from Nigeria to Pakistan to Indonesia being funded by Saudi extremists preaching hate. We are told of Muslim rage on every street...There are, of course, books and articles that reject this framework and posit a different reading of Islam and the past, that suggest the compatibility of Islam and democracy and Islam and the West, but it is fair to say that these have not gained the same level of influence as their more shrill counterparts.
>
> The history of conflict is not untrue. It is incomplete. By the same token, the reality of religious extremism in the modern world cannot be and should not be downplayed. There are radicals who will dedicate their lives to inflicting pain and death on those who do not agree with their vision. And there is a still-simmering Arab-Israeli conflict that remains a source of pain and anger for all involved. Nonetheless, there are other stories that garner less attention but are no less part of the tapestry.[6]

This is a balanced and sober assessment of the relationship between Islam and the West. In the violent words and actions we have heard and witnessed in recent years, it is easy to get swept away by emotional responses without pausing for a reality check. After the enormity of the 9/11 attacks, it became commonplace to ascribe terrifying military capability to Al Qaeda and its offshoots. But the reality is that all the jihadi organizations with global agendas and reach put together do not match the military power of a medium-sized military power. And to put things in perspective, the United States spends as much on defence as the next 20 countries put together. So the fear-mongering in the West is vastly exaggerated: jihadis are hardly the existential threat to America and Europe they have been hyped up to represent

One idea we need to get used to is that tomorrow's world will be a far more dangerous place than it ever was. As the population grows, water availability falls, and other natural resources are

---

[6] *People of the Book*, op. cit., p. 280.

depleted, inequalities and competition between and within nations will intensify. Life in much of the developing world will be even more difficult, with dysfunctional governments increasingly unable to cope. The number of economic refugees will multiply. This dystopian part of the planet will be a breeding ground for crime, extremism and chaos. Deprived young people with few opportunities will lash out against the status quo. Much of this discontent will be amplified on the Internet, while satellite TV beams images of the good life in rich nations.

In the Malthusian nightmare that will stalk parts of the developing world, we can safely expect extremist groups to exploit poverty and poor governance. But generally speaking, they will have local agendas and grievances. After the death of Osama bin Laden, and the increasing irrelevance and impotence of Al Qaeda, we can expect the frequency and ferocity of attacks against the West to decline. Without Bin Laden's charisma, fewer young Muslims will be attracted to the banner of global jihad. Another reason, of course, is the massive intelligence and security apparatus now in place in America and most European countries. And as we have just speculated, the success of the Arab Spring in spreading democracy across many Muslim countries will starve extremist groups of oxygen in the form of anti-American propaganda. Finally, the worldwide crackdown on funding to front groups collecting money for terrorist outfits has been very successful in turning off the spigot. There is now a much closer scrutiny of electronic fund transfers then ever before.

There will still be voices in the Muslim world calling for the faithful to establish the supremacy of the Caliphate and the rule of Shariah laws by force. But they will be ignored by the vast majority of Muslims, just as they are today. If and when much of the Middle East and North Africa emerge from their despotic past, the grim reality is that extremism will thrive largely in dysfunctional countries like Somalia and parts of Pakistan, Afghanistan and Yemen. But it will pose a far greater danger to the people of these unfortunate states than to the rest of the world.

Of course we must expect the occasional terrorist plot to succeed. Given the number of disturbed young people out there, it would be wishful thinking to assume that just because of Bin Laden's exit from the stage and the Arab Spring, all will be well. But we are constantly at risk from criminals and nuts of all kinds, and not just from jihadis plotting the return of the Caliphate and the triumph of their particular vision of Islam. Consider, for example, the fact that more than 40,000 Americans are killed in car crashes every year, and more than 30,000 die in gun-related incidents. Neither cause of needless fatalities has attracted the kind of national rage and diversion of resources as Islamic terrorism has. However, both the United States and Europe experienced terrorist attacks long before 9/11. These have come from a variety of groups that had nothing to do with Islam or Muslims. The Red Brigades, the IRA and the Basque separatists have long terrorized European countries, while a large number of right-wing and left-wing radical groups and individuals have regularly carried out terrorist attacks in the United States. As the Norwegian right-wing terrorist Anders Breivik so shockingly reminded us in July 2011 by massacring scores of young people, mindless violence is not the monopoly of jihadists alone.

According to the Council for Foreign Relations (CFR), citing FBI statistics, two-thirds of terrorist attacks in the United States between 1980 and 2001 were carried out by non-Muslim groups and individuals; this figure shot up to 95 per cent between 2002 and 2005.[7] In other words, the hundreds of billions spent to safeguard America after 9/11 have been mainly directed at the 5 per cent of all terrorist threats emanating from Muslim groups. I can imagine Osama bin Laden chuckling in his watery grave.

The question to ask is how long the West will remain hostage to a threat that has lost much of its potential to cause mayhem. I have argued that part of the menace of Islamic terrorist groups stems

---

[7] http://www.cfr.org/terrorist-organizations/militant-extremists-united-states/p9236

from stereotypes created over centuries of conflict between Islam and Christendom. While many jihadi groups are clearly armed and very dangerous, none of them has ever posed a serious threat to America, its democracy, or its way of life as many alarmists—including George W. Bush—have suggested. This is not to minimize the danger they pose, but to put it into perspective. If we allow some vague, distant fear to dominate the public discourse and force a disproportionate and permanent drain on resources, then these terrorist groups will have succeeded in dictating terms to civilized society.

Select Bibliography

Atwan, Abdel Bari, *The Secret History of Al-Qa'ida*, London: Saqi, 2006

Barber, Benjamin R, *Jihad vs. McWorld: how globalization and tribalism are reshaping the world*, New York: Ballantine Books, 1995

Bergman, Ronen. *The Secret War with Iran: The 30-year covert struggle for control of a 'rogue' state*, Oxford: Oneworld Publications 2008

Caldwell, Christopher, *Reflections on the Revolution in Europe: Can Europe be the same with different people in it?*, London: Allen Lane, 2009

Fatah, Tarek, *Chasing a Mirage: The tragic illusion of an Islamic State*, Toronto: Wiley, 2008

Fletcher, Richard, *The Cross and the Crescent: Christianity and Islam from Muhammed to the Reformation*, London: Allen Lane, 2003

Gul, Imtiaz, *The Al-Qaeda Connection*, New Delhi: Penguin, 2009

Halliday, Fred, *Islam and the Myth of Confrontation*, London: I. B. Tauris, 1996/2003

Haqqani, Husain, *Pakistan: between Mosque and Military*, Lahore: Vanguard Books, 2005

Hardy, Roger, *The Muslim Revolt: A journey through political Islam*, London: Hurst & Co., 2010

Hussain, Zahid, *The Scorpion's Tail: The relentless rise of Islamic militants in Pakistan—and how it threatens the world*, New York: Free Press, 2010

Karabell, Zachary, *People of the Book: The forgotten history of Islam and the West*, John Murray, 2007.

Kennedy, Hugh, *The Court of the Caliphs: The rise and fall of Islam's greatest dynasty*, London: Weidenfeld & Nicolson, 2004

Kennedy, Hugh, *The Great Arab Conquests: How the spread of Islam changed the world we live in*, London: Weidenfeld and Nicolson, 2007

Lawrence, Bruce (Ed.), *Messages to the World: The statements of Osama bin Laden*, London: Verso, 2005

Lieven, Anatol, *Pakistan: A hard country, London*: Allen Lane, 2011

Lyons, Jonathan, *The House of Wisdom: How the Arabs transformed Western civilization*, London: Bloomsbury Publishing, 2009

Memon, Muhammad Umar, *Ibn Taimiya's Struggle Against Popular Religion,* Paris: Monton & Co., 1976

Mir, Amir, *The Fluttering Flag of Jihad*, Lahore: Mashal Books, 2008

Nawaz, Shuja, *Crossed Swords: Pakistan, its army and the wars within*, Karachi: Oxford University Press, 2008

Qutb, Sayyid, *Milestones*, New Delhi: Islamic Book Services, 2001

Rana, Muhammad Amir, (as translated by Saba Ansari). *A to Z of Jihad Organizations in Pakistan,* Lahore: Mashal, 2004

Roy, Olivier, *Globalised Islam: The Search for a New Ummah,* London: Hurst & Co., 2004

Sfar, Mondher, *In Search of the Original Koran: The true history of the revealed text,* New York: Prometheus Books, 2008

Shahzad, Saleem. *Inside Al-Qaeda and the Taliban: Beyond bin Laden and 9/11,* London: Pluto Press, 2011

Vidino, Lorenzo, *Al-Qaeda in Europe: The new battlefield of international jihad*, New York: Prometheus Books, 2005

Wheatcroft, Andrew, *Infidels: The conflict between Christendom and Islam* 638-2002, London: Viking, 2003

Wright, Lawrence, *The Looming Tower: al-Qaeda's Road to 9/11*, New York: Alfred A. Knopf, 2006

Index

Acknowledgments

I have been fortunate in growing up in a home full of books. My father was a Sanskrit scholar, literary critic and short story writer, and I often picked up volumes from his library too advanced for my age. My brother Salman shared our father's deep interest in history, and built up his own extensive and wide-ranging collection. My mother began writing and publishing shortly after my father died when she was seventy-two, and didn't stop until a couple of years before she died at ninety-one. She always said that writing for newspapers was all very well, but I should settle down and write a book.

In many unconscious ways, all three have shaped some of my thoughts and ideas, and I am deeply sorry none of them are alive to see this book.

And I am grateful to my wife Charlotte for all her love and support over the years.

PRAISE FOR THIS BOOK

'As a school leader with a passion for teaching and learning, this book gives much to think about.'

Jo Fox, Deputy Headteacher, Ian Ramsey Church of England Academy

'McGill has truly brought together the science behind teaching AND learning.'

Sam Martin, Senior Assistant Headteacher (Teaching & Learning), Kennet School

'Ross has done it again! Grounded in cutting-edge neuroscience, his book turns fMRI research into practical, inclusive strategies that educators can use immediately in their classrooms to support all learners.'

Trudi Fisher, Lead Practitioner, Harrow Way Community School

'For years, as a teacher trainer, I have recognised, and taught, the importance of neuroscience, but we have generally lacked a clear, simple and up-to-date book. Ross Morrison McGill is now about to launch what is set to be one of the most definitive guides to cognitive science.'

John Viner, Adept Education Associates

'Reading this book was like being given the best advice from your most admired colleague. It opens your eyes to the treasure trove of scientific research into learning and gives you the confidence to use this in your everyday practice.'

Laura Marshall-Smith, Assistant Headteacher, Fakenham Academy

'[The book] does not disappoint, grounded in a deep understanding of how students think and learn. Ultimately, it doesn't ask teachers to do more, it helps us do what we already do, better.'

Kate Monin, Science teacher

‘This is the kind of book that should be part of every teacher training course and found in every staffroom library.’

Harsha Patel, Headteacher, Acton Gardens Primary School

‘As more students are identified as neurodivergent, this book offers a truly informative and practical approach to supporting all learners in the classroom. It’s already changed my teaching practice and how I help other teachers develop.’

Emma Chadwick, Assistant Headteacher, The Maple School, Synergy Education Trust

‘Ross expertly connects the art and science of teaching, making neuroeducation clear, practical and immediately useful for educators, leaders and CPD leads who want to better understand how learning happens and how this can strengthen classroom practice.’

Rebecca Bierton, National Director of Primary and Safeguarding, Ormiston Academies Trust

‘The beauty of this book is that it breaks down and supports how we learn. As ever, Ross has given really clear models that are easy to understand and apply, to work with driving improvement at a whole school level!’

Chris Stainsby, Deputy Headteacher, Queen Elizabeth School

‘Ross has produced something that allows us to fully understand how we learn with tangible and focused opportunities to put it into practice. A helpful and informative book that reminds me why I teach, while showing how to make processes simpler.’

Victoria Ayres, SEND teacher, Esland Bedford School

‘The connection between neuroscience and practical pedagogy is blended seamlessly, from the “debunking board” to useful classroom checklists. This guide stands out by offering educators an entirely different way to understand thinking, memory and learning.’

Kate Jones, Education adviser, former teacher and leader, and author

THE TEACHER TOOLKIT GUIDE TO THE SCIENCE OF LEARNING

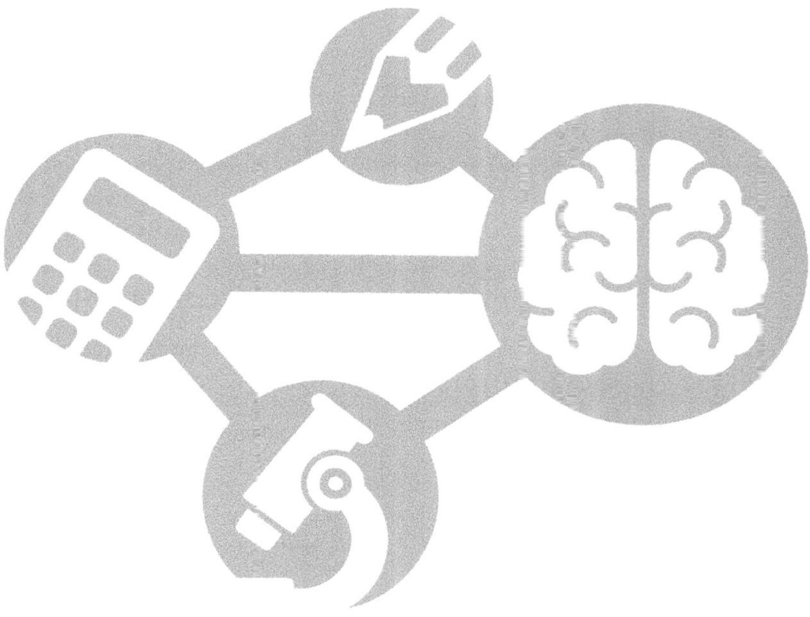

ROSS MORRISON McGILL

BLOOMSBURY EDUCATION
LONDON OXFORD NEW YORK NEW DELHI SYDNEY

BLOOMSBURY EDUCATION
Bloomsbury Publishing Plc
50 Bedford Square, London WC1B 3DP, UK
Bloomsbury Publishing Ireland Limited
29 Earlsfort Terrace, Dublin 2, D02 AY28, Ireland

First published in Great Britain, 2026
This edition published in Great Britain, 2026 by Bloomsbury Publishing Plc

A catalogue record for this book is available from the British Library

ISBN: PB: 978-1-80199-899-4; ePub: 978-1-80199-897-0
2 4 6 8 10 9 7 5 3 1 (paperback)

Cover design by James Fraser
Text design by Marcus Duck
Typeset by Marcus Duck

Printed and bound in Great Britain by TJ Books, Padstow, Cornwall

MIX
Paper | Supporting responsible forestry
FSC® C013056

To find out more about our authors and books visit www.bloomsbury.com and sign up for our newsletters

For product safety related questions contact productsafety@bloomsbury.com

CONTENTS

ACKNOWLEDGEMENTS

This book represents the culmination of several years of curiosity, reading and conversations with teachers and researchers. What began with a simple question – how does learning happen? – has evolved into a much deeper exploration of what might be happening in the brain when we teach. It is perhaps one more connection formed in my own long-term memory, bringing together what works, why, how, where, and when.

I remain hugely grateful to the community of neuroscientists, psychologists, and researchers whose work has helped shape my thinking. In particular, those who have published research using fMRI and other neuroimaging tools. Their work continues to fire new ideas, challenge assumptions, and strengthen neural pathways that underpin this book. While I have attempted to translate these complex ideas into something practical for teachers, it is their research that provides the prior schema!

To the many schools and colleges who continue to invite me to work alongside their staff, thank you. Your trust and support sustain my work and give me the time and space to think, research, and write. Every training session, conversation, and classroom visit adds another layer to this process – like a kind of professional retrieval practice that continues to shape my understanding. Thank you also to the thousands of teachers who engage with my work. Your questions, reflections and challenges have helped encode and sharpen the ideas throughout this book.

I would also like to thank Emily Evans and Susannah Fountain for their editorial expertise. Their attention to detail, thoughtful questioning and guidance have helped organise a manuscript that may have overloaded working memory into something coherent for teachers.

Finally, to my family, Jenni and Freddie, for your love. You have been part of every book publication to date, providing the humour, perspective and emotional regulation that keeps everything in balance.

INTRODUCTION

HOW fMRI SCANS CAN TELL US MORE ABOUT WHAT IS HAPPENING IN THE CLASSROOM

Over the last 15 years, I have been increasingly absorbed by the world of **cognitive science**, **cognitive neuroscience**, **psychology**, and **neuropsychology**. In this book, my intention is to explore the intersection between these different disciplines, their importance, how they can help you understand the ways in which students learn, and how you can make that learning effective and efficient.

In my work supporting teachers in schools and colleges across the UK, and in the contextual research I have undertaken, one key question persists: *How does learning happen in the classroom?* What are the processes taking place when you, as teachers, do this, or do that, at a particular point in the lesson, or in response to students at another point?

While many of you are, without doubt, becoming increasingly exposed to the concepts of **working memory** and **cognitive load theory (CLT)**, I would argue that this is likely to be only at a superficial level. In my training sessions, I have enjoyed showing teachers the practical applications to help bring teaching concepts alive by unpicking the decisions they make in the classroom that may either *support* or *hinder* the learning process. There has been significant traction gained over the five years following the COVID-19 pandemic; the world has become better connected, ideas have spread further, and it is possible to access improved professional development, even outside your own workplace, simply through online communication.

For definitions of key terminology, please consult the **Glossary** on page 149. Glossary terms are highlighted in **bold** the first time they appear in the book.

The 'what', the 'why', and the 'how' inside this book

My key objective for this book is to wrap the 'what', 'why', and 'how' of **neuroimaging** altogether, grounding these questions in research from relatively new interdisciplinary areas of study: **neuroeducation** and **neuroliteracy**. These are still emerging as fields for educators and researchers who are particularly interested in the brain and how these fields relate to classroom environments. I have spent time studying research from **fMRI scans (functional magnetic resonance imaging)** to see what impact specific conditions have on students with, for example, **attention deficit hyperactivity disorder (ADHD)**. I have also explored how neuroscientists use **electroencephalograms (EEGs)** to record brain activity using electrodes to detect electrical signals in the brain.

Analysing this brain activity helps us to understand not only the decisions we all take, but also what is happening in the brain, and how it responds to different stimuli. For example, when you deliver a **retrieval practice** activity, or a sequence of quick-fire questions in the class to groups or individuals, what is happening with students' attention? Which parts of their brains 'fire up' neurologically? My hope is that my research into some of the brain's functions will help classroom teachers understand what is *really* happening inside the brain during everyday classroom scenarios.

Is teaching an art or a science?

The 'art or science' debate pervades across social media, and it has made me think deeply about the art of teaching, and the science behind that teaching. It is also worth exploring what 'art' or 'science' are in practical and academic terms before we immerse ourselves in the details of this book; this is something I will look at in Chapter 1.

Why write this book?

I wanted to write this book for the following four reasons:

1 Since the publication of *The Teacher Toolkit Guide to Memory* (2022), the book and its resources have been the most popular training topic I have delivered in schools and colleges across the country. Each time I deliver sessions, I delve more deeply into how the strategies I have created evolve to suit a variety of contexts. This macro-understanding, and range of experiences, have widened my research and have informed *this* book.

I have analysed the varying levels of expertise among primary teachers, secondary or further education teachers, and lecturers. I have also analysed what pedagogy looks like in classroom settings. But what does the science of learning look like across these institutions and in individual classrooms? The science of learning now provides the basis of training for all new teachers across England, but even experienced teachers are still playing catch-up.

As a follow-up from *The Teacher Toolkit Guide to Memory* (2022), I began to think increasingly about one of the greatest assets you, as teachers, have – your voices. This led me to publish my next book, *The Teacher Toolkit Guide to Questioning* (2023). Asking numerous questions in class doesn't necessarily mean that we are actually *good* at asking questions! Having posed a question in class, knowing then how to respond or adapt in the moment, is something we could truly define as 'adaptive teaching'. I believe that this understanding of how to respond is missing if teachers are unaware of '*how* learning happens', explicitly at a neurological level.

2 Secondly, and more importantly for this book, I want to provide you with a bank of evolving neuroliteracy – key neuroscientific terms that blend fields of study, but with clear connections to the classroom (hence, neuroeducation).

What is still evolving is the relationship between cognition and the functions of the brain and, importantly, what this looks like in the classroom. Expert knowledge in this area is still lacking across the teaching profession. What's even more concerning is that we are still unclear about what cognitive **neuroscience** can actually do to improve teacher performance and student outcomes.

3 In this book I want to go further to explain some of the most popular strategies and prevailing **neuromyths**, to provide you with a personal or whole-school implementation plan to help make changes to your teaching practice. I will also provide you with an overview of working memory and, in particular, attention, and how (as teachers) we can manage students' focus in the classroom, with consideration for neurodivergent learners.

4 While my books are always aimed at the general teaching population, as a former school leader, I always consider how these ideas should be received strategically. This is especially the case for schools and colleges that want to consider how to embed concepts across the whole school, with clear implementation plans that are embedded into weekly teacher training sessions that you host in-house. As such, this book will help teachers, leaders, and schools and colleges unlock the power of cognitive science.

Defining terms

Circling back to the start of this introduction, here are introductory definitions to some of the terms you will encounter in the book within the context of cognitive science, cognitive neuroscience, psychology, and neuropsychology.

- **Cognitive science** is the study of thought and mental organisation; there is a large community of English teachers already confident in this area who are working in this space. It is an interdisciplinary field, concerned with attention, memory, reasoning, language, and emotion.
- **Cognitive neuroscience** is more focused on the biological aspects of all of the above, using EEG and fMRI scans to see what happens neurologically (physically) in the brain when various conditions are applied. This field also draws on brain injury, growth, or decline. *Applied* neuroscience considers the mechanisms and treatments of various diseases of the brain and our nervous system.
- **Psychology** is the study of our emotions and behaviours, using scientific methods to explain our conscious and subconscious decisions.
- **Neuropsychology** is a field of psychology focusing on how a person's cognition and behaviour is related to the brain and the nervous system – specifically brain injury responses and functions.
- **Neuroeducation** draws from cognitive neuroscience, developmental cognitive neuroscience, psychology, technology, and other related disciplines to explore the interactions between biological processes and learning.

Put simply, this book is about neuroeducation – all of the above disciplines – and what we do in the classroom, what is potentially happening in the brain at that point in time, and why.

What the book will cover

My aim is to help you move to a stage of confidence with your understanding of cognitive science. There is an enormous body of work and, as it is a relatively new field of academic study, it continues to grow at a rapid pace. My intention is to signpost some of the material I have been researching, outlining the key questions I've asked along the way, what I've discarded, and what I keep revisiting and exploring in greater depth. This book will give you the confidence you need to discuss these concepts with your teaching colleagues.

We will cover key concepts and also dispel some popular neuromyths. I have read and researched topics about memory and learning, attention, **cognitive load**, and processing, particularly with **neurodiversity** and associated ethical implications in mind. This included analysing how fMRI scans and EEGs can help us to understand teacher decision-making, and student attention span.

In *The Teacher Toolkit Guide to Memory*, I stated that the adolescent brain was 'approximately between 13 to 25 years old' (as defined by Blakemore, 2019); that this 'differs from those of children and adults' and that 'neural synapses are [still] forming' (McGill, 2022, p. 51). Yet emerging research (Mousley et al., 2025) from the University of Cambridge suggests that the brain goes through five distinct phases, and adolescence actually spans into your early 30s!

This means that you are not entirely your adult self until your brain is fully rewired for adulthood. The topology in your brain 'is particularly distinct, indicating that the network is becoming both more globally efficient and more locally specialized with age' (Mousley et al., 2025, p. 7). This remains stable until your mid-60s, after which a gradual decline in brain efficiency begins. The research identifies key neurological changes and 'these turning points define five major epochs of life' (Mousley et al., 2025, p. 4):

1. Childhood – from birth to nine years.
2. Adolescence – from nine to 32 years.
3. Adulthood – from 32 to 66 years.
4. Early ageing – from 66 to 83 years.
5. Late ageing – from 83 onwards.

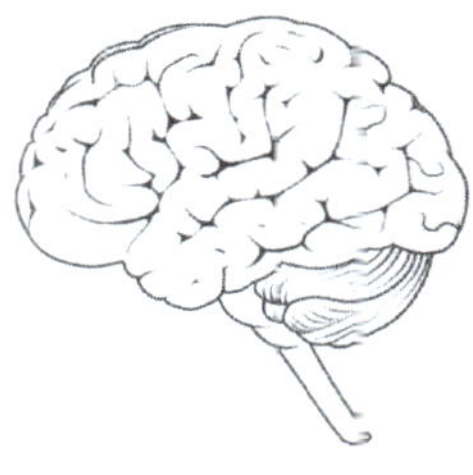

I will also help bring the concept of **metacognition** to life. It's a phrase I have grappled with for quite some time, but now have an understanding of its value across a variety of classroom settings. Interestingly, the etymological meaning of the word 'meta' means 'beyond', but it also means a 'change' in condition. In simple terms, metacognition is being aware of your own thinking: recognising your capabilities, understanding the problem in hand, and deciding which strategies might help you solve it. Metacognition involves drawing on prior knowledge and experience to plan, monitor, and evaluate your approach:

- What happens when we do things automatically?
- What happens when we transfer what we already know and apply it to a new situation?
- How do we describe this?
- What does it look like practically in the classroom?
- How does it translate into practical resources and techniques for students?

Like me, I suspect these are important questions you have also asked.

Bringing this all together, we will then consider how students can develop **self-regulation**, and unpick the science behind motivation and emotion in learning – all essential ingredients to the learning process. I will offer you a neuroscience curriculum that you can use in your classroom, including ways to develop your own neuroliteracy confidence. It is my hope that the teaching profession can develop more 'evidence-informed' approaches grounded in cognitive science and neuroscience.

What you will take away from this book

In past publications, I challenged outdated ideas about the way students study and I unpacked the cognitive science behind knowledge retention. This book goes one step further and critically revisits the research that underpinned *The Teacher Toolkit Guide to Memory* (2022).

With more practising teachers publishing work, there is an abundance of research now available. It's important to ask what still holds up, what needs rethinking, and what, if anything, we have missed altogether?

For example, **MRI (magnetic resonance imaging)** is still relatively new in the grand scheme of the history of the brain. MRI scans provide a snapshot of brain anatomy using a still picture to understand physical structure. However, fMRI (functional magnetic resonance imaging) is largely unknown; it relies on a **blood oxygenated level dependent technique** to generate fMRI images, and 'relies on regional differences in cerebral blood flow' (Atabek et al., 2022, p.2) to understand dynamic changes in brain activity.

We have learned more from brain visualisations in the last 50 years from MRI and fMRI scans than we have as a human species across 4,000 years of written history. I believe the ultimate question to answer is not 'How does learning happen?', but 'What happens to learning when teachers do X, Y or Z?'; fMRI research can offer some guidance.

I will provide you with enough research information, explained in pragmatic terms, to help unpick complex language for non-specialists. I'll provide you with the data, a balanced argument, a large number of reflection questions as well as some practical strategies and blank templates throughout this book. As always, the message from me is not *what* or *why* you do something in the classroom, but *how you do it*, considering *when* and *where* any of my recommendations are suggested, and how they should be tweaked to apply when working with a four or 44-year-old student in the classroom.

The Teacher Toolkit Guide to the Science of Learning explores how study strategies can be adapted for all learners, across all subjects, in real classrooms. This is not a 'revision' guide – it's a guide for teachers who want to make evidence-informed decisions about how students learn best, especially **neurodivergent** students, and how to bring this to life across the entire teaching sector.

When you reach the book's conclusion, you will understand why all teachers should be provided with a general overview of neuroeducation in any teacher training qualification. Managing behaviour and commanding your subject knowledge isn't enough in today's classroom landscape. If we want to encourage absent students back into class and address increasing home-learning demands, we, as teachers, must better understand *attention* to meet increasing neurodiverse needs. With the endless, and unknown, implications of artificial intelligence (AI), there is a potential existential crisis about the purpose of school, whether or not we need students to collectively gather inside a building, or if knowledge should be taught when students have Google or ChatGPT. My belief is that explicit knowledge should be taught by a human expert, in person, and that the emerging research on using AI suggests that relying on AI to do the thinking for you increases **cognitive debt** – a condition that develops if a person relies on AI, rather than using cognitive effort required for thinking. In a recent study, people who used their brain 'reported higher satisfaction and demonstrated higher brain connectivity' (Kosmyna et al., 2025, p.153). Put simply, when you stop using your brain to solve problems, the neurological connections that you have put in place weaken over time.

Abbreviations

It's worth sharing a few abbreviations and key terminology used throughout the book. I suggest bookmarking this page for reference as you move through the chapters.

- **CLT:** Cognitive load theory
- **CPD:** Continuing professional development
- **EEG:** Electroencephalogram
- **EYFS:** Early years foundation stage
- **fMRI**: Functional magnetic resonance imaging
- **IQ**: Intelligence quotient
- **KS1–KS5:** Key stages 1 to 5
- **LTM:** Long-term memory
- **MRI:** Magnetic resonance imaging
- **NFC:** Need for cognition
- **SEND:** Special educational needs and disabilities

I hope this book brings you hope, joy, and the reassurance to make your working life in the classroom that little bit easier.

Don't forget to share your views using #**GuideToLearning**.

HOW TO USE THIS BOOK

What you'll find in each chapter

In this book, I will share with you the conclusions I have drawn not only from my classroom experience and my training sessions with teachers, but also from the ideas pulled from the academic research I have read. This includes research into 'how learning happens' by examining, at a biological level, the anatomical changes that occur in the brain.

I will also explain why understanding the science of learning has the power to transform what we all do in the classroom. I'll show you how this knowledge of basic neurology can help you make more informed teaching decisions which will support your students. Taking a closer look at fMRI scans allows us to have a better understanding of what is happening when the blood flow changes during brain activity.

You'll be introduced to fMRI data that shows changes in blood oxygenation associated with neural activity and might help to explain what goes on in the brains of teachers and learners in the classroom. For example, if I give you a non-verbal 'glower' or a 'finger-wag' across the classroom, I may be wrongly assuming that you are misbehaving and not paying attention. I believe this could be critical knowledge for teachers working with neurodivergent learners, and for those managing student anxiety.

Another key objective is to show you how you can become an even better teacher by understanding what the available research can offer. I have condensed the academic research into pragmatic language, key recommendations, and practical ideas that you can adopt and implement immediately.

Each chapter is divided into four key sections.

1 Explainer

The first part of each chapter covers *what you need to know* about the discussed topic. We'll delve into fMRI research and examples of good (and bad) cognitive science. We will look at cognitive load theory, dual coding, retrieval practice, and working memory limitations.

2 Practical idea

After the explainer, we'll consider a practical idea that turns the science of learning *theory into practice*. There will be examples of how to use retrieval practice, reduce extraneous cognitive load, and how to design tasks that support **encoding** into **long-term memory (LTM)**. At the end of the idea, you'll find a set of *toolkit tips*, which are practical takeaways to support you when putting the idea into practice in your classroom.

3 Worked example

I'll give you a *clear example* of how the practical idea could work in practice. In these sections, I will provide you with classroom scenarios (from early years, primary, secondary, and further education) that show how you might adapt your lesson using knowledge of **working memory**, and how you might build a mixed approach to, for example, retrieval practice.

4 Template

At the end of each chapter, a *blank template* is provided to help you plan how to implement the practical idea in your classroom. Use the template to contextualise the idea for your students. When you're delivering the practical ideas or using the templates with your students, it's helpful to name the technique you are using, for example, the Debunking Board (see Chapter 3) or the Five Minute Inclusive Planner (see Chapter 7). This will help your students, or colleagues you are working with, identify each technique and enable them to learn how to respond and understand what is expected of them. Blank versions of the templates are also available online, so you can download and print them. Scan the ***QR code*** next to each template for access.

Bringing it all together

In the final part of the book, I will explain to you how to integrate all the practical ideas into your long-term curriculum plans and professional development. By embedding these ideas over time, and linking them to how the brain works, you can develop deeper neuroliteracy, improve retention, and enhance long-term student outcomes.

CHAPTER 1
THE SCIENCE OF LEARNING

I've come to believe that the best teaching methods blend both *art* and *science*. The *art* of teaching evolves from your lived experiences, whereas the *science* of learning uses academic evidence to validate your decisions. As teachers, we observe each other's teaching across the curriculum, and how we work with different age groups; this collective observation helps us to develop experience about what works best in our own classroom, with our own students. Teachers have always been learners, but the phrase 'science of learning' is now everywhere – in **continuing professional development (CPD)** sessions, teacher blogs, books, and even political agendas. But what does it actually mean in practice?

In this chapter, I will unpack the core ideas behind 'the science of learning' (cognitive science). I'll signpost you to some key pieces of research in this field that will help bridge the gap between research and classroom reality. I'll also discuss one of the most influential studies of the last decade (*Improving Students' Learning with Effective Learning Techniques* – Dunlosky et al., 2013) to examine how its recommendations shape policy and practice, and what has changed since then. If we are to be evidence-informed as a teaching profession, we must first understand the science behind the claims. I encourage you to be a critical consumer of research to inform your practice.

In the next chapter, we'll dive deeper into the specifics of memory, motivation, and attention, but for now let's step back and ask: What do we mean by the *science* of learning, and how does it relate to the *art* of teaching?

For centuries, teaching has been considered a craft – a series of instincts and improvisations shaped by experiences and intuition that respond to the moment. Today, we are surrounded by a growing body of cognitive science research that claims to show us how learning *actually* works. Over the last five years, I've taken a closer look at fMRI scans (functional magnetic resonance imaging) to see if there is neurological evidence that shows what happens during learning, specifically in the context of teacher decisions, or from various experiences, such as stress. The English government, and school inspectors, also have an interest in this area, and this has resulted in their recommendations for teacher training, classroom practice, and evidence-based policies. As a result, schools, colleges, and teachers restructure their thinking and actions around these teaching recommendations, but can scientific evidence ever truly capture the messiness of a real classroom?

How have the ideas around cognitive science entered the classroom? The review of learning techniques outlined in the research carried out by Dunlosky et al. (2013) spoke of renewed interest in evidence-informed teaching, but it also led me to question what works, for whom, and in what context. The research paper tended to draw conclusions from high schools and college classrooms, typically outside creative subjects. I was left with the question: What advice could I give a primary teacher, or someone who taught a creative subject?

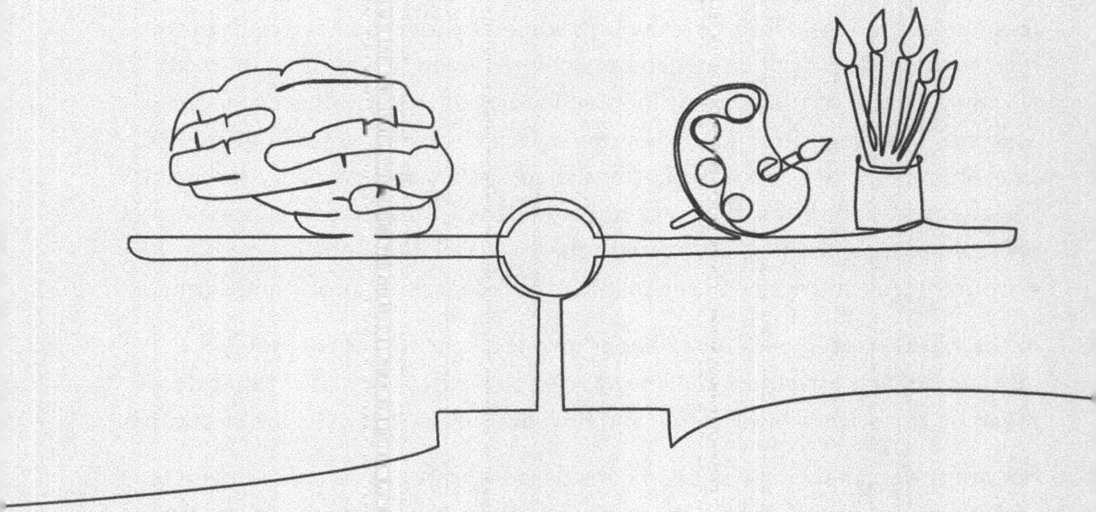

EXPLAINER

It has only been over the last few years that I have been able to articulate the differences between the art of teaching and the science of teaching. In layperson terms, the art of teaching is often associated with judgement, adaption, and responsiveness, whereas the science of teaching draws on research into instruction, memory, attention, and learning.

Alexander Makedon defined the *art* of teaching as 'an attempt to help our students learn' based on how we have observed them (1990, p. 13). Having read the available research, I now realise that learning is likely more of a science than an art. However, if teaching simply conveys information with no particular emphasis on *how well* students learn, then teaching becomes an expression of feelings, whether learning is effective or not. One could therefore argue that teaching is an art form.

The art of teaching

To simplify this further, I often describe the *art of teaching* as experiences gathered over time, which are difficult to measure. As teachers, we make so many idiosyncratic decisions using our internal database, that much of it becomes automatic over time, thus reducing our workload.

As an example, let's say that you're sitting in my classroom misbehaving. I look across the classroom directly at you, pause from my whole-class instruction, raise my eyebrows and gesture a pointed finger, while wagging my hand at you. You know that the 'finger wag' means I won't tolerate any nonsense. As a teacher, I know it works and it improves your behaviour, and as the student you know that you're now being closely monitored. There's no science here to back up this experience, but it's a valid classroom experience that all teachers rely on.

The science of teaching

In contrast, the *science of teaching* is rooted in evidence: the cognitive science, psychology, and neuroscience that tells us how memory works, how attention is captured, and how knowledge is best stored and retrieved.

The science of teaching is about understanding the research on:

- **retrieval** (see Chapter 2), actively bringing information to mind from memory
- **dual coding** (see Chapters 2 and 8), combining words with visual images to enhance understanding
- **spacing** (see Chapter 3), a learning technique that spreads studying evenly
- **cognitive load** (see Chapter 4), the mental effort required at any given time.

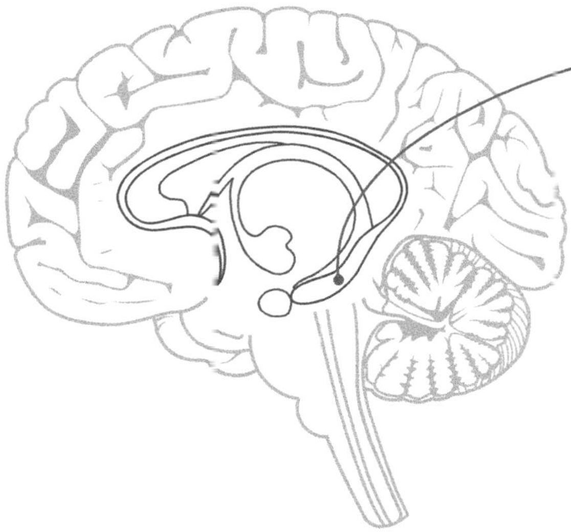

This study of teaching is critical in finding out why certain strategies work (or don't), for whom they work (or don't), and under what conditions they work (or don't). This book focuses predominantly on the science of teaching, but uses some of what we might describe as the art of teaching, backed up with scientific evidence. Recent neuroimaging research shows that when students retrieve knowledge, instead of just reviewing it, greater activity is observed in the **hippocampus**, a region strongly involved in memory formation and retrieval; they are more likely to be able to make connections across regions of the brain. In neurodivergent students, these activations may differ between individuals, reinforcing the need to evaluate how study strategies work for different learners rather than assuming one uniform response.

Two fMRI studies

Two separate fMRI studies help to explain what is happening in the brain when we experience high stress (workload), and how we process language.

High stress

From an fMRI perspective, what impact does workload have on teachers beyond their mental health, wellbeing, general health, and teacher attrition? According to research by Jang et al., 2025, overwork might structurally change areas of the brain linked to problem-solving and emotion, providing a 'biological basis for the cognitive and emotional challenges often reported in overworked individuals' (p. 110). This is preliminary evidence that teachers being overworked results in emotional drain and poorer performance.

Processing language

In the second study, infants' brain responses to speech analysis of auditory and motor systems were used to understand how infants process language (Kuhl et al., 2014). They used **magnetoencephalography (MEG) – a** non-invasive neuroimaging technique to measure faint magnetic fields produced by electrical currents in the brain. The purpose was to determine the value of gestures and speech modelling in classroom teaching, especially among young or neurodiverse learners. The researchers were particularly interested in whether babies simply *hear* the sounds or if their brains also stimulate the act of speaking them. The research found that even before infants can talk, they 'use prior speech production experience to generate internal motor models of speech as they listen to us talk' (Kuhl et al., 2014, p. 7). Their brains are preparing for language by internally rehearsing how to produce those sounds.

Further evidence of using neuroimaging to inform classroom methods can be found in tracking real-world interactions in the classroom. If brain activity is synchronised across students, can it predict class engagement and social dynamics? In *Brain-to-Brain Synchrony*, Dikker et al. (2017) discovered 'the extent to which brain activity is synchronised across students [and] predicts both student class engagement and social dynamics' (p. 2). In the experiment, high-school students wore portable EEG devices to record brain activity during regular classroom activities over the course of a term. The research demonstrated that student engagement is reflected in *shared* neural activity, meaning that when students are genuinely engaged in an activity, their brain waves synchronise. This is robust evidence for classroom strategies to improve attention, emotional connection, and a shared focus.

In another MRI study that used infrared **spectroscopy** to look at how students responded to different instruction-giving methods, 'participants watching videos of peer interactive group discussions demonstrated stronger brain activation than those watching videos of teacher-student interactions' (Zhang et al., 2025). Spectroscopy (the study of matter using wavelengths) was used to measure the changes in oxygenated blood flow in the brain – essentially those areas that are more active under different instructional strategies.

Students who engaged in peer discussions showed significantly more activation in the **prefrontal cortex**, situated in the front area of the brain. The prefrontal cortex is responsible for motivation, cognitive effort, and executive function (which coordinates with other brain regions to regulate attention, memory, and decision-making).

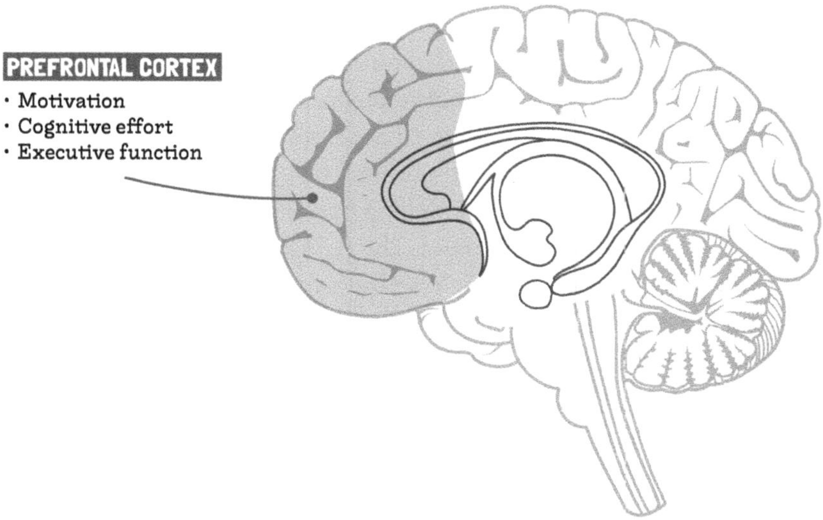

When students just watched a lecture, their brains worked harder; they used more effort and strain to sustain attention. The study observed that 'passive knowledge elicits aversive experiences' (Zhang et al., 2025, p. 17). However, when students were actively involved in questioning and dialogue, this 'activated brain regions linked to positive emotional experiences and mentalization' (Zhang et al., 2025, p. 21). Their brain activation pattern shifted, suggesting that there was more engagement rather than avoidance. This reinforces a growing body of evidence that critical thinking is not just a cognitive ideal; instead, it is something that leaves measurable neural footprints. It also suggests how higher-order thinking skills, like problem-solving and reasoning, rely heavily on our working memory capacity.

For teachers, this neuroimaging research in the classroom has practical implications. Interaction stimulates more neural activity than passive instruction. We therefore need to move beyond simply 'covering content'. Instead, we must create space for students to explain, discuss, and reason with one another – not just as a teaching strategy, but as a cognitive accelerator.

Post-COVID-19 pandemic, with rising anxiety levels and absenteeism, helping students actively engage in thinking is more than a pedagogical choice; it's a resounding necessity. Critical thinking needs to be taught, modelled, and practised – not just assessed.

Knowing that neuroimaging is already being used to determine what is working in the classroom, let's consider the ten study skills offered by Dunlosky et al., (2013).

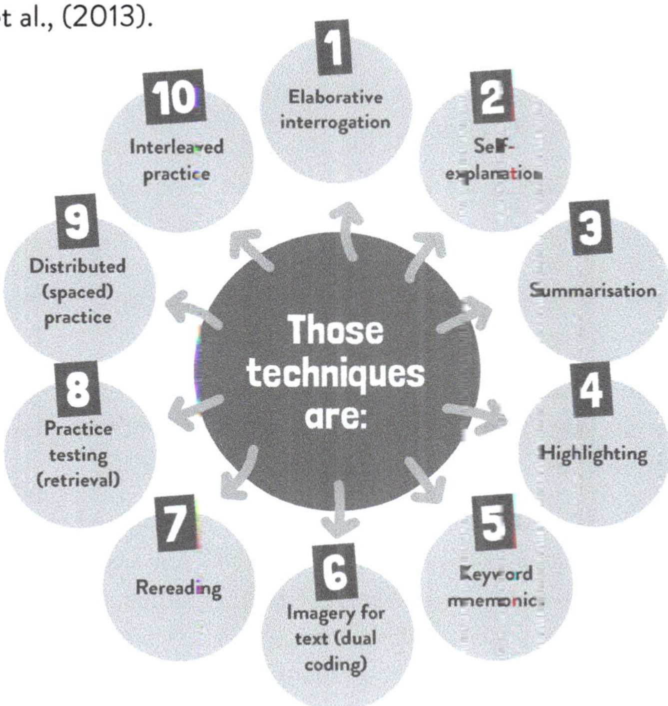

With the use of fMRI, we can evaluate which of these techniques is used in our classrooms, when they are used, how they are used, and most importantly, what happens inside a student's brain. Teaching as an art (by experience) is no longer enough. We also need the science of teaching to inform our decision-making.

In the next section, we will explore what the science of learning looks like 50 years after fMRI scans became available, and how cognitive science can influence classroom teaching.

PRACTICAL IDEA

Classroom learning charter

Let's revisit some of the most popular teaching methods and pair those with strategies for learning. For example, when a teacher delivers instructions to the class, students might select self-explanation, elaborative interrogation, or retrieval as a study technique.

The aim is to create a classroom culture rooted in evidence-informed study strategies by developing a shared language of learning, underpinned by cognitive science.

What would happen if teachers created classroom norms based on evidence-informed principles? For example, in:

- **spaced practice** in which learning is spread out over time
- **retrieval** in which students actively recall information from memory
- **cognitive load**, which describes the mental effort being used in students' working memory.

With this in mind, it is critical that schools and colleges develop a language for learning and a lens for embedding learning activities throughout the year (see the example of an implementation plan in Chapter 10).

More than a decade after Dunlosky et al. (2013) first ranked the effectiveness of ten study skills (outlined on page 7), many teachers still haven't seen this research. The researchers plotted efficacy of the ten skills based on how they were used in classrooms across several high schools and colleges. The following step-by-step guidance demonstrates how Dunlosky's study skills come alive in real classrooms, and how recent research 'offered by fMRI has meant that [they have] swiftly become a primary tool for investigating the inner workings of the mind' (Smallwood and Schooler, 2015, p.3). Neuroimaging can offer additional clues about the neural processes associated with some learning techniques.

Step 1: How would you introduce the ten study strategies to students (e.g. in EYFS)?

1. Elaborative interrogation → explain why
2. Self-explanation → tell me in your own words
3. Summarisation → condensing content into memorable chunks
4. Highlighting → key concepts and terminology, for example grammar
5. Keyword mnemonic → creating a mental shortcut
6. Imagery for text (dual coding) → aligning images with words
7. Rereading → restudying again after initial reading
8. Practice testing (retrieval) → low-stakes quizzes; no grade
9. Distributed (spaced) practice → sequencing content over time
10. Interleaved practice → mixing similar topics to strengthen schema

Rather than labelling the strategies as 'good' or 'bad', the research goal was to evaluate each technique based on evidence from a wide range of learner profiles and academic contexts. Retrieval, spaced and **interleaving practice** were identified as the most impactful, but we should question the context. Do these ideas work in a primary classroom, in an art classroom, or for a mathematics student in a further education college tackling a maths resit for the third time?

The reality? Different techniques may work better for different subjects, different learner profiles, and different contexts. If we consider that 'combining fMRI data with anatomy information is tremendously helpful' (Seghier et al., 2019, p. 6), it becomes clear that *how* the technique is used is just as important as *which* technique is selected.

Step 2: Student audit (metacognitive reflection)

Here are three key questions you should ask your students:

1. Which technique have you used before?
2. Which do you find most helpful?
3. Which do you want to learn more about?

Use '**exit tickets**' (short end-of-lesson checks of understanding) for small-group discussions, or to help you systematically check students' understanding. Online, evaluation forms and QR codes can be used to gather student views about learning to build a picture of data and habits over time.

Step 3: Classroom charter co-creation

As a teacher, you are the expert, so there's some critical information at this stage that would be non-negotiable. However, if you want to help students enjoy being in your classroom, it's important to agree on a set of shared 'learning goals' and norms and allow them to be part of this process. These might include:

1. We will always use retrieval to review previous learning at the start of every lesson.
2. We will space out our practice throughout every lesson, and every week, instead of cramming it all in at the end. This means sometimes you would've seen things before, and the goal here would be to test if you actually know it.
3. We will explain our thinking aloud when solving problems.

Once you have agreed a set of principles with your class, display the charter and refer to it regularly with your students.

Note: Adaptations may be required for younger/older students.

Step 4: Teach the techniques in context

Model each study strategy explicitly – nothing should be open to interpretation!

- In maths: Use retrieval with a 'Do Now' starter activity.
- In history: Use elaborative interrogation with 'Why did this happen?' questions.
- In art: Use dual coding by sketching key concepts.

Let's consider two very popular teaching ideas:

1. 'I do, we do, you do'
2. Think-Pair-Share

Try using the **'I do, we do, you do'** scaffolding methodology, moving from teacher-led guided practice towards independent practice.

- The logic behind this simple, yet very powerful teaching principle is that the teacher models the task and solution first talking through their decisions during the first stage, 'I do'.
- In step two, 'We do', the teacher guides the students through each stage, one step at a time, asking questions along the way. Modelling together reduces risk for students, and enables opportunities for questions and problem-solving queries along the way.
- In the final step, 'You do', the teacher steps back and asks students to complete the task on their own, perhaps offering some modified instructions to increase difficulty, or to adapt to a new problem. The teacher would navigate the classroom to provide support and challenge.

The **Think-Pair-Share technique** provides the students with valuable thinking time. I would always recommend setting the conditions for success during the setup. For example, 'I am about to ask you a question about the solar system.' You haven't told the students the question yet, but you are activating their prior knowledge (retrieval). You can then explain to the students what is going to happen. 'I will ask you the question, then I will finish with a long pause to give you time to think. During this stage, don't call out. Don't put your hand up, think first.'

You then pose the question, insisting on silence where needed. A long pause is added before you say, 'Now, write down your answer.' Follow this with another brief pause. 'Okay, pair up with your partner and share your thoughts.' During this time, you can scan the room and start to check engagement and participation.

The final step requires you to state, 'Now, write down your final answer and be prepared to show me your replies on a mini-whiteboard.' Having something written down is concrete. Demanding that all students show their reply pulls the information out of the student's head. After a brief '3-2-1', the students raise their responses into the air and the teacher systematically checks at once before moving on.

Step 5: Practise, reflect, and refine

1. Each week/lesson, spotlight one study strategy for your students.
2. Model the strategy with a live example piece of work; use the 'how to do this' in stages. Show what happens, what works, what went wrong, and what options are available.
3. Help students to reflect at key stages: 'Did this strategy help me to remember more?'
4. Adapt your classroom charter as needed, based on student age, subject, and student feedback and outcomes.

Step 6: Review the impact

Nothing is worth pursuing without any evidence or impact. Ask: 'Are you better off since... [this was introduced]?' After a half-term, revisit your original checklist or classroom charter and ask:

1. Has student confidence improved?
2. What strategies are mostly embedded?
3. What impact does retrieval have on the start or end of the lesson?
4. How do mini-whiteboards build knowledge-confidence with my students?
5. How do low-stakes quizzes assess retention, not just performance?

I often describe Dunlosky's research in the context of teaching sex education. We don't necessarily use the nicknames of our body parts, even though some of these phrases might be used regularly at home; instead we teach students the biological names. We use the correct terminology to avoid developing further misconceptions.

I liken this example to the word 'revision'. Although there is nothing wrong with this word linguistically, it is *not* the language for learning. I would also add that the 'science' behind revision has not been explicitly taught, so depending on where you went to school, who taught you, and the circles around your education network, you may or may not have been taught 'how to learn'.

Instead, in today's classrooms we might use 'retrieval' as an evidence-based technique for building knowledge confidence. This word derives from the

French word, *retrouver* which translates 'to find again'. This is an expressive analogy to understand the science behind retrieval: 'What did you have for dinner last night?', 'What date is your birthday?' One of these questions you might struggle with, whereas the other I would expect you to easily answer within a couple of seconds. Why is that?

In essence, we are finding this information again, and pulling it from our long-term memory (LTM), manipulating this information in our working memory and pulling it out from our heads – either by writing it down (**procedural knowledge** – how to perform a skill or process), or saying it out loud (**declarative knowledge** – the conscious knowing of concepts, rules, and facts). The challenge is that if any information is not stored in our LTM, then it is likely to be forgotten, whereas information can be easily retrieved if it has been stored. When information is deeply embedded into our LTM (our schema), we can build on it – very much like *building a brick wall*. What we learn is built upon what we already know!

The term 'retrieval' is used in the field of cognitive science, and on my travels and visits into the classroom, I now hear this word being used by Year 3 and Year 4 students in classrooms. The message? Our teachers are beginning to teach our students the language of learning, and this links directly to Dunlosky's ten study skills cited earlier.

While this language isn't used everywhere, I do see an underground revolution taking place in many classrooms across the country. I am optimistic that the current generation of students are being given the tools for learning, yet we 'intermittently fail to take stock of where [our] minds are currently residing' (Schooler and Schrieber, 2004, p. 27). Increasingly, our teachers today are developing these tools to help sustain motivation and attention, and by understanding more about attention, this knowledge should start to ripple through each generation of teachers trained in the future.

Neuroimaging evidence can explain why certain techniques work, and knowing more about attention can help us understand how we focus or why we daydream, or from an fMRI lens, how some neurodivergent students may appear to struggle across aspects of our curriculum. Mind wandering 'experience is costly in educational contexts' (Smallwood and Schooler, 2015) and we need to understand how this happens. In the same research, Smallwood and Schooler state that, although the benefits of daydreaming are less understood, 'mind wandering may have some important functions including contributing to future planning and creativity' (p. 25). We know retrieval practice lights up memory centres in the brain, and dual coding links verbal and visual systems. How do we use fMRI to build neuroliteracy confidence for all teachers, families, and students? (We will touch further on neuroliteracy in Chapter 2.)

TOOLKIT TIPS

1. Teach the language of learning explicitly. Move beyond generic terms like 'revision' and switch to cognitive vocabulary such as 'retrieval', 'spacing', and 'interleaving'.
2. Pair your teaching methods with learning strategies. For example:
   - Direct instruction → self-explanation
   - Questioning → elaborative interrogation
3. Co-construct a learning charter with your class. Create 2–3 non-negotiable norms, rooted in evidence.
4. Model thinking out loud; avoid playing guesswork!

WORKED EXAMPLE

In this chapter, I have explained why introducing cognitive science principles to students and encouraging them to engage with the ten study strategies to create a classroom learning charter helps develop a shared language of learning and boosts student agency as learners. Through talking more about the learning experiences, both teachers and students see learning as an active, and iterative, process.

So now, here is an example of a teacher working with Year 8 students in a science classroom, developing a learning charter with the students.

Miss Patel teaches Year 8 science and wants to boost knowledge retention well before the summer exams. Guided by the teaching and learning team, educational research, and her developing understanding of memory processes, she constructs a 'learning charter' with her students.

Step 1: Audit existing strategies/diagnose existing habits

Miss Patel starts with a class discussion: 'How do you revise at home?' Students mostly state that they reread their exercise books and highlight text they have made from writing up additional notes. Some of them also say they like to complete some of the online quizzes, but sometimes they find it 'a bit boring'.

Step 2: Build a charter together

Over two lessons, Miss Patel introduces research-informed study techniques and asks students to discuss how many they are familiar with. She then leads her class to create three shared learning norms following a discussion on revision myths:

1. We use retrieval starters every Monday and Thursday.
2. We use dual coding to revise processes, combining flow diagrams with keywords.
3. We use elaborative questioning when working in pairs: 'Why does this happen?'

Step 3: Teach through practice

Miss Patel begins each lesson with a 'Do now' quiz. (Some schools and colleges might call this a retrieval practice exercise, a starter activity, or something similar.) She models self-explanation during the worked example demonstrations, for example, 'I am explaining this out loud because...' and sets homework to redraw diagrams from memory using dual coding.

Step 4: Review and reflect

After half a term, she revisits the charter with students. A student feedback survey reveals that students now feel more confident recalling processes like 'photosynthesis'. She adjusts the charter slightly, removing one strategy that wasn't working and adding interleaving between biology and chemistry topics. The updated charter is added to her slide deck, and is also pinned to the wall at the front of the classroom.

This process has helped to embed cognitive strategies into Miss Patel's classroom routines, with students owning the language for learning. For decades, we've used the word 'revision', but a more appropriate term for learning in this context would be 'retrieval'.

TEMPLATE

Science of Learning Classroom Charter

Use the template to help plan your own classroom charter. The template is practical, flexible, and deeply rooted in research, and it forms pedagogy without being overly academic. Ask yourself:

1. How will your charter be displayed or revisited?
2. How will students reference this charter during lessons?
3. How will you review its impact and when will you review it?

The balance you strike in your classroom will make a big difference to your students' motivation. I would strongly encourage you to involve students in the process, no matter how old they are.

Scan the QR code for a downloadable copy of this blank template.

Stage	Prompts and guidance	Your notes/ reflections
Strategy focus	Co-construct or select 1–3 strategies to embed in your classroom with students: ☐ Cognitive load reduction ☐ Dual coding ☐ Elaboration ☐ Engagement ☐ Highlighting ☐ Interleaving practice ☐ Motivation ☐ Mnemonics ☐ Rereading ☐ Retrieval practice ☐ Self-explanation ☐ Spaced practice ☐ Summarisation	Example: Retrieval and dual coding for half-term three
Context	Define your teaching context here.	Example: Year 8 science in the biology lab; aim is to use and apply photosynthesis knowledge and recall key process and stages
Learning norms (co-constructed with students)	Work with your class to agree on 2–3 learning principles linked to the appropriate strategies above. Remember, these need to be applicable to the students age, time of year, and subject.	Example: 1. We start every Monday with a retrieval quiz. 2. Draw diagrams from memory at the end of every lesson. 3. We use 'because' in every answer to explain our decisions and understanding.

Stage	Prompts and guidance	Your notes/ reflections
Weekly lesson routines	Plan how the strategies will appear regularly.	Example: ☐ Retrieval starter every Tuesday ☐ Strategy spotlight display ☐ Weekly sketch note task ☐ Peer pair share explanation ☐ Interleaved quiz across topics
Impact and review	Define how you measure impact: • Define what success looks like. • How will you gather feedback? • When will you review?	Example: ☐ Exit tickets and weekly quiz ☐ Student voice survey after six weeks ☐ Witness a change in data and improved long-term recall in the topic ☐ Student confidence ☐ Attendance

CHAPTER 2
MEMORY AND FORGETTING

When we talk about how the brain processes and learns new information, it's tempting to retreat into comforting metaphors such as, 'the brain acts like a sponge' or 'neurons that fire together, wire together'. In truth, learning is messier and slower than this. There are thousands of books published about how we learn, topics about the brain, how to teach students better, and how to get them to remember more. In contrast, there are very few books published about the importance of 'why we forget', or why forgetting is very much part of the learning process. And why are training sessions about 'forgetting' rarely organised?

Significant advances in neuroimaging, fMRI, and EEGs may help answer this question. Some fMRI studies demonstrate how 'participants' thoughts wander freely' (Seghier et al., 2019, p. 5), reshaping our understanding of memory formation, attention, and even the emotional weight of a 'lightbulb moment'. We are all prone to 'mind wandering' in our daily lives, and know too often, what 'detrimental consequences' (Smallwood and Schooler, 2015, p. 25) it has on our attention span. A lack of focus tends to 'disrupt memory, comprehension, [and] intellectual functioning' (Smallwood and Schooler, 2015, p. 25) and – crucially – participation in the classroom.

How can we make sense of fMRI insights without falling into neuromyths or neuroscience novelties? In this chapter, we will move beyond slogans and scan images to explore what we really know about how learning occurs in the brain, and what still remains uncertain. This isn't about turning teachers into neuroscientists; it's about building neuroliteracy – the ability to interpret research critically and apply it ethically, while always keeping students at the centre of our classroom decisions.

EXPLAINER

Let's look at the biology of how the brain processes information. Learning is a mixture of memory systems, cognitive constraints, and environmental factors. Neuroscience allows us to peek inside the black box of learning, while interpreting what we see with caution.

In recent years, researchers have taken neuroimaging out of the lab and into the classroom, using tools like EEG to measure real-time brain activity during lessons. Neuroeducational studies are helping us to understand what is happening in the brain when pedagogical decisions are made. This is enabling teachers to better understand memory, processing, and brain plasticity.

The science of memory

Teachers have grappled over the last five to ten years with the neuroliteracy around working memory and cognitive load theory (CLT). The seminal study 'The effect of cognitive load on the retrieval of long-term memory: An fMRI study' (Sisakhti et al., 2021) discusses the link between neuroscience and practical classroom implications. In this study, the researchers discuss how students often appear to 'forget' content during lessons or tests not because the information has disappeared, but because their brains are overloaded with competing demands. The fMRI used in the study determined 'the mechanism by which a difficult-to-retrieve memory is handled is mainly by elevating the activation of the responsible brain areas and not by getting other brain regions involved' (p. 1). This research helped to demonstrate that when cognitive load increases, students' ability to retrieve long-term memories diminishes.

Research by Smallwood and Schooler (2015) tracks changes in attention and neural activation when a person moves from focusing on a task to having unrelated thoughts.

The fMRI scans they took demonstrated an increase in blood flow when the brain was working harder and using more oxygen compared to when people are less focused on a task. So when a student starts daydreaming during a lesson (for example, thinking about what is for lunch!), the brain activates a different area compared to when they are focused on the classroom tasks.

This area is called the default mode network which is a network of the brain areas involved when your mind is not focused on the outside world (e.g. reflecting, thinking about yourself, or thinking about others).

Using fMRI allows us to see these changes, and, importantly, it tells us that daydreaming isn't lazy thinking; it's measurable and is (critically) a neurological state that is an *essential* part of brain activity. However, this is different from being interrupted, where someone else actually changes your thinking state. This, of course, is challenging to measure, but using fMRI may help explain when someone is focused or not.

Neural efficiency

As our understanding of working memory continues to evolve, the role of neural efficiency in learning becomes more significant. A recent study poses a question I have previously asked myself as a teacher: Is neuroimaging ready for the classroom?

In a systematic review of **hyperscanning** studies in learning (Tan et al., 2023) (in which brain activity between two or more students is recorded at the same time when they are talking to each other), researchers used fMRI technology to explore how working memory capacities perform under cognitive load and emotional distraction.

The research suggested that 'teacher-student [inter-brain synchrony] over the **frontal, occipital and parietal regions** of the brain was greater when teachers used videos during lessons than when teachers gave lectures' (Tan et al., 2023, p. 6). See the figure on the next page to learn more about these regions.This is vital for teachers, as it sheds light on why some students can sustain focus or complete tasks efficiently, while others become overwhelmed – even if the tasks appear identical on the surface. It also supports the idea that working harder doesn't always mean learning better, particularly when cognitive load is too high. For teachers, this reinforces the importance of instructional clarity, scaffolding tasks and reducing extraneous distractions that could disproportionately affect students with lower working memory capacity or attentional control.

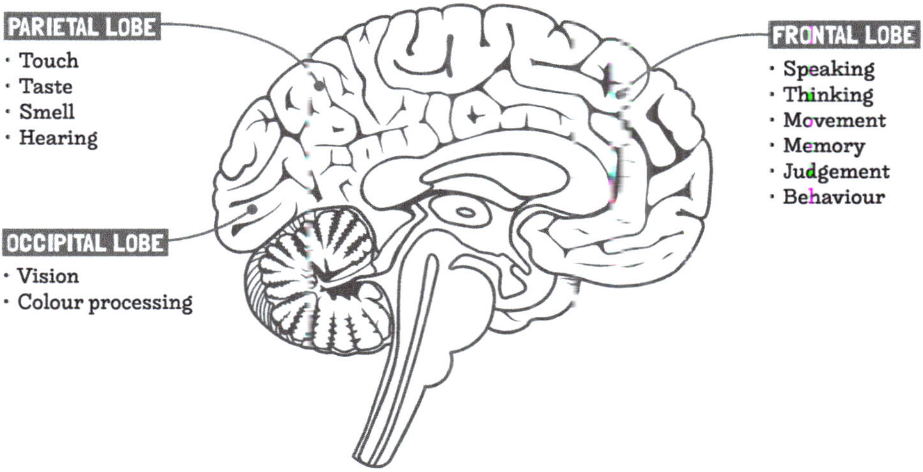

Real classroom scenarios

Let's be honest, very few teachers have access to an fMRI machine, but that doesn't mean neuroscience has no place in the classroom.

In 2020, I hosted a podcast with Professor Barry Carpenter CBE, who had conducted research into the cognitive functioning of premature children. This conversation made me reflect more deeply on my own son's extreme prematurity and the questions it raised about his cognitive development. It is Barry's belief that 'all headteachers should receive a psychological report and an MRI scan with a neuroscientific analysis of the brain function of their pupils' (Carpenter, 2020). So, what if fMRI scans could give teachers clues about how brain activity relates to classroom behaviour, especially under different instructional conditions, and individual brain health? For example, when students experience high cognitive load, neuroimaging shows reduced activity in regions responsible for retrieving long-term memory (LTM). How should teachers adapt when working with vulnerable students for example, or those with neurodiverse needs? How could teachers reduce students' stress and anxiety in order to boost retrieval? In retrieval practice, one of the most evidence-backed techniques in educational research, Simić and Manenica (2012, p. 70) demonstrated that students experienced 'higher stress in the first minutes of the exam', and they measured heart rate as 'a good indicator of students' stress in classrooms'. We know the 'testing effect', often called retrieval practice, has specific 'effects on learning and intellectual skills' (Atabek et al., 2022, p. 2). I have been exploring and trialling ideas with teachers working with neurodiverse students in early years settings, alternative provision, and with teachers supporting disaffected students in further education college settings. Retrieval practice is an effective strategy, but unsurprisingly it requires mixed methods and, importantly, low stress, with no grade.

What would happen if we tested retrieval practice with a more efficacious study technique, for example, elaboration? In a meta-analysis, 'Retrieval practice versus elaborative encoding', researchers learned that:

> **'the typical positive effect of retrieval practice is substantially reduced relative to encoding tasks known for decades to promote retention... [The] provision of feedback and the adoption of free recall for performing retrieval practice were essential for preserving that effect.' (Gonçalves et al., 2025, p. 45)**

In other words, elaboration (tell me why/how) was just as effective as retrieval practice.

Although very few studies have directly measured the benefits of retrieval practice using fMRI, indirect findings strongly suggest that effortful recall strengthens neural connections. We can infer that when a student practises low-stakes quizzing, brain activity likely consolidates memory more effectively than passive review like highlighting or rereading. Similarly, dual coding – the combination of verbal and visual information – is supported by CLT. When executed carefully, it reduces the burden on working memory by spreading input across multiple channels. What if fMRI could show that using either dual coding or retrieval practice as a strategy physically shows that the technique activates the brain? Thinking and working like a cognitive scientist, and using neuroscience research in education allows us to become much more intentional in our pedagogical decisions.

Neuroimaging and fMRI

The research paper, 'The concreteness effect: Evidence for dual coding and context availability' (Jessen et al., 2000) tested dual coding using neuroimaging to determine how students engage with words. Brain scans suggested increased activity not just in visual areas, but in spatial regions of the brain, particularly the right parietal lobe, responsible for processing and interpreting information.

The results suggested students weren't just seeing a flat image, they were mentally mapping ideas in a 3D space. Dual coding isn't just about slapping a picture next to some text on a presentation slide; it's about helping students construct mental models that are rich, spatial, and deeply memorable. Think Venn diagrams, labelled timelines, or even physically moving around a concept. When teachers get this right, it is not just 'decorating' learning; it is activating deeper cognitive pathways to support LTM.

Emotional and environmental factors

Conversations about working memory and CLT dominate much of the current educational landscape, but rarely do we consider emotion part of the same conversation. Think about how learning happens when students feel happy, safe, angry, or hungry? Emotional states, whether anxiety, excitement, or boredom, directly influence how information is processed, encoded, and retrieved.

Research into affective neuroscience shows that when students feel psychologically safe, their brains are more receptive to new learning. Conversely, stress floods the brain with cortisol, disrupting the hippocampus (responsible for memory consolidation) and impairing the working memory. This is why classroom dynamics and teacher-student relationships matter as much as the content being delivered. A teacher might be modelling a perfect retrieval strategy, but if a student feels overwhelmed, or perhaps ashamed that they're not understanding the point being made, their brain isn't primed to learn.

Alongside emotion, recent research suggests that the learning environment itself; noise levels, lighting, classroom layout, even temperature, can either enhance or inhibit cognitive performance. The landmark HEAD (Holistic Evidence and Design) project (Barrett et al., 2015) analysed over 150 classrooms across 27 English primary schools and found that classroom design alone accounted for '16 per cent of all influences on the variation in pupils' academic performance' (p. 127). This is the equivalent of a full term's worth of additional learning! The researchers identified three key design principles:

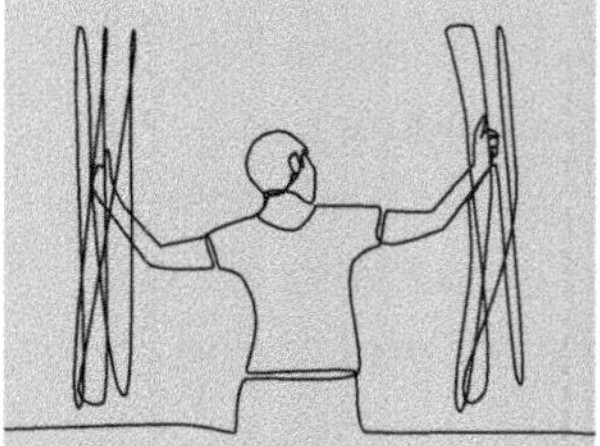

1.
Naturalness
(lighting, air quality, temperature)

2.
Individualisation
(student ownership and flexible layout)

3.
Stimulation
(colour and visual complexity)

While these may sound like environmental luxuries, they are in fact cognitive tools, working in tandem with students' emotional states and attention systems. When we neglect the physical context of learning, we risk overloading students with invisible barriers. If we can optimise these conditions, through better lighting, air, comfort, and a sense of belonging, you can unlock more of your students' working memory, motivation, and attention. We must seriously consider classroom design as a forethought, rather than as an afterthought, and start recognising the environment as an essential component of CLT in action.

In the next section, we will consider key study skills and how these methods 'light up the brain' for students in the classroom.

PRACTICAL IDEA

Memory maps and cognitive warm-ups

In this section I will help you create low-effort routines to prime the **encoding** and **retrieval** stages of the learning process. I will help you to prepare students to learn challenging information and retrieve it in various circumstances, whether this is online, in the classroom through questioning in front of their peers, or in a high-stakes exam. I will offer a chunked curriculum overview, memory recall starters, and visual memory aids that are all rooted in cognitive and working memory limits and provide you with examples that you can apply to different subjects and key stages.

First, let's consider the three most popular study skills: retrieval practice, spaced practice, and elaboration (Dunlosky et al., 2013), and unpack why these are good techniques for all teachers to use, across the entire sector.

Retrieval practice, or working memory training, is a great classroom technique to boost knowledge. Takeuchi et al. (2010) suggest that our 'individual capacity of working memory is associated with the integrity of white matter in our frontoparietal regions' (p. 3297). Takeuchi and colleagues reported that after working memory training, 'white matter structure changes' occurred in the brain. This is an example of how rehearsing material actually changes white matter, which is a type of brain tissue made of nerve fibres (axons) in your brain. White matter is important because it's where signals are transmitted to other parts of the brain relating to memory, attention and critical thinking.

Many neuroimage studies show activation of the hippocampal regions when effortful recall (hard thinking) is used. For example, when a teacher organises a retrieval practice quiz, the students have to 'find again' information from the LTM and manipulate this information in their working memory to solve the problem at hand. It is recommended that teachers keep the challenge high, but reduce the stress, as this is one of the best ways to achieve success.

The challenge for teachers is how to do this systematically. You are, after all, one teacher, working with countless students. You could use low-stakes quizzing methods such as 'thumbs up' or 'thumbs down', or 'Show me what you're thinking' on your mini whiteboard, or by completing a 'Do now' activity, designed for students to complete immediately on arrival to the lesson, with no teacher direction or input.

In one of my favourite teaching books, *Powerful Teaching: Unleash the Science of Learning* (Agarwal and Bain, 2019, p. 28), the authors write that 'retrieval and the process of getting information out is so simple, intuitive, and flexible' and is an intuitive way for teachers to build memory strength with their students. 'Power tickets' (think small question cards handed back to the teacher) are paper or online tools designed to retrieve and strengthen knowledge; they are used to connect feedback, retrieval, spaced, and interleaving practice all in one place. How the 'tickets' are designed can also build in the theory of dual coding prompting responses from students via text or images. Imagine having one resource that uses five evidence-based ideas from the science behind learning? Power tickets are worth trialling in your classroom! See an example here: **https://tinyurl.com/CognitiveWarmUp**

'Retrieval grids' are another effective technique I've seen used in classrooms, inspired by teacher and author Kate Jones and quoted in *Powerful Teaching* (Agarwal and Bain, 2019, p. 166). 'Retrieval grids' as questions about information learned 'Last year, last term, last month, last week, last lesson, today' are a fabulous resource for all student ages. This resource and technique could look like this:

	Today	Last lesson	Last week	Last month	Last term	Last year
Image						
Write one fact						
Write a paragraph						
Label the diagram						

To increase success, I would always encourage you to give students something to write down, as well as saying something out loud. By writing AND saying, we are pulling the information out of someone's working memory. In the above example, you could pose a question every other lesson, or every five minutes depending on the context of the lesson, and ask students to respond to each row and column. This can be used as a cognitive warm-up to map what students know from memory, to help connect schemas, and to identify current misconceptions and gaps in their knowledge.

1. Give a blank template to each student.
2. Pose a question, a statement that is true or false, or provide the student with a detailed instruction.
3. The student then responds on their own document in or out of the lesson.

The goal is for the student to have a full sheet of responses, evolving in accuracy over time, that can be used as a learning aid for reference, or for the individual to gauge their current understanding. In this example, each cell should only take a few moments to complete, with responses shared with you, with other students, or the class.

When you design and lead retrieval practice as an exercise to develop cognition, keep it subject- and age-specific, using a range of methods. Retrieval practice should never come with a formal assessment.

At times, you will want to encourage your students to correct their work or ask them to formally assess one another's responses. It should be a self-diagnostic tool as students identify the correct knowledge and gaps in their learning. You must also *avoid* leading the same retrieval practice exercise, in the same format, at the beginning or end of every lesson. It will lose its value and impact!

What would happen if you created low-effort routines that primed encoding and retrieval? How could these routines be embedded across the curriculum and chunked into one-off lessons? How can you include memory recall starters and visual memory aids, all rooted in cognitive load and working memory limits according to students' ages? Using the 'Last term, last month' approach means you are not formally assessing students, but you are keeping the challenge high, with mixed retrieval practice opportunities. By removing any formal assessment, you are reducing the stress associated with getting all the correct answers, 'speaking aloud' publicly to peers, or completing the entire grid. Remember, retrieval is a learning strategy, not an assessment strategy. Consider how you could use this template to cover subject content across a half-term, with students completing multiple versions of the resource for future reference.

TOOLKIT TIPS

1. Build 'forgetting' into your curriculum. Plan retrieval deliberately across time intervals (last term, last month, last week, last lesson) to revisit material strategically.
2. Reduce cognitive load before demanding any retrieval. For example, simplify your instructions, chunk tasks, combine words and visuals intentionally, and remove all distractions.
3. Keep retrieval low stakes, not high pressure. Remember, retrieval practice *never* comes with a grade!

WORKED EXAMPLE

One day, in Mr McGill's Year 9 geography classroom…

1. Mr McGill teaches Year 9 geography. At the start of the spring term, he decides to use 'memory maps' and 'cognitive warm-ups' to improve long-term retention of key concepts. His class has struggled with cumulative recall across topics, particularly before their summative assessment.
2. He begins by embedding a weekly cognitive warm-up using the 'last term, last month, last week, last lesson, and today' structure. Every Monday, students complete a warm-up grid during the first five minutes of the lesson. Each row requires them to recall one fact, label a diagram, or write a short explanation link to previous content.
3. Mr McGill differentiates opportunities by offering image prompts for students, including support for EAL (English as an additional language) and **SEND** learners, and models his own responses live.
4. No grades are given. Instead, the class checks their own answers from peer questioning, using mini-whiteboards, or cold calling (or another 'check for understanding process').
5. Over the half term, this teaching routine grows into a powerful metacognitive habit. Students start noticing gaps in their knowledge, identifying what they should do next – 'I forgot live volcanoes differ from dormant volcanoes' – and they begin self-quizzing using questioning grids before lessons.
6. To reinforce the retrieval further, Mr McGill layers in weekly 'power tickets'. Students write one challenging question linked to each time interval, which he collates. Families are then invited to try 'home quizzes' based on their child's latest memory map.
7. By the end of term, assessment scores rise, but more crucially, students describe greater confidence in 'connecting the dots' between old and new knowledge.

A key point to emphasise here is that there is NO work to be marked. The purpose of retrieval is to 'pull information out' of your students' heads and ask them to write it/say it out loud. Remember, retrieval is a learning strategy, NOT an assessment strategy, and this means it should never come with a grade.

TEMPLATE

Memory map and cognitive warm-up

Here is a template of a memory map and cognitive warm-up you can use or adapt in your own classroom. Use the QR code to download a printable version of this warm-up grid and adapt it for your students/subject or revision cycle.

Scan the QR code for a downloadable copy of this blank template.

This is a great resource to use as a questioning methodology, or you can ask students to respond or a mini whiteboard, or print this off on plain paper and ask the students to complete it across a lesson, over the week, or over the term, and help them build up a bank of responses. *Remember, you don't need to mark this – it's for student self-reflection and will reduce your workload!*

Section	Prompt	Your plan
1. Define curriculum focus	1. Which unit or topic are you supporting? 2. What key concepts must students retain across time?	E.g. Plate tectonics – types, causes, effects
2. Choose memory stages	1. Which intervals will warm up students' engagement? 2. What templates or techniques could you use?	☐ Last term? ☐ Last month? ☐ Last week? ☐ Last lesson? ☐ Today?
3. Choose response types	Select two to three formats to embed into your resource grid.	☐ Label diagram ☐ Recall one fact ☐ Recall two facts ☐ Paragraph ☐ Draw out concept ☐ True or false? ☐ Keyword definition ☐ Extended essay ☐ Performance ☐ Image/video ☐ Other ________
4. Frequency and format	1. How often will this routine happen in your lessons? 2. How will students record this? 3. How can you mix it up?	E.g. Every Monday; A5 book; first five minutes of the lesson.
5. Support and access	1. How will you scaffold for different students' needs? 2. How will you adapt in the moment? 3. Where and when will you use dual coding?	E.g. Icons or images on whiteboard; adapted worksheet; sentence stems. You could adapt dual coding to anchor concepts, e.g. tectonic plate = shaking earth symbol.

Section	Prompt	Your plan
6. Feedback method	1. How will students self-assess? 2. Is there an opportunity for pre-assessment?	☐ Cold call ☐ Peer marking ☐ Self-assessment ☐ Modelled answers ☐ Visualiser demonstration ☐ WAGOL (What A Good One Looks Like) ☐ Class discussion ☐ EBI (Even Better If) ☐ Take it one step further ☐ Other ____________
7. Power ticket extension (optional)	1. Ask students to write one quiz question per memory stage. 2. Build revision banks over time.	E.g. Collect digitally using QR forms, online survey, paper tickets, or evolving booklets to use later on for revision.
8. Family link (optional)	1. Suggest one question families could ask at home based on each week's grid. 2. Which concept do you remember best, and why? 3. Could your family design a difficult question to pose back to the rest of the class?	E.g. What did you remember from last month's lesson?

CHAPTER 3

NEUROMYTHS AND MISCONCEPTIONS

Neuromyths are false beliefs about how our brains function. One of the most prevalent is the notion that teachers should work to each student's preferred (learning) modality, e.g. audio, visual, and kinaesthetic. I analysed two meta-analyses, each of which had drawn opposite conclusions (McGill, 2025).

The first paper, peer-reviewed and drawing from a widely published work, said: 'There is no support for the matching claim that students with different learning styles need different forms of teaching matched to their style' (Hattie and O'Leary, 2025, p. 14).

Conversely, another published paper (not peer reviewed) stated that 'learning-style based instruction makes a positive contribution to academic success in every field, [suggesting a] highly statistically significant effect' (Erdem and Kaf, 2023, p. 35). What are we to believe from these conflicting findings? It's very difficult to know which argument to believe, but a good rule of thumb is to seek research that uses published work and is peer-reviewed.

Other such neuromyths include the suggestion that we use 'only 10 per cent of our brain' (Dhawan, 2014, p. 47), and that 'left-brained students are more logical, and that right-brained students are more creative' (Jarrett, 2014). These claims have often been presented as common knowledge in news outlets and social media; they are then picked up and repeated by parents, students, and teachers, despite being debunked by the scientific community. The persistence of neuromyths is more than a harmless quirk; it's a professional risk, and they undermine the hard work that teachers do every day. Believing in pseudoscience can lead adults to misdiagnose students' needs, waste precious planning time, or implement strategies that are off-the-mark, potentially damaging, or a waste of time and money. There may be damaging impacts on neurodiverse students who need early, targeted support rather than generalised reforms.

In this chapter, my aim is to separate fact from fiction by drawing on evidence from cognitive neuroscientific research.

EXPLAINER

Despite advances in educational research, perhaps the most enduring of all classroom myths is the belief that teachers should adapt their instruction to match visual, auditory, or kinaesthetic learning styles. This idea has now been thoroughly debunked and yet it continues to appear in school policies, teacher training sessions, and commercial CPD programmes. There are even academic papers still being published on it in 2026!

Hattie and O'Leary's review of 17 meta-analyses (covering over 100,000 students) offers a stark conclusion: 'There is little to no impact of matching teaching with preferred learning style', and a 'negligible effect size' on outcomes (Hattie and O'Leary, 2025, p. 15). What makes this more troubling is the persistence of such beliefs, not just in professional discourse but in teacher training and performance management frameworks. So, why does it stick? The answer lies not in evidence, but in emotional and intuitive appeal. Learning styles *feel* inclusive, different, and student-centred. But they also promote unhelpful stereotypes, limit expectations, and divert attention from strategies that actually work. Hattie and O'Leary argue that this is not simply a pedagogical issue, but a scientific literacy one, e.g. that teachers need to be taught how to interpret, challenge, and apply educational research more critically.

Erdem and Kaf (2023), in a meta-analysis of Turkish studies, found a large positive effect size for learning-style-based instruction. However, their study relies heavily on unpublished data and non-peer-reviewed research. This contrast is an ideal case study to explain why *neuroliteracy* – the ability to evaluate scientific evidence – is an essential teacher competency in a world saturated with educational claims, algorithms, and misinformation.

Adding further weight to the call for critical thinking, neuroscience and fMRI research shows that popular myths like 'left-brain/right-brain learning' also lack scientific support. The idea that some students are left-brained (logical) and others are right-brained (creative) has been dismantled by decades of neuroimaging studies. fMRI data shows that complex tasks like reading, problem-solving, or creating art activate multiple interconnected brain regions across *both* hemispheres. There is no evidence that teaching in ways that cater to a student's brain dominance enhances learning, and yet 'one-third of academics [state] that they would continue to use learning styles despite being presented with all the evidence' (Newton and Miah, 2017, p. 1). Even more powerful is recent research using fMRI and EEG to examine how specific pedagogical choices affect the brain. For example, Zhang et al. (2025) and Sisakhti et al. (2021) show how cognitive load and task complexity affect memory retrieval and attention in the classroom. These insights reinforce the need to prioritise instructional clarity, reduce distractions, and avoid misdirected effort across all learners.

An important systematic review of 24 fMRI studies and 401 participants in 'Can we predict real-time fMRI neurofeedback learning success?' looked at how the brain is activated during different learning processes (Haugg et al., 2020). The review helped to determine which brain regions are consistently involved in learning, and how different types of learning tasks activate different neural circuits. 'More than 20 different cortical and subcortical regions' associated with behavioural functions were analysed to provide neurofeedback about behavioural functions (p. 3343).

The challenge is how do we interpret fMRI results and apply them meaningfully in education. In Haugg et al.'s (2020) study, a 'slightly positive correlation between pretraining activity [brain activity measured before neurofeedback training] and neurofeedback [using brain activity or real-time fMRI brain feedback] learning success' was observed, but there were *no* common 'brain-based success predictors' (p. 3840). The message? Even though we are continually gathering enhanced brain data, understanding how learning actually happens in the brain does not provide a reliable, general predictor of who learns to regulate successfully. We can, however, understand that when feedback or reward is involved in learning tasks, the prefrontal cortex is active (see Chapter 1, page 6[illegible]), suggesting immediate feedback will enhance engagement and consolidation.

Remember fidget spinners?

Fidget spinners were successful toys 'said to have good impact on attention for children with ADHD and hand motor control' (Narukawa et al., 2023, p. 1), with 'future research required to examine the biological mechanisms behind the potential benefits' (p. 6). fMRI scans have shown that there are different levels of activation in the supplementary motor area (SMA) of the brain using different types of fidget spinners, e.g. 'eccentric' fidget spinners (custom-designed and engineered), versus standard, symmetrical fidget spinners. The SMA of the brain plans, sequences, and initiates complex movements and speech.

In another study, 'an improvement in fine motor control may have been due to the manipulation of the fidget spinner' (Koiler et al., 2022, p. 4). The research results 'suggested that using fidget spinners improved neural efficiency for simple motor tasks in an ADHD sample' of individuals (Koiler et al., 2022, p. 97). This dispels the idea that these are marketing gimmicks and may provide parents and special educational needs services with the evidence they need to support neurodivergent learners. The growing body of evidence in this area helps us to make the case for a neuroliteracy curriculum for teachers: a sustained CPD programme that helps teachers move from myth to method.

Ask yourself: 'What does [a certain] activity do to my students' attention, memory, and motivation?' or 'Is this strategy supported by evidence or assumption?' Most importantly, 'What teaching practices am I doing/not doing that might get in the way of learning?' These are essential questions for all reflective teachers.

Reassessing learning styles, brain dominance myths, and pseudo-neuroscientific beliefs is not just about 'debunking' myths, it's about redirecting professional learning towards what is proven to help. Most importantly, this is also about protecting the integrity of our classrooms, ensuring time, energy, and effort are spent where they can have the greatest impact. fMRI scans show how working memory and cognitive control is activated during learning, but as they cannot inform us how to improve our teaching, understanding any connections between neural activity and classroom practice remains inconclusive and indirect. At the time of writing, fMRI studies should be treated with caution, while still being a topic of interest.

In the next section, we will tackle neuromyths and exploit some techniques to equip teachers and students for the classroom.

PRACTICAL IDEA

The debunking board: A classroom wall of myths and facts

Empower your students to critically reflect on their work by identifying common learning myths. In this section I will help you develop a classroom display and interactive space that explicitly challenges misconceptions and replaces them with research-backed truths. This can be used throughout the academic year to help students build a bank of study skills.

Rereading and *highlighting* are two of the most widely used revision strategies in our schools and colleges. But they are also two of the least effective when used in isolation. Many students rely on highlighting and rereading techniques because they feel safe, productive, and familiar. However, Ruiz-Martín et al. (2024) found in their study of over 5,000 Spanish secondary students, that students who relied primarily on these techniques performed lower academically. The study also highlighted that 'secondary school students in our sample [who] clearly pursue performance goals over learning goals' showed weaker beliefs about learning itself (p. 12); they seemed to be more interested in receiving high grades than actually learning and understanding the content. The study also found that retrieval practice and elaborative strategies were consistently linked to higher achievement and more positive learning attitudes. This gives teachers crucial insight: it's not that students are lazy, it's that many have never been taught the alternatives, or shown *how* to turn passive strategies into active ones. The 'how' for me always points back to that abstract concept of metacognition (see Chapter 5). How do we teach students how to learn, not just what to learn?

Modelling alone isn't enough

Today, many of you are becoming accustomed to showing students a worked example: 'This one got a Grade A'. Showing students concrete examples, or how to complete tasks in stages, is critical to the success of the classroom.

You could also demonstrate two revision techniques side by side:

- Student A rereads a passage and highlights everything.
- Student B closes their book, writes down what they remember, then checks it.

Ask students whether they think Student A or Student B will retain more. Model their effectiveness in the classroom. This introduces metacognition to students, thinking about how they study, not just what they study.

Teach rereading as preparation for retrieval

Rereading is not harmful; it's just overused and ineffective when used in isolation. Reposition this technique as a warm-up instead. For example: reread once, then quiz yourself. Or reread, then explain it to someone. Link this to 'elaborative interrogation': Why is this true? How does this connect to what you already know?

Reboot highlighting with purpose

Most students highlight far too much, and they don't use the variety of colours effectively if no methodology is attached. I've been there too, creating a 'sea of yellow colour' across the page with no structure. Instead, teach students to highlight no more than two or three key ideas in each paragraph. Then ask them to rewrite the key ideas in their own words on a separate sheet. This makes the act of highlighting a preparation for elaboration, which is one of the most impactful study techniques.

Bridge to retrieval

Link all of the above low-utility strategies to retrieval. For example:

Highlight text → Hide text → Recall key points

Reread → Close book → Sketch it out from memory

Read → Cover text → Write it down (check the answers)

These simple and small shifts preserve students' preferred techniques but increase the cognitive demand, thereby reinforcing long-term memory.

Share the research

Use posters or classroom displays to communicate what the research says. For example:

1. 'Did you know rereading feels productive, but testing yourself on the material works better?'
2. 'Are you highlighting everything and remembering nothing? Less is more!'

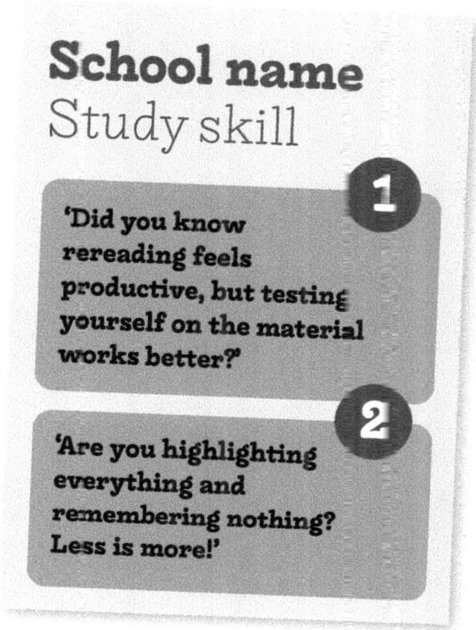

Make it part of CPD

As part of a CPD session, invite staff to complete a self-audit or quiz to explore which study strategies they model most often in their classroom. Use the results to help teachers retrain their students in evidence-backed habits without starting from scratch.

Why does this matter?

Changing study habits, particularly across the school or college organisation, is going to take a long period of time. But rather then banning ineffective strategies outright, reframing approaches allow you to build on students' existing routines and perceptions, helping them evolve rather than abandon what they know. For students, especially those preparing for high-stakes exams, this approach builds cognitive confidence. They begin to understand *why* a method works, not just *how* to use it. This is a great way to start teaching the essence of becoming a self-regulated learner (see Chapter 5).

Here is a step-by-step guide to help you bust some learning myths with your students:

1. Create a space in your classroom, perhaps a spare wall, a display board, or a shared online folder to create a 'Debunking learning myths' board or display.

2. Select common myths that tackle strategies students typically use. Consider what families say to you about studying and tackle the most popular only. Consider beginner and advanced strategies depending on expertise. Some examples might include learning styles, or left/right brain as a starting list.

3. Pair each myth with a research-backed fact. Include a brief explanation and, where possible, a reference to a research paper with a key headline. For example, Hattie and O'Leary (2025): 'No impact of learning styles'.

4. Lead a learning quiz: Turn some of these facts into retrieval starters to help reinforce key study skills. Design it as a warm-up exercise or a weekly quiz.

5. Make it interactive: Encourage students to contribute myths they've heard from their peers and tackle the research facts in class or for homework.

6. Link to study skills: Use myths like rereading and highlighting to teach retrieval practice and metacognitive strategies such as interleaving and dual coding.

7. Link to professional development: Share the ideas in department meetings or whole school/ college training. Invite colleagues to reflect on how they model study strategies in class. Develop a whole organisational approach so that study skills are explicitly taught.

8. Review an update regularly: Rotate displays and content so the ideas stay fresh and continue to prompt critical thinking; this allows students to start regulating their own learning patterns.

TOOLKIT TIPS

1. Teach scientific literacy, not just strategies, and always evaluate with scepticism and curiosity.
2. Replace brain myths with mechanisms. For example, don't just say 'learning styles don't work', instead explain attention, working memory, and cognitive load.
3. Students often rely on rereading and highlighting because they feel productive. In class, turn these techniques into active recall.
4. Use fMRI insights cautiously, but purposefully. Brain scans will never tell you how to teach, but they can inform your planning and delivery.

WORKED EXAMPLE

Mrs Rodriguez started to recognise that misconceptions about effective learning were common in her Year 10 RE lesson. Students often claimed, 'I'm a visual learner' or 'I use pink and green highlighters to revise'. Recognising the persistence of these myths, Mrs Rodriguez introduced a '*Debunking board*' in her classroom which she placed with some engaging pictures to spark conversations at her classroom entrance. The purpose was to challenge popular neuromyths and start a classroom conversation about how learning actually works.

She selected five common learning myths her students often talked about. With input from other colleagues, and references to recent research studies (including Hattie and O'Leary's meta-analysis of learning styles), she created a *myth/fact* poster with QR codes to quizzes, one-minute video explainers and hyperlinks to short blog posts that she and her department started to publish on the school website.

Every week, a new myth was added. Mrs Rodriguez used the posters during lesson starters. Students guessed whether a claim was true or false, then discussed the evidence behind the correct answer. In the first week, the class explored the myth 'You only use 10 per cent of your brain' to help challenge misconceptions about learning. Using an interactive quiz, she followed up with students questioning one another on how different parts of the brain activate during problem-solving activities. Mrs Rodriguez provided students with a simple fact sheet and questions that could be used to learn the truth. Some were factually accurate, while others were misleading to help students determine what correct questions they should now be asking, and which they should be avoiding.

She also gave students practical revision advice. Instead of telling them to avoid highlighting completely, she modelled how to use it effectively by highlighting one or two keywords, using a particular colour for adjectives and another colour for subject keywords. She encouraged them to create a key for reference. For example:

- blue highlighter = terminology
- pink highlighter = facts
- red highlighter = myth.

After modelling how to use this technique effectively, she then hid what she had completed, waited five minutes in the lesson, then modelled what she now knew from memory, with students firing lots of questions to try and see what information she had forgotten. As you can imagine, the students loved trying to catch her out!

On completion, the worksheet and website could be used for future reference when students were studying alone, with each week building on the next myth. Over time, students started to build a bank of key strategies, and the classroom display became interactive. Students started to submit their own 'learning myths' at home from their family, or from online survey responses. For example, 'Cramming last minute works if you focus hard enough!' said one student. Each of these submissions were added and shared in rotation back in class.

Eventually, Mrs Rodriguez turned the board into a retrieval starter, asking students: 'Which myth was challenged last week?' or 'Can you explain why learning styles aren't supported by research?' The classroom display started to inform parents' evenings and other colleagues in the department. When families were introduced to the top five revision myths at parents' evening, they were shown alternative effective techniques. Mrs Rodriguez challenged any misconceptions, promoting metacognitive habits instead. The leadership team witnessed her success and started to roll out some of the great work going on across the entire school/college.

Fact or myth exercise

Some of the points in this exercise are drawn from sources that have inspired me while researching the neuroscience of teaching and learning. If I had to recommend two books in particular, they would be:

- *How learning happens* (Kirschner and Hendrick, 2020)
- *How the brain learns, sixth edition* (Sousa, 2022).

Now, let's see which myths you can spot on the table on the next page. Remember, I have included some facts and myths about learning as a worked example, suitable for you reading this book. In the template section, I strongly recommend you come up with your own version to suit your students' age, knowledge, and current ability. See the answers on page 148.

Effective learning habits	Fact or myth?
1. Cramming last minute always works!	
2. Multitasking is an effective way to study.	
3. Aligning words and images is good for learning.	
4. Everyone learns best when listening to music.	
5. Mixing up your study techniques can improve your learning.	
6. When testing yourself, always give yourself a grade.	
7. Rereading is not the most impactful study skill.	
8. Highlighting information in different colours helps you learn it better.	
9. New learning happens when it is anchored to prior knowledge.	
10. Your brain is not fully developed until your early 30s.	
11. Increasing time on a specific task increases retention of new learning.	
12. The brain goes through physical and chemical changes each time it learns something new.	
13. You either have a fixed or a growth mindset.	
14. Your frontal cortex, the front end of your forehead, is the last part of your brain to grow.	
15. It's recommended that you find a quiet place to study.	
16. When students receive prompt feedback, they continue to improve.	
17. When a student cares about their work, they achieve more.	
18. The faster a learner retrieves information from memory suggests how intelligent they are.	
19. Learning and retention are different. We can learn something for just a few minutes and then lose it forever.	
20. Chunking information is an effective way of enlarging working memory capacity.	

TEMPLATE

Good learning habits

Use the template below as a classroom display or as a lesson planning resource. Use it weekly or termly to keep the conversations fresh about good learning habits. The ideas in the second column will help you to get started.

Scan the QR code for a downloadable copy of this blank template that you can adapt for your own students and subject.

Section	Ideas
Myth	Write one myth you want to challenge (e.g. 'I am a visual learner').
Fact / Research insight	Replace the myth with a research-backed claim (e.g. 'There is no evidence for learning styles').
Evidence source(s)	Add a simple URL source or 30-second summary.
Teaching strategy	How will you use this in class (e.g. retrieval quiz, discussion prompt, task activity)?
Student response prompt	What question were you asked in order to prompt metacognitive reflection?
Link to study skill	What strategy does this connect with (e.g. retrieval, elaboration)?
Staff CPD links	How will this myth inform wider staff development?
Curriculum rotation plan	When will this myth be displayed? Where? Weekly? Monthly? Assemblies?
Family extension task	Optional takeaway myth-busting tip for home or revision guide (e.g. send by text message).

CHAPTER 4

COGNITIVE LOAD AND ATTENTION

Cognitive load theory (CLT) suggests that the new information we process and learn has a limited capacity. When too much information is given at one time, it's difficult for a person to engage with it all. They need enough time and space between instructions for their brain to hear and process what the new information is telling them. When a person reaches their capacity for taking in new information, they are more likely to lose attention; 'when the mind wanders, [our] attention drifts' (Smallwood and Schooler, 2015, p. 3). **Meta-awareness** is the ability to notice when you, or someone else, is daydreaming. Research into CLT was first published in 1988 (see below) and, since then, CLT has become one of the most quoted research principles in staff rooms over the last decade and in teacher training slides across the country. Too often, however, it's cited rather than understood. Have you read the research and can you describe the research to another teacher in 30 seconds? Has it made a difference to how you teach? These are important questions you should be asking about all research generally; it is vital to understand how key messages are filtered, translated, and communicated.

CLT was originally developed by John Sweller (1988) and today, it seems to be used to justify everything. When a student turns to you while you are mid-explanation and says, 'Miss, what did you just say?', that's not laziness, it's a cognitive overload queue. Their working memory has maxed out.

In this chapter, we will look at Sweller's original research, interrogate how our attention and memory are managed in real time, and bring in fMRI and EEG data to offer a richer picture of how cognitive load unfolds neurologically in order to move beyond teaching and learning techniques, and into the biology of learning.

EXPLAINER

What happens to our attention span when we make a decision? 'When humans are provided with ample time to make a decision, individual differences in strategy emerge' (Barnes et al., 2014, p. 1). For example, if you and I both decide spontaneously to go to the cinema, you may decide to choose a film there and then, whereas I may want to search the internet to read reviews. So, what problem-solving strategies are we both using? To help explain how people arrive at certain decisions and the strategies they take to get there, Barnes et al. (2014) carried out some fMRI research to test the neural basis of decision-making in quick scenario situations. The researchers were interested in understanding what happens in our brain networks and regions when making decisions. They found that there was a 'stronger activation of sensory brain regions in participants who used a "wait and see" strategy' (Barnes et al., 2014, p. 9). How our brains are wired, influences whether we make quick decisions, or pause to gather more information.

So, how does the fMRI study help you as a teacher? In practical terms in the classroom, students may adopt consistent ways of making decisions (quickly acting or, alternatively, waiting for more information). These habits are shaped by how their brains are already wired before the task begins.

Consider how we process information when decisions are made. This might be reading film start and end timings when visiting the cinema, reading questions during an exam, or understanding signs and signals while driving a car on the road. Longitudinal research using fMRI has shown that reading interventions can reduce cognitive load by making the process of decoding and comprehension more efficient. Meyler et al. (2008) demonstrated that for struggling adolescent readers, 'intensive reading intervention, leads to significant and enduring changes in brain function among poor readers', supporting the view that 'reading intervention promotes change in the neural systems that support skilled reading' (p. 12). This research suggests that teacher instruction does indeed make all the difference and that poor readers make substantial gains in reading ability as a result. Teaching students how to read, manage their attention, and learn how to make decisions is metacognition in action and are the building blocks for long-term success.

So, how do we teach those attention and decision-making habits? In Chapter 10, I offer an implementation plan for whole-school and college professional learning. The month-by-month calendar (page 140) could easily be adapted to create a student version that helps develop attention and decision-making habits, alongside taught study strategies.

Handwriting versus keyboard

If we consider how students complete work in and out of the classroom, what is more likely to yield better results for the individual: the pen or the keyboard? Which is more beneficial for attention span? 'Using a pen involves paying attention to motor aspects such as drawing letters legibly, controlling the pressure of the tip on the paper, following lines and spaces on the page, and coordinating thought, action, and vision' (Marano et al., 2025, p. 23), yet it differs from using a keyboard that requires 'motor programming, and fine motor development'. The research suggests that 'once automatic control of the graphic gesture is achieved, minimal cognitive effort is required' (p. 23). Think about how long you have been using a keyboard and how often you automate your fingers in a specific region as you type. This is in contrast to the fine (motor control) art of moving a pen to create individual letter shapes to construct the words. This recent fMRI study provides compelling evidence that 'handwriting activates a broader network of brain regions involved in motor, sensory, and cognitive processing, contributing to deeper learning, enhanced memory retention, and more effective engagement' (Marano et al., 2025, p. 23).

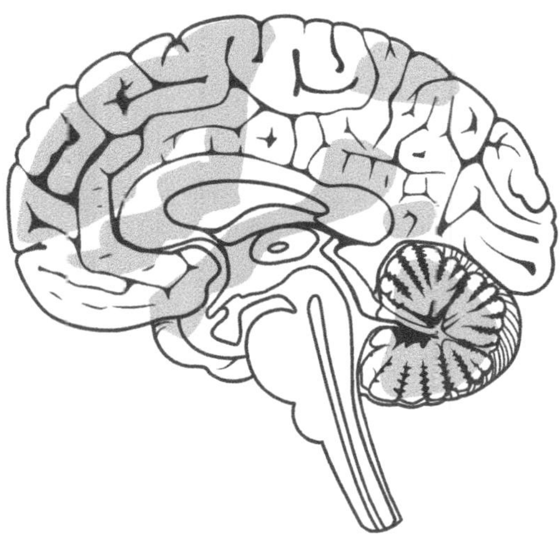

Brain regions associated with handwriting, adapted from Figure 2, Marano et al. 2025, p. 10

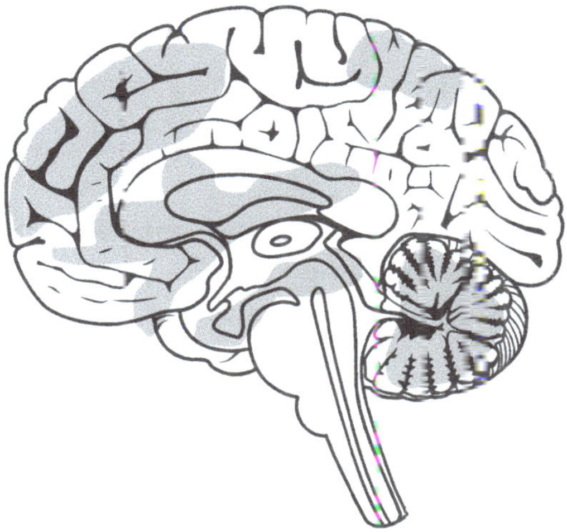

Brain regions associated with typewriting, adapted from Figure 2, Marano et al. 2025, p. 10

When I revisited Sweller's original research ('Cognitive load during problem solving: Effects on learning', 1988) I had no idea at the time that this piece of research would influence my views on attention span.

CLT is one of the most powerful ways to understand why some lessons fly and others flop. The basic idea? Our working memory is extremely limited. Whatever your age, research suggests that you can only hold between three to nine pieces of information in your working memory at any one time. However, it all depends on what the information is, what you already know, and if you are a novice or an expert in that topic. Add to that the type of classroom environment involved, the way the material is taught, as well as any emotions that need to be taken into consideration. Once that limit is reached, learning stops. That's not just a theory, it's also the biology of the brain.

CLT breaks the demands on our working memory into three categories:

1. Intrinsic load – the complexity of the task itself.

2. Extraneous load – the way the information is presented; this is often the parts that we, as teachers, have control over. For example, how would you teach photosynthesis to a group of thirty 11-year-olds in a secondary school biology lab? You can be exciting and engaging, or you might rely heavily on teaching from the textbook, which isn't always the best way to make new unknown concepts easy to understand. We all have a choice to make in the classroom about how to bring material to life.

3. Germane load – the productive mental effort needed to form and connect new knowledge. Remember, learning something new is built upon the foundations of what you already know.

Unless students already have some schemas – mental frameworks for understanding a problem – asking them to solve a novel problem 'using means-end analysis' (Sweller, 1988), or solving one step of the problem at a time, is too challenging.

What does this mean for curriculum and lesson planning?

CLT suggests that complexity should be managed. It means chunking information. It means building from the known to the unknown, not overloading slides, worksheets, or classroom instruction. Teachers can and should reduce extraneous load wherever possible: cut cluttered visuals, simplify instructions, avoid split attention (text over here, diagram over there, jazzy gifs and sounds on your slides). Keep the learning simple and ensure the learning details are explicit.

In *From Cognitive Load Theory to Collaborative Cognitive Load Theory* (Kirschner at al., 2018), the researchers argue that 'task complexity is key. Collaboration will occur when the task is complex enough to justify the extra time and effort involved in collaborating with others' (p. 226). Even collaborative learning can create collective cognitive overload if not carefully structured by the teacher.

In classroom studies involving fMRI scans, we can understand how increasing load not only reduces memory retrieval but decreases activity in key brain regions. We have visual proof that learning collapses when load is too high (Sisakhti et al., 2021) and evidence that increasing cognitive load impairs the performance of the long-term memory retrieval process by decreasing activation in key brain areas.

Retrieval practice

Need for cognition (NFC) is a personality trait describing how much people enjoy and engage in thinking. For example, when introducing new information, some students might want to know other contextual details to help them understand, whereas others are content with the straightforward information that will help them to answer a question. What would happen if we examined whether students who score high or low on NFC benefit differently from retrieval practice? Recent fMRI research suggests that retrieval practice leads to learning gains across all students, regardless of their appetite for cognitive effort. This is a reassuring message for teachers: effective strategies like retrieval practice don't just work for motivated or high-ability students – it works for everyone. But there is a critical caveat. While students may show similar test results, what's happening inside their brains may differ depending on factors like NFC. As Wiklund-Hörnqvist et al. (2022) remind us, 'behavioral equivalence does not always correspond to neural equivalence' (p. 3). Remember that just because two students perform similarly doesn't mean they processed or experienced the learning in the same way. Effective instructional design must consider cognitive efforts, and that retrieval practice is a universally beneficial strategy, even for students who don't believe they like to learn (or think hard).

This brings us to *attention span*, a topic I began to explore in *The Teacher Toolkit Guide to Memory* (McGill, 2022). How do the pedagogical techniques we use influence students' attention spans? We are getting closer to a position in which cognitive science and, specifically, brain neuroimaging (fMRI and EEG data) will be able to suggest to us what is working, why, and how. We should be cautious, however, specifically about how results from lab-based neuroimaging studies can meaningfully translate into classroom settings. While educational neuroscience has begun to recognise that there is 'no single brain region or connection indicative of individual learning capacity' (Seghier et al., 2019, p. 7), the 'ultimate aim is to identify the exact brain circuitry that can sustain a given mental process'.

Tan et al. (2023), in their review of hyperscanning studies in learning (see Chapter 2, page 22), found that teacher–student brain synchrony increased when lessons were scaffolded clearly and paired with multimodal input like video. What this tells us is that students don't need more chalk and talk, they need clarity, support, and space to think.

What does this mean for teachers?

CLT is *not* a one-size-fits-all solution – 'it is <u>not</u> a theory for everything' John Sweller said in an interview (2012) – but it is important as it reminds us to design lessons with students' minds at the heart of the curriculum process. It is all too easy to forget that we are experts in our subject matter, and the students that we are working with are novices. When you're an expert, you can hold your attention span for much longer than a novice. Added to that, if you are an expert, you can work forwards to solve a problem; as a novice, you need to work backwards from the solution. All expert teachers should help students work in stages, explaining and modelling in chunks to support the learning process. Instead of assuming students are not interested or inattentive, we should question whether the lesson activity is negatively creating cognitive overload. Consider whether your students are novices or experts in this topic. Have you reduced all the unnecessary distractions?

Curriculum leaders should question whether they have overplanned. Are their schemes of learning dense with objectives but light on processing time? Lesson planning becomes less about the number of activities and more about sequence and scaffolding. Even classroom layout and displays come into play; overstimulating rooms contribute to extraneous load, particularly for neurodiverse students.

In short, CLT theory states: teach less to teach more. Start with memory retrieval. Build schemas. Reduce clutter. Never underestimate how heavy a worksheet or a five-minute teacher explanation can feel to a student's mind. You are probably already applying CLT without even knowing it, for example every time you model a worked example, use dual coding, or pause to let students process. If you are doing those things in your classroom, you are already managing cognitive load.

In the next section, we will consider how you can manage cognitive load with practical strategies for the classroom.

PRACTICAL IDEA

Cognitive load audit of classroom materials

In this section, I invite you to review and redesign existing presentation slides, handouts, or worksheets using CLT (intrinsic, extraneous, and germane load). Use this as a department or key-stage-wide moderation, or in a CPD session.

The aim is to help you reduce unnecessary cognitive demands in your classroom materials and instructions. This can be used as a standalone CPD activity for yourself, as a department-wide curriculum review, or as a planning tool when working with early career teachers.

Please see the next page for a detailed step-by-step guide.

TOOLKIT TIPS

1. Design your lessons so you teach in chunks with the content sequenced from simple to complex.
2. Be ruthless about reducing extraneous load. Minimise all distractions on worksheets, slides, and in your instructions.
3. Sequence content before you scaffold new concepts, e.g. provide visual models, guide the practice, and remove any abstract representations.
4. Retrieval works for everyone! Keep it low-stakes and mix your methods.

1. **Choose your material:** Select one recent lesson resource such as a presentation slide deck, hand out, or worksheet to review.

2. **Print it out or display it with annotations:** Work in printed or digital format where you can make notes directly on the resource.

3. **Discuss the key differences in cognitive load theory:** Explain what intrinsic load is (the complexity) and what extraneous load is (the presentation).

4. **Audit the extraneous material:** Highlight the extraneous load and anything adding unnecessary demands on the students (e.g. too much text, not enough space in between the text lines, over-cluttered visuals, unnecessary animations, sounds or transitions in presentations, confusing fonts or colour schemes).

5. **Audit the intrinsic material:** Ask yourself what intrinsic load is in this content. Is it too complex for a novice learner? Have you introduced too many concepts at once? Can you sequence this scaffolded material more effectively? Is there a sufficient challenge for an expert student?

6. **Audit the germane load:** Identify places in the material where you can increase productivity. Where are the opportunities to add new knowledge? Have you added prompts for students to connect ideas? Are there worked examples followed by partial or independent practice? Have you built in space for reflection, with dual coding summaries?

7. **Redesign the material:** Using your annotations, simplify the layout, chunk the content into manageable parts, and add space for guided processing. Reduce unnecessary mental effort while preserving the challenge.

8. **Peer review:** Pair up with a colleague. Ask them to critique your material and offer feedback on how cognitive load could be reduced or germane load enhanced.

9. **Test the material with your students:** Pilot the redesign material with your class. Gather feedback on the clarity of instructions, the workload involved for students to understand material, and how engaging the content is. Ask students whether they found it hard to understand? Or, if not, what made this easier?

10. **Create a cognitive load checklist:** Use my checklist from the next section as a starting point to review new materials, resources, lesson plans, or slide decks you are planning to use with your students. Turn these audit findings into a departmental or key stage checklist for building future curriculum materials.

WORKED EXAMPLE

Here is an example of navigating cognitive load in the classroom. You can use this for evaluating your lesson materials and decision-making when planning lessons or resources.

Ms Harris is a Year 5 teacher and is preparing a lesson on adding and subtracting fractions with the same denominator. She selects a worksheet and a presentation she used last year, and her goal is to order the materials through the lens of CLT, ensuring clarity for all learners.

Step 1: Choose your material

Ms Harris selects a worksheet with ten fraction calculations and a presentation containing four teaching slides introducing key steps.

Step 2: Audit extraneous load

She notices the presentation uses a variety of fonts and unnecessary clipart (e.g. 'whooshing' noises and bouncing animations). The slides have been downloaded from a third-party platform and are quite generic. One slide includes a long, wordy explanation of equivalent fractions which duplicates what she plans to say aloud. Ms Harris knows that her students already understand a good definition of fractions and denominators. The worksheet has no consistent layout and requires students to navigate between number lines, shaded bar models, and abstract notation with no structure. Now she understands more about CLT, she is surprised she used the worksheet (successfully) at all in the past.

Action

Ms Harris simplifies the visuals by aligning number lines and fraction bars side-by-side. She uses a single font consistently throughout, that is large enough to be seen from all areas of the classroom. She removes all unnecessary clipart, and adds one key image to support key terms. She replaces any cartoons with clear fraction models. She also shortens explanations into clear and concise, numbered bullet points. Each stage of the process is also bulleted by numbers or letters.

A poor example of instructions on the resources might look like this:

- Turn to pg 2.
- Complete the sentence in B.
- Answer Q 3 and 6.

The simple action of adding letters or numbers makes it easier to process information and organise tasks.

A good example is shown in this improved format:

1. Turn to Page 2.
2. Complete the sentence in Section B.
3. Answer Questions 3 and 6.

The simple, yet important adjustment of bulleting by numbers or letters, and being clear with the wording, helps people to process information much more effectively.

Step 3: Audit intrinsic load

The core objective and concept of this lesson (e.g. to add fractions with the same denominators) is manageable, but misconceptions often arise when bridging from visual to abstract representation.

Action

Ms Harris sequences her classroom teaching as follows:

1. Visual representation and demonstration.
2. Fraction bar model guided practice.
3. Abstract notation, with time built-in for independent practice and targeted questioning.

Step 4: Audit germane load

To enhance schema (knowledge) building, Ms Harris includes a 'my turn, our turn, your turn' structure for building worked examples into the lesson, and she uses a variety of prompts to help answer the questions that many students ask: 'Why can we add the numerator but not the denominator?'

Action

Students complete partially completed bar models before attempting full questions. Ms Harris includes a reflection prompt on a key slide with little distraction; she offers one key image as a clue to the solution: 'What part of today's lesson helped this topic make sense for you?'

Step 5: Peer review and quiz

Ms Harris shares her revised worksheet with another primary colleague who suggests adding a glossary box to help build student subject literacy and confidence. She adds a 'Remember' strip at the top of the worksheet:

Same denominators = just add the numbers on the top half

During the lesson, students ask fewer clarification questions, complete the task more confidently, and they switch from monological and declarative questions towards dialogical responses that 'encourage open-ended inquiries and foster [not only] a two-way exchange of ideas' (Soysal and Soysal, 2023, p. 20) but also metacognitive question-asking in the classroom – 'a questioning technique that encourages students to think about their thinking and reflect on their learning processes' (p. 25). The students are so engaged and motivated that they begin to ask metacognitive questions of one another.

Download the blank template in the next section and design your own version once you've tried using this example to evaluate your most-used classroom resources.

TEMPLATE

Cognitive load audit template: Evaluating classroom materials

Use this five-step audit to redesign your lesson materials through the lens of cognitive load theory. Select one resource – a worksheet, slide deck, or homework activity – and follow the prompts below.

Each time you complete the table, save the audit as evidence of curriculum planning, or use it for future professional development sessions. Make sure you continue to repeat the process termly with different materials, and share your ideas with other colleagues.

Scan the QR code for a downloadable copy of this blank template

Focus area(s)	Reflection prompt	Notes / Actions
Select the material	- What classroom material are you reviewing? - When was it last updated? - When was it last used?	
Intrinsic load (How difficult the topic is to you [expert] or the student [novice].)	- What is the core concept? - Are there common misconceptions? - Is the material sequenced from simple to complex? - How is the content adapted for various needs?	

Focus area(s)	Reflection prompt	Notes / Actions
Extraneous load (How you choose to teach the topic/material. How do you make it accessible regardless of expertise?)	• Is there anything decorative, distracting or redundant? • Is the layout, font, or instruction structure confusing? • Could any audio/visual elements in the materials lead to distraction?	
Germane load (How do you help students make connections between knowledge?)	• Does the material promote deep understanding or connection to prior knowledge? • Are worked examples included? • What metacognitive prompts were used to guide thinking?	
Peer review and trial	• Have you shared this updated material with a colleague for feedback? • What did students say during or after the lesson? • What will you tweak next time? • Does it need to be presented differently? • Is the material still current and relevant for the curriculum?	

CHAPTER 5

METACOGNITION AND SELF-REGULATION

What is metacognition and how might fMRI help us understand it?

Metacognition is the ability to reflect on one's thought processes, and regulate decision-making. Remember, 'meta' means being aware of our thinking, and by examining our own thinking processes, we can modify them and improve them. Generating personal thoughts is an essential part of our working memory process and is distinct from external distraction. Emerging fMRI studies suggest 'rapid progress [has been] made within the past 15 years' (Katyal and Fleming, 2024, p. 226) in the ways we understand metacognition from a neurological perspective.

An interesting graphic inside 'The future of metacognition research' (Katyal and Fleming, 2024) offers a glimpse into the process of metacognition, attention space, working memory, and decision-making, e.g. that metacognition encompasses both stable beliefs about one's cognitive abilities (metacognitive knowledge) together with an evaluation of performance (metacognitive experiences).

The graphic (see page 63) shows how metacognition sits on top of ordinary thinking and decision-making. The bold arrows show metacognitive evaluations before or during a task, and the dashed line shows retrospectively what one could be thinking after the task when evaluating their performance.

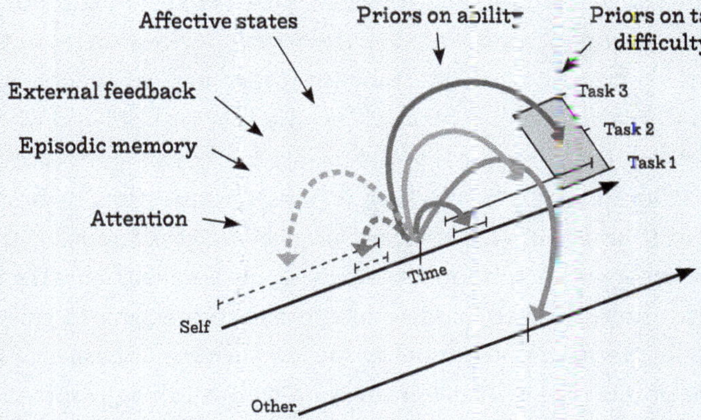

Adapted from Katyal and Fleming, 2024, Figure 1

First, we perform a task which draws on our attention and working memory. Then, a higher-order system evaluates that performance, judges our confidence, effort and likely success. This neuroimaging study explores the neural correlation of metacognitive processes especially in the prefrontal cortex (the evaluative layer) of the brain which is responsible for judgement, empathy, and decision-making. In simple terms, one part of our brain does the work, considering the time to complete the task, the scale of the task and target for completion. Another part of the brain checks our performance, shaped by feedback, emotion, memory, and prior success.

What this means is that learners bring with them a 'mental map' built from:

- what they believe about their own ability
- what they expect the task will be like
- how they felt about previous or similar tasks
- whether they have succeeded or failed
- the feedback they received
- where they should focus their attention.

This all influences how motivated and prepared someone feels for what comes next. Expert learners do not react to various tasks, they predict what to do based on past experiences, emotion, memory, and previous feedback. In essence, you learn based on what you already know.

So, what should you, as teachers, do for novice learners? You should break down the learning into smaller steps, working backwards from the solution. We have different types of 'thinking states' and, as teachers, we can understand *where attention is focused* (on the task or not) and *where the thought is coming from* (external input or internally/self-generated). For example, a student might be working on a maths question, saying the numbers aloud in their head. This is something called 'task focus'. If that same student hears a mobile phone vibrating which breaks their attention, this isn't because they chose to, it's because they are reacting to something external that pulls them away from being focused. These 'measures provide detailed information on the cortical processing that is taking place during mind wandering' (Smallwood and Schooler, 2015, p. 9). Look at the top-left and top-right images to understand the difference between self-generated thoughts (metacognition) and externally guided ideas (distractions).

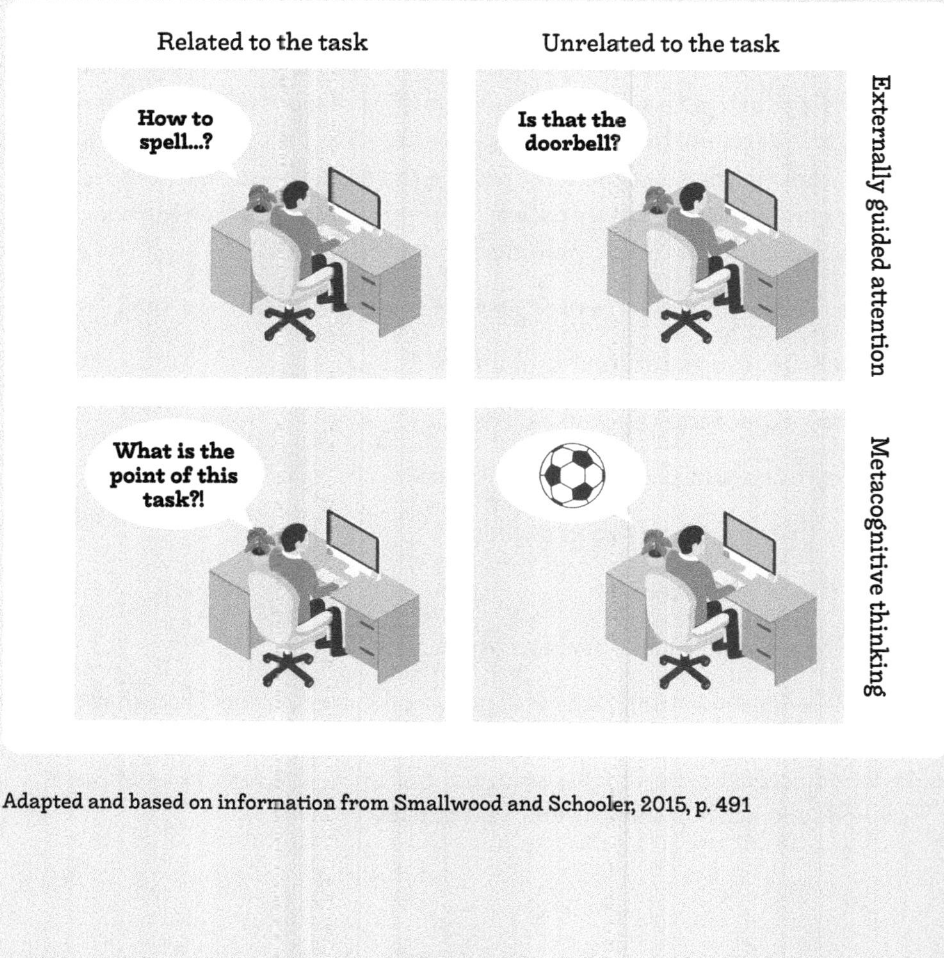

Adapted and based on information from Smallwood and Schooler, 2015, p. 491

In the bottom-left image on the diagram the student is thinking about the task and remains engaged. They are still engaged and the question itself has value. In the bottom-right image, the student is physically present but mentally elsewhere (daydreaming). Their thoughts are self-generated but unrelated to the task, so learning has passed, which is difficult for the teacher to detect because they're physically there, although mentally daydreaming. The teacher doesn't notice because they are not disrupting the lesson. We have ALL been here!

How can we use metacognition effectively?

Metacognition is much more than just thinking about thinking, it involves being able to regulate your learning and decision-making and is the golden thread that runs through all great teaching, and all the research I have read.

Metacognition is actively monitoring, planning, and evaluating how you learn, and it's the difference between a student asking, 'Do I know this?' versus 'How will I know if I've understood this well enough to apply it tomorrow, or in a future scenario?' It's a shift from performance to process. Self-regulation sits alongside metacognition: it's the behavioural and emotional control that underpins sustained effort, from managing distractions to deciding to review a mistake without giving up. Metacognitive skills can and should be taught explicitly. The key question is, how?

Whichever age group you teach, I'll share techniques you can model, embed and revisit. Metacognition is teachable, visible, and useful to every student, especially those who find learning boring, or challenging. I will explain how metacognition and **self-regulation** are explicitly connected to motivation, feedback, and cognitive load.

EXPLAINER

Metacognition

Metacognition is not a bolt-on to learning and it's likely that you provide metacognition strategies without even realising it. For example, 'Tell me why' is an excellent elaboration response to learning, or 'Explain this to me in your own words' is also an excellent strategy to encourage students to explain new information. You can implement these techniques into your conversations with students but doing it on a daily basis is more of a challenge. I would therefore remind you to put some prompts (or posters) on display, not just to remind yourself, but also your students.

Other strategies include breaking down a task and showing students how to plan, tackle, and reflect. By doing this, you are embedding self-regulation into the fabric of your classroom. Every time you model something, you're thinking out loud to students, or guiding them through ways of tackling a problem; you're making the invisible visible, and that's metacognitive teaching. When a student gets stuck and you ask, 'What do you already know that could help here?', you're not just helping them recall facts, you're encouraging them to monitor their own strategy and shift their approach.

In one fMRI study, the research sought to 'investigate if metacognitive ability relies on similar brain regions across a variety of tasks' (Molenberghs et al., 2016, p. 1949); it investigated individual differences, and discovered that feeling confident about one's choices was linked to increased activation in reward, memory, and motor-related brain areas, including the hippocampus (which is responsible for memory retrieval and consolidation).

Self-regulation

When teachers understand how students' brains develop, not just cognitively, but emotionally and physically, they are far better equipped to design lessons that reduce fear and anxiety. We have all seen how stressed or overwhelmed students and adults become, for example, when learning maths. In 'The effect of anxiety on mathematical thinking' (Atabek et al., 2022), 68 17-year-olds participated and reported high or low maths anxiety. The research used fMRI scans and found that students with higher anxiety levels showed 'high activation levels in the frontal cortex (the front part of our brain that is responsible for problem-solving) during thinking on mathematical problems', particularly for adolescents. The implication is that when anxiety is present, the brain might be working quite hard but not necessarily using its resources efficiently to problem-solve.

However, if teachers are aware of potential learning anxieties that their students face and have a more detailed understanding of cognitive processes, it is...

'...possible that anxiety and fear during learning and performance will be replaced by curiosity, enthusiasm and high motivation.' (Atabek et al., 2022, p. 10)

We can, therefore, act on what we know from research to make teaching more informed, with compassionate decisions. This starts by recognising that motivation is deeply connected to how students experience safety, challenge, and support in our classrooms.

Motivation

Neuroscience suggests that motivation is not a fixed trait and 'one way to encourage autonomy may be to develop students' motivation to learn' (Spratt et al., 2002, p. 19). Motivation is situational, malleable, and can be heavily influenced by how we structure lessons, feedback, and relationships. The more we help students feel a sense of autonomy, purpose, and success, the more likely they will stay engaged and attend class. 'If students achieve their goals after trying, then it is likely that they attribute their success to that effort' (Ruiz-Martín et al., 2024, p. 14).

This is where metacognition and self-regulation play a powerful role: students who are motivated when they can monitor their own progress, plan their time, and reflect on what's working have the tools to track their own efforts and improvement. At the same time, you can nurture their motivation, rather than just handing it out like a reward sticker or a stamp. Zarrinabadi and Rezazadeh (2023, p. 588) found that the effectiveness of teacher feed-forward enhanced 'participants' motivation' and 'that providing comments on learners' invested effort and persistence in doing writing' increased learner interest.

Feedback

Feedback without metacognition simply becomes a one-way monologue from you, as the teacher, to the student. As metacognition is about students thinking for themselves, feedback must therefore be a dialogue. For example, metacognitive prompts from you could include, 'What would you do differently next time?' or 'How does this feedback help you move forward?' These are simple and powerful questions that you should have up your sleeve to help build metacognitive capacity. In *The Teacher Toolkit Guide to Feedback* (McGill, 2024), I introduced a new perspective on feedback in the classroom: how we can move beyond the notion that written feedback is the only way to assess a student's piece of work. Pedagogical phrases, including feed-up (where am I going?) and feed-forward (where to next?) are absent from most teachers' vocabulary, and thinking about what these look like as classroom strategies isn't as hard to achieve as you would think. Just like maths, we often experience students who have negative feelings towards English or detailed writing. Research in this area (of Level 2 writing) suggests that 'groups who received feed-up and feed-forward significantly improved in terms of writing motivation' (Zarrinabadi and Rezazadeh, 2023, p. 575).

Research consistently shows that feedback has the greatest impact when students are taught how to interpret, apply, and reflect on what actions are provided. Remember that it doesn't matter what type of feedback you give, whether it's written, verbal, or non-verbal. The most important points to remember are:

1. Do your students trust your feedback?
2. Do they know how to act on the feedback?

If you want your students to self-regulate, you have to create space for them to think about what they've done and what to do next. It's not just feedback, it's about feeding-up and feeding-forward.

Cognitive load

Cognitive load theory (CLT) (see Chapter 4) reminds us that learning is effortful and, most importantly, that it is built upon what we already know. However, not all the effort we put in leads to effective learning. For example, when students highlight or reread material, the perception that they are using their time wisely is often misdirected effort. As mentioned in Chapter 3, Ruiz-Martín et al.'s (2024) research across 27 Spanish secondary schools (5,063 students) assessed how students develop self-regulation, and looked at the study techniques they were using, particularly what was associated with school achievement and their attitudes towards learning. What study techniques do your students use? Which techniques have misdirected effort?

Visit this link to see scatterplots showing the correlations between the study techniques and academic achievement (Ruiz- Martín et al., 2024, Figure 1)

The scatterplot tells a story: lots of students are working hard, but not necessarily in useful ways. Each dot is a learner. If they're high up and to the right, they're using a strategy often and it's working. But look at highlighting and rereading, which are used frequently; those dots are scattered widely, and lower, and 'yielded no significant correlation with achievement in spite of the large sample size' (Ruiz- Martín et al., 2024, p. 13). The dots in the bottom-left of these graphics represent the learners who coloured notes with highlights or reread material; those students saw no gains in performance. Although it would have felt like studying, it was not sticking.

That's effort without outcome. Effective study techniques aren't always popular with students who are novice learners. High-impact strategies like retrieval practice and elaboration need to be explicitly taught and modelled in classrooms. Students might believe they are busy when rereading or highlighting, but it's not paying off. This research paper also stated that retrieval practice could reduce anxiety, and that students with 'higher reported levels of examination anxiety are more likely to be using unsupported techniques' (Ruiz-Martín et al., 2024, p. 15).

More teachers are familiar with cognitive load, but very few are aware of *Cognitive Apprenticeship: Making Thinking Visible* (Collins et al., 1991), another seminal piece of research on CLT: 'In short, coaching is the process of overseeing the student's learning' (Collins et al., 1991, p. 2). It's worth mentioning that when we teach metacognition in our classrooms, bringing curriculum concepts to life through modelling and worked examples, teachers are making invisible concepts, rules, and facts in the curriculum visible, with real-life scenarios and problem-solving. This is what 'cognitive apprenticeship' is all about. It 'is not a model of teaching that gives teachers a packaged formula for instruction. Instead, it is an instructional paradigm for teaching' (Collins et al., 1991, p. 17).

When a student learns how to learn, they pause, check their understanding, and adopt or adjust their chosen strategy. They're not just learning content, they are learning how to learn, and self-regulating their decision-making.

In the next section, we will explore how metacognition and self-regulation can be translated into practical strategies for the classroom.

PRACTICAL IDEA

Metacognitive routines

Let's now consider how to embed metacognitive routines into every lesson, helping you to model self-questioning prompts and reflective check-ins to help build student self-regulation. These low-effort strategies build over time and increase student self-awareness and planning ability.

You can develop a reusable toolkit of sentence stems and reflection frames that students can use before, during, and after classroom tasks to monitor their thinking. The crux is that you make the learning visible and build explicit routines into your teaching.

Step-by-step guide

1. Begin with a simple prompt routine

Develop some retrieval prompts or a bank of key phrases you can use with students to activate their prior knowledge, or to help plan their study approach. Examples might include:

- What do I already know about this?
- What do I need to focus on most in this lesson?
- Which part of the task looks the most challenging?

2. Introduce metacognitive pause midway into your lesson routines

Consider this stage a '*metacognitive moment*'. Build in a deliberate break in the task where students pause and reflect. This must be a curriculum-related activity because we want to avoid students going off on tangents or being distracted with irrelevant conversations or notifications. You might use a prompt slide or hand signal to ask:

- What strategy are you currently using?
- Which is working, and how do you know?
- Should I keep going, change strategy or ask for help?

3. End the lesson with a reflection exit

End the lesson with a short reflection frame using any of these prompts:

- Write down one thing you have done well today...
- Next time, I will try to...
- One question I still have is...

Ask your students to plan-do-review.

- **Plan:** How did I approach this task?
- **Do:** What should I do next?
- **Review:** Did my strategy work; what will I change next time?

4. Encourage students to complete a reflection journal or a practical diary

In some examination subjects, this is an assessment component, and in my view it is an excellent process for building metacognition. It provides students with an example and a simple journal with numerous prompts and blank spaces where they can log daily or weekly stages in the learning process.

The journal can be digital or on paper, and you should encourage them to write about key decisions that they've made in the lesson or process; perhaps snap a photograph of their work at a particular stage, evaluate success, what strategies they have used and what future adjustments they need to make. The aim is for students to start to articulate what is helping them or hindering them in the learning process. It is a robust way to help build and embed self-regulation habits.

5. Model 'think aloud' in every lesson

Never play 'Guess what's in my head?' with your students. Instead, externalise your decision-making and articulate your thoughts so that students can see not just the answer, but the route you take to arrive at the answer.

- Demonstrate your thought processes live during each lesson.
- Narrate how you approach a question and what decisions you face, and which decision you choose and why.

Involve the students and ask them which decision they recommend you make as you model the learning process.

Some prompts might include:

- 'First, I'm noticing these key terms...'
- 'Now I'm thinking about what this reminds me of...'
- 'If I get stuck, I'm going to try and break this down into smaller steps.'
- 'I'm not sure what I should do here, if I make this decision that might happen but I think I need to go with this choice because...'

An important point is to ensure the learning is effortful on the students' part too, not just from your modelling to the class. Learning should be 'desirably difficult' and 'optimizing learning and instruction often requires going against one's intuitions' (Bjork and Bjork, 2011, p. 3).

6. Display metacognitive sentence stems

Place these in a prominent display in your classroom. They will act as prompts and visual nudges for both students and teachers. Examples include:

- Before the task: What do I already know?
- During the task: Is this helping me learn?
- After the task: How could I improve next time?

7. Reinforce with feedback loops

Integrate this strategy into your feedback commentary and student reflections. For example:

- After peer assessment, ask your students: 'What feedback did you receive, and how will you use it in your next lesson?'
- Afterwards, ask: 'Which part of your work shows the greatest progress?'

It's worth auditing yourself here and asking whether you gave the students enough time to reflect on their learning and the strategies used.

8. Make all the above habit-forming

Like all routines, techniques need repetition so that it builds into a habit. When habits form, expertise kicks in, and any new schema (germane load) is built. When new schemas are added to prior knowledge, past work which was harder to complete the first time around, is now made easier because it is automated, embedded, and you learn and build upon what you already know. When embedded consistently, these habits can foster powerful long-term changes and how students think about their learning.

TOOLKIT TIPS

1. Make thought processes visible by explaining the strategy and how you reached the solution.
2. Teach students to predict possible outcomes before they perform a task. For example, ask 'What might be difficult?', 'What do you think might happen?'
3. Move from reflections to regulation. Instead of asking 'What did you do?', ask 'What would you do differently next time?'
4. Neuroimaging suggests metacognitive judgements engage prefrontal regions involved in evaluation and regulation. Design classroom tasks that require students to estimate, justify, and revise strategies.

WORKED EXAMPLE

Building metacognitive habits

This example, written for an **early years foundation stage (EYFS)** context, will demonstrate how you can start to build metacognitive habits from a very early age.

Mrs Roberts is an EYFS teacher working with a Reception class. Her aim is to introduce very young children to early metacognitive routines without overloading them with abstract language. This is a very delicate and challenging task. Mrs Roberts decides to embed her approach through storytime and creative play.

Step 1: Modelling 'thinking out loud'

During a storytime session with *We're Going on a Bear Hunt* by Michael Rosen, Mrs Roberts pauses and narrates her thinking aloud:

> **'I wonder what they will do when they reach the river? I think I would try and find a bridge. Hmm... would I get wet if I walked through the water?'**

This modelling demonstrates decision-making, curiosity, and strategy checking. At the same time, Mrs Roberts is animating her facial features, looking up to the classroom ceiling to suggest her thinking, while using her forefinger to tap on the bottom of her chin. She knows the 'Hmm...' emphasis will encourage students to put up their hands.

Step 2: Metacognitive prompts

After the story, she asks the following questions:

1. What part of the story do you remember the most?
2. What part of the story made you smile, or made you feel sad?
3. Was there a bit that was tricky to understand?
4. What did you do when you weren't sure?

These questions are asked in child-friendly language, linked to the emotional tone of the story.

Step 3: Reflection routine

Later in the lesson, during a construction play activity, Mrs Roberts hands out small laminated 'thinking tokens' with pictures and simple phrases such as:

- 'I tried something new.'
- 'I kept going even when it was hard.'
- 'I asked a friend for help.'

Children in the class are invited to put a token on their play mat and share why they chose it. In this way, Mrs Roberts is embedding self-regulation vocabulary early.

Step 4: Repetition and celebration

Across a sequence of lessons, Mrs Roberts builds 'thinking' with student reflections using drawings and photos. She also celebrates metacognitive behaviour ('You remembered to stop and think first, and think about what might work best. Well done!'), embedding this language into praise and classroom routines.

TEMPLATE

Embedding metacognitive routines into every lesson

Scan the QR code for a downloadable copy of this blank template.

Aim to fill it in and adapt the prompts to match your context.

Stage	Prompts and guidance	Notes / Planning prompts
1. Planning prompt	What do I want students to reflect on before the lesson or task?	E.g. What do I already know? What do I need to focus on?
2. During-task check-in	What self-questioning prompts will I embed in the middle of the activity?	E.g. Is this strategy working? Should I try a different approach?
3. End-of-task reflection	What metacognitive sentence stem or activity can I use to support reflection?	E.g. One thing I would do differently next time is...
• A. Student reflection tool	What tool will students use?	E.g. Journal, exit slip, token, sketch note, Think-Pair-Share.
• B. Think aloud modelling	In which part of the lesson will I rate my thought processes?	E.g. Live modelling of writing, problem-solving, decoding a text.
• C. Display / Visual prompts	Which visual prompts will reinforce these routines?	E.g. Poster, sentence stems, anchor chart.
• D. Feedback links	How will I link this to feedback?	E.g. What feedback did you get? How will you use that next time?
• E. Habit tracking	How will I ensure this becomes a routine?	E.g. Weekly reflections, class review, parental feedback.

CHAPTER 6

MOTIVATION, EMOTION, AND ENGAGEMENT

How do our feelings affect learning? What could fMRI research tell us about relationships in the classroom?

We often think of learning as a purely cognitive task – something to be broken down, stored, and retrieved. But learning doesn't happen in a vacuum. It may be charged with emotion, shaped by relationships, and driven open (or blocked) by motivation. This is always what makes classroom life a fascinating space!

Many of the human factors in our classrooms have countless variables. For example, while it may be recommended to deliver retrieval practice at the start of every lesson, this may not always be possible. On Monday mornings my students are half asleep, and in period 5 on Fridays, after fish and chips, they are full of life! There are many variables that can add value, or be detrimental to learning; research may help guide our decisions as teachers.

Motivation isn't just about getting students to care. It's about helping them persist through difficulty, recover from setbacks, and take ownership of their learning. I firmly believe that learning is an emotional process. Emotions are *not* a distraction to learning, rather, they are deeply entwined with how memories are formed, how attention is sustained, and how students behave. Science is catching up to what great teachers have always known: that if a child feels unsafe, unseen, or unsure, learning takes a back seat.

In this chapter, I want to explore what research suggests about motivation, emotional learning, and engagement in the classroom. This may include the impact of stress and anxiety on memory and attention, and how rewards, relationships, and routines influence motivation. We will also look closely at intrinsic versus extrinsic drivers, the power of autonomy in learning, and the dangers of **toxic positivity** or 'learned helplessness'.

Most importantly, I'll aim to answer how you can nurture motivation and emotional safety in the classroom.

EXPLAINER

Motivation

The research into the neuroscience of motivation helps to explain what teachers have always believed: that emotions and motivation are deeply connected to learning. Yet, in our current system of exams and school/college accountability, it's easy for students to become over-reliant on external validation rather than having the motivation to learn for learning's sake.

Research by Ackerman and Kanfer (2009) stated that 'Test takers are likely to experience cognitive fatigue during longer tests' (p. 177). However, it should be noted that the research went on to say that 'experience of fatigue during testing does not appear to be, in and of itself, detrimental to test performance' (p. 177).

With all this in mind, how do we motivate students to want to attend school and to do well in their examinations? Motivation is linked to a dynamic process influenced by our biology, our social relationships as humans, and the routines in our everyday life, particularly the classroom. Our motivation to complete goals can also be closely linked to emotion and fatigue. In another fMRI study using electroencephalography, the research showed that students' 'goal-directed attention [was] negatively affected by mental fatigue' and that behaviour was 'caused by an inability of fatigued subjects to allocate their attention efficiently' (Boksem et al., 2005, p. 114).

So, practically, what should you do in the classroom with this research in mind? Teachers will tell you that it is very hard to motivate students who are tired or hungry, and that tests are good for students, but that accountability can often get in the way of great teaching and learning. We often talk about motivation as if students either have it or they don't, but in reality, motivation fluctuates for us all constantly. It's situational. It's emotional. It's contextual. Crucially, it is something we can develop and manage.

There are two broad types of motivation: **extrinsic** and **intrinsic**. The simplest way I can break this down for you is to think about the first two letters of each word, 'ex' and 'in' – one is **ex**ternal and the other **in**ternal. Extrinsic motivation might be driven by rewards and consequences. For example, the first person to read this entire book receives a £100 voucher, or if you don't read this book by the end of this working week, you'll receive a £100 penalty. In essence, when you finish the task, you will either receive a reward or a sanction. Intrinsic motivation, however, comes from within. What was the original reason you grabbed a copy of this book? 'I'm reading this because it interests me, or I want to improve my understanding of the science of learning.' For me, my motivation for writing this book is that I care profoundly about teaching and learning, and I want to share my understanding of neurology and how it connects to pedagogical techniques in the classroom, e.g. neuroeducation.

In another fMRI study, research suggests that while extrinsic rewards can *initiate behaviour*, sustained engagement relies more heavily on intrinsic motivation. Although mental fatigue typically reduces both task performance and brain activity, this effect can be temporarily reversed when a reward increases the value of a task: 'although task performance as well as the activity of many brain regions decreased as fatigue emerged, we found the opposite pattern when an incentive (i.e., monetary reward) increased the perceived benefit of task performance' (Darnai et al., 2023, p. 8). This means that fatigue is the problem, and reward is a short-term solution.

From a neuroimaging perspective, Darnai et al. (2023) used fMRI to investigate how mental fatigue and motivation influence brain activity. Notably, the 'results showed reduced activity in non-specific brain areas' associated with effort and reward processing (p. 7). When we engage deeper into a reflective thinking task, this activates more regions of the brain with a change in blood flow (with more oxygen required), compared to simply performing a task.

The research indicates that metacognition is neurologically distinguishable from basic task performance, and that more demanding tasks require more cognitive effort. To develop our brain health, we should be attempting tasks that require more neural challenge and coordination.

A positive classroom environment

When students feel safe, respected, and competent, their brain is more open to taking risks and remaining focused. The limbic system, which processes emotion, works hand in hand with the prefrontal cortex in the top front side of our brain, which is responsible for reasoning and decision-making (see page 6). There is established evidence that 'motivation may lead to autonomy or be a precondition for it' (Spratt et al., 2002, p. 18). It's not a pedagogical preference; instead, the link between autonomy and motivation is not one-directional but mutually reinforcing in the classroom, for you as the teacher and for the entire class. A motivated learner is more likely to choose challenging tasks and work through them independently. For this to be achieved, classroom culture also matters, with autonomy 'demonstrated across cultures and across disciplines ranging from STEM (science, technology, engineering, and math) to foreign languages' (Cullen and Oppenheimer, 2024, p. 1).

A positive classroom environment to help motivate and engage students isn't just about displays, beanbags, or jazzy whiteboard presentations, it's about emotional safety. Students who fear failure, those who experience repeated corrections without support, or who feel misunderstood by their peers or by adults, may withdraw or continue to struggle in the classroom. Mental health struggles can be an invisible barrier to learning. As a profession, we are becoming better equipped in understanding the needs of neurodivergent students including the strategies that will protect their wellbeing and help them manage challenging situations.

Rewards and praise, as well as excellent teaching, requires careful consideration when we are thinking about emotion and engagement in the classroom. While positive reinforcement has a place, research can also suggest that overuse of praise (toxic positivity) can reduce intrinsic motivation. This is especially so if praise is generic, for example, 'Good job', or when it is not linked to effort. Positive praise strategy, especially when used as scripts to improve teacher workload, can motivate students to do more work.

In the next section we' l look at some practical ideas for providing feedback and praise, unpicking the differences between extrinsic and intrinsic examples.

PRACTICAL IDEA

Motivational climate checklist

In this section, I will provide you with a diagnostic test to assess classroom 'climate', and the language and task-design that affects motivation. This will include reflections on praise, challenge, autonomy, in-class participation, and failure response.

1. Start with a learning temperature check

Start each lesson with a 'learning temperature check'. Ask students to reflect (either privately or collectively) on how motivated they feel to complete today's task. This activity can take one minute or five minutes to complete, whatever is sufficient to create the emotional space to help students uncover invisible barriers to learning. This could be achieved with a silent hand signal, with students displaying one to five fingers, using a mini whiteboard, writing a sentence or target into a learning journal, or completing an online survey.

2. Observe and record your language

Jot down or audio record three or five key phrases and words you use when giving praise, correcting behaviour or motivating students. Later ask yourself: are these mostly extrinsic ('Well done for finishing fast...'), or are they intrinsic ('You've worked hard to improve your writing structure.')?

3. Analyse the task structure

Does this task offer a choice or autonomy? Is it too easy or too difficult for this group? Where can I build in purposeful struggle or low-stakes challenge?

4. Review feedback opportunities

Reflect on how feedback was delivered. Did it support student autonomy? Did students know how to act? What opportunities have been provided for students to revise or improve their work?

5. Use a diagnostic tool

Complete a one-page checklist that prompts reflection (praise, prompt, tone) to use in the classroom for task design when seeking opportunities for reflection and student autonomy.

6. Adjust the lesson plan

Based on student reflections and your evaluation, make adjustments to your next lesson. Simplify the task, add different choices that are clearly connected to success criteria, introduce new feedback prompts to help students take action, and change how you open or close the lesson.

Other factors to consider include the social and emotional aspects throughout the lesson. What data can you garner in the moment from students? Are they focused? Is the pitch and challenge appropriate without adding too much stress? How does adjusting the pace of the lesson impact on the student's progress? What Plan B do you have if you have to scrap the original plan in the lesson?

Putting it into practice

A great climate for learning includes, for example, a structured start and end to the lesson, providing students with the tools to be successful. Overall, continual feed-forward (asking a student what they can do next to improve) should be at the heart of the learning process, and should give students a sense of autonomy over their progress. It's not just about what they've got wrong or helping them choose what to do next, it's also about helping students know how to act that matters the most.

This idea is to provide a useful approach for you to work across a key stage or department with other teachers, allowing you to have a consistent approach. Of course, emotional checks may differ in early years compared to students in Key Stage 4 or in further education, so context is key, and remember to adapt it to suit your context.

In the next section, I will show you a worked example that you can use for inspiration, or adapt using the template in this chapter.

TOOLKIT TIPS

1. Build motivation before demanding any performance. Start lessons with a motivational temperature check.
2. Use rewards sparingly and strategically. Replace generic praise with effort-linked feedback.
3. Aim to reduce anxiety without lowering the challenge. Rather than question publicly, turn retrieval practice quizzes into secret post-box ballots.
4. Anticipate what cognitive load a novice learner might experience. Start planning to teach content from this position.

WORKED EXAMPLE

Mr Sampson teaches Level 2 Motor Vehicle Mechanics at a large further education (FE) college. Neurodiverse learners in FE have often either been recently diagnosed (and are only beginning to understand their own cognitive profile), or have experienced fragmented or inconsistent support earlier on in their education, resulting in a need to navigate a more independent learning environment. Mr Sampson is conscious of this, and he wants to ensure his unusual classroom space is as inclusive as possible.

Mr Sampson's learners are aged between 16 and 19 years old, with a wide range of educational history. Some students have diagnosed conditions such as ADHD and dyslexia. Other students have no formal diagnosis, but show signs of **executive dysfunction**, sensory sensitivity or difficulties with processing instructions He teaches in a very large workshop space with vehicle bases that can host ten cars, tools, and diagnostic equipment. It is a noisy, unpredictable, and highly physical learning environment.

Step 1: Plan with variability

Mr Sampson avoids teaching to labels and, instead, uses the *Five Minute Inclusion Planner* (see page 101) to proactively plan for variability. This means anticipating a wide range of cognitive, emotional, and sensory needs, rather than reacting to them. With this in mind, he adapts his lesson plan daily and anchors his planning to three key aspects:

1. **Cognitive access**: Reducing overload in instructions and technical terms.
2. **Emotional regulation**: Managing learner anxiety, especially around practical assessments.
3. **Sensory diversity**: Reducing auditory and tactile overstimulation; providing ear defenders, goggles, and coloured screens, where necessary.

Step 2: Adjusting the physical and emotional climate

Knowing that the workshop can feel chaotic, Mr Sampson designs a quiet prep zone with visual prompts for each stage of the task. A poster-sized *task flow* using icons (e.g. tyre, lift, inspect, report) is displayed prominently to show particular sequences. He also uses colour-coded systems on whiteboards around the large classroom space to chunk instructions between key stages, depending on where resources and tools are situated around the room:

1. prepare (orange)
2. perform (yellow)
3. reflect (green).

He offers noise reduction ear defenders for any student who prefers them, and builds in pre-task metacognitive prompts such as:

- What tools do you need before you begin?
- What might go wrong if you skipped 'this XYZ' step?

Step 3: Targeting executive function and memory

Instead of verbal lists, instructions are visual and sequenced using magnetic task strips on each whiteboard around the workshop. Every learner moves their name tag along the strip to show where they are in the process. This gives Mr Sampson and all of the students an overview of everyone's progress. He then provides personal checklists that are laminated and attaches them to various toolkits around the room (e.g. five checks before a learner starts working on a particular vehicle). These not only support working memory, but also build procedural fluency over time, together with student confidence. It makes Mr Sampson's workload easier too!

Step 4: Feedback and self-regulation

At the end of each practical task, Mr Sampson schedules five minutes of silent reflection, with prompts including:

1. What helps you stay focused?
2. Did anything make you lose focus?
3. What part was challenging?
4. How did you overcome any difficulties?
5. What would you do differently next time?

By using the following simple exit tickets to help reflection: 'One thing I did well/One thing I'd like help with next time', he threads the responses into his next lesson plan. Over time, students become more aware of what is working for them.

Step 5: Peer learning and trust

Mr Sampson notices that his neurodivergent students often thrive more when they are paired with people they trust or have been reliant on in the past. The task doesn't dominate this decision, but by pairing students, it helps with pace and prompting in such a large open space. He carefully structures buddy systems that offer support without dependency, which are rotated where needed.

Mr Sampson also creates 'How I stay focused?' cards at the start of the term that help students describe the methods they use to stay focused. This isn't to help promote learning style myths, but to tackle them head-on and to help neurodivergent students. In an FE setting in which dependence on the teacher may be reduced, such methods help build confidence and remind students to stay focused, reflect on their progress, and commit to challenging instructions and tasks. Mr Sampson then uses this information to shape curriculum planning and support patterns offered in class.

Why does this work?

By designing for variability from the outset, Mr Sampson avoids last minute accommodations and instead creates a workshop where every student can engage immediately. His approach is principled, planned, and perceptive; designed to get the best out of his students. Crucially, this approach meets students where they are, and supports them to achieve the highest possible level of success in their chosen curriculum area.

TEMPLATE

Motivational climate checklist

This template is formatted as a table so it can be easily recreated in your context and used as a practical tool to promote inclusion.

Scan the QR code for a downloadable copy of this blank template.

Planning element	Teacher notes / Prompts	My plan
Lesson topic	What is the focus of the practical task? What cognitive demands are involved?	
Cognitive access	How would I reduce working memory overload? Are key terms explained in plain language?	
Emotional regulation	What are the likely points of anxiety or frustration in this activity? How will I support students to manage these?	
Sensory diversity	What visual or tactile resources could be overwhelming? What adaptations can I offer?	
Task-flow: Visual sequencing	Can I break the task down into steps? How can I display instructions more clearly?	

Planning element	Teacher notes / Prompts	My plan
Classroom layout considerations	Where do all students go to prepare, perform, and reflect? Can I create zones or key signposts for each stage?	
Working memory supports	What visual aids, checklists, or anchor points are needed? Can these be attached to various work stations?	
Self-regulation prompts	What questions will I ask you to reflect on, focus on, or challenge? And to strategise before, during, and after the task?	
Peer support structures	How will I structure peer support or body systems? How will I avoid dependency while offering scaffolding?	
Student voice and personal profiles	What tools will I use to collect information about individual needs? How am I currently using school or college information?	
Exit reflections	For a quick review of feedback tools, will I use it at the end of the session? How can I reduce anxiety but keep the challenge high?	
Adjustments for future lessons	What will I carry forward or adapt for the next lesson? How will I use student responses? Where and when do I need to involve other colleagues?	

CHAPTER 7

NEURODIVERSITY AND THE ETHICS OF LEARNING

How inclusive are your classrooms and your classroom decisions?

Since the publication of *Just Great Teaching* (McGill 2019), I have seen the conversation around SEND and mental health shift dramatically from a quiet whisper on corridors to national headlines and frontline exhaustion. Anxiety and ADHD are no longer niche diagnoses that are discussed in the inclusion office; these learning needs are the reality of every classroom across the country. But are we meeting this need with care or confusion?

In recent years, I've watched teachers carry the emotional load of a system that cannot keep pace. The government white paper 'Every child achieving and thriving' provides major reforms to the system that supports children and young people with SEND in England (DfE, 2025). The SEND Code of Practice (DfE, 2024) asks schools to identify and respond to young people with special educational needs, but what happens when waiting-lists stretch to years, and support services are paper-thin? Currently, there is an emerging discourse that our young people are easily labelled, questioned for their anxiety, and told to 'toughen up'. This is misdirected effort. Instead, we must ask: are our students really self-diagnosing, or are they simply articulating emotions we've long failed to legitimise?

This chapter explores the ethical imperative for the teaching profession: to see beyond the label and respond to the learner. When I deliver teacher training across the country, more and more teachers are asking me to dig deeper into **neurodivergence** based on my work in cognitive science. There is an enormous gap in teacher knowledge, with 30 per cent of teachers wanting SEND to be on their training agenda (DfE, 2023).

In this section, we will examine what cognitive diversity looks like in classrooms, challenge reductive behaviour policies, and ask what inclusive practice really demands. Neurodivergence is not a barrier to learning, the infrastructure available across education is. If we are to support every student, we must reimagine what 'achieving' looks like in our schools and colleges, and how we redesign an education system that meets the needs of every person.

EXPLAINER

I want to look at who we design education for, rather than how we get students to learn. I will dig deeper into neurodivergence by looking at the research from fMRI scans of students with, for example, ADHD, dyspraxia, dyscalculia, or dyslexia. I will also look at what we can learn from electroencephalography.

Neurodivergence reframes learning differences not as deficits, but as natural variations in human cognition. The term 'was collectively theorised and developed by autistic activists' (Botha et al., 2024, p. 1592) and from the 'first known sociological study of the neurodiversity movement' (Botha et al., 2024, p. 1593). The key principle is that '**Neurotypical** is not the only way to be, or even the best way' (Singer, 1998, p. 50); that neurological differences are part of human variation, not problems to be fixed. In one fMRI study on ADHD, the researchers found that struggling learners 'cut across any traditional diagnostic boundaries' (Astle et al., 2019, p. 11), suggesting that teaching should respond to thinking *profiles* rather than *labels*.

In another fMRI study that evaluated attention and motor control in adults with and without ADHD, the research suggested 'statistically significant differences in the brain activation patterns' (Berberat et al., 2021, p. 9) during cognition, regulating emotions, and planning. Importantly, even when behaviour may look similar, and when medication alters neural activation patterns, neural effort differs between ADHD+ (medicated) and ADHD- (unmedicated) people. The research demonstrated that some brains need to work harder, or recruit different networks, to achieve the same cognitive control. Interestingly, executive function is not located in one part of the brain, but relies on a coordinated network moving across the **corpus callosum**: the nerve fibres that communicate between each brain hemisphere.

In a further fMRI study, 'Impaired neural networks for approximate calculation in dyscalculic children' (Kucian et al., 2006), cerebral mechanisms underlying developmental dyscalculia (DD) were analysed. This was looking at what happens in the brain for people who struggle to acquire maths skills. The study indicated that 'findings in patients with dyscalculia suggest that defects in parietal areas seem to be particularly responsible for arithmetic problems' (Kucian et al., 2006, p. 3). The study 'investigated brain activation in 18 children with DD and 20 typically achieving school children during different numerical tasks' (p. 3).

The research found that there were specific regions of the brain that exhibited 'weaker brain activation in almost the entire [brain] network for approximate calculation in children with DD' (Kucian et al., 2006, p. 9). Scans revealed how different people responded to answering a task, how long they took to respond, and how they adapted in decision-making.

The researchers concluded that 'differences appear to reflect a deficiency in recruitment of neural resources designated for the processing of analog numbers' (Kucian et al., 2006, p. 15). In other words, the brain is not activating the relevant neural networks strongly or consistently enough.

From a teaching perspective, this challenges the dominant models of 'intervention' used in schools and colleges. Traditionally these have been deployed *after* failure, but increasingly, if targeted earlier, intervention has helped students succeed. If we know that processing time, sensory overload, or executive dysfunction are common cognitive traits for some students, the real issue isn't their diagnosis, it's how we adapt our systems in and out of the classroom.

Research suggests that when classroom structures are adapted for neurodivergent learners, all students can benefit. Crucially, neurodiversity invites us to not just ask ourselves *'What do students need?'*, but it also challenges the assumptions that are deeply engrained into our definitions of ability.

In some of our schools and colleges, behaviour policies prioritise eye contact to 'track the speaker', stillness, or quick oral responses such as 'Cold call', and while these have some merit, they don't necessarily factor in neurodivergent learners. Emerging research on behaviour and exclusions in English state schools is crystal clear on the 'detrimental use of internal exclusion in mainstream secondary schools' with a 'disproportionate application with vulnerable/marginalised population subgroups' (Thornton et al., 2025, p. 21). We know SEND students are much more likely to be excluded from school than any other group of students. Perhaps some of the policy decisions we make inadvertently punish students whose brains are wired differently to those who are neurotypical. On the surface, a neurotypical teacher or learner simply views that the neurodiverse learner cannot keep up, or doesn't want to take part in the learning process. The education system is calibrated around neurotypical norms.

Cognitive science has sometimes been misused to reinforce these norms. What could fMRI scans reveal about our decisions in the classroom? For example, working memory research tells us that all learners have limited cognitive bandwidth. But for neurodivergent students, this bandwidth may be further narrowed by anxiety, sensory input, or the effort needed to regulate attention. This doesn't mean they cannot learn; it means they need teaching to be designed for how their brain *actually* works, not for how neurotypical people *wish* it would work.

Motivation, too, looks different. A student with ADHD may appear 'unmotivated' or 'inattentive', but research suggests there is no lack of willpower. In the research paper 'Toward systems neuroscience of ADHD: A meta-analysis of 55 fMRI studies' (Cortese et al., 2012), researchers looked at MRI studies of ADHD. Rather than a lack of willpower, ADHD involves 'altered connectivity within and among several neural networks rather than abnormalities of discrete, isolated brain regions' (Cortese et al., 2012, p. 1). This helps to explain why some students struggle with executive function and self-regulation. While students with ADHD are often perceived as lacking motivation, neuroimaging research reveals a more nuanced picture. Functional MRI studies demonstrate that individuals with ADHD are 'unable to expand the required effort in challenging energetically and suboptimal tasks' (Ariyarathne et al., 2020, p. 32).

Teacher expectations

How we see our students matters, and decades of research suggests that the expectations we set as teachers can shape students' trajectories. Published in 1968, the highly influential educational psychology study 'Pygmalion in the classroom' by Rosenthal and Jacobson is named after the popular 1912 play *Pygmalion,* in which a woman is coached to speak in a certain way. The research introduced the idea that teacher expectations can shape student achievement, just like the storyline in the original play. In the study, teachers were told that certain randomly selected students were likely to show rapid intellectual growth. In reality, the students were chosen at random and the test used to identify them was fictitious. Students who were labelled as 'capable' showed significantly greater gains in IQ over an academic year, and that 'one person's expectations of another's behavior may come to serve as a self-fulfilling prophecy' (Rosenthal and Jacobson, 1968, p. 5). This demonstrated that the way students were perceived by their teacher had an impact on their academic performance. When teachers expect a student to succeed, they may unconsciously treat them in ways that encourage success. For example, more feedback, more attention, higher expectations.

This has profound implications when we consider students with neurodivergent needs. A student may be perceived as disruptive or unmotivated, but what if they were instead perceived as capable and curious? This isn't just a mindset shift; it's backed by evidence.

Teacher expectations shape classroom dynamics, but they often do so in ways we don't consciously register. This is particularly significant when working with neurodivergent students who may already face lower expectations due to misunderstandings or stereotypes.

Over 50 years later, on closer inspection, how does the theory of the Pygmalion Effect stand in today's classroom? 'Questioning Pygmalion in the twenty-first century' (Murdock-Perriera and Sedlacek, 2018) argues that the original research had methodological flaws. Despite this examination and evidence, the Pygmalion Effect remains influential: 'Rosenthal and Jacobson's (1968) methodological choice of communicating IQ test scores via informal conversations demonstrated that this type of transmission could create expectancy effects' (Murdock-Perriera and Sedlacek, 2018, p. 12). For teachers, the way expectations were seeded, not through formal instruction but in passing comments and casual exchanges, was enough to shift how teachers interacted with their students. This raises important ethical questions. If casual remarks or non-verbal cues can alter a student's potential, what happens when those expectations are shaped by ableist assumptions, neurotypical norms, or unconscious bias?

What can we do?

The ethics of the classroom in the modern world are clear. Inclusion is not about paperwork; it's about epistemology – that is, what counts as knowledge, who is positioned to succeed, and how progress is defined. Neurodiversity requires more integration into an existing system. It needs transformation and adapting education; structures to meet diverse learner needs that are largely unmet, underfunded, and increasing in complexity.

Any so-called 'SEND crisis' is often framed in terms of rising diagnoses and stretched funding, but it also reflects a system struggling to align pedagogy, policy, and cognitive understanding. There is a need for a 'greater collaboration between educators and neuro- and cognitive scientists' (Hardiman et al., 2011, p. 4), which has lagged behind the urgent unmet needs of SEND students in the classroom. I see increasing numbers of teachers translating neuroscience findings from the laboratory to the classroom for themselves, and becoming more 'thoughtful and informed consumers of research from the neuro- and cognitive sciences' (Hardiman et al., 2011).

We don't want simplified information; instead, we want to be able to understand cognitive science and its implications for the classroom. You undoubtedly want to know where it is best to focus your efforts – for example, how to avoid neuromyths (Chapter 3), and how to develop better neuroliteracy to help guide your teaching. We must also seriously consider the neurological ethics associated with implementing fMRI research in the classroom, or how it is used to inform teaching practice. In the current landscape, 'without the help of translators in the short-term and more rigorous teacher preparation in the long-term, neuroscientists and cognitive scientists will continue to work in a vacuum, and teachers and the public may make false inferences' (Hardiman et al., 2011, p. 142).

A society that values all aspects of academic and creative subjects, all routes in and out of the classroom, and a wide breadth of student support systems can only be positive, and this is what our profession needs more than anything else. At the time of writing, Professor Becky Francis has completed and published the *Curriculum and Assessment Review* on behalf of the government (DfE, 2025). In the 40-page 'easy-read', a parent- and teacher-friendly summary is offered, providing approximately 25 recommendations. It concludes that the English education system has many strengths, but that it does not work equally well for all students, particularly those from disadvantaged backgrounds and those with SEND. The review confirms improvements for inclusion, **oracy**, and digital literacy, as well as refining assessment and widening post-16 pathways.

PRACTICAL IDEA

Designing for variability: An inclusive lesson plan

In this section, we will consider how you can design learning for variability. The flexible lesson plan template prompts you to plan with neurodiverse needs in mind from the outset, not as a bolt-on. It includes prompts for sensory needs, processing differences, cognitive load, and emotional regulation. As teachers, you are often told to teach study skills, but many of you have not been equipped with the strategies to adapt the classroom for learners who think, feel, and focus differently. Adapting teaching strategies means designing for variability from the start.

If you are planning lessons without consideration for neurodiverse learners, then you're only planning for a percentage of students. The resource offered in the next section is a thinking tool you can use time and time again.

The Five Minute Inclusion Plan

1. Use the template in this chapter

With the template, consider the students in your class and the following key points:

- objectives
- cognitive access
- emotional access
- sensory needs
- reflection and self-regulation.

Key questions to ask yourself: What's the topic you're teaching? How does this link to prior knowledge? Who are the learners in your classroom? What considerations have you made for their processing time, fatigue, and sensory needs? What barriers already exist? What strengths can be leveraged?

2. Define the learning objectives

Ensure these are flexible, not fixed. For example: students will demonstrate an understanding of cell structures in multiple ways (verbal, written, performance).

Key questions to ask yourself: How will you break content into small, manageable chunks so that you don't overload students' working memories?

3. Audit for cognitive access

Not all students can process information at the same pace. Therefore, teachers must break information down into smaller steps.

Key questions to ask yourself: How will you show students the learning process? Consider the transitions and attention span between activities: What's your buffer strategy?

4. Plan for emotional access

Include strategies to reduce stress and enhance motivation. Provide optional group or solo tasks, and plan activities to boost confidence. Remember, a low-stakes, high-challenge approach results in improved in-class participation and success rate.

Key questions to ask yourself: How do I reduce the stress but keep the challenge the same? How do you include dual-format recall opportunities (verbal and visual) to support neurodivergent students?

5. Design for sensory diversity

Include planning prompts such as, 'Is the environment overly stimulating?', 'Is the lighting, noise or seating plan adaptable?', 'Can students access tools and resources to reduce any potential stimulation (e.g. ear defenders or fidget tools)?'.

Key questions to ask yourself: Do you consciously pause between key instructions? Mary Budd-Rowe states that 'The accumulation of pauses after student utterances before the teacher spoke again in most recordings averaged 0.9 seconds!' (Rowe, 1986, p. [illegible]).

6. Plan to support executive function

Consider using timers and visual countdowns, to break the learning tasks into various checkpoints with success landmarks. Provide worked examples and models for planning various responses by students. Give students a checklist to help track progress.

Key questions to ask yourself: How do you model the learning process? 'I do, we do, you do' works very well (see Chapter 1, page 11).

7. Build in metacognitive reflection and self-regulation

Provide students with an opportunity to reflect on their learning. This can be a simple end-of-lesson question and evaluation using a mini whiteboard, or a thumbs up or thumbs down. Alternatively, you could ask students to write something privately to document their success, any challenges, and what they will do in the next lesson. You could also include an 'exit ticket' reflection question that you can monitor privately.

Key questions to ask yourself: How do you anticipate cognitive overload? Research suggests that as a student develops expertise, you should fade away the support to help build schema and metacognition. Cognitive apprenticeship is 'a model of instruction that works to make thinking visible' and is central to 'integrating knowledge and skills in order to accomplish meaningful tasks' (McGill, 2022, p. 104).

8. Use this plan in meetings or professional development

Share the plan with your colleagues and ask for their feedback to understand how you could improve it further. Consider using it in department evaluations and lesson reviews. Create a shared bank of inclusive lesson planning templates. Encourage your special needs coordinator (SENDCo) to lead the modelling sessions using this plan.

Key questions to ask yourself: How can students access the lesson differently? What's the regulation plan for emotionally overwhelmed students? What strategies will help them learn and be understood?

Finally, as highlighted in point 6 above, it is important for all teachers to consider the sequence and flow for the lesson. Think carefully about cognitive routines. How could you chunk the lesson into 'now, next, and then' to help signpost students throughout the process. How could you ensure you build in timers, checklists, and predictable patterns to support cognition, not hinder it? Understanding working memory and how learning happens is an essential part of the teaching process.

TOOLKIT TIPS

1. Teach the student, not the label. Plan for patterns of strengths and difficulty rather than assumptions about neurodivergent needs.
2. Assume a difference in everyone's cognitive needs. Executive function relies on distributed brain networks, so approach lesson planning as a novice, acquiring mastery over time.
3. As the Pygmalion research (1968) suggests, expectations matter. Make sure you share your ambitions with every student, even when they challenge your patience.
4. Design lessons for variability, not a linear pathway. Chunk instructions, offer options A, B, and C, and reduce all unnecessary distractions from your resources. Add processing time delays between instruction and task.

WORKED EXAMPLE

Mr McGill is planning a Year 8 science lesson on the digestive system. Using the Five Minute Inclusion Plan he begins with the big picture: this is a new topic, and several students in his class have an EHCP for autism, ADHD, and sensory sensitivity. He has these key considerations for lesson planning to ensure that he is being truly inclusive of all student needs.

1. Lesson objectives: 'Students will describe the function of key organs in digestion'. Access goal: 'Students have access to learning using dual-coded slides and embedded retrieval techniques at the start and end of the lesson.'
2. Cognitive access: He strips his presentation free from transitions and unnecessary animations. Diagrams only have keywords and necessary descriptions, removing any redundant information. He uses colour-coded notes and dual-coded retrieval grids that students will have to hand.
3. Emotional access: A visual task board breaks down the lesson into clear segments. 'Now, Next, Then' is visible throughout and students can work independently or in pairs during the task section.
4. Sensory needs: The classroom lights are dimmed, or the blinds are lowered. Noise cancelling headphones are available if needed. Mr McGill allows movement breaks and has a corner with printed materials.
5. Executive function: Mr McGill uses a step-by-step scaffold adopted for the relevant age to help students write up the functions of the organ, using sentence starters. He also models an exemplar paragraph under the visualiser and allows students to use a visual checklist at each stage of the demonstration. Classroom timers are used to help students switch between tasks and keep on track. This also helps with motivation.
6. Reflection: He provides students with exit slips with various prompts for students to respond to. For example, 'What helped you stay focused today?' and 'What one thing did you understand clearly?'

Why does this work?

The template helps teachers build a quick-win thinking strategy that they can use time and time again. Perfect for reducing workload!

TEMPLATE

The Five Minute Inclusion Plan

This template aligns with my famous Five Minute Lesson Plan used by teachers all over the world. Remember, this is a thinking methodology to take you through the planning process to become more inclusive in your practice. Use this template to help embed inclusive thinking at the beginning, not the end, of your planning process.

The template prompts you to consider emotional access, cognitive load, sensory diversity, and emotional function in your classroom context. In just five minutes, reading this document through will help you plan proactively for the widest range of learners, before the lesson even begins. What other aspects do you need to consider?

Scan the QR code for a downloadable copy of this blank template.

THE FIVE MINUTE INCLUSION PLAN

1 The big picture
- What are you teaching?
- Who are the learners?
- What barriers already exist?
- What considerations are needed?

2 Define objectives
- How will you break them down?
- What reflection prompts can you add?
- How will you check for understanding?

3 Cognitive access
- How will you dual code?
- How will you show the learning process?

4 Emotional access
- How will you retrieve?
- Oral or written?
- Safe spaces?

5 Sensory diversity
- Ear defenders?
- Lighting/sounds?
- Use of wait time for processing?
- Slides and worksheets?

6 Executive function
- 'I do, we do, you do'
- Visual countdowns
- What will you say out loud?

7 Metacognition prompts
- How to reveal answers?
- How to self-correct?
- Key reflection questions?
- Reduce cognitive load?

8 Classroom strategy
- How to implement?
- Routines used?
- Backup plan?

9 Interventions
- The plan for overwhelmed students?
- Use of second adult?
- Alternative spaces?

10 Stickability
- What needs to stick?
- Next lesson? Next month? Next term?

11 Sequence/flow
- Beginning or end?
- Other times of day?
- Curriculum alignment?
- Other formats?

CHAPTER 8
THE EVOLVING ROLE OF STUDY SKILLS

It has been my experience not only as a teacher but also now as a trainer, that there is insufficient teaching of effective study skills. By the time exams are happening, it's too late. My belief is that we are so focused on delivering the curriculum, we have left *how we learn* to chance.

We need to stop teaching students what study skills work best, and start teaching them *how to use those skills* in a variety of ways. This, I believe, needs to start from the beginning of primary school. Many of us during our school and college years, myself included, relied on intuition, not instruction.

I still recall to this day having a pack of highlighters for my A-Level exams, believing that colour-coding every line of my notes was an effective revision approach. I wasn't taught otherwise. But research has long since shown that highlighting and rereading, while popular, are among the least effective strategies when used in isolation.

Instead, we should be telling students how to use these skills strategically, in tandem with more powerful methods like retrieval practice and elaboration (see Chapter 2). There has been no explicit study-skills implementation in schools to teach students these skills before they reach college. The focus is largely on teaching the curriculum. But a small revolution is happening in some schools where teachers are increasingly immersed with cognitive science and are understanding ways we can teach students *how* to learn, alongside learning the curriculum. Despite this good news, we still have a skills gap to narrow; we need all students to receive these skills in the classroom well *before* they reach higher education. Unless schools make a personal choice to begin teaching 'how to learn' as part of their curriculum experiences as early as EYFS, students will continue to be left with a mixed experience. During these early years of education, children are developing cognitively at a rapid pace so it is important for schools to include explicit, cognitive support with learning from the outset.

In this chapter, I will be revisiting the cognitive science of study techniques; I will explore the quiet revolution I see happening in classrooms across the country, where children as young as Year 3 or 4 now talk about retrieval, instead of revision. The language of learning is already happening in our classrooms and I will explore the research, bust some myths, and offer practical ways to embed study skills meaningfully across the curriculum, from EYFS to further education.

EXPLAINER

Over a decade ago, Dunlosky et al. (2013) sparked a quiet revolution by rating the effectiveness of ten study techniques. Since then, thousands of teachers, myself included, have tried to integrate their findings into classroom practice. But what does new research say? Let's look at two recent studies.

The first study, from the University of Wisconsin (Bartoszewski and Gurung, 2015), surveyed over 300 college students. The surprising headline from the research findings? While many students *believed* self-explanation and keyword mnemonic were most effective, the only technique that *actually* predicted exam performance was elaborative interrogation – that is, generating an explanation for why a concept is true (Bartoszewski and Gurung, 2015, p. 2) – and even then, its increased use correlated with *lower* exam scores. The study's real insight was this: academic performance had more to do with teaching quality and student self-efficacy than the use of specific techniques. The key message? The way teachers teach study skills and habits – and the belief we build around them – may matter more than the technique itself.

The second, more recent study explained in chapters 3 and 6 (Ruiz- Martín et al., 2024) surveyed over 5,000 secondary students across 27 Spanish schools. The findings indicated that retrieval practice and elaborative strategies were positively linked to both academic performance and healthier learning attitudes. Meanwhile, rereading and highlighting, though frequently used, lagged behind. The critical insight was that many students still rely on ineffective techniques not because they're lazy or ill-informed, but because those methods *feel* productive. It's comfortable for all of us to reread material. It's also easy to highlight text. But, what we call the **illusion of learning** is not true learning. In essence, students who misdirected their effort in fact achieved lower outcomes.

Retrieval practice activates brain regions linked to memory consolidation, and long-term learning. Neuroimaging studies show that retrieval practice engages the prefrontal cortex and hippocampus, areas central to memory integration and cognitive control. Indeed, the findings of Wiklund-Hörnqvist et al. (2022) provide 'behavioural and brain-imaging evidence that retrieval practice is effective also for individuals with lower levels [of cognition]'

(p. 1). Furthermore, 'repeated retrieval... also... linked to subcortical brain regions' and to 'more detailed representations after retrieval practice (Wiklund-Hörnqvist et al., 2022, p.2). This suggests that retrieval practice strengthens the quality and structure of stored information, and offers new ways of understanding why some study strategies work better than others. In addition, students who engaged in retrieval practice showed 'blood-oxygen-level-dependent signal[s] in several left hemisphere regions that have been linked to language processing and semantic retrieval' (Wiklund-Hörnqvist et al., 2021, p. 6). These areas of the brain are associated with deeper learning and memory consolidation. This adds a neurological dimension to what many teachers already observe in the classroom: students who quiz themselves or others, elaborate answers aloud, or practise recalling key concepts tend to retain information more effectively. Neuroimaging now reinforces this, offering a compelling argument for embedding retrieval into revision timetables and classroom routines.

Emerging fMRI studies further strengthen these links by showing that active study strategies such as retrieval and elaboration stimulate specific brain regions associated with memory consolidation and long-term retention. While fMRI scans cannot be used as classroom tools, they help us better understand what is happening beneath the surface when students do indeed learn effectively. In summary, 'retrieval practice study produces superior retention' (Wiklund-Hörnqvist et al., 2021, p. 7); it improves test scores and activates specific areas of the brain linked to memory and cognitive control, reinforcing long-term learning at a neural level.

One key point for you to consider is how to blend your methods between the time of day, the knowledge being tested, your location, the task, and the format. A mixed approach to retrieval is more likely to yield improved results to support knowledge transfer to long-term memory, rather than using the same methodology time and time again. Note that retrieval, of course, will be very different in an Early Years environment compared to a further education classroom, and will vary significantly between subjects. I've suggested key study skills on the next page, that take into account a variety of phases, subjects, and contexts. (See Chapter 1, page 9 for ten study skill definitions offered by Dunlosky et al., 2013.)

By phase

Primary (Early Years and Key Stage 1)

1. Retrieve information through oral recall, songs, or movement-based routines. For example, 'What did we learn yesterday?'
2. Scaffolded visual tools. For example, story maps, talk partners.
3. Emphasise verbal self-explanation: 'Tell me how you work that out.'
4. Embed regulation through routines. For example, tidy up time or self-scoring smiley faces.

Primary (Key Stage 2)

1. Introduce basic study strategies like spaced practice through weekly review quizzes.
2. Begin dual coding. For example, diagrams, timelines, visual narrative pairings.
3. Model metacognitive talk: 'How did you check your answer?'
4. Encourage personal goal-setting using traffic-light targets or exit tickets.

Secondary (Key Stage 3 to Key Stage 4)

1. Retrieval: Frequent low-stakes quizzing, brain dumps, flash cards.
2. Elaboration: Connect learning to real-world problems.
3. Interleaving: Mixed practice across units (e.g. topics in maths or science).
4. Promote active note reflection over passive rereading.

Post-16/Further education

1. Encourage self-testing over rereading (e.g. use of practice papers).
2. Promote elaborative interrogation: 'Why does this idea make sense?'
3. Model spaced learning in revision plans.
4. Empower students to review their own misconceptions using mark schemes.

By subject

English and humanities

1. Use narrative techniques for memory: timelines, story retelling, concept mapping.
2. Encourage dual coding: Essay structures with visual outlines.
3. Use elaboration: 'How does this connect to what we studied before?'
4. Interleave topics. For example, comparing themes across texts.

Maths

1. Spaced retrieval through mixed-topic starter questions.
2. Use worked examples: Show steps, then remove scaffolds over time.
3. Encourage metacognitive reflection: 'Which part of the method was hardest? Why?'
4. Highlight cognitive load: Avoid presenting new methods with high distractions.

Science

1. Apply retrieval through practical write-ups or keyword recall during practical experiments.
2. Model sequencing: Breaking complex problems into steps.
3. Embed visual study strategies. For example, labelled diagrams, flow charts.
4. Promote reteaching of misconceptions through elaboration.

Languages

1. Retrieval through oral recall, translation drills, vocabulary flash cards.
2. Use spacing with weekly reviews of past units.
3. Dual coding with gestures or imagery to link key language words.
4. Encourage low-stake peer quizzing to reduce anxiety.

Creative arts/PE/Technology

1. Use modelling narrating decisions aloud during creation or performance.
2. Encourage rehearsal logs and practical diaries: What worked? What changed? What's next?
3. Retrieval through technique drills, self-recorded feedback and video diaries.
4. Space repetition of core routines. For example, warm-ups, scales, drills.

By context

SEND/Neurodiverse learners

1. Chunk retrieval tasks into manageable units.
2. Use visual prompts and concrete examples over abstract explanations.
3. Use plenty of considered pauses and 'time to think' about what is being said.
4. Use metacognitive sentence stems: 'First I tried... then I noticed...'.
5. Repetition with variation practice in multiple formats (text, audio, movement).

Low motivation/Disengaged students/Poor attendance

1. Use self-scoring quizzes to build confidence and agency.
2. Set personal retrieval goals. For example, 'three things I remember from last week'.
3. Explain the science behind the strategy: *Why* it works to build buy-in.
4. Scaffold independence with collaborative peer tasks first.
5. Think carefully about students' intrinsic motivation. For example, build this into your planning. Why do they want to learn this information?

High attaining/Exam focused

1. Focus on optimising strategy choice: When to use, and why.
2. Refine elaboration: Deeper synthesis, not just surface links.
3. Self-monitoring checklist to evaluate retrieval quality.
4. Train students to avoid illusions of competence (e.g. the belief that rereading material is good-quality revision, in favour of 'Can I do this without my notes?').

I will explain how to do all of this in the next section.

PRACTICAL IDEA

Study-strategy audit and planner for all key stages

How can you help students to choose the most appropriate method for any given problem? In the following section I suggest ideas and techniques, and offer guidance for when to introduce these. This should encourage independent learning from your students. I will also provide suggestions for developing a **study-strategy audit** and planner for all students and key stages you teach. This will enable students and teaching colleagues to review current study habits and select high-impact strategies (retrieval, spacing, dual coding, interleaving etc.) aligned with their subject and key stage. The audit will also include suggestions for family involvement at home.

The core goal is to raise awareness of high-impact strategies (retrieval, spacing, elaboration, dual coding, and interleaving) while reducing dependency on low-utility habits (highlighting, rereading, copying). Most importantly, the strategies will help you to support students to understand *why* a particular strategy works and *how* to apply it flexibly across various contexts. Let's get started!

Step-by-step guide: Study-strategy audit and planner

1 **Complete a study-strategy audit (baseline):** Use a short survey or visual checklist to prompt students to reflect on their current habits. Questions might include:

1. When you revise, what's the first thing you usually do?
2. Which of these do you use: rereading, highlighting, flashcards, past papers, self-quizzing, watching videos?

2 **Teach the Big Five:** Introduce each of the five most effective study strategies (retrieval, dual coding, elaboration, interleaving, spacing) on a systematic basis, aligned to your curriculum plans. Rather than covering them all at once, use classroom examples and modelling to demonstrate a 'strategy of the week'.

3 **Match study strategies to subjects and age groups:** Different strategies suit different tasks. Use simple tools to help students align strategies with their age and subject. For example:

1. Retrieval = for quick quizzes in core subjects.
2. Dual coding = for visual prompts in a target modern foreign language (MFL).
3. Elaboration = for comparing and contrasting characters in an English text.
4. Interleaving = for mixed-topic activities in maths or PE, or blended across both subjects.
5. Spacing = for developing personal revision timetables as students move closer to their first set of formal examinations

4 **Scaffold strategic planning:** Once study strategies are introduced, help your students build a study planner using spaced intervals across a number of weeks or months. Start simply by:

1. Planning three sessions (five–15 minutes) every week, rotating strategies.
2. Including time for self-quizzing and reflection.
3. Using prompts: 'What did I recall today?' or 'What helped me remember?'

5 **Bridge the gap between home and school:** Share the audit and planner with families. Explain how retrieval, elaboration and spacing trump rereading, highlighting, or cramming. Offer home-friendly versions that encourage families and students to:

1. Quiz each other over family meals.
2. Teach parents how to ask elaborative questions (e.g. 'Why do you think that's true?').
3. Use colour-coded flashcards for low-stakes recall.

6 **Integrate into curriculum time:** This is an important way of delivering study skills using a more explicit, consistent, and inclusive approach for all students, in all schools. Study-skill planning should be part of a weekly timetable, not an optional extra left for schools to consider. Retrieval techniques are beginning to be embedded in every lesson in most schools and, eventually, spaced recall and 'Do now' activities, quick flashcard checks, mini whiteboards, and visual consolidation tasks (thumbs up/down) will become part of every lesson. Encourage metacognitive talk: 'I'm asking you to recall yesterday's content because it strengthens your long-term memory by reviewing the material we covered in the last lesson.'

7 **Review and reflect:** Students should revisit their study plan every half term. What worked? What didn't? What new strategy will they try next? Use a strategy-swap activity in tutor time or in specific lessons.

8 **Whole-school or college CPD:** Ensure professional development time is protected to train all school/college staff on using the same audit. Encourage departments to map where and how study strategies are taught. Ask:

1. Where do we model them in our lessons?
2. Where do we leave them implicit?
3. How do we build a bank of study-skill resources by subject and age group to be used across the school/college?

Why this matters

This approach doesn't just improve study outcomes; having study skills explicitly linked to a curriculum plan, and to teaching, builds long-term habits, metacognitive awareness, and confidence among students and families. If every student left school and entered college or a career with a working understanding of how their brain learns, how many more would thrive later in life? What impact would this have on our society?

TOOLKIT TIPS

1. Teach 'how to learn' as part of your curriculum delivery.
2. Model strategy selection during problem-solving, not just strategy use.
3. Design a study-strategy audit to evaluate effective/ineffective skills.
4. Bridge the gap between home and the classroom; share with families how learning happens to help build social capital in the home.

WORKED EXAMPLE

In a Year 10 English lesson, Miss Jackson's students are revising for their GCSE English Literature exam. Miss Jackson is aware that many of her students default to rereading and highlighting as a study skill, especially when under pressure. Instead of focusing on the content alone, she begins the term with a study-strategy audit.

Step 1: Baseline audit

Miss Jackson uses a visual checklist through an online survey to ask her students:

1. What's the first thing you do when you revise?
2. Which of these techniques do you use most: highlighting, rereading, flashcards, past papers, quizzing?

She learns that over 80 per cent of her class prefer to highlight and reread material, while only a few use retrieval or elaboration strategies.

Step 2: Teaching the 'Big Five'

Over the next half term, Miss Jackson introduces one new strategy each week:

- Week 1: Retrieval practice
- Week 2: Spacing (via 'Do Now' quizzes)
- Week 3: Dual coding (laminated quote maps for character themes)
- Week 4: Elaboration (why did this character act in this way?)
- Week 5: Interleaving (mixed practice on speaking and listening components that students can use in their GCSE Language exam)
- Week 6: Repeat elements where required. Ask students to design and make their own flashcards. Complete online retrieval quizzes.

Step 3: Planner building

Students build their own revision planner using a scaffolded template with three 15-minute sessions a week, choosing one of the five strategies for each session.

Step 4: Home–school links

Miss Jackson communicates with home and shares a revision guide for families. They are prompted to ask their child:

1. What three things do you remember from yesterday's lesson?
2. Name one thing you can remember from the lesson last week?
3. Give me one fact from a lesson last month?

This simple and effective method encourages retrieval practice and metacognition in the home. Miss Jackson holds families to account, checking in with students each lesson to see what progress is being made in between lessons.

Step 5: Reflection and revision

Every half term, students reflect on the following:

1. What worked?
2. What strategy helped me remember the most information?
3. What will I try next?

Regular reflection builds metacognitive awareness and shifts revision habits from passive to active, ensuring they are also selecting the most effective study skills.

TEMPLATE

Study-strategy audit planner

This template can be adapted for Key Stage 2 to Key Stage 5 students (seven–18 years old), and embedded into any pastoral opportunities (tutor time, assemblies, homework diaries).

Scan the QR code for a downloadable copy of this blank template.

Section	Prompt	Example / Notes:
Study habits audit	• What do I usually do first when revising? • What study strategies do I enjoy most? Why?	☐ Reread ☐ Highlight ☐ Quiz myself ☐ Past papers ☐ Flashcards ☐ Other ____________
Learning the Big Five	• Which of the following have I tried? • Which one works best for me? Why?	☐ Retrieval ☐ Spacing ☐ Dual coding ☐ Elaboration ☐ Interleaving ☐ Other ____________
Strategy planner	• Week 1 plan • Week 2 plan • Week 3 plan	For example: • Mondays – retriever quiz (15 mins) • Wednesdays – dual coding mind map (15 mins) • Fridays – past papers (15 mins) • Repeat and adapt • Try something new

Section	Prompt	Example / Notes:
Subject strategy match	• English • Maths • Science	• Retrieval and elaboration (character comparison) • Interleaving in spacing • Retrieval and dual coding (diagrams)
Family strategy ideas	• Ask your family to ask you what you remembered from class today?	• Provide flashcards or quote cards for parents to quiz their child
Reflections	• What helped me learn this week? • What will I try next?	• Your comments:

CHAPTER 9

APPLYING COGNITIVE SCIENCE ACROSS THE CURRICULUM

Many teachers still feel underprepared for curriculum reform. In the *Curriculum and Assessment Review* (DfE, 2025), the report cites 'low subject knowledge among non-specialist teachers and little access to relevant professional development' (p. 89), particularly, in how to build and sequence knowledge. Long-term curriculum planning must be rooted in how learning happens, and curriculum coherence matters just as much as innovation. This means 'curriculum fads' should be addressed at a national level, with further guidance published to support all schools and colleges. It's one thing to understand the theory of cognitive science. It's quite another to apply it well in a noisy, time-poor, 30-student classroom.

This chapter offers practical help for you to bridge research and reality; the research into cognitive science isn't a one-size-fits-all toolkit, after all. While it is vital that you become a critical consumer of research, it's also important that the research findings are adapted for your subject, age, learner profile, and context. The biggest challenge I hear in schools and colleges isn't 'What is retrieval practice?' or 'How does dual coding work?', it's 'How do I use this in drama?' or 'What does metacognition look like in design and technology?'

The research is clear that while some techniques, such as retrieval and spaced practice, are effective across subject-specific areas, they won't look identical in every subject. That's why the practical focus of this chapter is subject-based application models and I will suggest how to adapt principles to your curriculum or key stage area. Here are some examples:

- In art, a mind map isn't just a study aid, it might chart the evolution of an artist's influence, or the planning of a new composition and, in so doing, combines cognitive load reduction with creative freedom.
- In English, retrieval might involve low-stakes quizzes on literary terminology, but also verbal recall of plot points and author intent before students need to write an analytical response.
- In science, self-explanation can be taught explicitly during practical lessons, asking students to verbalise why each step in the experiment matters, linking theory to action.
- In PE, interleaving practice may include combining tactics from different sports to test adaptability and decision-making, improving long-term memory transfer.
- In music, spaced practice is vital, teaching students to revisit and rehearse short sections regularly, building fluency over time without cognitive overload.

Each of these examples takes a cognitive principle and reshapes it to fit the discipline command – not the other way around. The art of teaching, therefore, is how to apply the science of learning. It requires experimentation, collaboration, and context.

EXPLAINER

In the *Curriculum and Assessment Review* (DfE, 2025), a critical theme emerged from the extensive research carried out: namely that there is a need for a curriculum across England that reflects the diversity of the learner population and puts equity, evidence, and coherence at its heart. With an examination system that places a very large time burden on 16-year-olds, there was a call to Ofqual to consider 'the volume of exam assessment at the heart of assessment design' (DfE, 2025, p. 135). While I'm torn between exams being a fair and (relatively reliable) method for evaluating student knowledge, especially in the world of misinformation and artificial intelligence, we also need to become richer in our approaches to assessment for all students, whatever their individual needs. How do we develop a systematic approach to curriculum and assessment that meets the needs of our students today and those of the future?

Every curriculum review should continue to challenge current high-stakes assessment practices in light of increasing student anxiety, exclusions, and attendance. Assessment should support deep learning and inform teaching.

But where might fMRI research fit in, and what insights can the teaching profession learn from it? One of the strongest arguments in the curriculum review is that curriculum is not the same as content; it's about progression and how we as teachers amass knowledge and understanding over time.

There's a clear need and demand by teachers to have an evidence-informed profession – one that draws on research about cognition, language development, and neurodiversity.

Oracy

Oracy continues to stay on the national curriculum agenda. Although young people are more likely to pick up a digital device than they are a physical book, we still need to consider how students process language and how they communicate face-to-face and in the online world.

Like metacognition, developing oracy helps students articulate their thinking, deepen understanding, self-regulation and motivation, not just in English but across the curriculum and in the real world. Teaching metacognitive strategies within subjects helps students apply self-regulation in their everyday learning.

Curriculum reforms should value communication and language development, and are a cognitive tool, not simply a speaking skill. Speaking supports thinking, self-regulation, metacognition and learning across all subjects. Therefore, applying cognitive science across the curriculum should include structured opportunities to ensure that all classrooms are speech communities. In the next section, I'll explain how you can bring metacognitive research into classroom practice. Applying the science of learning doesn't mean adding more. It means doing better with what we already do.

It's worth noting that key stage and subject specificity are also important:

1. Science and maths benefit from worked examples that reduce extraneous load and retrieval practice that supports complex **schema formation**.
2. English and history lend themselves to elaboration and interleaving, helping students link texts and ideas across different units.
3. Art and design, PE and DT align well with cognitive apprenticeship – modelling expert performance, then scaffolding practice. For example: 'Here is one I made earlier. This scored a Grade 8.'
4. In languages, space retrieval and dual coding are essential for vocabulary acquisition. I am a huge fan of scripts and choral recitals for developing schema. Shall we sing aloud our ABCs?
5. In PSHE and RE, metacognitive talk helps students reflect on values.

While checklists or knowledge organisers have their place in the classroom, true curriculum implementation succeeds when schools build shared language, offer real examples, and allow teaching staff to adapt whole-school documentation into strategies that work for their students and their subjects: 'Teachers needed sufficient time to participate in interventions. Time was so important that it was described as "the most crucial condition" for success' (Sims et al., 2021, p. 54). This matters even more in an education system where we struggle to recruit teachers, and we are still at the very beginnings of applying the science of learning across curriculum areas.

Working memory

The working memory model reminds us that the brain is limited by how much new information it can hold and manipulate. Students 'can hold up to two additional items with no impairment in their [verbal] reasoning speed' (Baddeley and Hitch, 1974, p. 6). You experience this every day: the glazed eyes during a detailed explanation, the middle of the lesson drift, or the chaos of too many instructions at once. It's not necessarily bad teaching; it's cognitive overload in a school system that struggles to adapt to endless scenarios. You do a remarkable job considering all of this!

Cognitive science

Cognitive science tells us that effective teaching lightens the load. We reduce split attention, provide scaffolding, chunk instructions, and revisit content to support information transfer to the students' long-term memory. This is the foundation of classroom strategies like dual coding, modelling, worked examples, and low-stakes retrieval. But simply knowing about these isn't enough. Good implementation asks the following:

1. Is this teaching idea grounded in replicated, peer-reviewed evidence?
2. Can it be applied practically within the daily rhythms of classroom life?
3. Does this idea help students remember and apply knowledge more efficiently?

In an evolving world, influenced by misinformation and artificial intelligence, applying cognitive science and neuroeducation into classrooms and across the curriculum is increasingly important. Not all brains learn in the same way, nor do we teach in the same way, and with neurodiverse learners who process and regulate attention differently, many of the fMRI studies I've shared throughout this book have identified functional differences in working memory and reward networks. For example, as ADHD comes 'under closer examination in cognitive neuroscience' (Cortese et al., 2012, p. 1047), research will continue to explore the **frontoparietal network** to understand how ADHD brains are wired. The hope is that this type of research can then be integrated into classrooms around the country.

PRACTICAL IDEA

Curriculum mapping through a cognitive science lens

When viewed through the lens of cognitive science, schemes of work can help reduce forgetting and build fluency. They can also offer retrieval-rich opportunities to help students retain and transfer prior learning. Individual schemes of work should be interconnected into a whole school or department curriculum mapping document. They all connect together.

In this practical section, we will consider a whole-school/college approach to curriculum mapping through a cognitive science lens. I'll provide you with a subject-specific framework for reviewing your curriculum, helping you reflect on what is taught, when, and how. The step-by-step curriculum mapping activity is designed to help teaching staff adapt cognitive science principles to their own subject demands and student needs, ensuring that memory, motivation, and metacognition are not left to chance. The key message: curriculum is more than content; it's the architecture of how learning is built, retrieved, and transferred to long-term memory.

Step-by-step: Applying a cognitive science lens to curriculum design

1 **Clarify core knowledge (Encode):** Start with the essentials. What must students remember long after the lesson ends? Identify the threshold concepts – those sticky, powerful ideas that underpin deep understanding. I like to think of building knowledge as a spiderweb. The anchor points must be fixed first, with the thread across the top providing a 'bridge'. This analogy could be akin to your curriculum web across the year or key stage: how everything connects together to help students move from A to B. Without these anchor points moored to a fixed location, the entire web wobbles, and once those key points are anchored, more schema (the spider's spiral threads) can be connected.

2 **Identify where and how content will stick (Store):** Core knowledge needs to be identified, but equally so does how you bring the content to life using your resources and teacher instruction (storytelling). Consider

mapping where cognitive load is highest. What topics are tricky? Where might students' working memory be overwhelmed? Where do misconceptions typically arise? Use this to embed the following:

1. worked examples in maths and science
2. dual coding in geography and MFL
3. scaffolded prompts and templates in PSHE
4. oracy and retrieval in English and RE.

Be selective. Some of these points don't need to appear in every lesson, however, they should thread deliberately across units, reducing cognitive load and reinforcing schema.

3 **Plan when and how knowledge will be revisited (Retrieve):** Too often, schemes of work cover content and sometimes fail to plan for forgetting. Remember that forgetting is part of the learning process, so it is essential that you plan for spaced practice before revisiting material. One approach is to consider interleaving practice by mixing related topics or problem types over time, without adding any unnecessary distractions to learning. For example:

Week 1	Week 2	Week 3	Week 4	Week 5	Week 6
Introduce new concept	Apply concept to existing knowledge		Revisit concept in another context		Check retention of new concept

By using the example table, you are building cognitive science principles into your curriculum planning, rather than bolted-on techniques.

4 **Build in flexibility for reteaching and greater depth:** Avoid rigid checklists. Effective schemes of work should offer structured freedom, with built-in time for review, challenge, and reflection. For example: 'If students go below X in this assessment check, should I return to teaching Y before moving onto Z?' or 'This lesson offers extension tasks linked to common misconceptions identified in a previous class'. Remember that a good scheme of work should serve the teaching process and should be adapted accordingly, not be a static document that prevents you from responding to your students.

5 **Flag concept links across units or subjects:** Students rarely learn in a neat order. Highlight overlaps across disciplines to help connect schemas. For example, energy transfer (science) can be reinforced in:

1. a PE lesson warm-up
2. an English lesson in which you build a narrative structure
3. a history lesson in which timelines and storytelling is revisited
4. a DT lesson in which you are helping to nurture students' ideas around product-concept development
5. a geography lesson in which students are evaluating primary and secondary sources of evidence.

6 **Use student and staff feedback to refine the curriculum plan:** Ask students which lesson helped them remember the most information, and why? Ask staff: In which areas do students typically forget or misunderstand information? Which topics tend to lead to more challenging behaviour?

Use these core questions to adapt your curriculum map by adding more retrieval opportunities, simplification, or reteaching of concepts.

7 **Make the learning process visible:** When you are an expert, you can move forwards and immediately solve a problem. When you are a novice, and do not have the prerequisite knowledge to solve problems, you need to see the end goal and work backwards in stages from the problem in order to understand the learning process. This is best achieved when teachers show step-by-step what to do. Imagine being asked to make a milky and sweet cup of tea. If you've never made one before, you will need to be shown the steps to do this. Once you have made a number of cups of tea over time, imagine being asked to make 100 cups of tea for an event in a 15-minute break? If you are an expert, you can draw on your experiences to connect ideas and solve this problem. Using visuals is a good idea here, such as a set of IKEA instructions to show the learning process. Step-by-step instructions enable more people to become experts in building furniture.

Ask yourself: Where are key ideas introduced? When are they revisited? How are misconceptions flagged? Where is a deeper application expected? Over time, this strategy will help you and your students build shared mental models for curriculum progression.

8 Use the spiderweb analogy:

1. Anchor points/Frame = the big ideas.
2. Spokes/Spiral = interleaved knowledge threads.
3. The full spiderweb = growing schema, repaired over time and strengthened.
4. Gaps/Broken parts = misconceptions, missed lessons.

This spiderweb metaphor should remind us that curriculum plans should hold learning together and should not be rigid. No spiderweb is built in the same location, or the same size. Schemes of work that are built on cognitive principles guide content delivery and support effective teaching. They help novice students become experts, reduce teacher workload through smarter sequencing, and embed the science of learning into everyday practice.

TOOLKIT TIPS

1. Adapt cognitive science principles to your subject and key stage. For example, do not assume retrieval practice works as a quiz that you use only at the start of lessons.
2. View your curriculum as knowledge progression, not content. It's not a list of topics to be taught, but the spiderweb architecture that builds over time.
3. Lighten the load: What would be the benefit of having short (curriculum-related) brain breaks in class? How can you reduce split attention?
4. Balance all assessment with learning opportunities. Make the implication of formative or summative assessment practical, and adaptive to your students' needs. For example, mix the ways you might assess what students know.

WORKED EXAMPLE

Applying curriculum mapping in an MFL lesson

Mrs Warbrook teaches Spanish to Key Stage 3 students in a mixed-ability Year 8 class. Her goal is to revise and deepen vocabulary knowledge for the topic 'Mi Ciudad' (My City), while embedding cognitive science principles into the curriculum plan.

Step 1: Core knowledge (Encode)

Mrs Warbrook identifies key vocabulary and sentence structures (e.g. 'hay una piscina', 'no hay un cine') as anchor points. These are the threshold concepts for future speaking and writing topics. She prioritises high-frequency words and provides chunks of targeted vocabulary in the spoken language rather than isolated nouns.

Step 2: Storage strategies (Store)

She highlights topics that generate misconceptions – for example, gendered nouns and verb placement. Mrs Warbrook adjusts her scheme of work to include dual coding techniques (e.g. simple icons for places in the city) and worked examples that show common translation mistakes.

Step 3: Retrieval planning (Retrieve)

Her department's schemes of work were outdated, but have now been improved with cognitive science principles for effective learning. Identifying explicitly where encode, store, and retrieve occur in current documentation helps sharpen the progression of knowledge. There are schedules for retrieval practice quizzes that are planned collectively, not ad-hoc surprises in class, with interleaving prior topics like 'asking for directions' and the 'names of shops' found on the high street. Each unit ends with a mixed topic low-stakes quiz and a speaking challenge using multiple chunks of vocabulary together.

Step 4: Flexibility and depth

Mrs Warbrook's lessons now also include optional tasks: 'If confident, add an opinion using "porque es…".' Gaps are flagged after formative assessments, and 'reteaching weeks' are mapped in, with 'low-stakes quizzing weeks' later being the priority.

Step 5: Cross-curricular opportunities

The MFL department identifies links with geography (urban versus rural), history (local heritage), and maths (ordinal numbers for directions), and sequences vocabulary accordingly.

Step 6: Feedback loops

Students annotate vocabulary organisers weekly, reflecting on fluency and accuracy. Staff review common errors and suggest department-wide tweaks to sequence terminology in their curriculum planning. Teacher workload improves, and staff report feeling happier and more engaged in the materials they are sharing with their students.

TEMPLATE

Curriculum mapping template (based on cognitive science principles)

Here is a template designed to help you develop your curriculum mapping for the year ahead. Use this with a key stage group of students to develop a cognitive science perspective in your planning. The template provides some examples, and follows the structure of existing research recommendations for how learning happens – encoding, **storage**, and retrieval.

Scan the QR code for a downloadable blank copy of this template.

Section	Prompts to complete	Teacher notes
1. Define core knowledge	• What must my students know by the end of this unit? • What is the minimum knowledge required to progress? • Which core knowledge or anchor points should be highlighted?	• Think about encoding – what reaches our long-term memory?
2. Reduce cognitive overload	• Where might my students experience unnecessary complexity or confusion? • How will you reduce extraneous load?	• Consider lesson materials, displays, and tasks
3. Plan for misconceptions	• What common errors or misconceptions do students make in this topic? • How are these flagged and pre-taught or revisited?	• Use past assessment data and teach insight/ experiences

Section	Prompts to complete	Teacher notes
4. Embed retrieval practice	• What retrieval methods will you use during the unit? • When, and how often, will you revisit key knowledge from this and previous topics?	• Plan spaced and interleaved tasks
5. Incorporate dual coding	• Where can diagrams, images, models, or gestures support conceptual understanding? • Are visuals paired with words clearly and consistently?	• Support memory and comprehension
6. Structure for challenge and support	• How is the scheme adaptive? • Are there stretch tasks for deeper thinking? • What scaffolds exist for students with SEND?	• Avoid one-size-fits-all design
7. Sequence with purpose	• Does the order of content build logically? • How are ideas or skills revisited over time? • Is the **curriculum spiral**, **linear**, or **thematic**?	• Sketch a mini sequence if useful
8. Plan for feedback and review	• When and how will student understanding be checked? • What opportunities exist for reflection, reteaching, or self-regulation?	• Highlight what CPD or department discussions are needed
9. Connect to other subjects	• What interdisciplinary knowledge exists? • Where are the links? • How might prior knowledge from other subjects enhance understanding of this topic?	• Add depth and transfer opportunities
10. CPD / Department review	• What do all staff need to know to teach this topic consistently? • What training is required? • How often will the scheme be reviewed, updated, or co-planned?	• For whole school alignment

CHAPTER 10

A TEACHER TOOLKIT FOR THE FUTURE

I firmly believe that the future of teaching will *not* be powered by robots. We are a species built on relationships and, as such, we need (and thrive on) human contact. A world in which students study at home and work online with their teacher would be catastrophic for everyone's mental wellbeing. The pandemic gave us a glimpse into what that world might look like, so switching to online schooling is something we should avoid at scale if we want our young people to be able to contribute to a real-world existence.

In this chapter, we will explore how you can prepare for the changing classroom, not by chasing trends, or by avoiding the **fourth industrial revolution**, but by focusing on what works best for the young people you teach, whether that's AI, or new approaches to teacher professional development and curriculum delivery. What matters most is how we interpret and implement research in real classrooms, how our government can support the teaching profession, and how routines, relationships, and opportunities can all promote student reflection and reframe future potential. Some questions to consider include:

1. What should be in every teacher's toolkit? What kind of training actually improves long-term practice?
2. How do we ensure AI enhances learning for our students, rather than undermines it?
3. How should we use academic research to influence the classroom in a landscape of AI technology, algorithms, and misinformation?
4. How do we ensure that all teachers are equipped to be neuroliterate?

It is my view that the education system must evolve with the world our students now live in, a world that is increasingly shaped by artificial intelligence, shifting education policies, online learning, and increasing mental health needs. This final chapter is about how teachers, schools, and families can embed evidence-informed strategies that are resilient, flexible, and future-facing.

The chapter will examine what a teacher toolkit looks like in an age of AI-generated content, algorithmic feedback, and constant digital distraction. How do we prepare students not just to recall knowledge, but to navigate it ethically and critically? In the following sections we will explore implementation plans, models for whole-school professional development, and practical takeaways for classrooms, homes, and virtual learning spaces. The science of learning is not static, and neither should our teaching be.

EXPLAINER

We are only a few years into the artificial intelligence revolution, despite its origins in the 1950s, and at the time of writing, I would confidently say that we are saturated with mobile applications, website platforms, and day-to-day decision-making. Even our everyday chores, such as online-banking and household lighting can now predict and analyse data for us – online metacognition by robot!

There is a growing promise that 'AI will have an enormous impact on what we teach, as it will impact many occupations' (Holmes et al., 2019, p. 3) with ethical warnings long before AI reached general public use. AI will transform education, with platforms 'trained on data which contains human bias' (p. 170). Most research currently agrees it will be teachers who decide whether AI changes meaningful curriculum choices and teaching and learning in the classroom. AI tools can provide adaptive teaching and retrieval practice resources, taking the 'heavy lifting' out of many tasks, but can they truly personalise classroom cycles and reduce teacher workload? In addition, there is still limited evidence that these platforms outperform human-led feedback, particularly when teachers themselves adapt and scaffold the details in person, in the classroom. We must prioritise technology that enhances memory metacognition and feedback loops, and continue to avoid platforms that promise quick wins without any peer-reviewed pedagogy.

Implementation science – the study of how methods and strategies are actually used in real-life settings is clear: short-term CPD doesn't change long-term practice. Instead change occurs with sustained, subject-specific, and instructional coaching. At the end of this final chapter, I will provide you with a template that allows you to interrogate all the ideas in this book and design your own implementation plan for professional development.

Study skills, home learning, and the digital world

As teaching and learning slowly moves more into a hybrid model, and with the risk of AI replacing (some) teachers, the ability to manage time, motivation, and memory outside the classroom is now on the core curriculum agenda. Students need support in learning *how* to learn, not just *what* to learn. Retrieval practice, spaced learning, and self-explanation remain the most effective study strategies, but many students still default to highlighting and rereading, especially when learning independently.

Neuroimaging evidence suggests that retrieval activates key memory regions, and successive relearning taxes 'brain regions such as the hippocampus that are known to be important for memory formation and retention' (Wiklund-Hornqvist et al., 2021, p. 7).

The neuroimaging studies showed that students who learned using retrieval practice had significantly greater activation in the posterior hippocampus (the rear part of the brain which is the brain's key region for detailed memories) compared to those who simply read the material.

The link between student agency and their encoding of information is crucial. How we integrate explicit study strategy instruction into curriculum time, especially for disadvantaged learners, is something that we should all be trying to improve.

Equity and the future of education

Any future model for learning must be grounded in equity. Digital poverty, neurodiversity, and cultural bias all shape how students access and engage with learning. AI-trained models often replicate data with bias, while commercial edtech can exclude learners with SEND. As highlighted in Chapter 7, future-facing teaching must move beyond one-size-fits-all assumptions. Instead of a flexible, accessible pathway into the curriculum, the *Curriculum and Assessment Review* highlights the need for 'curriculum clarity and coherence' to reduce cognitive load and increase the opportunity for all to study to a wider range of subjects, 'made accessible for pupils with SEN' (DfE, 2025, p. 20). We must also make space for multiple voices and models of learning, not rigid delivery or diagnostic labels. Schools and colleges must work towards creating a future-proof implementation plan to help you, as teachers, manage all of these challenges.

PRACTICAL IDEA

Future-ready CPD: Your implementation plan

I think you'll agree that you don't need yet another presentation slide deck, or a training session; what you really need is time, trust, and tools to turn evidence into action. In this section, I will help you to build a long-term implementation plan for the future, for your personal professional development, as well as at a whole-school, or college, level. I will also offer you a step-by-step framework for organisations and individual teachers to apply the insights from this book into monthly CPD cycles. We'll look at how to blend tech tools, AI reflection, and research translation into sustained practice.

What is the goal?

The goal is to create a personal framework to help embed cognitive science, curriculum planning, and education research strategies into sustained professional development.

Step-by-step: A future-ready CPD framework

1 **Clarify your CPD goal:** Choose one cognitive principle or chapter from this book. Retrieval? Cognitive load? Metacognition? Start small. Choose one idea that aligns with a known need in your classroom, school, or college. For example, exam anxiety, SEND access, poor recall in Year 9.

2 **Define your implementation lens:** Now ask yourself, is this about your knowledge (awareness), classroom practice (behaviour), or long-term culture (habits)? For example, metacognition may begin as you model (behaviour) but may grow into a whole school reflection routine (culture).

3 **Build a monthly CPD calendar**: Split the year into six or eight mini-implementation cycles that align with the school academic year. Each one should focus on one cognitive principle (e.g. spacing), one model or technique (e.g. quizzing), and one subject-specific adaptation (e.g. science versus drama).

4 **Implementation plan, month-by-month**: An example of what this might look like is demonstrated in the table below:

Month	Focus	CPD format	Application task
September	Retrieval practice	Staff twilight	Departments plan x3 methods
October	Cognitive load	Peer observation	Redesign one slide deck
November	Metacognition	Video modelling	Staff reflect via surveys
December	Motivation	Coaching pairs	Develop 'Do Now' check ins
January	Dual coding	Department modelling	Redesign one worksheet
February	Feedback	Book looks	Apply a mixed-feedback matrix method
March	Spaced practice	Observations	Scaffold weekly review tasks
April	Revision techniques	Student voice	Develop revision cards
May	Curriculum	Whole-school audit	Map by department or key stage
June	Behaviour for learning	Staff twilight	Student feedback and surveys
July	Neurodiversity	SEND audit	External agency

5 **Try the 3-tool technique (Theory – Translation – Trial):**

1. Theory: What does the research say?
2. Translation: What does it mean for our subject?
3. Trial: How will we know it is working?

Build and protect time for trialling ideas, providing feedback, and reflecting on small wins. At this stage, it isn't perfection that you're looking for from the outset. Teaching study skills cannot be left to chance. It needs to be explicit.

6 **Add family-friendly strategy guides:** Involve families with simplified 'Try-at-home' versions and consider using the following:

1. Monthly flyers: For example, 'This month we are teaching retrieval. A question to ask [your child] at home might be "What did you remember from last week's lesson?"'
2. Evening routines: Teach your family one idea you learned in class today.
3. Online dashboards: Use school or college platforms to share weekly memory tips with your family.

7 **Reflect, record, refine:** Use staff voices and student feedback to revisit impact. Key questions to ask include:

1. What do teachers now do differently?
2. What do students notice in lessons?
3. Where is there curriculum coherence or cognitive drift?

Why does this matter?

Implementation is often the missing link in all school/college policies, and the research on implementation science tends to suggest that it takes 18 months to four years before you see any meaningful change on the ground. If we want to embed cognitive science in our schools and colleges, we need more intelligent routines, clear CPD feedback loops, and leadership that encourages teachers to reflect on their practice. You do not need to be overwhelmed with additional material that makes no demonstrable difference. Schools and colleges that embrace evidence slowly, carefully, and together build staff cultures that last beyond inspection cycles. Embedding neuroeducation and developing teachers who are neuroliterate isn't about doing anything trendy or creating a headline for CPD, this is about building a long-term habit of learning for teachers (**andragogy**), for students (pedagogy), and for their families.

TOOLKIT TIPS

1. AI can generate content, but it cannot replace human experience or expertise. Teach students how to use the tools ethically and effectively.
2. Implementation beats inspiration; one twilight training session will not change practice. Revisit concepts in staff professional learning to influence habits.
3. Build study skills into your curriculum plans. Think in cycles, not initiatives. Design any programmes with equity built in from the start. This ensures all students are exposed to various strategies throughout the academic year.

WORKED EXAMPLE

At McGill Academy (fictional), a mixed-comprehensive in North London, SLT were concerned about curriculum inconsistency and teacher workload. Feedback from staff highlighted low student recall, with teachers feeling unprepared for implementing retrieval-based teaching approaches.

Using the future CPD framework, the deputy headteacher launched a staff-wide plan centred on monthly mini themes, drawing directly from cognitive science principles. In September, retrieval practice was introduced. The department created three methods tailored to their subject. Teachers tried one method for two weeks, reflected, then fed back to all other staff.

In October, the focus shifted to cognitive load. Teachers reviewed their slide decks and reduced visual clutter, provided worked examples, and trialled new ways to break down complex tasks e.g. introducing worksheets one at a time. By December, video modelling was used to develop metacognitive talk, to allow teachers to see each other in action. Teachers recorded their own thinking aloud during planning, with modelling and self-reflection demonstrations provided using visualisers. Monthly flyers were sent home to parents. 'Ask your child how they remembered today's lesson?' became a weekly nudge, shared through the academy website. A short home-study guide was published, explaining cognitive science terms such as retrieval, dual coding, and spaced learning, including short videos published on the school's social media channels. These videos featured school and college staff in light-hearted roleplay scenarios to boost engagement and student motivation.

The approach was structured, consciously slow, and sustainable, in keeping with the research on implementation science. Rather than introduce multiple initiatives at once, they focused on one initiative each month. This provided the opportunity for the plan to evolve into a permanent fixture threaded through all aspects of school life. The leadership team at McGill Academy reported not only an improvement in student grades, but a renewed attitude to learning from student voice surveys, and an uplift in attendance. This was a direct result of a more conscious approach to curriculum implementation, a developed staff confidence in neuroliteracy, all of which resulted in happier students in classrooms, with better behaved corridors. A win-win overall!

TEMPLATE

Implementation guide

In my teacher training sessions, when I share my implementation guides, they often elicit a 'light bulb moment' for teachers and school/college leaders. They suddenly see the big picture, and how each individual chapter or idea connects together, with each idea building on another.

My advice would be to use this in your own classroom and practice across the academic year. Or, if you have a leadership team who are engaged with cognitive science, they might find this useful as a whole school/college approach for professional development, and potentially as a quality assurance process for introducing key ideas on a monthly basis.

Choose your ideas carefully, aligned with your students and school/college context, and seek to introduce, refine, revisit, and re-engage each of the ideas on a monthly basis, where each strategy or concept best fits in with your priorities.

Scan the QR code to download a blank template and redesign your own implementation schedule.

Month	Classroom focus (e.g. retrieval, dual coding)	Cognitive science principle (what does the research suggest?)	CPD plans	Application task (e.g. flyer message, text alert, redesign slides, trial quiz)	Family engagement (e.g. try this at home)	Department / Key stage	Lead staff	Evaluation method (e.g. observation, work scrutiny; how will you evidence any impact?)
September	Retrieval practice	Testing effect/ memory strength	Staff twilight	Departments design x3 retrieval tasks	Parent flyer	Whole school	Deputy headteacher	Staff show and tell
October	Cognitive load	Working memory limits	Peer observation	Teachers redesign one slide	Newsletter	All departments	Departments	Lesson feedback
November	Metacognition	Modelling thinking Monitoring learning	Video modelling CPD	Teachers record 'think aloud'	Parent prompt text alert	KS3 – KS4	Lead practitioners	Staff survey
December	Motivation and engagement	Self-regulation Goal orientation	Coaching pairs	Introduce 'Do Now' activity	Weekly parent portal reminders	Whole school	Pastoral leads	Student feedback
January	Dual coding	Combining verbal and visual processing	Department modelling	Teachers redesign one worksheet	Examples on school website	Departments	Curriculum leads	Work scrutiny
February	Feedback	Effective feedback cycles	Book looks	Trial mixed-method matrix approach	Parent guidance publication	KS4 focus	Senior leaders	Student voice
March	Spaced practice	Spacing effect for long-term retention	Lesson observations	Introduce weekly routines	Parent prompt text alert	Whole school	T&L team	Retrieval quiz data
April	Revision techniques	Retrieval and spacing combined	Student voice workshop	Students develop revision cards	Parent revision guidance	KS4	Year lead	Mock exam performance
May	Curriculum coherence	Knowledge sequencing and curriculum mapping	Whole-school audit	Department map knowledge progression	Curriculum overview shared with parents	Whole school	SLT	Curriculum review
June	Behaviour for learning	Inclusive cognitive design	Staff twilight	Trial student surveys	Parent behaviour update	Whole school	Behaviour lead	Student behaviour data
July	Neurodiversity	Divergent cognitive abilities	SEND audit	Scaffold and support plans	SEND family workshop	Whole school	SENDCo	SEND provision review

BRINGING IT ALL TOGETHER

What should you do now?

Since *The Teacher Toolkit Guide to Memory* published in 2022, the topic of *how we learn* has preoccupied my everyday writing, reading, and conversations with teachers. My whole career in education seems to have led to this simple question: *'How does learning happen?'*

Asking questions, sharing ideas, and listening to feedback – drawing from both the art and science of teaching – has empowered me to move away from generic advice to something deeper. If you are a teacher striving for meaningful impact, you must regularly interrogate the hallmarks of effective teaching and learning, and ask: 'What truly works, for whom does it work, and in what context does it work?'

A recent podcast interview stuck with me. The host decribed me as 'a teacher who researches, who is now a researcher who teaches'. It was a 'eureka' moment for me, or what I would now describe as a new connection of established neurons! This line sums up the essence of what I hope you will take from this book: that by reading and learning these neuroscience insights, you will build and shape your own classroom practice. It is through my accumulation of knowledge (the science), combined with my 35 years in education (the art), that I feel empowered to shift mindsets, challenge ideas, and work towards positive, practical improvements in teaching.

Over the last decade, the English teaching profession has shifted from 'what works' to explore 'why' and 'how' we seek solutions for various classroom conundrums and methods. With increasing access to educational research, neuroscience and fMRI scans, educators can move *towards a deeper look inside the brain and understand learning processes better*.

Clearly, there are ethical considerations associated with fMRI research in the classroom, and it's difficult to gather live data from brainwave readings and electrical signals during live instruction. Instead, this book draws on relevant academic research and extrapolates the findings into practical classroom solutions (even for that last period lesson on a Friday afternoon).

When we discuss 'How learning happens?', it is important for all teachers and leaders to ask the following five questions:

1. '**What** is it 'specifically' that we are learning?'
2. '**Who** is learning it?'
3. '**Where** are they learning it?'
4. '**Who** is teaching it?'
5. '**How** are they teaching the material, where, and for how long?'

But most importantly, we should *start with*, 'What do students already know?'

Reflecting on these questions will allow you to dig deeply into cognition, improve your evaluations, and discover more effective ways to teach your students.

Why is this work important?

Drawing from my growing interest in cognitive science, psychology, neuropsychology, and the emerging interdisciplinary field of neuroeducation, this book builds on the foundation laid in *The Teacher Toolkit Guide to Memory* (McGill, 2022), *The Teacher Toolkit Guide to Questioning* (McGill, 2023), and *The Teacher Toolkit Guide To Feedback* (McGill, 2024). I've aimed to bridge classroom practice with the science of the brain – not just to offer strategies, but to cultivate an opportunity for you to develop your own neuroliteracy.

The ideas at the heart of this book are about empowering you with the language and tools to think critically, adapt confidently, and understand your students at a deeper level. Doing this from an fMRI-informed perspective remains underexplored across education. In a world of information overload, improved neurodiversity awareness, and rapid technological change, understanding how learning happens – and how the brain responds to instruction – remains *an urgent and underdeveloped gap* across teacher training.

We now have technologies that allow us to explore learning at a neurological level, and while fMRI tools are *not classroom instruments*, they can inform how we think about teaching, learning, and professional development. Insights from neuroimaging deserve a place in shaping the future of teacher education.

CONCLUSION

How this book can become a professional development opportunity

As this book comes to a close, remember that the science of learning is not just about memory or metacognition. It's about humanity. Teaching and learning are human processes, and as humans we are social creatures. This book is about understanding what happens in the brain so we can better reach the hearts of our students. We are teaching at a time in which:

- fMRI scans can now map how the brain encodes feedback
- neuroscience can show us how study skills impact long-term recall
- AI can write lesson plans, but it still cannot replace the teacher who knows their students, adapts in real time, and builds relationships that spark curiosity.

This book offers you a toolkit for the future of the classroom – an approach that is grounded in inquiry, evidence, and teacher empowerment.

As teachers, you are already researchers. You hypothesise daily, make decisions in milliseconds, gather feedback from eye contact and silence. This book doesn't ask you to change the focus of that expertise. Instead, it enhances what you already do, with more clarity and confidence. In teaching, there is rarely a perfect time to embed anything, especially more complex ideas like cognitive science, fMRI-informed insights, or metacognitive routines. But where you seize the day in those classroom moments, that's enough to start with. The future of teaching and learning rests with you becoming more expert, more connected with students and more neuroliterate. This is my invitation to you, to lead from the classroom, inside out, rather than wait for government directives.

This book provides professional development that can evolve over time. You're encouraged to trial one idea at a time, to align it to specific classroom needs, and to reflect on its impact – individually or collectively. Successful professional development not only requires that you build new knowledge, but also that you revisit prior learning. All internal teacher training events should revisit past knowledge to ensure nothing is a one-off. You are more likely to invest in, and use, ideas if you 'move from dependency toward increasing self-directedness' (Knowles, 1970, p. 43). However, in some schools/colleges, teacher autonomy can be lost when priorities and external pressures get in the way. Teacher wellbeing and collective teacher efficacy is hindered when CPD becomes a one-way street, rather than co-constructed. How often are you encouraged to bring your life experiences to the learning process? Effective CPD must be *goal-oriented* and *relevancy-oriented* to the individuals involved. This means you need to see an *immediate application* of the idea, and the *reasoning* for learning something. This is something Knowles (1970) described as andragogy (adult learning). If you believe these hallmarks are in place, you are more likely to be motivated by the professional development provided for you, and to be an active participant.

In Chapter 10, I shared a calendar as a tool for curriculum planning, performance management, or collaborative CPD. The model offers a practical pathway to embed cognitive science into your school or college culture by focusing on small, iterative changes, and revisiting core ideas throughout the academic year. This approach will empower you to develop deeper expertise and stronger neuroliteracy. It's not about adding more to your workload, but about working smarter with the research already available – and most importantly, protecting your time and trust, while providing you with the tools you need to lead your own development and improve outcomes for all learners.

Limitations

All published research has its limitations, and in the spirit of research integrity, I believe it's important to acknowledge mine. This book is not a clinical study, nor is it the result of a long-term academic research trial. I'm not a neuroscientist or a cognitive psychologist. I am, however, a qualified teacher with 35 years of experience in education. I am continually building my neuroliteracy through extensive reading, conversations with experts, and professional training. I have written this book within an academic year, drawing together available research, translating my accumulated knowledge and complex ideas into the emerging field of neuroeducation. My intention has not been to make any new claims; instead, it has been to bridge the gap between science and the classroom to provide you with practical techniques that you can apply immediately to your own classroom setting. I have synthesised the information already available, and I have reframed it *through the lens of neuroeducation and neuroimaging* to support you every day in your teaching.

I have explored the views of teachers across the UK and gathered a small amount of qualitative data from them on neuroeducation, cognitive science, and how confident they feel in applying this knowledge to their practice. At the time of writing, over 1,500 pieces of data have been collected, and the survey remains open-access for you to contribute. **Visit: https://bit.ly/McGill2026**

All participants have shaped the questions and insights throughout this book, and I will share the full research data in my teacher training travels across the country.

It is also important to acknowledge the practical and ethical constraints of this work. I'm not suggesting that fMRI scans become part of classroom practice. However, we should acknowledge that we can gain a great deal of insight from the studies, and that it must begin to inform our thinking, and teacher training, particularly as a response to an increasing awareness of neurodiversity in our classrooms. As with any limitations being identified, I believe this allows the reader to identify any gaps and where someone else can contribute new knowledge. This, after all, is how ideas generate from one another, how neurons connect, and how the human race evolves.

As a teacher and someone who is continually critically examining work and practice across the education system, I hope this book offers food for thought and future opportunities. If I had more time and funding, or if I ever have the opportunity to work in a neuroscience lab, I would like to build more formal research around the ideas shared in this book. My belief is that if teachers had the opportunity to work more closely with researchers in the fields of cognitive neuroscience and educational psychology, they could build more robust evidence based around the neurological impact of classroom practices. In the meantime, I hope this book serves as a much-needed bridge between the lab and the classroom, between the science and the student, between the science of learning and the art of teaching, and between theory and practice.

Taking it further

I invite you to continue asking deeper and more meaningful questions after reading this book. From staff appraisal to postgraduate study, there are countless ways to reframe this content into actionable research. Whether you're mentoring an early career teacher, or pursuing a doctorate, I want to leave you with some of the most pressing and powerful inquiries to consider for your own research. Remember to share your views online using the hashtag, **#GuideToLearning**.

Research questions

These questions are deliberately open-ended, and are designed to stretch both classroom practice and theoretical understanding. Each of these questions can be scaled for school-based inquiry, performance management, MA/EdD research projects, or even longitudinal PhD studies. All these questions and more are areas that I would want to research if I could double the word count to this book – backed by fMRI data, of course – and are designed to push the teaching profession forward towards a more scientific, personalised, and equitable understanding of learning.

1. What neurological responses can be observed when students are exposed to different types of questioning techniques?
2. What is the cognitive load threshold for an 11-year-old during a typical 60-minute lesson, and how can it be optimally managed?
3. To what extent does retrieval practice in GCSE lessons engage the prefrontal cortex compared to passive notetaking?
4. How do individual differences or teaching techniques affect attention and memory consolidation in classroom environments?
5. What impact does a teacher's own neuroliteracy have on their student outcomes?

The big shift: From curiosity to action

If time, funding, or access to neuroscience labs were not constraints, I would want to explore these questions further with teachers across the education system. I would build collaborative research trials that integrate classroom observation with neuroimaging insights. I would test interventions informed by cognitive science in real-time teaching environments. I would also seek to co-design teacher training programmes that respond not just to a policy, but to the biology of learning itself.

Yet even without the lab coat or any funding, I believe every teacher can start now. We all have the tools to be curious, to test ideas, and to use evidence to improve outcomes – ethically and intelligently. This book, I hope, provides a structure and the spark for doing exactly that.

A final thought

What if every teacher was trained in the basic anatomy of the brain? What if every school tracked not just exam results, but also had their pedagogy aligned with memory science? What if we saw professional development not as a compliance-driven event, but as an invitation to explore the very thing we all care most about – how people learn?

We have never had more access to research, tools or collective insight than we do today. And yet, we have barely scratched the surface of understanding how classroom decisions impact the mind. This is our opportunity. Not just to teach better, but to teach smarter, to ask better questions, and to take ownership of what comes next.

I hope this book inspires this journey for you, and that 'fMRI' becomes part of your professional language and pedagogical reflections. I hope it leaves you with more questions than answers, and that, dear reader, is exactly where learning begins!

ANSWERS TO 'FACT OR MYTH?'

Here is a list of correct answers to the 'Effective learning habits: Fact or myth?' table from Chapter 3, page 46). How many did you, your colleagues, or your family get right or wrong?

As with all research, you will find arguments both for and against these statements, as well as established and emerging findings. These answers are based on all the research quoted throughout this book.

1. Myth 2. Myth 3. Fact 4. Myth 5. Fact 6. Myth 7. Fact 8. Myth 9. Fact
10. Fact 11. Myth 12. Fact 13. Myth 14. Fact 15. Fact 16. Fact 17. Fact 18. Myth
19. Fact 20. Myth

GLOSSARY

Andragogy: The theory and practice of adult learning (coined by Malcolm Knowles).

Attention deficit hyperactivity disorder (ADHD): A neurodevelopmental condition that impacts on attention, energy, and impulse.

Blood oxygenated level dependent technique: Used in fMRI imaging to measure blood flow and oxygen levels. More active areas in the brain consume more oxygen.

Cognitive access: Reducing unnecessary cognitive load to make instructions and content easier to understand.

Cognitive debt: Failing to engage with a subject (e.g. by using AI instead), which replaces cognitive effort for thinking.

Cognitive load theory (CLT): Research that explains how the limits of working memory affect learning.

Cognitive load: The demand placed on working memory during learning.

Cognitive neuroscience: A sub-field of cognitive science; the biological focus on mental processes.

Cognitive science: The study of human cognition from a variety of perspectives e.g. psychology, philosophy.

Continuing professional development (CPD): Adult professional learning.

Corpus callosum: Thick nerve fibres connecting the different brain hemispheres.

Declarative knowledge: The conscious knowing of concepts, rules, and facts.

Dual coding: A strategy that combines visual and verbal formats to support students' understanding.

Early years foundation stage (EYFS): The framework for the development and care of children from birth to age 5.

Electroencephalogram (EEG): A technique for recording electrical activity in the brain.

Emotional regulation: The ability to manage and respond to emotional experiences appropriately.

Encoding: The process of converting information into a form that can be stored in memory (or transmitted and later retrieved).

Executive dysfunction: Difficulty in planning, organising, prioritizing, and executing tasks.

Exit tickets: A way to gather feedback from students at the end of a lesson.

Extrinsic motivation: External factors which influence a person's reasoning.

fMRI: A technique that measures changes in blood flow and oxygen levels to show brain activity.

Fourth industrial revolution: Also known as 'the Intelligence Age', it describes rapid technological advancement in the 21st century.

Frontal lobe: The area of the brain that manages our higher mental functions: concentration, planning, judgement, emotional expression, creativity, and inhibition.

Frontoparietal network: The network in the brain responsible for cognitive control, executive function, and goal-directed behaviour.

Hippocampus: A brain component that consolidates short-term memories into long-term memory.

Hyperscanning: Two or more brains being simultaneously scanned to investigate neural connections.

'I do, we do, you do': Scaffolding methodology to help teachers show the learning process.

Illusion of learning: The belief that mastery has been achieved using ineffective study techniques.

Implementation science: The study of methods and strategies used to facilitate the uptake of research findings.

Interleaving practice: A mixed and sequenced approach to practising different concepts, rules, and skills.

Intrinsic motivation: Engaging in an activity because it is inherently interesting, enjoyable, or satisfying in itself.

Linear curriculum: A straight, sequenced approach to learning, no revisiting; structured, step-by-step.

Long-term memory (LTM): A high-capacity system for storing information, experiences, and skills over long periods.

Magnetoencephalography (MEG): A non-invasive technique that measures the magnetic fields produced by electrical activity in the brain.

Meta-awareness: Awareness of one's own thought processes, such as recognising when your mind has wandered.

Metacognition: The ability to reflect on and regulate one's thinking and learning.

MRI: Magnetic resonance imaging are scans showing a snapshot of brain anatomy using a still picture to understand physical structure.

Need for cognition (NFC): A person's tendency to engage in and enjoy effortful thinking and cognitive activity e.g. a crossword.

Neurodivergence: Refers to individuals whose neurological and cognitive profiles differ from what is considered typical e.g. people with ADHD, autism, dyslexia or dyspraxia.

Neurodiversity: Refers to the *full range* of human cognitive variation. This definition includes **every** one of us. **Neuro** = nervous system and **diversity** = variations and differences.

Neuroeducation: Explores the interactions between biological processes and learning.

Neuroimaging: A range of techniques used to visualise brain structure or measure aspects of brain function.

Neuroliteracy: The ability to interpret research critically and apply it ethically, while always keeping students at the centre of classroom decisions.

Neuromyth: A false belief or misconception about how the brain works.

Neuropsychology: A field of psychology focusing on how a person's cognition and behaviour is related to the brain and the nervous system.

Neuroscience: The multidisciplinary scientific study of the nervous system.

Neurotypical: A term used to describe individuals whose brain function and cognitive development align with what is considered typical or standard for the majority of the population.

Occipital lobe: The area of the brain that manages our visual processing: sight, image recognition, and perception.

Oracy: The ability to articulate ideas, engage with others, and develop understanding through speaking and listening.

Parietal lobe: The area of the brain that supports sensory processing, spatial attention and the integration of information, such as touch, body position, and temperature.

Prefrontal cortex: The area of the brain that manages our executive functions e.g. self-control, planning, decision-making, and problem-solving.

Procedural knowledge: Knowledge of how to perform tasks or skills, often carried out automatically without conscious thought.

Psychology: The study of our emotions and behaviours, using scientific methods.

Retrieval: The process of accessing and bringing stored information from memory into conscious awareness.

Retrieval practice: A learning strategy in which information is actively recalled from memory to strengthen learning and improve long-term retention.

Schema formation: The accumulation of interconnected, organised networks of knowledge.

Self-regulation: The ability to manage thoughts, emotions, and behaviours.

Sensory diversity: The natural variation in how individuals perceive and respond to sensory input, such as sound, light, touch, taste, and smell.

Spaced practice: A considered approach to retrieving information at intervals over time to support long-term retention.

Special educational needs and disabilities (SEND): A term used to describe learning difficulties or disabilities that require additional support for children and young people aged 0–25.

Spectroscopy: The study of how substances absorb or emit light to show what they are made of.

Spiral curriculum: Key concepts revisited multiple times with increased complexity each time.

Storage: The active, physical process for maintaining encoded information over time.

Study-strategy audit: A self-reflection and assessment process for reviewing study habits and techniques.

Thematic curriculum: Learning surrounding a central topic.

Think–Pair–Share technique: Providing students with the opportunity to retrieve information in a non-threatening situation.

Toxic positivity The pressure to maintain an unrealistically positive outlook while dismissing genuine negative emotions and difficulties.

Working memory: A limited-capacity system for temporary holding and manipulating information.

REFERENCES

Ackerman, P. L. and Kanfer, R. (2009). Test length and cognitive fatigue: An empirical examination of effects on performance and test-taker reactions. *Journal of Experimental Psychology: Applied, 15*(2), 163–181. https://doi.org/10.1037/a0015719

Agarwal and Bain (2019). *Powerful Teaching: Unleash the Science of Learning*. California: Jossey-Bass.

Ariyarathne, G., de Silva, S., Dayarathna, S., Meedeniya, D. and Jayarathne, S. (2020). ADHD identification using convolutional neural network with seed-based approach for fMRI data. *ACM International Conference Proceeding Series*, 31–35. https://doi.org/10.1145/3384544.3384552

Astle, D. E., Bathelt, J. and Holmes, J. (2019). Remapping the cognitive and neural profiles of children who struggle at school. *Developmental Science, 22*(1). https://doi.org/10.1111/desc.12747

Atabek, O., Şavklıyıldız, A., Orhon, G., Colak, O. H., Özdemir, A. and Şendil, U. (2022). The effect of anxiety on mathematical thinking: An fMRI study on 12th-grade students. *Learning and Motivation, 77*, 101779. https://doi.org/10.1016/J.LMOT.2021.101779

Baddeley, A. D. and Hitch, G. (1974). Working memory. *Psychology of Learning and Motivation - Advances in Research and Theory, 8*(C), 47–89. https://doi.org/10.1016/S0079-7421(08)60452-1

Barnes, K. A., Anderson, K. M., Plitt, M. and Martin, A. (2014). Individual differences in intrinsic brain connectivity predict decision strategy. *Journal of Neurophysiology, 112*(8), 1838–1848. https://doi.org/10.1152/JN.00909.2013

Barrett, P., Davies, F., Zhang, Y. and Barrett, L. (2015). The impact of classroom design on pupils' learning: Final results of a holistic, multi-level analysis. *Building and Environment*, 89, 118-133. https://doi.org/10.1016/j.buildenv.2015.02.013

Bartoszewski, B. L. and Gurung, R. A. R. (2015). Comparing the relationship of learning techniques and exam score. *Scholarship of Teaching and Learning in Psychology, 1*(3), 219–228. https://doi.org/10.1037/stl0000036

Berberat, J., Huggenberger, R., Montali, M., Gruber, P., Pircher, A., Lövblad, K. O., Killer, H. E. and Remonda, L. (2021). Brain activation patterns in medicated versus medication-naïve adults with attention-deficit hyperactivity disorder during fMRI tasks of motor inhibition and cognitive switching. *BMC Medical Imaging, 21*(1). https://doi.org/10.1186/s12880-021-00579-3

Blakemore, S. J. (2019). *Inventing Ourselves: The secret life of the teenage brain*. London: Transworld.

Bjork, E. and Bjork, R. (2011). Making things hard on yourself, but in a good way: Creating desirable difficulties to enhance learning. *Psychology and the Real World: Essays Illustrating Fundamental Contributions to Society*. 56-64. New York: Worth Publishers.

Boksem, M., Meijman, T. and Lorist, M. (2005). Effects of mental fatigue on attention: an ERP study. *Brain Res Cogn Brain Res*. 25(1):107-16. https://doi.org/10.1016/j.cogbrainres.2005.04.011

Botha, M., Chapman, R., Onaiwu, M. G., Kapp, S. K., Ashley, A. S. and Walker, N. (2024). The neurodiversity concept was developed collectively: An overdue correction on the origins of neurodiversity theory. *SAGE Publications, Autism*, 28(6). https://doi.org/10.1177/13623613241237871

Carpenter, B. (2020). 'Podcast 81 Working with society's most vulnerable children', *Teacher Toolkit*. Available at: www.teachertoolkit.co.uk/2020/04/26/podcast-81

Collins, A., Brown, J. S. and Holum, A. (1991). Cognitive apprenticeship: Making thinking visible. *American Educator*, 15(3), 6–11, 38–46.

Cortese, S., Kelly, C., Chabernaud, C., Proal, E., di Martino, A., Milham, M. P. and Castellanos, F. X. (2012). Toward systems neuroscience of ADHD: A meta-analysis of 55 fMRI studies. *American Journal of Psychiatry*, 169(10), 1038–1055. https://doi.org/10.1176/APPI.AJP.2012.11101521

Cullen, S., and Oppenheimer, D. (2024). Choosing to learn: The importance of student autonomy in higher education. *Science Advances, 10*(29), 6759. http://doi.org/10.1126/sciadv.ado6759

Darnai, G., Matuz, A., Alhour, H. A., Perlaki, G., Orsi, G., Arató, Á., Szente, A., Áfra, E., Nagy, S. A., Janszky, J. and Csathó, Á. (2023). The neural correlates of mental fatigue and reward processing: A task-based fMRI study. *NeuroImage*, *265*, 119812. https://doi.org/10.1016/J.NEUROIMAGE.2022.119812

Department for Education (DfE) (2023). *Working lives of teachers and leaders: Year 1 research report*. Available at: www.gov.uk/government/publications/working-lives-of-teachers-and-leaders-wave-1

Department for Education (DfE) (2024). *SEND code of practice: 0 to 25 years*. Available at: www.gov.uk/government/publications/send-code-of-practice-0-to-25

Department for Education (DfE) (2025). *Curriculum and Assessment Review: Final report*. Available at: www.gov.uk/government/publications/curriculum-and-assessment-review-final-report

Department for Education (DfE) (2026). *Every child achieving and thriving*. Available at: www.gov.uk/government/publications/every-child-achieving-and-thriving

Dhawan, V. (2014). Education and neuroscience. *Research Matters: A Cambridge Assessment publication*, 17. Available at: www.repository.cam.ac.uk/bitstreams/92a6da8a-a315-4a6[illegible]-[illegible]731-[illegible]7d50556101d/download

Dikker, S., Wan, L., Davidesco, I., Kaggen, L., Oostrik, M., McClintock, J., Rowland, J., Michalareas, G., van Bavel, J. J., Ding, M. and Poeppel, D. (2017). Brain-to-brain synchrony tracks real-world dynamic group interactions in the classroom. *Current Biology*, *27*(9), 1375–1380. https://doi.org/10.1016/J.CUB.2017.04.002

Dunlosky, J., Rawson, K. A., Marsh, E. J., Nathan, M. J. and Willingham, D. T. (2013). Improving students' learning with effective learning techniques: Promising directions from cognitive and educational psychology. *Psychological Science in the Public Interest: A Journal of the American Psychological Society*, *14*(1), 4–58. https://doi.org/10.1177/1529100612453266

Erdem, E. and Kaf, Ö. (2023). Effect of learning styles on academic achievement: a meta-analysis. *Türk Akademik Yayınlar Dergisi (TAY Journal)*, 7(1), 26-43. www.tayjournal.com/files/74/manuscript/manuscript_3730/tay%20journal-3730-manuscript-155019.pdf

Gonçalves, A., Muniz, B.F.B. and Jaeger, A. (2025). Retrieval practice versus elaborative encoding: A systematic and meta-analytic review. *Educ Psychol Rev* 37, 100 (2025). https://doi.org/10.1007/s10648-025-10[illegible]76-6

Hardiman, M., Rinne, L., Gregory, E. and Yarmolinskaya, J. (2011). Neuroethics, neuroeducation, and classroom teaching: Where the brain sciences meet pedagogy. Neuroethics. 5(2). 1–9. https://doi.org/10.1007/s12152-011-9116-6

Hattie, J. and O'Leary, T. (2025). Learning styles, preferences, or strategies? An explanation for the resurgence of styles across many meta-analyses. *Educational Psychology Review*, *37*(2), [illegible]–26. https://doi.org/10.1007/S10648-025-10002-W

Haugg, A., Sladky, R., Skouras, S., McDonald, A., Craddock, C., Kirschner, M., Herdener, M., Koush, Y., Papoutsi, M., Keynan, J. N., Hendler, T., Cohen Kadosh, K., Zich, C., MacInnes, J., Adcock, R. A., Dickerson, K., Chen, N. K., Young, K., Bodurka, J. and Scharnowski, F. (2020). Can we predict real-time fMRI neurofeedback learning success from pretraining brain activity? *Human Brain Mapping*, *41*(14), 3839. https://doi.org/10.1002/HBM.25089

Holmes, W., Bialik, M. and Fadel, C. (2019). *Artificial Intelligence in Education: Promises and Implications for Teaching and Learning*. Boston, MA: Center for Curriculum Redesign.

Jang, W., Kim, S., Kim, Y. J., Lee, S., Choi, J. Y. and Lee, W. (2025). Overwork and changes in brain structure: a pilot study. *Occupational and Environmental Medicine*, *82*(3), 105–111. https://doi.org/10.1136/OEMED-2025-110057

Jarrett, C. (2014). *Great myths of the brain*. New Jersey: Wiley-Blackwell.

Jessen, F., Heun, R., Erb, M., Granath, D. O., Klose, U., Papassotiropoulos, A. and Grodd, W. (2000). The concreteness effect: Evidence for dual coding and context availability. *Brain and Language*, *74*(1), 103–112. https://doi.org/10.1006/BRLN.2000.2340

Katyal, S. and Fleming, S. M. (2024). The future of metacognition research: Balancing construct breadth with measurement rigor. *Cortex*, *171*, 223–234. https://doi.org/10.1016/j.cortex.2023.11.002

Kirschner, P. A., Sweller, J., Kirschner, F. and Zambrano, J. R. (2018). From cognitive load theory to collaborative cognitive load theory. *International Journal of Computer-Supported Collaborative Learning 13*(2), 213–233. https://doi.org/10.1007/S11412-018-9277-Y

Knowles, M. S. (1970). *The Modern Practice of Adult Education*. New York: Association Press.

Koiler, R., Schimmel, A., Bakhshipour, E., Shewokis, P. A. and Getchell, N. (2022). The impact of fidget spinners on fine motor skills in individuals with and without ADHD: An exploratory analysis. *Journal of Behavioral and Brain Science*, *12*(3), 82–101. https://doi.org/10.4236/JBBS.2022.123005

Kosmyna, N., Hauptmann, E., Yuan, Y. T., Situ, J., Liao, X.-H., Beresnitzky, A. V., Braunstein, I. and Maes, P. (2025). *Your Brain on ChatGPT: Accumulation of Cognitive Debt when Using an AI Assistant for Essay Writing Task*. Available at: http://arxiv.org/abs/2506.08872

Kucian, K., Loenneker, T., Dietrich, T., Dosch, M., Martin, E. and von Aster, M. (2006). Impaired neural networks for approximate calculation in dyscalculic children: A functional MRI study. *Behavioral and Brain Functions*, *2*(1), 1–17. https://doi.org/10.1186/1744-9081-2-31

Kuhl, P. K., Ramírez, R. R., Bosseler, A., Lin, J. F. L. and Imada, T. (2014). Infants' brain responses to speech suggest analysis by synthesis. *Proceedings of the National Academy of Sciences of the United States of America*, *111*(31), 11238–11245. https://doi.org/10.1073/PNAS.1410963111

Makedon, A. (1990). *Is teaching a science or an art?* Paper presented at the Annual Conference of the Midwest Philosophy of Education Society (Chicago, IL, November 10, 1990). Available at: https://files.eric.ed.gov/fulltext/ED330683.pdf

Marano, G., Kotzalidis, G. D., Lisci, F. M., Anesini, M. B., Rossi, S., Barbonetti, S., Cangini, A., Ronsisvalle, A., Artuso, L., Falsini, C., Caso, R., Mandracchia, G., Brisi, C., Traversi, G., Mazza, O., Pola, R., Sani, G., Mercuri, E. M., Gaetani, E. and Mazza, M. (2025). The neuroscience behind writing: Handwriting vs. typing—who wins the battle? *Life*, *15*(3), 345. https://doi.org/10.3390/life15030345

McGill, R. M. (2019). *Just Great Teaching*. London: Bloomsbury Education.

McGill, R. M. (2022). *The Teacher Toolkit Guide to Memory*. London: Bloomsbury Education.

McGill, R. M. (2023). *The Teacher Toolkit Guide to Questioning*. London: Bloomsbury Education.

McGill, R. M. (2024). *The Teacher Toolkit Guide to Feedback*. London: Bloomsbury Education.

McGill, R. M. (2025). 'Learning styles: Two studies, Two Conclusions'. *Teacher Toolkit*, May 20. Available at: www.teachertoolkit.co.uk/2025/05/20/learning-styles-research-comparison

Meyler, A., Keller, T. A., Cherkassky, V. L., Gabrieli, J. D. E. and Just, M. A. (2008). Modifying the brain activation of poor readers during sentence comprehension with extended remedial instruction: A longitudinal study of neuroplasticity. *Neuropsychologia*, *46*(10), 2580–2592. https://doi.org/10.1016/j.neuropsychologia.2008.03.012

Molenberghs, P., Trautwein, F. M., Böckler, A., Singer, T. and Kanske, P. (2016). Neural correlates of metacognitive ability and of feeling confident: A large-scale fMRI study. *Social Cognitive and Affective Neuroscience*, *11*(12), 1942–1951. https://doi.org/10.1093/scan/nsw093

Mousley, A., Bethlehem, R. A. I., Yeh, F.-C. and Astle, D. E. (2025). Topological turning points across the human lifespan. *Nature Communications*, *16*(1), 10055. https://doi.org/10.1038/s41467-025-65974-8

Murdock-Perriera, L. A. and Sedlacek, Q. C. (2018). Questioning Pygmalion in the twenty-first century: the formation, transmission, and attributional influence of teacher expectancies. *Social Psychology of Education*, *21*(3), 691–707. https://doi.org/10.1007/s11218-018-9439-9

Narukawa, S., Nishimura, M., Kuze, I., Ohno, I., Fukunaga, M., Kobayasi, K. I. and Murai, S. A. (2023). Cortico-striatal activity associated with fidget spinner use: an fMRI study. *Scientific Reports*, *13*(1), 1–10. https://doi.org/10.1038/S41598-023-43109-7

Newton, P. M. and Miah, M. (2017). Evidence-based higher education - Is the learning styles 'myth' important? *Frontiers in Psychology*, *8*(MAR), 444. https://doi.org/10.3389/FPSYG.2017.00444

Rosenthal, R. and Jacobson, L. (1968). Pygmalion in the classroom. *The Urban Review*, *3*(1), 16–20. https://doi.org/10.1007/BF02322211

Rowe, M.B. (1986). 'Wait time: Slowing down may be a way of speeding up!', *Journal of Teacher Education*, 37(1), 43–50.

Ruiz-Martín, H., Blanco, F. and Ferrero, M. (2024). Which learning techniques supported by cognitive research do students use at secondary school? Prevalence and associations with students' beliefs and achievement. *Cognitive Research: Principles and Implications*, 9(1), 1–21. https://doi.org/10.1186/S41235-024-00567-5

Seghier, M. L., Fahim, M. A. and Habak, C. (2019). Educational fMRI: From the Lab to the Classroom. *Frontiers in Psychology*, 10. https://doi.org/10.3389/FPSYG.2019.02769

Šimić, N. and Manenica, I. (2012). Exam experience and some reactions to exam stress. *Hum Physiol* 38, 67–72. https://doi.org/10.1134/S0362119712010161

Sims, S., Fletcher-Wood, H., O'Mara-Eves, A., Cottingham, S., Stansfield, C., Anders, J. and van Herwegen, J. (2021). *What are the Characteristics of Effective Teacher Professional Development? A Systematic Review and Meta-analysis*. London: Education Endowment Foundation. Available at: https://educationendowmentfoundation.org.uk/education-evidence/evidence-reviews/teacher-professional-development-characteristics

Singer, J. (1998). *Odd people in: The birth of community amongst people on the autism spectrum*. Honours thesis. University of Technology Sydney. Available at: https://terapiastimulus.fi/wp-content/uploads/2023/07/Odd_People_In_The_Birth_of_Community_amo.pdf

Sisakhti, M., Sachdev, P. S. and Batouli, S. A. H. (2021). The effect of cognitive load on the retrieval of long-term memory: An fMRI study. *Frontiers in Human Neuroscience*, 15, 700146. https://doi.org/10.3389/FNHUM.2021.700146

Smallwood, J. and Schooler, J. W. (2015). The science of mind wandering: Empirically navigating the stream of consciousness. *Annual Review of Psychology*, 66, 487–518. https://doi.org/10.1146/annurev-psych-010814-015331

Soysal, Y. and Soysal, S. (2023). The art of asking good questions in the classroom: A phenomenographic study of teacher educators' recommendations. *ECNU Review of Education*. https://doi.org/10.1177/20965311231210008

Spratt, M., Humphreys, G. and Chan, V. (2002). Autonomy and motivation: Which comes first? *Language Teaching Research*, 6(3), 245–266. https://doi.org/10.1191/1362168802LR106OA

Sweller, J. (1988). Cognitive load during problem solving: Effects on learning. *Cognitive Science*, 12(2), 257–285. https://doi.org/10.1207/S15516709COG1202_4

Sweller, J. (2012). An interview with John Sweller. YouTube video (added by Veritasium). Available at: www.youtube.com/watch?v=3bZOdZ8cBOk&t=961s

Takeuchi, H., Sekiguchi, A., Taki, Y., Yokoyama, S., Yomogida, Y., Komuro, N., Yamanouchi, T., Suzuki, S. and Kawashima, R. (2010). Training of working memory impacts structural connectivity. *Journal of Neuroscience*, 30(9), 3297–3303. https://doi.org/10.1523/JNEUROSCI.4611-09.2010

Tan, S. H. J., Wong, J. N. and Teo, W. P. (2023). Is neuroimaging ready for the classroom? A systematic review of hyperscanning studies in learning. *NeuroImage*, 281, 120367. https://doi.org/10.1016/J.NEUROIMAGE.2023.120367

Thornton, E., Cheng, Q., Demkowicz, O. and Humphrey, N. (2025). Lost learning: Prevalence, inequalities and outcomes of internal exclusion in mainstream secondary schools. *British Educational Research Journal*. https://doi.org/10.1002/berj.70049

Wiklund-Hörnqvist, C., Stillesjö, S., Andersson, M., Jonsson, B. and Nyberg, L. (2021). Retrieval practice facilitates learning by strengthening processing in both the anterior and posterior hippocampus. *Brain and Behavior*, 11(1). https://doi.org/10.1002/BRB3.1909

Wiklund-Hörnqvist, C., Stillesjö, S., Andersson, M., Jonsson, B. and Nyberg, L. (2022). Retrieval Practice Is Effective Regardless of Self-Reported Need for Cognition - Behavioral and Brain Imaging Evidence. *Frontiers in Psychology*, 12. https://doi.org/10.3389/FPSYG.2021.797395

Zarrinabadi, N. and Rezazadeh, M. (2023). Why only feedback? Including feed up and feed forward improves non-linguistic aspects of L2 writing. *Language Teaching Research*, 27(3), 575–592

Zhang, Y., Guo, W., Tara, A. N., Cao, X., Wu, H. and Shi, H. (2025). The effects of different instructional strategies on the college students' critical thinking learning experience and neural correlates using functional near-infrared spectroscopy. *Education and Information Technologies*, 30(14), 20467–2049[illegible]. https://doi.org/10.1007/S10639-025-13566-W

FURTHER READING

Agarwal, P. K., Finley, J. R., Rose, N. S. and Roediger, H. L. (2017). Benefits from retrieval practice are greater for students with lower working memory capacity. *Memory*, *25*(6), 764–771. https://doi.org/10.1080/09658211.2016.1220579

Alkoby, O., Abu-Rmileh, A., Shriki, O. and Todder, D. (2018). Can we predict who will respond to neurofeedback? A review of the inefficacy problem and existing predictors for successful EEG neurofeedback learning. *Neuroscience*, *378*, 155–164. https://doi.org/10.1016/J.NEUROSCIENCE.2016.12.050

Andersen, I. G. (2018). Pygmalion in instruction? Tracking, teacher reward structures, and educational inequality. *Social Psychology of Education*, *21*(5), 1021–1044. https://doi.org/10.1007/S11218-018-9452-Z

Antony, J. W., Ferreira, C. S., Norman, K. A. and Wimber, M. (2017). Retrieval as a fast route to memory consolidation. *Trends in Cognitive Sciences*, *21*(8), 573–576. https://doi.org/10.1016/J.TICS.2017.05.001

Aspiranti, K. B. and Hulac, D. M. (2022). Using fidget spinners to improve on-task classroom behavior for students with ADHD. *Behavior Analysis in Practice*, *15*(2), 454–465. https://doi.org/10.1007/S40617-021-00588-2

Axmacher, N., Haupt, S., Cohen, M. X., Elger, C. E. and Fell, J. (2009). Interference of working memory load with long-term memory formation. *European Journal of Neuroscience*, *29*(7), 1501–1513. https://doi.org/10.1111/J.1460-9568.2009.06676.X

Bevilacqua, D., Davidesco, I., Wan, L., Chaloner, K., Rowland, J., Ding, M., Poeppel, D. and Dikker, S. (2018). Brain-to-brain synchrony and learning outcomes vary by student–teacher dynamics: Evidence from a real-world classroom electroencephalography study. *Journal of Cognitive Neuroscience*, *31*(3), 401–411. https://doi.org/10.1162/JOCN_A_01274

Bogdanov, P., Dereli, N., Dang, X. H., Bassett, D. S., Wymbs, N. F., Grafton, S. T. and Singh, A. K. (2017). Learning about learning: Mining human brain sub-network biomarkers from fMRI data. *PLoS ONE*, *12*(10). https://doi.org/10.1371/JOURNAL.PONE.0184344

Jerrim, J. (2025). *How engaged are low-income White children during secondary school?* ImpactEd Group. Available at: www.impactedgroup.uk/resources/report-mind-the-engagement-gap

Jiang, K., Yi, Y., Li, L., Li, H., Shen, H., Zhao, F., Xu, Y. and Zheng, A. (2019). Functional network connectivity changes in children with attention-deficit hyperactivity disorder: A resting-state fMRI study. *International Journal of Developmental Neuroscience*, *78*, 1–6. https://doi.org/10.1016/J.IJDEVNEU.2019.07.003

Koiler, R., Bakhshipour, E., Schimmel, A., Jones, A., Milla, K., Shewokis, P. A. and Getchell, N. (2021). Fidget Spinners May Decrease Prefrontal Cortex Activity During Cognitively Challenging Fine Motor Tasks. *Advances in Intelligent Systems and Computing*, *1201 AISC*, 69–75. https://doi.org/10.1007/978-3-030-51041-1_10

Pan, Y., Dikker, S., Goldstein, P., Zhu, Y., Yang, C. and Hu, Y. (2020). Instructor-learner brain coupling discriminates between instructional approaches and predicts learning. *NeuroImage*, *211*, 116657. https://doi.org/10.1016/J.NEUROIMAGE.2020.116657

Thalmann, M., Oberauer, K. and Souza, A. S. (2019). How Does Chunking Help Working Memory? *Journal of Experimental Psychology: Learning, Memory, and Cognition*. https://doi.org/10.1037/xlm0000578

Yamada, Y., Stevens, C., Dow, M., Harn, B. A., Chard, D. J. and Neville, H. J. (2011). Emergence of the neural network for reading in five-year-old beginning readers of different levels of pre-literacy abilities: An fMRI study. *NeuroImage*, *57*(3), 704–713. https://doi.org/10.1016/J.NEUROIMAGE.2010.10.057

Zhang, Z., Su, H., Peng, Q., Yang, Q. and Cheng, X. (2011). Exam anxiety induces significant blood pressure and heart rate increase in college students. *Clinical and Experimental Hypertension*, *33*(5), 281–286. https://doi.org/10.3109/10641963.2010.531850

INDEX

F

G

H

I

J

K

L

M

ABOUT THE AUTHOR

Ross is globally known as @TeacherToolkit, and over 21 million readers have visited his website.

He began teaching in 1991 and taught for 26 years in London's national-challenge (secondary) schools, including 20 years as a school leader.

A multiple award-winning teacher, blogger, and author, Ross was featured in *The Sunday Times*' '500 Most Influential People in Britain' (2015). To this day, he remains the only classroom teacher to have been included on the list. In April and July of 2025, Ross was invited by the Cabinet Office and the Department for Education to visit Number 10 Downing Street and meet the Prime Minister to share his social media expertise.

Today, Ross works with teachers and schools worldwide, enhancing teaching and learning, reducing workload, and improving teacher mental health. He is also the author of 13 books on education, and over 100,000 people have purchased his books, which continue to inspire and empower teachers globally.

Ross attended seven state schools as a free school meals pupil. His early experiences shaped his passion for education into a lifelong commitment to improving the lives of others through teaching and learning. At heart, Ross remains a design and technology teacher.